PINK BLOOD:
HOMOPHOBIC VIOLENCE IN CANADA

D0880164

Despite Canada's reputation as a beacon in the international struggle for gay rights, homophobia and homophobic violence remain major problems across the country. Since 1990, hundreds of gay, lesbian, bisexual, and transgendered people have been assaulted or murdered in Canada, but so far the phenomenon has been largely ignored in Canadian criminology texts and other scholarly works.

Pink Blood is the first book to analyse homophobic violence in Canada on a national scale. Douglas Victor Janoff uses legal records, case studies, and interviews with victims, activists, and police officers from thirty cities to convey the devastating impact this violence has had on queer Canadians and on the communities they inhabit. Janoff critically examines common public perceptions and police attitudes and practices, as well as hate crime legislation and policies that, despite good intentions, are often powerless to counteract this serious and complex social problem.

Drawing from a wide range of scholarship in law, criminology, sociology, psychology, philosophy, and social work, *Pink Blood* is a groundbreaking work from a respected researcher and community activist.

DOUGLAS VICTOR JANOFF is a policy adviser for the Government of Canada.

DOUGLAS VICTOR JANOFF

PINK BLOOD

Homophobic Violence in Canada

UNIVERSITY OF TORONTO PRESS
Toronto Buffalo London

© University of Toronto Press Incorporated 2005
Toronto Buffalo London
Printed in Canada

ISBN 0-8020-8781-7 (cloth)
ISBN 0-8020-8570-9 (paper)

Printed on acid-free paper

Library and Archives Canada Cataloguing in Publication

Janoff, Douglas, 1958–
Pink blood : homophobic violence in Canada / Douglas Victor Janoff.

Includes bibliographical references and index.
ISBN 0-8020-8781-7 (bound). ISBN 0-8020-8570-9 (pbk.)

1. Gays – Crimes against – Canada.   2. Homophobia – Canada.   I. Title.

HV6250.4.H66J36 2005   362.88′086′640971   C2004-906714-1

University of Toronto Press acknowledges the financial assistance to
its publishing program of the Canada Council for the Arts and the
Ontario Arts Council.

University of Toronto Press acknowledges the financial support for
its publishing activities of the Government of Canada through the
Book Publishing Industry Development Program (BPIDP).

I can't believe the things I hear
Falling from the atmosphere
Sexual atrocities are happening right over me
And I can't sleep.

Jann Arden

Contents

Acknowledgments

Since 1995, an incalculable number of people have assisted me in this project: victims, community members, activists, academics, researchers, and criminal justice officials provided me with the data that are at the heart of this book. Many friends and family members provided me with invaluable support over the years it took to research and write this book. Among the many, I would like to thank Karen Baldwin, Peter Bartlett, Ross Boutilier, Tracey Brown, Catherine Chase, Melvin Chuck, Vince Connors, Brian Coutts, Joe Crowell, Dean Cummer, Margaret Denike, Bob Fuguere, Anita Harper, Richard Hudler, Donna Huen, Martha Johnson, Randall Lampreau, Stephen Lock, John Lowman, Bruce MacDougall, Maureen Medved, Claudine Metcalfe, John Mitchell, Jane Mulkewich, Mark O'Neill, Michael Polowich, Lewis Poteet, Brian Preston, Bruce Ryder, Sandy Scott, Theressa Seto, David Sorlie, Debbie and Peter Smith, Scott Thompson, Lorna and Elmo Townsend, and Donna Wilson.

I would especially like to thank Karlene Faith – activist, author, teacher, and friend.

NECROLOGY

This book is dedicated to the memory of the victims listed below, killed in Canada since 1990 – and to those whom I was not able to list. Although most of these victims were gay, lesbian, bisexual, or transgendered, others were not. Some had a connection with the queer community; others were 'accused' or suspected of being queer. Some homicides generated extensive coverage, others very little. My apologies for the four victims at the end whom I was not able to name: all should be remembered.

Who	How	Where	Year	Chapter
Robert Annett	killed in his apartment	Toronto	2000	3
Stéphane Arcand	shot	Ste-Mélanie, PQ	1991	1
Willis Arcand	strangled and stabbed in the neck	Kemptville, ON	1994	1
Elexer Martinez Areya	kicked in the head ten times	Calgary	1994	5
Paul Armstrong	burnt beyond recognition	Toronto	1996	3
Larry Arnold	beaten	Toronto	1994	1
Robert Assaly	bludgeoned/stabbed	Montreal	1991	4
Garth Balderston	beaten	Ottawa	1990	4
Grayce Baxter	strangled/dismembered	Toronto	1992	3
Jack Bell	beaten	Toronto	1993	3
Anthony Bennett	killed in his apartment	Toronto	2000	3
Brian Booth	stabbed/suffocated	Montreal	1990	1
Michael Boley	suffocated	Toronto	1990	6
Marc Bellerive	stabbed 40 times and throat slashed	Montreal	1991	3
Lucien Bertin	stabbed 40 times	Halifax	1990	5
James Bewick	strangled/throat crushed	Swift Current, SK	1999	5
François Bolton	strangled with a necktie and coathanger	Vancouver	1993	3
Phillip Bright	beaten	London	1993	2
Kelly Bouboire	stabbed	Winnipeg	2002	7
Walter Bourbonnais	killed in his house	Montreal	1997	3
David Buller	multiple stab wounds	Toronto	2001	3
Jim Bwabwa	stabbed	Toronto	1998	2
Norman Cardwell	shot point-blank	Toronto	1991	3
Jean Chenier	stabbed/burned	Gatineau	1996	3
John Clarke	killed in his apartment	Toronto	1996	3
Stacey Clarke	beaten/choked/ crushed	Melfort, Sask.	1997	5
Roger Cloutier	shot	Ste-Mélanie, PQ	1991	1

Who	How	Where	Year	Chapter
Dennis Colby	beaten	Toronto	1995	3
Michel Comeau	kicked and beaten	Fredericton	1993	3
Virginia Coote	strangled	Toronto	1994	1
Pierre-Yvon Croft	stabbed 15 times	Montreal	1991	3
Gerald Cuerrier	shot in the head	Orleans, ON	1994	5
David Curnick	stabbed 146 times	Vancouver	1994	3
Derek DaCosta	strangled	Toronto	1990	5
Michael DeCarlo	disappeared	Toronto	1995	1
William Davis	punched/kicked/ burned/pierced	Duncan, BC	1999	2
Mario Desrosiers	strangled	Hull	1994	4
James Detzler	beaten/drowned	Toronto	1997	5
Cassandra Do	strangled	Toronto	2003	3
Harry Dolan	stabbed	Montreal	1993	7
Anthony Dowding	bludgeoned on the head 20 times	Toronto	1999	6
Henry Drosdevech	stabbed 68 times and castrated	Abbotsford, BC	1993	5
Henry Durost	strangled in his home	Toronto	2004	3
Rev. Warren Eling	strangled	Montreal	1993	2
Gaetan Ethier	bludgeoned/stabbed	Montreal	1991	4
Dennis Lee Fichtenberg	stabbed	Prince George, BC	1993	7
Mario Fortin	shot	Quebec City	1990	3
Rolland Gagné	bound and killed in his home	Montreal	1993	3
Alrick Gairy	shot	Toronto	2000	3
Normand Gareau	beaten	Montreal	1991	3
Dave Gaspard	stabbed 60 times	Vancouver	1994	5
Richard Gerlitz	shot in the head 23 times with a nailgun	Calgary	1993	6
Robert (Chantal) Gillade	beaten and stabbed	Vancouver	1995	3
Joseph Gligor	hacked to death with axe and knife	Kitchener	1991	6
Bill Goodwin	badly decomposed body discovered in his apartment	Ottawa	2003	7
Douglas Grass	hit on the head with a hammer 15 times	Stratford	1993	2
Réal Halde	throat slashed	Montreal	1996	3
Donald Hebert	strangled/ stabbed in the heart with a butcher knife	Ottawa	1993	4
Nigel Henry	shot	Toronto	1997	3
Garth Hill	strangled	Victoria	1994	2

Who	How	Where	Year	Chapter
Michel Hogue	beaten/stabbed	Laval	1992	3
Harry Isaac	stabbed/suffocated	Toronto	1994	1
Mario Joanette	stabbed	Montreal	2002	7
Gregory Jodrey	beaten	Wolfville, NS	1994	1
Richard Kall	multiple stab wounds	Toronto	2000	3
Kristine Kavanagh	killed in her apartment	Vancouver	1994	3
Shawn Keegan	shot point-blank	Toronto	1996	1
Stephen Kirby	beaten/kicked	Toronto	1994	5
Gordon Kuhtey	kicked/bludgeoned	Winnipeg	1991	1
Daniel Lacombe	beaten	Joliette, PQ	1992	6
André Lafleur	strangled	Montreal	1995	3
Yves Lalonde	bludgeoned with branches and a baseball bat	Montreal	1992	1
Michel Landry	shot	Quebec City	1990	3
Robert Lemay	stabbed	Shawinigan	1996	2
Roderick MacLeod	stabbed	Sydney, NS	1992	6
Jason Mason	beaten/stabbed in the heart	Salmo, BC	1991	2
Gerald May	beaten/stabbed	Vancouver	1990	4
Kenneth McDermott	beaten/stabbed	Edmonton	1993	1
Richard McIntyre	bludgeoned	Winnipeg	1990	1
Clifford McIver	bludgeoned/ strangled	Charlottetown	1995	6
Julieanne Middleton	strangled/drowned	Toronto	1994	1
James Miles	strangled	Edmonton	1999	1
Bruno Minici	body found a year after he disappeared	Greater Van-couver	1993	1
James Moffat	beaten	Sudbury	1992	1
John Mogentale	beaten/asphixiated	Vancouver	1995	1
Edward Yong Sua Mok	beaten/stabbed	Montreal	1990	3
Gerrard Morin	beaten/thrown off a highrise	Toronto	1997	3
Richard Niquette	Stabbed	Montreal	1995	3
Cornelius Otte	Beaten	Hamilton	1997	1
Christopher Palmer	shot five times	Toronto	2000	3
Yvon Parent	bludgeoned with ax handle	Hinton, AB	1991	5
Robert Panchaud	beaten/stabbed	Montreal	1992	3
Donald Pettipas	stabbed in the chest	Halifax	1992	2
Norman Rasky	stabbed/bludgeoned	Toronto	1992	4
Christopher Raynsford	strangled	Ottawa	2002	7
Robert Read	beaten/run over	Sackville, NB	1991	2
Guy Robert	throat slashed	Ottawa	1995	5
Andrew Robotham	shot	Toronto	2000	3
Clayton Russell	killed in his apartment	Toronto	1996	3
Jude Simard	killed in a park	Montreal	2002	Concl.

Who	How	Where	Year	Chapter
Tommy Simoneau	shot	Joliette	1991	1
John Somerton	skull smashed with iron bar	Toronto	1992	2
Richard Sneath	beaten to death	Ft. McMurray	2002	7
Maureen Sullivan	shot	Prince George	1992	2
Tracey Tom	found dead in a shopping cart	Vancouver	2003	3
Normand Trudel	killed in his home	Montreal	1996	3
Alexander Turner	suffocated	Windsor	1995	7
Gerson Acuna Ugalde	found dead in a swimming pool	Montreal	2001	3
Faye Urry	body found in the city's industrial area	Prince George	2002	3
Michael Vadeboncoeur	stabbed	Toronto	1991	2
Benoit Villeneuve	beaten	Ottawa	1993	2
Denis Villeneuve	strangled	Sudbury	1999	7
William (Kendra) Voght	strangled	Vancouver	1993	2
Garfield Walker	beaten/stabbed	Montreal	1991	3
Aaron Webster	beaten/bludgeoned	Vancouver	2001	7
Thomas 'Deanna' Wilkinson	shot point-blank	Toronto	1996	1
John Wilson	stabbed	Toronto	1994	3
Unnamed	stabbed in his apartment	Vancouver	1995	1
Unnamed	killed at the Salvation Army	Toronto	2000	3
Unnamed	shot at La Mallette bar	Quebec City	2000	3
Unnamed	unclear	Winnipeg	2002	7

PINK BLOOD:
HOMOPHOBIC VIOLENCE IN CANADA

Introduction

It is precisely at times such as these, when we live with the possibility of unthinkable destruction, that people are likely to become dangerously crazy about sexuality. Contemporary conflicts over sexual values and erotic conduct have much in common with the religious disputes of earlier centuries. They acquire immense symbolic weight.

Gayle Rubin, 'Thinking Sex'

Back in the 1990s, the Royal Hotel, with its high ceilings and signature portrait of the Queen on the back wall, was wedged between a falafel joint and a video arcade on Vancouver's Granville Street. By five o'clock on Friday afternoons, the spacious, friendly pub was already starting to fill up with work-weary customers ready to celebrate the end of the week. If you got there at six you might have to line up outside in the rain; by seven, you'd have to squeeze through the jovial crowd and elbow your way to the bar to get a pitcher of Kokonee. Although some women played pool in the corner, the crowd mainly represented a cross-section of Vancouver's gay male population – lawyers, truck drivers, waiters.

In 1992 I was also known to hoist a few pints there. I would meet up with a regular circle of buddies, including Reed, a playwright, and Steve, a hairstylist. One day Reed called to say that Steve had been gay-bashed. I found myself at the hospital, staring incomprehensibly at Steve's head, which was wrapped in bandages like a mummy. His arm was broken in three places and seven teeth were missing. After the shock wore off, I wrote about the incident in the *Vancouver Sun*:

At 3 a.m. on Aug. 5, in a dark corner of Stanley Park frequented by gay men, three young white males smashed Steve's face to splinters with a four-foot metal bar. Steve fell unconscious on his back in a puddle of blood; the men continued to pound the bar into his face.

Two horrified onlookers chased away the attackers, carried the victim to a car and rushed him to the emergency department of St. Paul's Hospital ...

Eight metal plates and 38 screws now hold Macklin's newly reconstructed face together.[1]

Nine months later, Reed published an update on Steve's condition:

Several weeks ago, he went in to have the metal plates in his temple and jaw replaced with plastic. Infection was discovered and a part of Steve's throat was taken to reconstruct the roof of his mouth.

At this moment Steve has more than 140 stitches on the inside of his mouth. But the repair job hasn't taken, so back he goes.

This will bring the total number of operations on Steven's face and head to more than six ... The cost of all this medical care is well into the hundreds of thousands of dollars.[2]

The attack occurred on the August long weekend. On that particular weekend, tens of thousands had come to watch an international fireworks display in the West End – the centre of Vancouver's visible gay male community. (There are fireworks displays in many Canadian cities. The situation is more tense in Montreal and Vancouver, where 'outsiders' pour into the queer neighbourhoods, which afford excellent vantage points.)[3]

On the Saturday night of that long weekend – minutes after the fireworks ended – three gay men were attacked by two men and a woman on Davie Street; later that night three men kicked a gay man on the ground while five others looked on. A St Paul's emergency physican said she attended to about ten gay-bashings that Saturday night, instead of the usual two or three.

And the next night Steve was almost killed.

It was obvious to us – to Steve's friends – that he had been gay-bashed. But that 'fact' was suddenly up for debate. Steve's wallet had not been taken, even though one attacker was heard to exclaim: 'Give me your fucking wallet!' Because the attackers did not utter the word 'faggot,' the Vancouver police did not consider it a hate crime. 'Robbery was the motive,' they said.

The case sparked a bitter outcry. A march was organized to 'take back' Davie Street. Reed complained that the police were more willing to arrest gay men for public sex than they were to defend them from bashers, whereas 'straight men have illegal sex available to them 24 hours a day on Richards Street, condoned by city hall.' Gay councillor Gordon Price bristled: 'It panders to the worst clichés about gay men, desperate for sex ... Do citizens have a right to walk through a darkened park at 3 a.m. and expect a high level of security? No, they do not. Do gay men having sex in a park at 3 a.m. have the right to a high level of security? No, they do not.'[4] What appeared to be a clear-cut case of 'gay-bashing' had suddenly become highly complex. A gay man attacked in a gay cruising area was being told his attack was not a hate crime. And Steve, who hadn't even been having sex in the park that night, was now fuelling a debate about prostitution and public sex!

Another troubling aspect of the crime was the behaviour of the witnesses. Two men saved Steve's life by carrying him to a car and driving him to the hospital. But having done that, they simply dropped him at the emergency room and took off – presumably, they were reluctant to explain their presence in Stanley Park at three in the morning. Although one man did call the police later that day, it made me wonder: Would the men have bolted so quickly if the victim had been Asian, elderly, or disabled?

Learning the Ropes

As a freelance journalist, I had published articles on AIDS and gay and lesbian issues for various publications. Now I wanted to learn more, so I returned to graduate school and began asking questions. My first question was why there was so little discussion of homophobic violence in the criminological literature. Faulkner notes that there is 'little or no recognition' of queer-bashing in most criminology texts, 'thus relegating discussions of heterosexed violence to the fringes of criminological investigation.'[5]

An analysis of textbooks used by law enforcement students in the United States found almost no mention of gay and lesbian issues; they discussed other minority groups at much greater length.[6] One Canadian textbook includes a few pages about sexual orientation, but gets the term wrong (the section is titled 'Gender Orientation'). One short essay in the text is based on four newspaper articles but makes no reference to recent Canadian research. The other two short essays were researched and written in the United States, and make no reference to Canada – this, in spite of the textbook's title.[7]

I also wanted to learn what was happening outside Vancouver. I went to Mexico and wrote about the dozens of transvestites, transsexuals, and gay men who had been murdered in the early 1990s.[8] I joined the national board of EGALE (Equality for Gays and Lesbians Everywhere), which is Canada's gay and lesbian equality rights organization, and participated in an Amnesty International conference in Amsterdam during the 1998 Gay Games. One afternoon I sat in a circle with activists from around the globe, all of whom had chilling stories to share.[9] In 2003 I moderated a roundtable discussion in Istanbul titled 'Extreme Violence in Homosexual Homicides.[10]

In 1997, I learned a lot by developing and teaching a criminology course at Simon Fraser University called 'Homosexuality and Social Control.' Although one American survey found law enforcement students to be more homophobic than undergraduates in other disciplines, my predominantly heterosexual students were very open-minded and eager to learn about queer issues. Guest speakers included a gay prison nurse, a transsexual police officer, a gay Crown prosecutor, a lesbian activist, and MP Svend Robinson. I also took my students on a tour of the West End. We visited Little Sister's bookstore, the queer community centre, and 'Boystown,' a section in Yaletown where male prostitutes ply their trade.

I pointed out to my students that if two male students left the classroom holding hands, they might get assaulted. The hand-holding experiment seemed like the perfect didactic exercise to demonstrate the dangers of being queer. I hesitated, however – chilled by the case of the late Michèle Pujol, a University of Victoria women's studies instructor who had given her students a similar assignment: 'Spend 10 minutes walking around campus holding hands ... Feel free to be demonstratively affectionate. Try to walk around crowded areas.' One student became indignant: even though she had been given the option of not doing the exercise, she complained that the course had a 'lesbian bias' and filed a sexual harassment complaint, later overturned.[11]

Where to Begin?

According to Faulkner, 'there is still a wide gap' in our knowledge of the extent of 'heterosexed violence in Canada.'[12] I needed to take a problem that I and my community 'know' is 'true' and 'prove' to a broader, more sceptical audience that it exists. This required a critical approach. Scott notes that people sometimes take this violence as a 'given' and assume 'that the facts of history speak for themselves.' This approach gives us an 'act of power or domination ... What we don't have is a way of placing those alternatives within the framework [of] dominant patterns of sexuality and the ideology that supports them. We know how they exist but not how they're constructed.'[13]

To analyse queer-bashing in Canada, I asked two research questions: How prevalent is homophobic violence in Canada? And how can homophobic violence be curtailed in Canada? These questions allowed me to take an exploratory approach, to cast a wide net into uncharted Canadian waters. The first question exposes how little we know and how disparate our information sources are. The second proposes a diligent application of this knowledge.

What's the Good Word?

Researchers in this area have had to confront a bewildering set of terms, each with its own advantages and disadvantages, each possessing different shades of meaning and 'qualifications for membership': *gay, queer, gay man, gay woman, lesbian, homosexual, bisexual,* and *MSM* – '*men who have sex with men.*' Over the past thirty years there has been a shift from a *gay movement* to a *gay and lesbian movement* to a *gay, lesbian, bisexual, transgendered (GLBT) movement* to *a queer movement.*

Academics have negotiated this semantic quagmire in various ways. Kinsman – the author of *The Regulation of Desire* and Canada's expert on the regulation of homosexuality – finds *homosexual* to be rather clinical, and prefers *gay* when referring to post–Second World War same-sex identities, which he associates with an affirmative social movement.[14] Mort sees the shift to *queer* from *gay and lesbian* as highly symbolic of a generational split: 'Gay politics has been cast as flabby and reformist; the product of comfortable, middle-aged men holding to a tired, 1970s sexual agenda ... It is queer that now signifies youth, style and vibrancy.'[15] MacDougall opts for *homosexual,* arguing that the term is more common in legal discourse than *queer* and less cumbersome than *gay, lesbian, and bisexual.*[16] Although many younger Canadians feel that *homosexual* is derogatory, graduate students and faculty use it liberally, especially disciples of Michel Foucault, whose English translations are filled with the word *homosexual,* rather than *gay* or *lesbian.*[17] (In French, the word *homosexuel* is more common and less pejorative.)

The terms *transgender* and *transgendered* have become increasingly popular over the past ten years, often serving an 'umbrella' function to cover the following terms: *preoperative (pre-op)* and *postoperative (post-op) male-to-female (MTF)* and *female-to-male (FTM) transsexuals,* as well as people who identify as *drag queens, drag kings, trannies, male impersonators, female impersonators, transvestites, cross-dressers, two-spirited, androgynous, intersex,* and *pan-sexuals,* who presumably transcend all previously noted categories! Although this *transgendered* category makes sense in theory, the transsexual women I interviewed (all of them over forty) never referred to themselves as 'transgendered.' They had put a lot of time and energy into being accepted as women and were proud to be known as transsexual women. (I also met someone who used the term *no-op.* He was taking female hormones to develop breasts but had no intention of undergoing the surgery.)

Queer, which I use often, is the most convenient and inclusive term, but also the most controversial, especially for those born before 1970, who remember *queer* as an extremely derogatory term. One Canadian academic told me:

> Not very fond of the term 'queer,' and it has not received general acceptance as of yet. I also disagree with some of the intended/purported purposes of its usage. In fact, I believe the different and unspecified communities/ identities it refers to do not in many cases want to be perceived as a 'whole,' as they have different ideologies, beliefs, goals, and ways of accomplishing goals. As 'gay' can be argued to be male-identified, so too can 'queer' be argued to be 'youth' and 'politically' identified. So how is that progress?[18]

As criminological literature on this topic proliferates, so do the terms. *Anti-gay violence* is obviously limited because it omits references to lesbians. The terms *anti-gay and -lesbian violence* and *violence against lesbians and gay men* are unwieldy, and furthermore, they omit reference to violence directed against the transgendered – who may not even be homosexual in their orientation, but whose victimization is often lumped together with statistics tracking *anti-gay violence. Sexual orientation victimization* (SOV) excludes the transgendered, who technically belong to a gender-identity category (since many continue to be attracted to the same sex they were attracted to before their sex change). *Queer-bashing* and *homophobic violence,* while not perfect, have a more inclusive feel.

Homophobia, Domestic Violence, and Female Victimization

I have tried to steer away from a discussion on domestic violence within the queer community – an often controversial topic. Paul Forseth, a Reform MP, accused gay men of being at least as violent as straight men, 'especially where you have alcohol and drugs, and mix that with very short-term changing sexual relationships and all the jealousies ... They are vengeful, and their health isn't very good.'[19]

Instead, I focus my attention on violence that is motivated by hate – on acts of violence against 'the other' because the victim is, or is perceived to be, queer. Incidents involving openly gay men and women who assault or kill their partners, although an important topic of research, are not analysed in this book. Of course, there will always be some overlap. A closeted homosexual who hates himself can kill his partner because he hates homosexuality. For example, 'Pete' told me he once dated a guy whom he discovered was a gay-basher; the man beat up two gay men in front of Pete in a park. Pete's own relationship with the man was abusive. Looking back on it, Pete felt the attacks were intended to keep him 'in line.'[20]

The lines were just as blurred when Wisconsin police were called to an incident involving an older man and a younger Laotian man. The older man was Jeffrey Dahmer. The police returned the young man to Dahmer's custody, having concluded that the incident had been a 'domestic' between two gay lovers. Unfortunately, Dahmer was a serial killer, and the young man would be his last victim.[21]

But what about a young, predatory man who claims to be straight, but who has a secretive, abusive, remunerative, on-again, off-again sexual relationship with an older gay man? In many of these killings, the young man is homophobic: although he has sex with the older man, he takes pains to distance himself from the victim's homosexuality. In these cases, the police often negate the possibility of hate motivation and label these killings 'domestic violence,' a crime of 'passion,' or a robbery gone bad. I believe this approach is overly simplistic. I prefer to place these incidents on a continuum of homophobia and to examine the extent to which the violence – or the investigation, prosecution, and public disclosure of the incident – is saturated with homophobia.

The degree to which each sex experiences homophobic violence is also a sensitive issue. Petersen questions the conventional wisdom that gay male victims predominate: 'Studies have served to reinforce that belief because the methodologies employed by researchers have produced distorted and gender-biased results.' Political, research, and media organizations have overrepresented gay male victims, having 'failed to recognize that lesbian-bashing is at least as pervasive as gay-bashing. They have not even considered the possibility that lesbians suffer greater victimization than gay men.'[22]

But what does 'lesbian-bashing' mean? A Montreal magazine surveyed lesbians and found the following:

- 63 per cent of the victims knew the perpetrators in cases involving a robbery
- 67 per cent of the victims knew the perpetrators in cases involving threats
- 100 per cent of the victims knew the perpetrators in assault cases[23]

A literature is emerging that explores the extent and nature of lesbian victimization.[24] One survey found that lesbians experienced significantly higher rates of non-sexual physical violence than heterosexual women.[25] Another article featured interviews with young activists in the 'Lesbian Avengers' movement, who spoke of the dangers they faced in their daily lives.[26] Ault points out that gay men's concerns dominate queer anti-violence projects, which downplay misogynistic violence: women are relegated to the role of the maternal 'emotional worker,' caring for gay male victims. Gay men's groups claim to promote an end to heterosexism, yet they fail to confront the issue of male domination.[27]

My own research methods, discussed in the next chapter, netted only a small number of female victims. As shown in table I.1, in the 335 queer-bashing cases I analysed, only 8.4 per cent of victims were female. Women figured even less significantly in the hundred homicides I analysed; as shown in table I.2, they accounted for less than 3 per cent of the victims.

I came across other lesbian homicide victims – killed by their female partners, female ex-partners, or female roommates – but these cases fell slightly outside the bounds of my research.[28] I was looking for homicides in which the killer appeared to target a woman *because* she was lesbian or bisexual, or because she expressed a desire to be with a woman.

An Overview

In the following chapters, I link theories and ideas with hundreds of 'real world' cases of homophobic violence that have occurred in Canada since 1990. Chapter 1, 'Methodology and the Media,' examines the myriad methodological conundra inherent in this type of research: invisibility, underreporting, and the lack of clarity regarding what actually consti-tutes a hate crime. I explain how I designed my research project and how I netted more than four hundred cases. Since many of these were culled

Table I.1
Number and sex of victims in queer-bashing incidents

No. of victims in an incident	No. of cases	%	Total victims	% of victims
1 male	239	71.6	239	56
2 male	45	13.4	90	21.2
3 male	14	3.9	42	9.9
4 male	2	0.6	8	1.8
1 female	17	5.1	17	4
2 female	8	2.4	16	3.7
3 female	1	0.3	3	.7
1 MTF transsexual	9	2.7	9	2.7
Total	335	100	424	100

Table I.2
Number and gender of victims in queer-bashing homicides

No. of victims in an incident	No. of cases	%	Total victims	% of victims
1 female	3	3	3	2.8
1 male	87	87	87	81.3
2 males	4	4	8	7.5
3 males	1	1	3	2.8
1 transsexual female	4	4	4	3.7
1 transsexual female and 1 transvestite male	1	1	2	1.9
Total	100	100	107	100

from the media, I also critically analyse media representations of homosexuality and homophobic violence.

There is no single theory that can explain all dimensions of homophobic violence. In chapter 2, 'Theories of Homophobia: Why Do They Want to Hurt Us?' I examine theories from a variety of disciplines: criminology, sociology, psychology, philosophy, and social work. These theories shed light on several key ideas: social control, sexual regulation, the social construction of homosexuality, queer theory, and theories of homophobia. Patrick Hopkins's concept of 'gender treachery' and Gail Mason's theory of anti-lesbian violence are powerful tools for helping demystify homophobic violence.

In chapter 3, 'The Horror of Homophobic Violence,' I apply theories of *abjection* to explore extreme homophobic violence. Then I enumerate various characteristics of homophobic crime and explain how specific subgroups are affected: youths, students, the transgendered, prostitutes, prisoners, and queer refugees.

Chapter 4, 'Law, Homophobia and Violence: Legislating against Hate,' reviews legal scholarship on how homophobia is reproduced in law. I provide examples of homophobic practices in the Canadian legal system. Jenness's research demonstrates trends in American hate-crime legislation; legal remedies for victims are also discussed.

Chapter 5, 'Homo-cide: Getting Away with It,' considers the hypothesis that men who kill queers 'get away with murder.' I describe the evolution of the concept of 'homosexual panic' and show how it masks and condones certain killings in Canada's criminal justice system. I also analyse more than a hundred homicides that have occurred in Canada since 1990.

In chapter 6, 'Homophobia, Violence, and Policing in Canada,' I investigate the legacy of police homophobia, the way police treat queer officers, and how the police target the queer community. I provide examples of police officers who have engaged in queer-bashing. I also evaluate the ability of twenty different police departments across Canada to keep track of hate crimes.

Chapter 7, 'Urban Cowboys and Rural Rednecks: Community Resistance to Homophobic Violence,' compares the distinct approaches to homophobic violence in Toronto, Montreal, Vancouver, and Ottawa. I demonstrate how these programs have evolved, and I reflect on how successful these approaches have been. I also consider how homophobic violence affects smaller cities, rural areas, and northern regions.

Finally, in the conclusion I review the most pressing issues that have emerged from my research. I suggest ways we can all learn from the horrors of homophobic violence – and how we can make Canada a safer place for young people.

CHAPTER 1

Methodology and the Media: Reading between the Lines

In this chapter I describe the methodological difficulties inherent in this research: invisibility, underreporting, and conflicting definitions regarding what constitutes homophobic violence. I explain how I came up with more than four hundred cases, and I critically examine the way homophobic violence is reported in the media.

In the following crime, the closetedness of the victim allowed events to go undetected. In 1998, nineteen-year-old Stewart Myers met his victim – a closeted, fifty-four-year-old man – outside a Water Street bar in St John's. They bought some beer and proceeded to a wooded area. Myers recalled: 'I thought he was gay. He was playing with my penis ... As he was taking a piss, he fell down, I reached over and grabbed a rock and hit him over the head ... Then I took the money out of his pocket. There was blood coming out of his nose, and I just left him there not knowing what would happen to him.' The victim, who had three teeth knocked out, staggered to a service station and called an ambulance, claiming that he had been assaulted at a local pub. He was hospitalized for a week with lacerations, a concussion, and chipped bones. It was only several months later that police realized the homophobic nature of the assault.

Myers later attempted suicide, after which he told a police officer at the hospital that he was a gay-basher – and admitted that he was confused because he had once kissed a man. His lawyer argued that the attack was a robbery and had not occurred 'because he hated homosexuals or wanted to hurt them.' The judge disagreed, stating when he sentenced Myers to three years for robbery: 'Sexual orientation may have provided the accused with an appropriate victim at least in his mind.'[1]

The Presumed Sexual Orientation of Research Subjects

The above case points to one of the major difficulties social scientists face when researching queer populations, whose visibility is contingent on social, cultural, and geographical factors, including self-identification. For example, according to Ross, a lesbian interview subject 'may build her emotional, physical and sexual life with another woman and yet not identify as either lesbian or gay.'[2]

As early as 1941, McHenry argued that when it comes to homosexual victimization, the 'casual reader' of the crime section should be 'sufficiently sophisticated to read between the lines.'[3] After a New York man was killed, police 'found numerous erotic pictures and photographs of stalwart nude males ... The dead man was obviously a homosexual, from the evidence, with a preference for more vigorous companions.'[4] In 1961, Reiss raised questions about the uneasy relationship between 'adult male fellators' and the young rough trade who preyed on them: 'The fellator risks violence, therefore, if he threatens the boy's self-conception by suggesting that the boy may be homosexual and treats him as if he were ... Violence ... integrates their norms and expectations by controlling and combatting behavior which violates them. On the other hand, it protects the boy's self-identity as nonhomosexual and reinforces his self-conception as "masculine."'[5]

Tearoom Trade – Humphreys's 1970 study of surreptitious homosexual encounters in public toilets – pried open the closet door and shone a very bright light inside. His unconventional research methods shook the social science community to its core – in fact, one of his colleagues actually punched him at an academic conference.[6] Humphreys observed hundreds of men having sex in 'tearooms.' He knew that since so many lived double lives, very few would consent to be interviewed. So he wrote down their licence plates, found out where they lived, disguised himself, and knocked on their doors, claiming to be doing a survey on 'men's health.' Humphreys justified his actions by stating: 'Clearly, I could not knock on the door of a suburban residence and say, "Excuse me, I saw you engaging in a homosexual act in a tearoom last year, and I wonder if I might ask you a few questions?"'[7]

Not surprisingly, Humphreys found that 54 per cent of his research subjects were married: 'Maybe, like some tearoom regulars, he will work with Boy Scouts in the evenings and spend much of his weekend at the church.'[8] In fact, many queer people spend all their lives 'passing.'[9] Berger attempted to measure the extent to which gay men attempt to 'pass,' and found that parents 'were among those less likely to know.'[10]

Invisibility and Underreporting: 'The Dark-Pink Figure'

The number of crimes that are never reported is called the 'dark figure.' Roberts offers three reasons why the dark figure for hate crimes is especially high: fear of additional victimization, fear that the report will not be taken seriously, and, in the case of gay and lesbian victimization, fear of homophobic police attitudes.[11] 'Gay-bashing is probably the least likely to be reported of all hate crimes,' he states. 'Gays and lesbians are less likely to trust the police than any other minority.'[12]

According to Sagarin and MacNamara, 'the homosexual victim may be ashamed, unable to face police, and frightened of complications threatening to his job or other aspects of his life that could arise as a result of making a complaint.'[13] An Edmonton police officer told me: 'It only comes to the attention of the police if the victim says it was hate-related. It doesn't get talked about unless the victim doesn't mind if everyone knows.'[14] A Winnipeg officer reflected: 'It's not so bad to say to the police that you're gay, but then the question is, "Is my lifestyle, my name and my family going to be dragged through court?"'[15]

Most surveys and opinion polls in the media use probablistic sampling – a random sampling of the general population, often with the help of postal codes or telephone numbers. However, since queers do not have a 'Q' beside their name in the phone book, random sampling is impossible. Harry observes that white, educated men between twenty-five and forty-five are usually overrepresented in surveys of the gay male community – which parallels an oversupply of white, educated research subjects in 'both probability and non-probability samples of the general population.'[16]

Victimization surveys in the queer community generally use non-probability or 'opportunistic' sampling. However, these surveys present a huge problem: lack of representativeness. Stanko and Curry put it bluntly: the surveys 'provide only a crude picture' because methodological problems 'plague' the projects.[17] Martin and Dean argue that because of the stigma attached to homosexuality, 'only a very select type of gay man would be willing to state his sexual preference or describe his sexual behavior during a brief screening interview.'[18] Herek and Berrill point out that representativeness can also be compromised by how surveys are distributed – for example, at a meeting of gay anti-violence activists. Other surveys may be biased simply because of their wording: even 'the words *gay* or *lesbian* ... may discourage closeted respondents.'[19]

Differing Definitions: What Constitutes a Homophobic Crime?

What queers perceive to be a crime may in fact be radically different from what the police or Crown attorneys perceive. At a radical 'kiss-in' at Toronto's Eaton Centre, filmmaker John Greyson, who was videotaping this demonstration of queer affection, was arrested and had his camcorder confiscated because the police declared it could be used as a 'dangerous weapon' – even though the CBC was shooting only a few feet away.[20]

Police sometimes have difficulty 'naming' violent behaviour that is perpetrated against homosexuals. In a 1995 survey, twenty-two police officers and prosecutors were asked: 'Is there hate activity in your region?' The following regions said 'No': British Columbia, the Northwest Territories, Saskatchewan, Ontario, and New Brunswick.[21]

I wrote to the Edmonton Police Service and asked a homicide detective whether any gay men had been killed in the city – and, if so, whether any of the homicides had been motivated by hate. Had any of the gay men been targeted by predators? James Miles, sixty-one, was on his list of six gay men who had been killed over a twelve-year period. Sabu Weerasooriya, a twenty-year-old Sri Lankan immigrant, was accused of strangling the victim after he and another man were discovered repeatedly withdrawing money from the victim's bank account.[22] Reflecting on the killings, the detective rejected the possibility of hate motivation: 'They all involved disagreements between lovers or sudden anger brought on by alcohol or drugs ... None of them ... involved predatory motivation on the part of the accused ... More along the lines of lovers' spats.'[23]

When I asked a Toronto hate crimes detective what he felt was 'the worst case' of gay-bashing he had ever heard of, he mentioned an assault in Los Angeles. When I asked him what he thought about two transgendered prostitutes who had been shot to death in Toronto at point-blank range, he explained that these homicides did not fall into his department's classification of a hate crime.[24] In fact, even though I gathered evidence on more than one hundred homicides for this book, not one of the twenty police departments I surveyed considered these killings as meeting their definition of 'hate-motivated.'

One of the few exceptions to this was in 2001, after Aaron Webster was killed in Stanley Park. An RCMP hate crimes officer in Vancouver made the staggering observation that 'if Webster was murdered because of his sexual orientation, it would be the first hate-motivated murder of a gay man in B.C. history.'[25] Of course, that was according to his own definition. If he were to ask the friends and families of the several other queer victims in B.C. whose killings are described in this book, he would no doubt get a different response.

Even some queer activists are reluctant to frame such killings as hate crimes. If you call The 519, Toronto's queer community centre, and ask them for statistics, they will tell you how many hate-related assaults, sexual assaults, and attempted murders have been committed. But if you ask them about murders, they will tell you, 'We don't keep track' – even though more than thirty queers have been killed in their city since the early 1990s.

If This Isn't a Hate Crime, Then What Is?

The following triple murder was never actually framed by the Toronto police as a possible hate crime. In 1996, Marcello Palma shot three street prostitutes: a woman, a pre-op transsexual named Deanna Wilkinson, and a transvestite prostitute, Shawn Keegan, whose nickname was 'Junior.'[26] The three bodies were discovered within hours of each other; each had been shot in the head.[27] A gay hairdresser claimed that two years before the murders, Palma had tried to pick him up on Church Street when the hairdresser was in drag, walking home from a club. Apparently Palma stopped his truck, chatted the cross-dresser up, and gave him his pager number. Palma eventually came over to his place, the hairdresser said, and wanted to have sex with him.[28]

Before the shootings, Palma had been undergoing psychiatric treatment. He told his psychiatrist he had had sex with 'prostitutes, transvestites and homosexuals' and that he wanted to kill street people and 'scum.' You would think this kind of talk, which recurred over several sessions, would have prompted somebody to check whether he owned any guns. In fact, he had 'six restricted weapons certificates and owned six firearms,' including the Sturm Ruger 57 he used – with illegal hollowpoint bullets – to kill all three victims. Before his arrest, he fled to Montreal, where he legally purchased a Winchester rifle and a box of ammunition with a firearm certificate.[29]

After a three-year delay, the case finally came to trial. Christie Blatchford said bluntly that Palma was 'a piece of work' and described his uncanny resemblance to Jack Nicholson in *The Shining*: 'He's Jack on steroids ... A similar wicked and endearing grin that splits his face, the same intense and unblinking stare.' The more the defence tried to demonstrate his insanity, the more it 'supports the prosecution view of him as a narcissist with a simmering rage, and not as someone who was, essentially, off his rocker.'[30]

One psychiatrist said that Palma 'was in a brief psychotic episode' at the time of the murders and was suffering from a 'dissociative disorder,' but added that he was not 'a psychopath or a schizophrenic.' Palma said that men had sexually abused him twice when he was a child.[31] After nearly five years of legal wrangling, the possibility that the killings had been motivated by hate had been successfully expunged from the public discourse. In 2001, Palma was found guilty of first-degree murder and sentenced to a minimum of twenty-five years. He was prohibited from possessing weapons for the rest of his life, and was required to give a DNA sample.[32]

Problematic Interactions between Victims and Perpetrators

Homophobic violence can happen randomly to people who are simply walking down the street, minding their own business. Police have known for years that queer neighbourhoods are magnets for queer-bashers; both gay and straight men place themselves at risk simply by walking alone on, say, Church Street in Toronto. Attacks can be triggered by a single glance, a verbal exchange, or nothing at all.[33] Some incidents can be traced to interactions with relatives, neighbours, or acquaintances.[34]

However, many cases in this book are less clear-cut; prostitution, robbery, public sex, drugs, alcohol, and rape must often be folded into the mix. In fact, 33 per cent of the hundred-plus homicides I analysed involved robbery or attempted robbery.[35] In 1994, for example, Henry Isaac, fifty, met a thirty-three-year-old prostitute named Leonard Welch at a Toronto gay bar and took him home.[36] Isaac was stabbed six times, but actually died of asphyxiation after being gagged with a dish towel.[37] His hands and feet had been bound. Welch was captured on videotape trying to withdraw money with the victim's bank card.[38]

To create one single category – Queer Victim – and another single category – Queer Basher – is to ignore the diverse and complex settings in which the Basher and the Bashed often find themselves. For example, in 1990 a Montreal chambermaid discovered the body of Brian Booth. His hands had been tied behind his back with wire, and a towel had been stuffed down his throat. He had come from Whitehorse for a convention. An article described him as a 'good family man,' active in the Royal Canadian Air Cadets. His family was understandably devastated.[39]

Reiss's research, although dated, details where 'queers' and 'peers' meet: 'Street corners, public parks, men's toilets ... parks or hotels.'[40] Many of the queers he observed did not seem to be participating in any overt or covert homosexual groups.[41] Sagarin and MacNamara hypothesize that homosexual victimization 'increases with casualness, anonymity, age discrepancy, sado-masochistic activity, alcohol and the "prostitutional" character of an interaction between two men. There is a class of criminals who prey on homosexuals.'[42]

Harry suggests that 'fag-bashing' is linked both to public sex and to 'the frequency with which a gay man visits places culturally defined as deviant, such as gay bars, or ... a known gay neighborhood.'[43] Miller and Humphreys observe that 42 per cent of the homicide victims they studied were 'overt homosexuals' who frequented gay-identified areas and were killed by gangs. In contrast, only 12 per cent of the 'covert' group met a similar fate.[44]

An analysis of seventeen homosexual murder victims in Amsterdam reveals that only one did not die in his own home; the exception was killed in a public toilet.[45] Over an eighteen-month period in Montreal's queer community, the perpetrator was listed as 'unknown' in only 28.6 per cent of the cases.[46] In a British survey of 'homosexually active' men who were sexually assaulted, consensual sex had immediately preceded more than one-quarter of the incidents.[47] An activist in Hamilton said that victims had come forward 'six or seven times' to tell him they had been bashed, but 'four or five of them admitted they fanned the flames.'[48] Clearly, these violent crimes fall into a grey area: Is the victim being assaulted because he's gay, or are other factors at play? For example, the following poster distributed in Toronto gay bars demonstrates how to 'date safe.'

> Assaulted or robbed by someone you picked up?
> You can do something about it.
> REPORT IT!

> - Find out who he is
> - Introduce him to others
> - Get/mix your own drinks
> - Trust your instincts[49]

Vancouver lawyer Ken Smith complains that police do not take assaults seriously if they find out a gay male victim voluntarily invited the perpetrator into his apartment: 'The implication is that we are the makers of our own destiny.'[50]

A tiny article in the *Vancouver Sun* is especially revealing because of what it *doesn't* say. A twenty-eight-year-old man was stabbed to death in his West End apartment: 'There was no indication the man was robbed or that the attack was a gay-bashing incident.'[51] The police never identified the victim as a gay man, so why would they go out of their way to tell the press that it was *not* a gay-bashing? Normally, this is police code for: 'The victim was gay, but there was no break-in. He appears to have voluntarily allowed the killer into his apartment; therefore, this is not a "hate crime" since it doesn't involve an "innocent" victim who arouses public sympathy.'

Designing a National Research Project

Academic Material

The preceding case warranted only a few sentences in the Vancouver papers. To write this book, I could not rely on superficial media reports or guarded police statements. I would have to use every medium available to me: scholarship, interviews, newspaper articles, and other documents. Over the past twenty years, little has been published in academe about queer-bashing in Canada.[52]

Legal Cases

A search of criminal and civil cases in the QuickLaw database netted several homicides that had already been reported in the media, but it also provided two murder cases from smaller B.C. communities that I probably would not have heard about otherwise.[53] R. v. Butler describes the brutal murder of Dennis Lee Fichtenberg, who met his fate in a trailer near Prince George. Butler, who was convicted of second-degree murder, claimed to be fending off a 'homosexual advance.' The appellate decision contains chilling excerpts from the killer's confession, in which he uses the euphemism *hit* to describe how he stabbed the victim.

> I reached over to pull out the knife to cut up the god damn onion and ... his hand brushed up against my leg. Now when you get all this fag talk going on ... I said to him, with the knife in my hand, don't fuck around ... So he walks over behind me and takes one of the knives out of the pot ... I sort of looked over the shoulder and he says, he says knives don't bother me ... I

grabbed onto the blade of his knife ... I hit him with the knife that I had, and ah, he looked at me and he said he was sorry and then I said to him, it's a little too late to be sorry now because I looked at the side where I hit him, the blood was just you know, coming out fast. I knew he was going to die, just from that wound ... I hit him again with the knife in the neck and he fell on the floor ... I was covered in blood ... and he was just laying there, I forgot the third time I hit him ... It was in the chest ... and I took his keys and his wallet ... Before I left he was laying down on the floor and there was a lot of blood and he was making wheezing noises, his lungs were filling up with blood from the first hit, and I went over and hit him a couple of more times in the chest and then I left.[54]

In the original trial, a mysterious spectator stomped out of the court-room, shouting: 'There's too many lies here. I have to get out.' Butler lost his appeal; his original sentence – ineligible to apply for parole for thirteen years – remained intact.

Interviews and Correspondence

I interviewed and corresponded with hundreds of Canadians, including queer-bashing victims, family and friends of homicide victims, queer activists, criminal justice personnel, academics, journalists, and other people affected by homophobic violence. This was the most time-con-suming aspect of my research, but also the most rewarding because it gave me an opportunity to engage with other concerned citizens: in each major city across Canada, I talked to at least one person from the queer community and at least one person from the criminal justice system.

This snowball method led to contacts in other cities and towns where it was more difficult to find people to interview. Most people allowed me to use their names, although one activist from a smaller Canadian city – who had recently been threatened and stalked – was understandably reluctant to do so. In this book, I use the names of homicide victims, but use the names of living victims sparingly, except in high-profile cases or when victims have expressly encouraged me to use their names. Many victims' lives have been permanently damaged; they are trying to put this trauma behind them.

Police Data

Talking to police departments was the most frustrating part of my re-search. It amazed me that nobody had ever picked up a phone and called across the country, asking the 'simple' question: 'How many homosexuals have been bashed in your jurisdiction?' The 'simple question' turned into a big deal: you would think I had been asking them to provide me with state secrets. By nature, police departments are quite bureaucratic and hierarchical in structure. In some cases I was referred to a person who knew nothing about the topic. Even though street cops are usually the most knowledgeable in this area, they are often not permitted to speak to civilian researchers. Some police departments called me back within hours of receiving my request; others engaged me warmly over the phone, but would provide no specific data. These data are analysed in chapter 6.

The Sudbury Police Department wrote to say that 'the questions have been reviewed and it is felt that there are too many personal opinions required. Also, the information you are seeking, regarding violence, may be obtained from Statistics Canada ... We do not wish to participate in this survey.'[55] The irony, of course, was that if Statistics Canada had been able to provide me with data on homophobic violence, I probably wouldn't have been writing this book in the first place! A year and a half later, I had a long conversation with a new Sudbury superintendant who was more politically correct.

Miscellaneous Data

This book also contains a lot of miscellaneous data collected from disparate sources. For example, representatives from the Hamilton liaison committee spent weeks compiling crimes that dated back fifteen years. A Calgary source prepared and faxed me a thirty-page report. Much of this information is one-of-a-kind; embedded in these documents are data that, when taken as a whole, provide a unique picture of queer-bashing in Canada. These documents include reports, correspondence, statistics, briefs, submissions, information downloaded from websites, newsletters, public relations materials, minutes and records kept by individuals and organizations, posters, training and procedural manuals, police files, and legal documents such as transcripts and affidavits.

After I mentioned to a Regina activist that I was having trouble getting data from her region, she passed along the request to her community. I received an e-mail from a woman with the names of two Saskatchewan gay men who had been murdered. She thanked me for doing this research and added: 'It gives me no pleasure to give you these names, but they must be remembered.' In the end, I felt honoured to have been so well received.

Table 1.1
Categorizing homophobic incidents

Type of crime	No. of cases	%
Threats	51	14.8
Threats with robbery/attempted robbery	5	1.5
Physical violence	229	66.8
Physical violence with robbery/attempted robbery	38	11.1
Sexual assault	12	3.5
Sexual assault with robbery/attempted robbery	2	.6
Other robbery incidents	6	1.7
Total	344	100

My Own Definitions of Homophobic Violence

I chose an arbitrary date: incidents that had occurred since 1 January 1990. Because I was relying on media reports or other people's descriptions of an incident, some details were inevitably missing. I realized I would be unable to divide them into precise Criminal Code categories. So I created my own system, which I followed throughout my research. Table 1.1 shows the breakdown of incidents by category.

I defined 'threatening behaviour' as verbal threats, written threats, or chasing, following, or spitting at the victim. Examples: one activist 're-ceived death threats at work after he wrote a gay positive letter to the Editor of the *London Free Press*'; others were threatened while entering London's gay and lesbian community centre.[56] Most of the incidents I analysed involved overt physical violence, which I defined as hitting, punching, shooting, stabbing, bludgeoning, pushing, spraying, and/or kicking.[57]

Almost 15 per cent of the incidents shown in table 1.1 involved a robbery or attempted robbery.[58] This number is similar to the results of a controversial American survey of the gay male community that explored promiscuity – a topic that many believe is unnecessarily judgmental, moralistic, and intrusive. Researchers asked 150 gay men, 'How many different men would you roughly estimate you have had sex with since you were 18?'

- 35 per cent said they had had sex with fewer than 100 men
- 42 per cent said they had had sex with between 100 and 499 men
- 23 per cent said they had had sex with more than 500 men (with one man reporting 10,000 sexual partners)

Overall, 21 per cent of the men sampled said they had been robbed; however, 41 per cent of the most promiscuous group reported having been robbed.[59]

Gay Men, Sexual Assault, and Homophobic Violence

According to my analysis, 4 per cent of the incidents involved sexual assault.[60] But this begs the question: When men are sexually assaulted by other men, is it homophobic violence? Or is it just violence? There doesn't seem to be any consensus on this issue.

Two incidents in St John's demonstrate how debilitating and complex sexual violence can be. In 1997 a young man in that city was lured into an alley and raped; prayers and religious words were used during the attack. 'The young man was hurt less physically (he didn't resist for fear of being seriously hurt) as much as emotionally. He was traumatized and confused. The religious aspect of this was quite disturbing.'[61] In 2000, a group of teenagers used a tree branch to anally penetrate another teenage boy. Newfoundland Gays and Lesbians for Equality (NGALE) declined to be interviewed by the CBC; they felt it wasn't really a gay issue and that it was beyond their expertise.

In their literature review, Stermac, Sheridan, and Davidson noted that links are rarely made between anti-gay violence and sexual assault. However, they also found evidence that men conflicted about their sexuality rape other men 'as a means of symbolically defeating some unresolved aspect of themselves.'[62] They studied twenty-nine male sexual assault victims in Toronto and found that the majority had been coerced into sex by male 'partners or acquaintances ... by use of threats of intimidation.'[63] Not all victims disclosed their sexual orientation, but those who did were all gay. Many victims said they had been sexually assaulted in gay cruising areas. The authors contended that 'these were not homophobic assaults ... victim and perpetrator were gay and initially consented to a casual pickup ... not suggestive of antigay violence.'[64]

However, this interpretation assumes that (a) any man who goes into a cruising area and seeks out a gay victim to sexually assault *must* be gay; and therefore (b) any resultant sexual assault cannot logically be a gay-bashing because it's two gay men having sex together. This is like saying, 'A man who picks up a prostitute and then beats her up is not engaging in misogynistic violence because the two of them knew what they were getting themselves into.' Here is an area in urgent need of research: Why do men go into gay environments, draw gay men into compromising situations, and then sexually assault them? And why do academic researchers not see these as gay-bashings?

A study of 287 gay men in Vancouver found that one-third 'had been forced to have sex against their will at least once in their lives.' One gay man with AIDS who had been sexually abused said: 'The only way I could be happy was to be accepted by other men, to allow other men to control me.' The researchers noted that it is difficult for some rape victims 'to fend off unwanted sex and insist that their partners wear a condom. It can also make people so depressed they don't care whether they get infected with HIV.'[65]

A San Francisco study of men who have sex with men found that those who had been sexually abused as children were more likely to engage in high-risk behaviour, defined as unprotected anal intercourse with a 'non-primary partner' or serodiscordant partner.[66] Gay men who have been sexually abused sometimes rationalize their victimization by saying: 'That's what you get for taking chances ... Life's an experience.'[67] A British article noted that 'fantasies of the sexually-forceful man, the pleasure of "being taken," and the excitement of power-driven sex are very common in gay culture and pornography. All these collective sexual fantasies normalize sexual abuse ... providing motivation, justification and normalization for the assault.'[68]

In this vein, the editor of a Toronto gay magazine complained that a straight male journalist who wrote a column about the gay scene was a 'dinosaur' and an 'old fart.' The editor suggested that 'to spice up his bland reputation,' the journalist should 'go to a bathhouse and put his saggy ass in the air, his face in a pillow and see who rams him from behind ... I will happily supply the condoms and a lot of lube (cuz God knows he'll need it).'[69] This perhaps helps explain a story recounted to me by one of my students: He interviewed a gay man who had been raped by someone who broke into his Vancouver apartment. The victim said that his friends, instead of providing emotional support, constantly repeated crude sexual jokes about the incident, insinuating that he must have enjoyed it. My student, who was heterosexual, asked me why gay men did this. I had no answer for him.

Hundreds of Media Sources

This book includes references to documentary films, transcripts of radio and television broadcasts, and more than five hundred mainstream and alternative newpaper articles. Because of my reliance on media reports, it is important to look closely at how the media frames homosexuality and homophobic violence.[70] A keyword search on various newspaper databases yielded some interesting results. For example, here is a snippet from a wire story from Windsor: 'Trouble started in the Little Memphis tavern July 19, 1992, when one of a group of four men was heard to shout: "Are you calling me a queer?"'[71] After being ordered out of the bar, one of the victims suffered a fractured skull and several broken facial bones. The judge said the attack 'was eminently forseeable' and ordered the bar to pay more than half a million dollars in damages.[72] Was this a 'real' case of queer-bashing? Or was it a regular barroom brawl in which men called one another 'queers'? I decided that even if it wasn't a queer-bashing case, it still had important implications for victims of homophobic violence, so I kept it in my data set.

My database search also turned up the unsolved murders of two Toronto women – Julianne Middleton and Virginia Coote – who were found strangled within four months of each other in 1994. All I had to go on was the following quote: 'An autopsy found [Middleton] had drowned and that the imprints on her neck were left by a would-be strangler. Both women were Parkdale hookers, both were lesbians, and both were addicted to crack cocaine.'[73] Although there was nothing to indicate that they had been queer-bashed, there was nothing to say they hadn't been – so I added them to my list.[74]

Sometimes the mainstream media served as sources for incidents that the queer community would not touch. For example, sixty-seven-year-old Cornelius Otte drove a church choir to Hamilton from Wisconsin in 1997. His body was found naked on his hotel bed; his jewellery and wallet had been taken. The victim had gone to a porn movie house three nights in a row and brought two men back to his hotel room for sex.[75] A year later, Cale Presnail, twenty-four, pleaded guilty to second-degree murder, with no chance of parole for ten years.[76] It appeared that the victim had been targeted because of his desire for gay sex; even so, Hamilton's gay and lesbian liaison committee did not want to get involved: 'There was no ownership of the issue in the gay community.'[77]

Media Representations of Organized Hate Activity

Quisenberry contends that television news coverage of hate crimes can have a positive, agenda-setting effect.[78] Jacobs and Potter counter that the print media have 'accepted, reinforced and amplified the image of a nation besieged by hate crime' by publishing 'alarmist articles' on the topic. The media play a generally uncritical role; they accept 'at face value advocacy organizations' assertions about epidemics of hate violence.'[79]

Judson and Bertazzoni examine 'the landscape of hate,' seen through the eyes of the American mass media. One problem they see relates to the media's efforts to 'balance' stories by profiling the killers and outlining the philosophies of organized hate groups. The latter, including white supremacist groups, use interviews to disseminate their website addresses, thereby generating nationwide publicity for their causes.[80] Only a handful of the queer-bashing incidents in my data set can be attributed to organized hate groups.[81]

I found only one killing that definitively linked skinheads to homophobic violence, and the media were deeply sympathetic to the victim. In 1992, Yves Lalonde, fifty-one, was jogging in a Montreal park[82] when six teenage skinheads 'struck him on the back of the head, causing Lalonde to collapse face-first onto the ground. The boys then took turns hitting Lalonde on the head and about the body with the baseball bat and with sticks, fracturing his skull and rupturing his liver.'[83] They were overheard bragging about the killing and planning another gay-bashing the following night.[84] One of the fifteen-year-olds arrested said he wanted to 'rid the park of faggots so children could play there again.'[85] Another fifteen-year-old told his lawyer that Jews control the country's finances; a psychologist said he 'gravitated to skinhead and White Power groups to compensate for lack of a father figure.' Four youths pleaded guilty to second-degree murder and got the maximum: three years in detention.[86]

Judson and Bertazzoni note that although the media often afford extensive coverage to organized hate activities, other cases of hate violence are given a much lower profile.[87] Two brutal murders in Winnipeg, spaced a year apart, demonstrate this difference. In 1990 an early-morning jogger found Richard McIntyre's body in a gay cruising area on the banks of the Assiniboine, 'battered by repeated blows from a tree limb and fists.' After Wallace McKay was arrested – and once it was determined that the victim had known him – the police declared that it was 'not a gay bashing.'[88] McKay was described as an 'ex-lover.' It is worth noting that with regard to the gay community, long-term spouses, prostitutes, extortionists, and one-night dalliances have all been described by the police and the media as 'ex-lovers.' The possibility that McKay had been motivated by hate was thereby neatly erased. He pleaded guilty to manslaughter and received forty-three months.[89]

The following year, Gordon Kuhtey was killed at the exact same spot. This time, the possible links to a neo-Nazi gang thrust the murder into the national spotlight. A witness saw four men kick the victim repeatedly, then beat him with 'a good-sized tree branch.'[90] Four people in a nearby apartment building saw him being beaten, and others were awakened by his screams.[91] Kuhtey's body was found floating at the river's edge with condoms in his jacket.[92] The media described him as a gentle man who cared for his ailing mother and who liked to take long walks in the middle of the night.[93] His family insisted he wasn't gay.

Five years later, four men were arrested, including James Lisik – who had been charged in another queer-bashing in 1993 but had had his charges stayed – and Matthew McKay, who had gained national notoriety in 1995 as a member of the Airborne regiment in Somalia. He had left the Canadian Forces after being caught on video making racist slurs.[94] The Crown claimed that the four suspects were neo-Nazis who would beat and rob gays for 'fund-raisers.'[95] Their case hinged on the testimony of a woman who claimed she had seen them beat Kuhtey. However, the defence proved she had been living in Vancouver at the time. The four were released, and the case remains unsolved.[96]

Not All Stories Are Created Equally

Judson and Bertazzoni point out the media's preference for 'breaking stories,' and their reluctance to follow up. Remarking on a hate killer who was caught and pleaded guilty, the authors noted: 'Such a denouement in the courtroom is much less interesting than either the frenzy that surrounded his initial hateful act, or a trial in which his hateful beliefs could have been aired.'[97] The following is a good Canadian example of this type of anticlimax. Brian Hickey met a man at a Vancouver gay bar and went back to the victim's house. At knifepoint, Hickey bound and gagged the victim, who later described Hickey as 'psycho' and 'absolutely full of hate. He is very violent.' In March 1995, Hickey pleaded guilty to unlawful confinement and was sentenced to eighteen months.

However, two months after being sentenced, Hickey picked up another victim, John Mogentale. In the victim's apartment, Hickey robbed Mogentale and then beat him to death. Police suggested a link to five similar robberies that had occurred in Vancouver over a two-year period. The headline in the *Province* screamed: 'GAY-BASHING "PSYCHO" ON THE LOOSE.'

Yet, despite the media blitz, the articles did not explain *why* Hickey was on the loose. He was supposed to have been in jail for eighteen months. Had he escaped from prison? Had some administrative mix-up allowed him to be released?[98] One activist said it was 'outstanding that the police went to the public to ask for help,' apparently unaware that the police had waited until a week after the murder to do so. Journalists didn't ask why the police had waited. Instead, they published interviews-with-fearful-gay-men-in-West-End-cafes: 'Very few gay-bashings go without retribution,' said one man. 'The cops better find him before we do. Anyone who thinks gays don't fight back is very foolish.'[99]

Meanwhile, the Q Street Patrol distributed three thousand posters with Hickey's photo. Although he had dyed his hair black, he was spotted at Wreck Beach a few days later.[100] At his sentencing hearing, Hickey said he had been raped at age twelve and was going to gay bars by the time he was fifteen. He pleaded guilty to second-degree murder, with no chance of parole for fifteen years. The *Province* buried this 'denouement' on page 42.[101]

Judson and Bertazzoni tackle another thorny question: Why do some horrific hate crimes get covered by the national media, while others remain 'local stories'? They point to the killing of Billy Jack Gaither, an Alabama gay man whose throat was slashed and whose body was set on fire on a pile of tires in 1999.[102] They note that although the murder was just as horrific as Matthew Shephard's, it garnered only a fraction of the media coverage. Several homicides I reviewed were paid relatively little attention by the media, including the case of Bruno Minici, twenty-three, whose body was found in a Vancouver-area park in 1993, nearly a year after he went missing.[103]

In another example, Christopher Sipes – a twenty-five-year-old in a rural area near Ottawa who apparently weighed about three hundred pounds[104] – killed Willis Arcand, who was sixty-six and much smaller. Sipes claimed he was very drunk and awoke naked to find the semiclad victim making a pass at him. Sipes stabbed Arcand in the throat with a gun-cleaning rod, then strangled him.[105] The same night, the victim's VCR and television went missing.

Sipes pleaded guilty to manslaughter and got a five-year sentence, which would allow him to apply for day parole within a couple of years.[106] A community member complained that the police were more concerned about Sipes's drug deals than they were about the killing itself.[107] The police and the Crown, in their apparent rush for a conviction, seemed to overlook the absurdity of the defendant's argument: that this huge young man's life was so imperilled by a senior citizen's grope that he had to kill him. Besides, what was the defendant doing with his clothes off? And why didn't the media pick up on these clues?

Heterosexism in the Mainstream Media

There are many ways the media can spread homophobia.[108] In rare instances, the intolerance is blatant. Watney points out that as recently as 1987, the *Sun* in London, England, offered free one-way airline tickets to Norway in order to encourage gay men to leave Britain for good, under the headline, 'Fly Away Gays – and We Will Pay!'[109] He also quotes another *Sun* headline: 'Gays in Fear: They Dread Revenge after Attack on Boy.' He complains that '*The Sun* is hardly siding with vulnerable gay men here: it is calling out for anti-gay violence, in a direct if crude discourse of revenge.'[110]

In Canada, I did not find many overt examples of homophobic media coverage. However, the *Winnipeg Sun* featured an interview with the father of a twenty-year-old gay-basher who beat his victim with a base-ball bat. In a story titled 'Dad Backs Accused Boy,' we are told that the father 'vows to support his son – even if activists call for his head to avenge all attacks on homosexuals.' Here, the paper was portraying the gay-basher as a potential victim of revenge – even though none of the activists interviewed in the article had suggested such a thing.[111]

There is little scholarly analysis that compares how homophobic violence is covered in the queer media with how it is covered in the mainstream media. That said, important connections can be gleaned from the media's representations of AIDS and homosexuality.[112] For example, McCallister compared how AIDS was covered in a medical journal, a gay newspaper, and the *New York Times*. He found that the gay newspaper was more critical of the medical establishment; the other publications tended to place medical researchers on a pedestal and rarely approached the gay community for quotes.[113]

In the earlier stages of the AIDS crisis, the British press routinely distinguished between 'innocent' and 'guilty' AIDS victims, suggesting that 'promiscuous homosexuals' should be sent to 'leper-type colonies.' Lawsuits and formal complaints eventually forced many newspapers, including the *Sun*, to tone down their rhetoric.[114] The Glasgow Media Group analysed the way news with homosexual content was produced, and found that news values are 'inflected with heterosexual assumptions.'[115]

I found that many Canadian media reports reflected strong hetero-sexual assumptions. For example, in 1992, forty-eight-year-old James Moffat was killed by Steven Lynn, twenty-three, who had lived in the victim's Sudbury house for a year – even though he didn't regularly pay rent. Lynn claimed that after a night of drinking, Moffatt grabbed his 'privates,' so he pushed the victim over the deck. The victim struck his head and died. Lynn hid the body in a woodpile, then burned it. He took his girlfriend on a three-day trip to Toronto and charged thousands of dollars on the victim's credit cards. He was eventually arrested in Vancouver. Although convicted of second-degree murder, he appealed and had his charge reduced to manslaughter.[116]

MacDougall comments on the inconsistency 'between killing a homosexual (supposedly out of panic) and robbing that person.'[117] How can the court be expected, on the one hand, to be lenient because of this supposedly spontaneous act of self-defence, but look the other way when the killer goes shopping with the dead man's credit card – and burns the corpse? The media missed some obvious clues. One headline read, 'Man Jailed for Lover's Murder,' thereby reducing the incident to a 'lover's quarrel.' If Moffat really had been the victim's 'lover,' why would he have claimed to be so horrified by the possibility of gay sex? And why didn't the media ask why the Crown had agreed to reduce the sentence on appeal?

Alternative Points of View

The Glasgow Media Group notes that it is hard to get queer-related stories into the media 'unless they are packaged in a certain way ... There is a temptation to go to an authoratative (i.e. non-gay identified) source rather than a gay organization when covering gay issues.' A journalist from a British gay paper complained that the media routinely stole AIDS stories from him: 'They don't want to be seen to be taking information from a gay publication or if they do, they'll say that you're "claiming that ..." or they'll distort the text to make it look as if you're coming from a non-factual point of view.'[118]

In Canada, regional gay and lesbian newspapers and newsletters are often the only source of information for bashing incidents; in Calgary, Saskatoon, Halifax, and St John's, queer activists and journalists often wear the same hat. An activist who wrote for the gay Atlantic Canada paper, *Wayves*, and its precursor, the *Gaezette*, observed that the Halifax dailies 'would print stories about trials where the truth was being distorted ... where the perspective of the mainstream media was fostering the assumption that gay men who cruise or gay and lesbian people who are beaten up or killed for their sexuality were somehow deserving of it. The [mainstream] media most often projected the assumption that the homosexual in any story involving violence had provoked the assault.'[119]

A reporter for the *Gaezette* provided an alternative point of view after attending the sentencing hearing of Larry McLeod, who met Gregory Jodrey at a Wolfville tavern in 1993. They ended up near Acadia University,[120] where McLeod – an amateur boxer – 'deliberately and methodically beat' Jodrey to death. McLeod's lawyer argued that his client was in a 'minor to medium range' homosexual panic and 'just lost it' after Jodrey raped him.[121] The reporter at the hearing noted that there was 'a great deal of emphasis on McLeod's heterosexuality.' McLeod's friends were asked if he was gay. In written statements, their responses varied from 'Absolutely not. Larry loved kids. He was our favourite baby-sitter ... He was not interested in boys or men. He had a lot of pride in himself,' to 'There was no evidence of it. He had an interest in meeting girls. He socialized normally. In every way he was a normal teenager.' The victim, on the other hand, was described as an 'aggressive homosexual' who, under the influence of alcohol, 'would stop at nothing to get what he wanted.' The Crown repeatedly referred to the victim as an 'admitted homosexual.'[122] McLeod was sentenced to four years.

The Glasgow Media Group discovered that some heterosexual reporters were forced to toe a homophobic editorial line. A British reporter was criticized for writing a lurid article that vilified gay men and IV users with AIDS. He defended himself by saying: 'It was that or my mortgage because the editor ... said, "I am not having any more of your gay loving, junkie loving pieces. We are going to tell it like it is."'[123] Perhaps an editor with similar values was the guiding force behind an article in the *Winnipeg Sun* about the near-murder of a lesbian. This was the lead: 'It was Shakespeare's classic tale of star-crossed lovers, but thanks to a modern-day twist it would have to be re-titled Juliet and Juliet.'[124]

The story described a lesbian couple in Sudbury, forced to flee after a family dispute. Earl Longpré, the stepfather of one of the women, followed the couple to Winnipeg along with two other disgruntled male family members. The men found the woman's lover in a Winnipeg furniture store and dragged her out to their car at knifepoint. They spirited her to a house, where they demanded that she end the relationship: 'When the complainant indicated that she was not going to end the relationship, the accused stabbed her while she was being held by persons whom she was unable to identify. She was repeatedly stabbed in the area of her heart. Her fingers on one hand were sliced off and her arm penetrated.'[125]

There are many ways the reporter could have approached this story. She could have used it as an opportunity to write about violence against lesbians, or about hate crimes in general. Yet instead of focusing on the victim's miraculous survival – and despite a stab wound three inches deep – the reporter zeroed in on the victim's past convictions. A horrific case of homophobic violence was reduced to tabloid fodder, a crime with a Shakespearean 'twist.' Longpré was sentenced to eight years for attempted murder.[126]

The Glasgow Media Group noted that British AIDS groups representing the queer community resorted to guerrilla tactics to get their message out to the mainstream media: they would sneak into government press conferences and distribute alternative literature, making themselves available for immediate comment. Activists also demonstrated in front of newspaper offices and broke into BBC studios to protest what they perceived to be biased reporting. In 1991 in New York, during the Gulf War, activists invaded network newsrooms and chained themselves to desks, chanting, 'Fight AIDS, not Arabs.'[127]

In Canada, queers sometimes question the heterosexist assumptions of the mass media, albeit in a more restrained fashion. In 1991, Xtra objected to a Toronto Sun headline, 'Gay killer.' John Rivest, a gay man from rural Quebec, had shot three gay men and a woman to death.[128] Xtra said the victim's 'sexuality had nothing to do with the story,' pointing out that most of the victims owed him money.[129] During a police standoff, Rivest said he was heading to the Gay Village in Montreal to shoot forty more people.[130] Then he stuck a .357 magnum revolver in his mouth and pulled the trigger.[131]

Rivest had been a psychiatric out-patient for six years. Police found a 9-mm pistol, five hundred rounds of ammunition, and a .22-calibre pistol at his home. The gun store manager said: 'None of us could imagine him doing something like this. He appeared to be so timid. He had effeminate manners.'[132] This case raises an interesting question: If a gay man kills three gay men – and is planning to shoot forty more – is he committing a hate crime? Or is he simply a mass-murderer who 'happens' to be gay?

Despite these criticisms, many cases I analysed – especially those involving transgendered victims – garnered sympathetic coverage.[133] Sometimes newspapers appealed to their readers for help. In 1995, police officer Joe Gateveckes wrote two Toronto Star columns about Larry Arnold, who was last seen at Traxx, a gay bar on Yonge Street, sitting with two men with French accents, approximately twenty-five and thirty-five years of age. He was seen leaving the bar with one of them. His battered body was later found in a Rosedale ravine. Two suspects were questioned, but no arrests were made. This crime remains unsolved.[134]

Summary

Social scientists face several barriers when researching queer populations: secrecy, invisibility, and conflicting notions about what constitutes a crime against the queer community. Homophobic violence is often disguised and/or combined with other crimes. Many robberies and sexual assaults involving queer victims may actually have homophobic motivations. In many cases, the victim and perpetrator are somehow acquainted – a fact that police, the Crown, and the media use to minimize or negate hate motivation. Although the mainstream media are an important source of queer-bashing incidents, in-depth interviews and alternative perspectives can help researchers read between the lines.

CHAPTER 2

Theories of Homophobia: Why Do They Want to Hurt Us?

Why does queer-bashing occur? In my view, it's a way of keeping us in our place. A broad range of scholarship in criminology, sociology, psychology, philosophy, and social work is necessary to explain this complex phenomenon, since people queer-bash in many settings and for many reasons. The theories in this chapter explore the following concepts: the social construction of homosexuality, heterosexual hegemony, masculinity, queer theory, lesbian-bashing, and Patrick Hopkins's theories of homophobia. I have interspersed these theories with contemporary Canadian examples of homophobic violence.

Although most people understand the concept of a 'hate crime,' many do not realize how difficult it is to 'prove' hate motivation. The hate element in the following homicide was obscured, since the Crown, police, and the media framed it as a 'robbery.' In 1994, James DeLorme and Roy Marshall drove 'down-island' from Nanaimo to Victoria to have some fun. They went to several drinking spots, including two gay bars, where they met their unfortunate victims – Garth Hill and his lover Ray Lycek – who offered to put the two men up for the night. On their way to Hill's place, they stopped at Lycek's for a few drinks.[1]

Lycek said afterwards that if robbery really had been the primary motive, the two assailants could have easily carried it out at Lycek's place. Instead, the four continued to Hill's house, where Lycek was smashed over the head with a bottle and strangled with a telephone cord. At least he survived.[2] The belt around his partner's neck was tightened and released for four long minutes. Lycek awoke to find his lover dead and the house robbed. After DeLorme and Marshall were caught, they claimed they had been highly intoxicated. DeLorme then added that he had been sexually abused as a child.[3]

The Crown and the police denied any hate motivation, but Lycek pointed out that the VCR was tossed into a ditch. 'This was gay-bashing,' he said. 'No doubt about it, and no one wanted to say that.' The two were sentenced to ten years each for manslaughter – which meant they would be able to apply for day parole within a few years.[4] The *Times Colonist* didn't explore the possibility that this was a hate crime – but they did manage to vilify the poor man who died. They dredged up an assault charge from five years earlier and mentioned that Hill had been HIV-positive – a fact unknown to the killers, so it really had nothing to do with the story.[5]

Homosexuality and Social Control

The criminal justice system's lame attempts to address homophobic violence, as seen above, reinforce the message that relatively little will be done to punish perpetrators. Negative images of homosexuality are firmly rooted in our culture and are reproduced through many institutions, including the media, organized religion, the medical profession, and the courts. Homophobia stigmatizes us, creates anxiety in men whose sexual identities are fragile, and fuels the masculinist ideology that underlies queer-bashing. Then we internalize these messages and blame ourselves for the victimization that occurs.

But how did this strategy of sexual regulation – of keeping us 'in line' – evolve? Many theorists have turned to the writings of Michel Foucault, a gay French philosopher who died of AIDS in 1984. Central to much of Foucault's work is the concept of *power/knowledge* – the idea that knowledge is power, that power and knowledge are inextricably linked. In 1978, the English translation of *La Volonté de savoir* was published as *The History of Sexuality,* Volume 1. Foucault focused on the late nineteenth century, which was marked by 'an explosion of the numerous and diverse techniques for achieving the subjugation of bodies and the control of populations.'[6] Sex was seen as a force so powerful and dangerous that it needed to be policed and administered on two fronts: by objectifying the body, and by targeting the population as a whole.

Individuals were encouraged to 'confess' to authority figures, including doctors, psychiatrists, and social scientists. The shift to a clinical setting meant that hidden sexual fantasies and practices could now be expressed in medical terms, 'as though it were an area of particular pathological fragility in human existence.'[7] What resulted was a power relationship that required an authority to interpret what the subject said. This new form of regulation, which Foucault called *bio-power,* spread through these specialists, part of a *pathologization* process that Foucault called the 'psychiatrization of perverse pleasures.'[8] A whole new universe of sexual anomalies was created: *misoscophiles, gynecomasts, presbyophiles, sexoesthetic inverts,* and *dyspareneunist women.*[9]

According to Foucault, sodomy laws were based on a biblical injunction, only sporadically enforced. Same-sex relations under the rubric of 'homosexuality' soon led to cures and incarcerations: 'the sodomite had been a temporary aberration; the homosexual was now a species.'[10] The label of 'pervert' was now 'scientifically' established: 'corrective technologies were applied ... The body, the new sexual science and the demand for regulation and surveillance were connected.'[11]

In 1899 the gay movement's first organization, the Scientific-Humanitarian Committee, was founded in Berlin by Dr Magnus Hirschfeld and his colleagues to resist Paragraph 175 – a law that had criminalized same-sex relations in Germany since 1871.[12] In 1929 this group finally persuaded a Reichstag committee to drop Paragraph 175, but then the Nazis came to power.[13] In 1932, gay bars were raided, and homosexuality was depicted as 'a disease alien to healthy village life, but easily spread through seduction and propaganda.'[14] Hirschfeld fled Germany in 1933 after his Institute for Sex Research was razed by a squad of Brown Shirts.[15] By 1934, Paragraph 175 had been extended to include a kiss, an embrace, or even homosexual fantasies.[16]

'Pink lists' were compiled, and 50,000 homosexuals were arrested during the Nazi reign. An estimated 5,000 to 15,000 pink triangle prisoners died in concentration camps after being subjected to disproportionate degrees of violence, starvation, and medical experimentation.[17] Shocking research into the castration of 'homosexuals' during the Nazi era reveals the 'unkindest cut' of all: 'a large proportion of those formally convicted of homosexuality by nazi courts were not actual homosexuals.' By 1935 the Hereditary Disease Law allowed for 'voluntary' (that is, forced) castration of men who had 'committed a crime "resulting from a degenerate sex drive,"' including men convicted of a single homosexual offence – sometimes before their cases had even gone to trial.[18] Even after the war, Swiss homosexuals 'were sometimes given the choice *by their employers* of castration or loss of job and pension.'[19]

Kinsman and the Regulation of Homosexuality

Kinsman uses 'hegemonic approaches ... to explore lesbian and gay oppression and resistance' and argues that 'coercive laws, police practices, "queer-bashing," and limited social options all attempt to make heterosexuality compulsory.' *Heterosexual hegemony* is produced when homosexuality is constructed as a sin, an illness, a congenital disorder, a deviance, or a symptom of social degeneration.

After the Second World War, Canadian psychologists and psychiatrists continued to root out and 'cure' gay men. Chenier describes the postwar construction of the male sex offender: sex crime was considered a mental health problem in need of a cure.[20] Homosexuals in the Canadian military were labelled 'anti-social psychopaths' and accused of having 'psychopathic personalities with abnormal sexuality.'[21] Kinsman demonstrates how the Canadian homosexual has historically been portrayed as a child molester, seducer, corrupter, communist, criminal, blackmail victim, or security risk, or as someone whose sex should only be tolerated in private.[22]

In 1952, Canada's Immigration Act was amended to exclude homosexuals.[23] Meanwhile, bookstores and nascent gay organizations were censored and charged with obscenity.[24] In the mid-1950s, the McRuer Commission examined the impact of 'criminal sexual psychopath' legislation, which ensnared adult homosexuals – even those engaged in consensual activity. Only two gay men were allowed to submit testimony to the commission – which was then ruled to be inadmissible. Yet Toronto's police chief was allowed to submit his own opinion: 'Homosexuality is a constant problem for the Police of large cities ... Homosexuals constantly corrupt others and are constantly recruiting youths into their fraternity.'[25]

In the 1960s the Royal Canadian Mounted Police – which banned homosexuality from its ranks until 1986 – commissioned a Carleton University psychology professor to devise the notorious 'fruit machine,' which attempted to detect homosexuals within police ranks. The project fell into disarray when the RCMP refused to furnish fifteen 'normal men' from the force to serve as a control group.[26] According to Kinsman, this was part of a broader effort by the Canadian state to construct gays and lesbians as 'national security risks' during the Cold War. By the time Pierre Trudeau was elected prime minister in 1968, 'the Directorate of Security and Intelligence reported having collected the names of close to nine thousand suspected and confirmed homosexuals in the Ottawa area.'[27]

Kinsman and Gentiles describe how the RCMP's witch hunt against Canadian civil servants and military members ruined the lives of many gays and lesbians in the late 1950s and early 1960s. Even now, many victims of that campaign are reluctant to talk about it.[28] The police pressured homosexuals to inform on one another in return for immunity.

Although many files have remained secret, Kinsman and Gentiles uncovered a four-hundred-page RCMP document that described police surveillance of a 1970s women's group that called itself Wages Due. Some of the members were referred to as 'dirty ... radical lesbians who have a perverse desire to de-feminize themselves.' The Coalition for Gay Rights in Ontario and the National Gay Rights Organization were also under surveillance.[29]

Social control sometimes led to physical control. As recently as 1968, Canadian gay men like Michael Riordon were undergoing aversion therapy. Three times a week for a year, 'I look at slides of naked men, and with each of them a sharp jolt of electricity is delivered to my leg.'[30] (In the 1970s, the South African army used a more brutal technique: 'When the subject was screaming with pain, the current was switched off and a *Playboy* magazine centrefold was substituted for the previous picture.'[31])

In 1977, Canadian media coverage of the murder of a twelve-year-old boy in Toronto linked homosexuality with child abuse. According to Kinsman, 'coverage of the "homosexual murder" served to focus hostility against the whole gay community ... The media portrayed the child molester or child murderer as a homosexual stranger.' The media failed to apply the same fervour when the Ontario government suppressed a report on the deaths of fifty-four children – most of whom had been abused and killed by their own families.[32]

The 1960s and Beyond

During the social upheaval of the 1960s, a more sophisticated social analysis emerged. The repressive nature of institutions came under scrutiny, highlighting the 'process by which rules are created that in turn provide the necessary, but not the sufficient, conditions for rule-breaking.'[33] As Becker observed, '*social groups create deviance by making the rules whose infractions constitute deviance, and by applying these rules to particular people and labeling them as outsiders.*'[34]

Instead of simply looking at the *behaviour* of a person deemed to be deviant, criminologists began to study the labelling process itself, the 'continuously shaped and reshaped outcome of social interaction ... the theoretical perspective of symbolic interactionism.'[35] Schur also developed the idea of homosexuality as a 'victimless crime.' He reflected on the people opposed to the decriminalization of homosexuality: 'Surely it is fantastic to think that enactment of the proposed reform would impel hordes of individuals immediately to discard their current heterosexual inclinations and activities for a life of homosexuality, thus precipitating the decline and eventual demise of the conventional family and of civilization as we know it.'[36]

Implicit in all this new analysis was the social construction of deviance. The publication of 'The Homosexual Role' by McIntosh in 1968 represented a turning point in the theorization of homosexuality and coincided with an increasingly vocal gay rights movement.[37]

Since the 1969 Stonewall riots in New York City, gays and lesbians around the world have gained an ever-increasing number of rights. For example, in 1973 the American Psychiatric Association removed homosexuality from the Diagnostic and Statistical Manual of Psychiatric Disorders.[38] However, Weeks notes that this was not a 'cool scientific decision,' but rather a 'response to a political campaign.'[39] According to Weeks, three elements have characterized the shaping of the modern gay and lesbian movement: 'a struggle for identity, a development of sexual communities, and the growth of political movements.'[40]

A strong Canadian gay and lesbian equality rights movement has had its own share of successes. In 1996, gays and lesbians successfully lobbied for sexual orientation to be included in the Canadian Human Rights Act, which governs federal jurisdictions.[41] As of 1998, Canada was one of only five countries to expressly forbid discrimination against gays and lesbians in the military.[42] Little Sister's, a Vancouver bookstore, sued the federal government to end customs censorship of gay and lesbian materials.[43] For many activists in Ontario, B.C., and Quebec, the court victories in 2003 and 2004 concerning same-sex marriage were the movement's crowning acheivement.

Masculinity and Its Discourses

Other theories focus on the links between gender and homophobia. Sumner argues that criminological theory has failed to recognize the hegemonic masculinity at its core: 'The ideological censure of women, femininity and subversive masculinities ... is basic to both the formation of gender division and the character of modern criminal law.'[44]

A close reading of criminological theory makes it abundantly clear that the most obvious question – why men and boys commit almost all crime – is assiduously ignored. Messerschmidt contends that traditional criminologists use an *essentialist* framework to explain why women commit so little crime.[45] Essentialism tends to explain away behaviour using an individual's 'innate' characteristics, related to the fact that a person is, for example, 'black,' 'gay,' 'female,' or 'Italian.' At the same time, the narrow concepts of patriarchy used in some feminist critiques 'explain away real variations in the construction of masculinity within a particular society and, consequently, encourage the theorization of one type of masculinity – the "typical (patriarchal) male."'[46]

Pronger playfully deconstructs the actions of gay male athletes, who quickly learn the 'standard language of masculinity,' which requires them to pass as straight. Gay athletes constantly subvert and reinterpret masculinity, using 'irony' to resist homophobia.[47] According to Griffin, 'young lesbian and gay athletes learn that secrecy is the only option if they are interested in pursuing a career in athletics.' Homophobia in the locker room keeps young men 'safely within the bounds of traditionally masculine and heterosexual attitudes and behavior in an emotionally and physically intimate setting.'

Young female athletes are stigmatized by their participation 'in an activity that already casts suspicion on their femininity and heterosexuality.' Meanwhile, lesbian coaches remain silent. 'The association of lesbians with athletics is enough to discourage many women' and causes some female athletes to 'display traditional heterosexual markers through clothing, hairstyles, and mannerisms.'[48] Morrow believes that physical education teachers have a golden opportunity to provide leadership in the reduction of homophobic behaviours.[49]

My research indicates that indeed, the volatile mix of sports, masculinity, and homosexuality can lead to violence. In 1996 a man assaulted one of the members of Montreal's gay hockey team. Apparently, he was aghast to discover that such a team even existed.[50] Canadian queer-bashing incidents have also occurred during activities linked to the World Cup[51] and the Grey Cup[52] (and, notoriously, the Stanley Cup riots in Vancouver in 1994).[53]

Queer Theories

The past decade has also seen an upsurge in the theorization of queer identity. Sedgwick lays out her own blueprint for social inquiry by analysing the silent discourses that flow from *closetedness:* 'The relations of the closet – the relations of the known and the unknown, the explicit and the inexplicit around homo/heterosexual definition – have the potential for being peculiarly revealing.'[54]

For Butler, 'heterosexuality is always in the act of elaborating itself,' which is proof positive that 'it is perpetually at risk ... that it "knows" its own possibility of becoming undone.'[55] She questions the validity of categories such as straight: 'What does it mean to avow a category that can only maintain its specificity and coherence by performing a prior set of disavowals?'[56] Instead of asking the question, 'Why is homosexuality stigmatized as such?' Watney wonders, 'Why has it been made so consistently to seem extraordinary, something quite out of the way of everyday life?'[57] He contrasts a homosexual identity, which is fundamentally sociopolitical, with 'the identity of the heterosexual, for whom heterosexuality does not designate desire for the opposite sex, so much as a rejection and denial of homosexuality.'[58]

According to Gamson, the gay and lesbian movement has created 'a quasi-ethnicity, complete with its own political and cultural institutions, festivals, neighborhoods, even its own flag,' which assumes 'the same fixed, natural essence, a self with same-sex desires.'[59] However, by creating a single category, activists 'simplify complex internal differences and complex sexual identities.' In civil rights discourse, 'the appearance of normality is central to gaining political "room" ... "We are everywhere," goes the refrain from this camp.' Although fixed identity categories provide legitimacy on the one hand, they can reproduce oppression on the other.[60]

Since the early 1990s, the emergence of queer identity has had an impact on the 'traditional' gay and lesbian movement. Queer theory demands liberation by disrupting the binary categories of man/woman, gay/straight. Moreover, the inclusion of bisexual and transgendered people in the movement is not simply an expansion, but a subversion of pre-existing identities. Lesbians are now accused of being 'sexist' for not accepting other groups into their fold, including transsexual women and bisexual women who are married to men: 'It is by keeping sexual and gender categories hard and clear that gains are made. Lesbian visibility is more recent and hard won ... Just as they are gaining political ground *as lesbians*, lesbians are asked not only to share it but to subvert it, by declaring *woman* and *lesbian* to be unstable, permeable, fluid categories.'[61]

An excellent example of this conundrum surfaced when a transsexual woman named Kimberly Nixon successfully challenged a rape crisis centre's decision to exclude her as a volunteer.[62] At a B.C. Human Rights Tribunal, Vancouver Rape Relief argued that its counsellors are required 'to have experienced all their life being treated as female.'[63] (Although the media was generally sympathetic, the *Vancouver Sun* referred to her as 'a former man' rather than a transsexual or transgendered woman.)[64]

Hausman observes: 'As queer approaches to the transgender phenomenon flourish, feminist ones wither.' Transgender social theory has in some ways eclipsed 'a certain problematic previously characterized by feminism as the "woman question," and then later as sexual difference, in the current guise of transgender.' In her review of several academic articles and books on transgender issues, Hausman notes that 'feminists are portrayed negatively in many of these texts – policing the genders in order to retain "woman" for itself, ignoring the plight of those who do not signify female or male biologically or socially, reserving heterosexual norms of feminity for genetic women only.' Hausman reviews *FTM*, by Holly Devor,[65] which Hausman considers a strong example of 'a feminist theorist taking up an advocacy position for transsexual and transgender experience.'[66] (Devor, a professor at the University of Victoria, made headlines in 2003 when she changed her name to Aaron and began to project a male persona.)

As Mort sees it, the irony of queer theory is that despite its notions of pluralism and binary opposites, what results is 'a polarised codification of sex. It has privileged the principle of sexual dissidence as *the* epistemology of sexuality, in such a way that the pervert ... has become the motif of sexual classification.'[67] In the future, queer theory will probably become more grounded as it continues to absorb non-Western, activist-oriented perspectives.[68]

The End of Gay?

In one study, a researcher identified a subgroup of bisexual men who never wore condoms – and who constantly switched back and forth between men and women.[69] As a way of reaching this subgroup, some health activists no longer aim their programs at *gay* or *bisexual* men, but at 'MSM' – *men who have sex with men*. This approach is especially useful in non-Western queer communities, and among male immigrants in Western countries who have sex with other men but don't identify as queer. Phellas has done in-depth research on the complex sexual identities of Cypriot men in London;[70] Fernandez's fascinating analysis of certain male same-sex relationships in Honduras highlights the dichotomy between the macho *hombre* and the passive, effeminate *loca*.[71]

Archer feels it is time to do away with identity categories altogether. *The End of Gay (and the Death of Heterosexuality)* is a reflection not just on 'how far we've come,' but on how much farther we need to go to erase the barrier between gay and straight, which Archer feels is no longer relevant. In fact, he thinks we should not be making such a big fuss out of sexual attraction: it is not 'especially relevant to your sense of self.'[72] He argues that sexual identity has been hijacked by academics and activists, often to little effect.[73] Although 'gay' has not yet died, 'the death of a movement, of a way of thinking and being, is usually a good thing, though it often doesn't seem so at the time.'[74]

Archer feels that many gays have conflated bisexuality with repressed homosexuality, instead of recognizing and appreciating the multiplicity of 'sexual pleasure and forms of human beauty.'[75] This either/or approach assumes 'that there are two possible states of existence for people who have same-sex sex, a dichotomy paralleling the one that separates gay and straight, dichotomies within dichotomies. You are either in the closet or you are out of the closet ... Being out is liberation, being in is oppression.'[76]

Archer criticizes 'mainstream' organizations like the Gay and Lesbian Alliance Against Defamation (GLAAD), which called on its members to protest against a *Newsweek* article about Matthew Shephard: 'Tell them this coverage was disrespectful and gratuitous.' He argues that the article was attempting 'to answer a few questions outstanding at the time about just why it was he went off with his murderers ... because it questions the wrong things, suggesting that Shephard may have had some self-destructive personal problems, that he was sad and lonely ... It is disrespectful and gratuitous. In GLAAD's eyes, those who are not part of the solution are part of the problem.'[77]

However, Archer is also wary of queer radicals who lament the disappearance of the 'gay-as-taboo or outlaw.' (He compares these activists to proponents of ebonics in the black community: 'segregationists who delay rather than encourage general acceptance of a larger issue.') He pleads for older gay and lesbian activists to put down their armour 'and settle into the sexual freedom and unity they've won for us through brutish and sometimes brutal expression of sexual division.' He ends on a depressing note, despairing that 'gay is, after certain fundamental victories are won, inherently more confining than liberating.'[78]

The Etiology of Homophobia

The search for the causes of homophobia has become a multidisciplinary project. One article, complete with two pages of mathematical equations, attempts to link economic downturns to outbreaks of hate crime.[79] Other researchers have explored the links between homophobia and belief in the devil. One survey found that men and women who believe in an active Satan are more intolerant toward lesbians and gay men.[80] For Herek, homosexuality is stigmatized because it violates gender norms and 'is equated with deviance and abnormality.'[81] Lehne believes that this stigmatization causes both heterosexuals and homosexuals 'to monitor their own behavior carefully to avoid any appearance of gender nonconformity.'[82]

It was Weinberg, in 1972, who coined the term homophobia, 'the dread of being in close quarters with homosexuals.' He points out that 'homosexuality is itself considered a problem; our unwarranted distress over homosexuality is not classified as a problem because it is still a majority point of view.'[83] Discrimination against lesbians occurs since many privileges are accorded only to women who marry. He lists five motives underlying homophobia: religion, the secret fear of being homosexual, repressed envy, the threat to values, and resentment stemming from the perception that homosexuals do not procreate.[84]

Homophobia among the educated classes is less brutal and more subtle, and expresses itself partly through those endless questions about how we got that way: 'This ostensibly valid intellectual inquiry is frequently an expression of hostilities or fears, which become presented as if they were part of a serious intellectual exploration.'[85] For example, Rupp, opening with a few choice lines from Leviticus, writes a 'scholarly' diatribe about violence as it affects 'a group of perverts with a common sexual aberration.' He uses a bad gay joke to make his point: '"Show me a happy homosexual and I'll show you a gay corpse." ... It makes mirth of a frightening truth ... of the clandestine nature of the gay world and the perverse activities which bind the group together.'[86]

Rupp claims that the 'general promiscuity and the transient attachments of the homosexual often lead to suspicion, jealousy and murder,' although he offers no empirical evidence. Suicide is very common, and 'sudden death' is 'not unknown' to occur during fellation: 'In such homicides police are entreated to check the trachea for the presence of sperm.' During sex, 'it is not unusual for the anal insertor to grasp the passive partner's neck ... or to twist a towel ... around the neck ... during the sex act. Occasionally too much force is applied and the receptor partner is accidentally strangled.' Homosexuals seduce unsuspecting youths, but the sex act is repeated over and over again until 'finally the response is conditioned. Once the aberration is fixed cure is virtually impossible. Herein lies the pernicious and insidious evil of homosexuality.'[87]

Religious doctrine also reproduces homophobic discourse. In 1994 the European Parliament recommended that gay and lesbian couples be free to marry and adopt. Pope John Paul II complained that the plan would confer 'institutional value on deviant behavior.'[88] An American religious group claimed 'that people living a homosexual lifestyle were responsible for 50% of all child molestation.'[89] To counteract this lie, researchers examined the hospital charts of all sexually abused children over a one-year period. Out of 269 cases, only two abusers were 'potentially homosexual or lesbian from the information provided by caregivers.' In contrast, 82 per cent of the cases involved 'a man or woman who was, or had been, in a heterosexual relationship with a relative of the child.' In other words, this scenario was more than one hundred times more likely.[90]

Watney complains that *homophobia* is a reductive term that has 'merely reversed the widespread tendency to pathologize all forms of homosexual desire and acts as symptoms of an underlying *perversion*.'[91] He points out that clinical phobias are 'generally extremely unpleasant and debilitating, and beyond their conscious control.' He believes that anti-gay sentiment is linked to the Freudian concept of 'reaction-formations' – obsessions that 'defend the individual against some repressed emotion or wish within him or herself, or else from other displaced and strictly speaking phobic anxieties projected onto gay men.'[92] He offers the example of a three-month sentence handed to a British eighteen-year-old who, fearing AIDS infection, punched and killed a gay man after inadvertently drinking from the victim's bottle.[93] To call these behaviours 'phobic' is 'to lend them a spurious psychological dignity which they do not deserve.'

Internalized Homophobia

As early as 1927, psychologists observed that the heavy drinking patterns of 'secret or partially repressed' homosexuals sometimes resulted in sporadic sexual encounters 'without destroying the masculine image. When sober, the sexual indiscretions can be conveniently disowned or "forgotten."'[94] Smith believes that homosexuals 'with maladaptive coping styles' become 'psychologically wounded' from stigmatization: 'This internalized homophobia becomes self-directed and plays a major role in the development of dysphoric states which must be worked through to attain stable adjustment.'[95] Young believes that stigmatization can also cause members of minorities to 'exhibit symptoms of fear, aversion, or devaluation toward members of their own groups and other oppressed groups.'[96]

Klein interviewed closeted, homophobic bodybuilders who prostituted themselves to gay men. Many of the athletes gravitated to bodybuilding to compensate for low feelings of self-esteem: hypermasculinity and homophobia were 'in part a reaction against feelings of powerlessness.'

They depended on gay men to admire them – but this admiration intensified their own homophobia, which acted 'as both a precondition and a
consequence of a weakness in the male identity complex.'[97] These bodybuilders coped by denying or compartmentalizing their secret lives, by
pretending to be 'heterosexual while abstaining from heterosexuality.'
Both gay men and hustlers were stigmatized in the process; the hustlers'
homophobia was intensified by their need to characterize gays as
'loathesome predators' who were corrupting them.[98]

One therapist has observed that some of his gay clients feel too powerless to stand up to gay-bashers, having 'consciously or unconsciously
accepted second-class citizenship.' One of Arey's clients saw himself as a
wimp, singled out because he was gay: 'From childhood memories of
being targeted for abuse for being "different" on the playground without
allies for protection, to the current reality ... of having no legal protection
or recourse, a mind-set is created and reinforced.'[99] Another client dated
abusive men and had compulsive desires 'to wear T-shirts with pro-gay
slogans on them, and to dress in ways that provoked homophobic men
... to snear or threaten violence.' He would hitchhike late at night, but
after being harassed and threatened, 'he blamed his victimization on
societal homophobia and saw no connection between his behavior and
the reactions.'[100]

Minimization: 'He Asked for It to Happen'

Howard Ehrlich suggests that 'three basic threats' provoke queer-bashing: 'violations of territory or property, violations of the sacred, and
violations of status.' Out of the 'need for affiliation and social conformity,' queer-bashers rationalize and downplay their violence.[101]

For example, two young men in St Catharines kicked a gay man thirty
times, causing brain damage. One of the bashers, sentenced to thirty
months, reflected stoically: 'The sentence is pretty harsh, but I'll get through
it.'[102] In Toronto, four men attacked a gay man on Yonge Street. One of
the bashers told police, 'I want to kill those fucking faggots.' Neverthe-
less, his lawyer continued to claim that the attack 'wasn't a case of "gay-
bashing" but an attack by men who were drunk.'[103]

The 1993 murder of the Reverend Warren Eling, a closeted Anglican
priest in Montreal, was also minimized by the killer. The victim was
found naked, bound with his underwear, and strangled with the belt of
his bathrobe, which had been wrapped five times around his neck and
then 'tightly knotted to the head of the brass bedstead.' Eling's collection
of 120 gay porn videos was discovered: 'Friends suggested his sexual

behavior had become compulsive, and they were especially distressed by his choice of street-toughened trade.' Danny McIlwaine, thirty-one, was a local crack addict who had first met Eling while hustling in the Gay Village. After their first sexual encounter, Eling had given McIlwaine his phone number.[104]

McIlwaine claimed that during their second and fatal encounter, Eling wanted him to administer 'auto-erotic asphyxiation' by inserting a dildo and tying the belt around his neck.[105] After he realized Eling was dead, he stole the victim's car keys and fled to Toronto. Back in Montreal, after reading in the paper that he had killed a priest, McIlwaine tried to kill himself by drinking six glasses of antifreeze. (McIlwaine said Eling had originally lied and told him he was a McGill professor.) He was arrested in the hospital, then tried to kill himself again. An old friend said McIlwaine was more upset about people finding out he was having sex with men: 'A murder rap, Danny could handle.'[106]

McIlwaine protested his innocence: 'I am not a killer and I will never admit to being one. What happened was an accident. He asked for it to happen.'[107] However, the Crown argued it was more than an accident resulting from kinky sex: the circumference of the tightened belt was 35 cm, while the normal circumference of the victim's neck was 37 cm.[108] The Crown said the killing was premeditated because McIlwaine had gone to see a store owner in advance to try selling some electronics. He refused to plead down and appeared stunned when the jury found him guilty of first-degree murder: 'What's going on? Is this possible?'[109]

In an interview with *Xtra*, McIlwaine denied he was a closeted gay man. After a downward spiral of crack addiction, he had lost his family and his job and was penniless. 'What was I going to do? Hold up a store, or sell my ass? So I hit the street. My pride was in the toilet anyway.' McIlwained described one queer activist – who had called him a gay-basher – as a 'clown': 'Now wait a minute, it wasn't a murder ... and don't use my situation as a soapbox about your cause.' McIlwaine said it bothered him to think that people actually thought he intended to kill Eling: 'I had no intentions of hurting him. I was just doing what he wanted to do.'[110] On appeal, a new trial was ordered. In 1997 the jury returned with a verdict for second-degree murder after deliberating for four days.[111]

Gender Treachery: Hopkins's Theories of Homophobia

One of my favourite novels, Margaret Atwood's *The Handmaid's Tale*, is set in a society in which homosexuals are labelled 'gender traitors' and executed. Atwood's book inspired the title of Patrick Hopkins's article, 'Gender Treachery: Homophobia, Masculinity and Threatened Identities.' This 'treachery' occurs when homosexuality, bisexuality, cross-dressing, and feminist activism challenge traditional gender categories, which determine 'individuals' physical, economic, and sexual situations' in addition to 'their own sense of personal identity.' This identity is regulated by the binary system of man/woman: 'For a "man" to qualify as a man, he must possess a ... number of demonstrable characteristics that make it clear that he is not a woman.'[112] Hopkins notes that being a man is portrayed as 'natural' even though 'masculinity is so valorized, so prized, and its loss such a terrible thing, that one must always guard against losing it.'[113]

The author draws a distinction between *heterosexism* – 'loosely characterized as valorizing and privileging heterosexuality' – and *homophobia*, which has evolved from its original clinical sense to denote 'acts of physical, economic and verbal assault.' Heterosexism, he argues, is the 'necessary precursor' to homophobia: although not all heterosexists are homophobic, they have created the conditions in which homophobes flourish. 'Homophobia is a product of institutional heterosexism and gendered identity.'[114]

Theory 1: 'The Closeted Gay-Basher' Theory

Hopkins deconstructs three explanations of homophobic behaviour. I accompany his analysis with examples from my own research. The first theory involves the belief, common among gay men, that queer-bashers are in the closet and lash out because of frustration and self-loathing.[115]

The 'repression hypothesis' theorizes that gay-bashers are secretly gay, 'overcompensating, metastasizing into toxic, hypermasculine, ultra-butch homophobes.' Hopkins admits that in some cases, repressed homosexuals 'marry, and live a lie, unfulfilled emotionally and sexually, deceiving their wives and children, sometimes having furtive sexual affairs with other men.' However, the closeted gay-basher theory could also be 'wish fulfillment on the part of some gays. Forced by necessity of survival to be secretive and cryptic themselves, many gay men find it eminently reasonable to suspect any man of potential homosexual desire.'[116]

Along these lines, researchers in one controversial study wired men's penises in order to explore 'whether homophobic men show more sexual arousal to homosexual cues than nonhomophobic men as suggested by psychoanalytic theory.' Homophobic men who claimed to be exclusively heterosexual demonstrated 'significant sexual arousal to male homosexual erotic stimuli.' The media seized on this finding, but downplayed the researchers' contention that anxiety in the clinical setting could also have caused stimulation in the homophobic group.[117]

Another study noted how difficult it is to measure 'arousal' when clinical subjects are suddenly exposed to explicit gay pornography.[118] However, many social constructionists have voiced concerns that this line of research risks 'excusing' the violence: by implying that homophobia has biological origins, this research threatens to gloss over the social roots of homophobia.

A classic example of the repression theory is the chilling murder of Kendra Voght, a pre-op transsexual on hormones. A Vancouver activist attended the trial and reviewed the evidence. Police found rope in the hotel room of Paul Savoy and found his fingerprints on a copy of the 'Kink Pages' – a sex magazine featuring ads for transsexual escorts. Witnesses saw Savoy and Kendra at Celebrities, which at the time was Vancouver's largest gay bar. The two stayed there for hours before taking a cab back to the Clarence Hotel.[119]

Despite this evidence, Savoy continued to claim he had no idea Kendra was transgendered; he contended that while receiving oral sex, he asked for intercourse and was informed that she was a he. 'Infuriated by the discovery, Savoy immediately grabbed the throat of Voght, who was kneeling, and throttled him until his body went limp.' He threw Voght's body out the window and onto a roof. Savoy was found guilty of second-degree murder, ineligible to apply for parole for ten years.[120]

Another variation on the repression theory posits that repressed homosexuals are liable to kill their wives. For example, an accused wife killer in California was 'exposed' by a tabloid. 'I Had Gay Sex with Laci's Hubby: Drag queen's shocking revelation about his wild night with Scott.' A psychiatrist suggested that if Scott 'was ashamed of a secret craving for gay sex, it most likely unleashed a murderous rage that led to the savage deaths.'[121]

Theory 2: The Irrationality/Ignorance Hypothesis

Another theory described by Hopkins posits that 'homophobia is an irrational fear, based on ignorance.' The stereotype here is of 'a little boy who grows up in a poorly educated, very conservative family, often in a rural area, who hears his parents and other relatives' bad-mouthing homosexuals. The boy gets peer approval by deriding faggots, and thereby internalizes the norms of 'traditional heteromasculinity.'[122]

Along these lines, a mother from a small town in the B.C. Interior publicly defended her gay-bashing son. A gay man who had gone to live in the Slocan Valley was bashed twice. In the first incident, three complete strangers came a-knocking on his door:

> The guy just walked in with two other guys – and he had a baseball bat ... I couldn't walk for three weeks ... This other one left the room, came back with a butcher knife and tried to stick it in me ... Trying to get me to admit that I was an AIDS-infected faggot ... So I'm being beat on for like over an hour.

His phone was smashed, but he managed to get a call through to an RCMP officer, who said: 'Well there's nothing we can do now; we'll come around at about 2 o'clock tomorrow and see what we can do then.' The victim had to drive himself to the closest ambulance, and was put into a cast. A month later, the same assailant came back with an accomplice:

> I saw these two fellows walking up the driveway and I got scared immediately ... I was in a cast up to my shoulders ... He just came right at me, with his fists and his feet – no questions or anything, just saying, 'You're a faggot, aren't you? You're a faggot!' ... Standing on my cast and kicking my head in. And he just wouldn't stop ... The phone rang and I managed to get it turned on and kicked under the coffee table, so my friend Michael was able to call the police.[123]

This time the victim was 'left with multiple bruises, a broken eye socket, a fracture under one eye and a possible fracture to the base of his skull.' His broken arm had to be reset. Brent Winje pleaded guilty to assault with intent to cause bodily harm and was sentenced to two years.[124] In a horrifying taped interview, Winje described how he drank all day and then sought out his victim.

> He fell against the couch and I closed my fist ... I used the back of my fist and sidestroked to each side of his head about between fifteen and twenty times ... His eye was swollen closed and discoloring. His nose was bleeding; his mouth was hanging open because he had a broken jaw; it was hanging open and these gobs of blood just coming out of his nose ... I was asking him, 'Do you have AIDS ...' that scares me very much.

The victim's friend, who had been staying with him, was also bashed during this period. Three local police officers are reported to have spread word throughout the valley that an HIV-positive man was living in the house. Winje said he figured it was true, since it was the police who told him.[125] Outside the courtroom, Winje's mother said: 'There are two sides to this. There has been political pressure to call this a gay bash but it was not a gay bash and it was not a gang. It was fear of AIDS.'[126]

Hopkins argues that the ignorance/irrationality theory, although no doubt true in certain cases, oversimplifies homophobia 'as learned but completely irrational, unfounded, arbitrary, ignorant, counterproductive, and dysfunctional.' However, homophobic activity is often frighteningly rational in its execution: it 'wins approval from peers and authority figures, protects one from becoming the target of other homophobes, and reaffirms one's place in a larger context of gender appropriate behavior.'

Theory 3: The 'Political Response' Theory

In this formulation, according to Hopkins, homosexuals present a political threat by seeking to end heterosexual privilege. Homophobia, it follows, is the only way heterosexuals can protect their power.[127] Canadian political discourse is rife with such examples:

- Reform MP Art Hanger, while discussing same-sex relationship recognition in the House of Commons, said: 'Homosexuality, to anyone who has not been brainwashed by the last decade of effective propagandizing by the gay lobby, is unnatural. It is a repudiation of nature.'[128]
- Dr Grant Hill, the Alberta MP who served as the Reform Party's health critic, stated that supporting gay rights legislation 'would only encourage a lifestyle known to spread disease.'[129]
- When MP Myron Thompson addressed cheering delegates at a Reform Party convention, he declared: 'I do not hate thieves, I hate thieving; I do not hate murderers, I hate murderering; I do not hate homosexuals, I hate homosexuality.'[130]
- Reform MP Randy White accused gays and lesbians of making up stories about homophobic violence: 'You have to dig up a lot of rocks to unearth a worm ... There are enough real victims of crime, gay and otherwise, for police to deal with, without seeking imaginary ones.'[131]

Bill C-41, the act that amended the Criminal Code's sentencing provisions for hate crimes, was hotly debated in 1994. Carmen Paquette and John Fisher spoke in front of a parliamentary committee on behalf of EGALE, the national queer rights group. The MPs used four discursive strategies to vilify queers and to minimize the problem of homophobic violence.

1. *The equation of homosexuality with pedophilia* simmered just below the surface. One MP asked Paquette if she would use the term pedophilia to define sex between a fourteen-year-old and a thirty-year-old. Paquette replied: 'In Canada, 98 per cent of pedophiles are heterosexuals who like young girls.' When asked to define the remaining 2 per cent, she replied: 'This has nothing to do with sexual orientation.'[132] Later, an opposing committee member, disgusted with the Reform Party's gay-bashing approach, said: 'This is a sentencing bill. I've never heard so much garbage in my life.'[133]
2. MP Chuck Strahl applied the *tautological approach*, blaming queer victims for not reporting: 'How, though, will this bill help if homosexuals routinely fail to go to the police with the complaint?'[134]
3. Strahl also raised the *freedom of expression* argument: Could the Old Testament be construed as hate literature – and thereby risk the wrath of federal authorities – because it admonishes sodomites be put to death?[135]
4. Another MP raised the ugly spectre of *straight-bashing*: 'Even though I have all my life considered homosexuality to be deviant behaviour ... is there a possibility of a backlash ... not gay-bashing but heterosexual-bashing ...? From the tone of your presentation today, I gather there might be considerable bitterness in the gay and lesbian community. Paquette protested: 'That minorities engage in backlash is another myth. I consider myself your equal and I want the law to recognize that.'[136]

Despite these examples, Hopkins argues that the political backlash theory 'endows homophobes ... with a hyperrationality that does not seem to be in evidence.' The theory assumes that homophobes actually perceive a threat to their power and privilege. Most homophobes, 'in fact, do not perceive any obvious threat from the people they attack.' He cites a television interview with a gay-basher who 'had little or no explanation for why he was doing what he was doing except that it was fun. When asked how he could have fun hurting people, he said that he had never really thought of queers as real people.'

Hopkins believes that gay-bashers do not reflect on the social significance of queers 'any more than people who kick dogs for fun consider the political and moral significance of dogs.'[137] He concludes by warning warns readers not to assume that violent homophobes are few and far between: 'Challenge the asumption that one must be sexed or gendered to be a person. Eliminate the binary and it would be impossible to have heterosexism or homophobia, because hetero and homo would have no meaning.' He then returns to his original point – that homophobia 'could not exist without the background assumptions of (heterosexist) masculine identity.' Homophobia cannot simply be eliminated through education and sensitivity training. The gender dichotomy itself must be eliminated.[138]

Theory 4: The 'Sexual Abuse Victim Who Bashes' Theory

Along with Hopkins's theories, at least three other theories of homophobia appear in the literature – and are reflected in my data set. The following theory involves men who were sexually abused by other men. Lew notes that some of these victims worry that the abuse has 'made' them gay: the 'anxiety may be acted out in fear and avoidance of gays ... or by more active, sometimes violent, forms of homophobia.'[139]

In an Australian study of gay homicide victims, some killers claimed that the sexual abuse they had suffered when younger somehow 'caused' the fatal incident. As a result, gay men were scapegoated, 'seemingly made to bear a form of collective responsibility for this abuse.'[140] In other words, as a child or teenager, A was sexually abused by a man named B. When A grew up he killed a gay man named C – completely unrelated to his life – because C's homosexuality in some way reminded him of what B did to him. Instead of getting therapy and dealing with his painful past, he inflicted violence on an easy target, then convinced himself and his lawyers that he was somehow righting a terrible wrong.

Katz refers to these types of homicides as *righteous slaughter*: 'a self-righteous act undertaken within the form of defending communal values.' The killer goes through an emotional process, one that transforms 'what he initially senses as an eternally humiliating situation into a rage.' What the killer is doing is 'captured by the concept of sacrifice: the marking of a victim in ways that will reconsecrate the assailant as Good.'[141]

For example, David Maltby marked his gay victim with a hammer. Back in 1986, he took over the Bahamian High Commission in Ottawa and held the vice consul hostage for fifteen hours – an event that was turned into a Canadian B movie.[142] Maltby was sentenced to eight years; by 1993 he was out. A few months later, he and an accomplice, Robert Gaunt, went on a crime spree. They ended up in Stratford. At a bar there they learned they could rent a room from Douggie Grass, a costume maker for the Stratford Festival, who, they were told, 'preferred young men.' Maltby used this barroom comment – concerning a man he had never met – to form a motive for the murder. Maltby bought a hammer, took it to Grass's home, and hit Grass on the head with it fifteen times. He and Gaunt then stole clothing, jewellery, and the victim's car.

Maltby later rationalized the murder, saying he killed 'to avenge the sexual abuse he suffered as a youth ... He was used as a child prostitute.'[143] He added: 'It's time there was justice for the victims and their families.' He got life with no chance of parole for twenty-five years. Gaunt pleaded guilty to manslaughter and was sentenced to thirteen years.[144]

Sexual abuse also emerged as the motive after Charles Webb, a twenty-six-year-old Halifax man, was charged in the 1992 killing of Donald Pettipas, a fifty-one-year-old VIA Rail bartender. The police issued a release stating that Pettipas – stabbed twice in the chest with a large knife – was a 'suspected homosexual' with 'considerable male traffic coming and going from his apartment.'[145] Police found photos of the victim posing with nude boys. Webb said Pettipas sexually and physically abused him as a teenager, then took pictures of him. He claimed that Pettipas demanded sex again, using the photos as a form of blackmail. He said Pettipas came at him with a knife, and in the struggle, Pettipas fell on it. The Crown objected: 'The knife was obviously plunged into the upper right part of the body with considerable force ... It pierced the body, went through the carpet, and even into the concrete.'[146]

'Bill' – a gay Haligonian who knew both men, told me that 'Chuck' was not exactly a coerced 'victim.' In fact, Bill said Chuck saw 'Donny' regularly over the years. In fact, one day Bill said he witnessed Chuck with his hands around Donny's throat. Bill said he never heard Chuck complain about abuse – until Chuck was arrested for the killing.[147] But the media seemed to take the killer at his word. One headline read: 'Man Who Killed His Molester Sentenced to Four-Year Term.' Webb pleaded guilty to manslaughter.

Homophobia was also downplayed in the killing of Phillip Bright, a drag queen in London, Ontario, who had worked as a prostitute and an escort. 'Pete,' a man who dated him off and on, told me that by the end of Phillip's short life, the victim was sharing a house with a woman and her kids.[148] One morning his roommate found him dead; he had been beaten, and died of a ruptured spleen.[149] Jesse Lee L'Ecuyer pleaded guilty to manslaughter and was sentenced to seven years.[150] The London Police were guarded in their comments to me, but wrote the following:

1) Sexual orientation played no part in this homicide. The victim and the accused were casual acquaintances for about six months prior to the incident. Their common interests had nothing to do with sex.

2) Motive for the homicide was revenge. To right a perceived wrong. The accused was under the influence of alcohol and wrongly believed that the victim had molested a child of a mutual friend. There was no homophobic motive.[151]

However, just because the killer and the victim weren't having sex doesn't mean sexual orientation played no role. Is it possible the accused 'wrongly believed' the victim was a child molester *because* he was gay? Gay men know what it's like to be called a 'pervert' and 'child molester.' It doesn't matter how many times you try to explain it, some homophobic people cannot – and will not – make the distinction.

Theory 5: The 'Macho Lesbian-Basher' Theory

The 'mainstreaming' of lesbian culture has led some scholars like Ann Ciasullo to analyze media representations of lesbians. Butch women tend to be overshadowed by white, femme, upper-middle-class lesbians who are almost indistiguishable from straight women.[152] Other researchers focus on how violence against lesbians differs from violence against gay men. Mason discusses two scenarios in which lesbians are assaulted. In both, the assault is 'a rejection or repudiation of the conventional systems of sexual and gendered order.'

Mason's first scenario is similar to 'classic' gay-bashing: 'attacks in public places by young men, often acting in groups, who are strangers.'[153] In Canada, lesbians have been targeted on the street in B.C. and Alberta, and close to lesbian bars in Vancouver and Ottawa.[154] As I stated in the introduction, 9 per cent of the assaults and 3 per cent of the homicides I analysed involved biological female victims. But women don't just get lesbian-bashed; they get gay-bashed, too. In Hamilton, two men were walking toward a 'boyish-looking' woman and 'out of the blue, one of them punched her in the mouth.' When they heard her voice and realized she was a woman, they ran.[155] Lesbians in the company of gay men have also been targeted by gay-bashers.[156] A close friend – a straight woman in Vancouver – told me three men mistook her for a 'faggot' one night while she was walking on Denman Street with her boyfriend, who was assaulted.

However, Mason points out that men bash lesbians not just because of their sexual orientation, but also because the victims' 'sexual attention is

turned away from men.'[157] For example, in 1992 a Toronto man pro-
cured the services of a female prostitute for an acquaintance of his, then
demanded sex with her as a kickback. The woman replied that she was a
lesbian and never had sex with men unless it was for money. The man
raped her and 'punched the woman with such force that her jaw was
broken; it was wired shut for eight weeks.' The assailant was sentenced to
four years.[158]

This leads to Mason's second scenario, in which a man – a would-be
suitor, an ex-husband, an ex-boyfriend, or an acquaintance – assaults
and/or rapes the victim. The violence seems 'to be tied to the assumption
that the woman has rejected, or might reject, the sexual overtures of the
perpetrator ... In both cases, the violent repudiation of homosexuality
may ultimately facilitate an affirmation of heterosexuality.'[159] Mason's
approach is nuanced: the concept of love 'may also help us understand
certain types of violence.' The love that a straight man feels may not
simply be for a particular woman, 'but also for the gendered system of
heterosexuality itself and the privileges it affords him: a love for a certain
kind of sexual love.' Certain women 'may well become objects of hate if
they threaten to deny or thwart the pleasure that this love promises.'

A key factor in this rapid shift from love to hate 'is the fear of
indifference – an indifference that lesbianism embodies.'[160] This indifference becomes painfully evident in an example from 1992. A Prince
George mechanic named Wayne Sullivan went out drinking with his wife
Maureen and her childhood friend, Sandi. He claimed afterwards that the
two women 'set him up' by 'talking suggestively about a threesome but
not coming through.'[161] Wayne said that at home, Maureen told him she
loved Sandi and not him – and that made him snap. Sandi heard a shot;
Maureen fell to the floor and died of a gunshot wound thirty-six hours
later.[162] Wayne ordered Sandi to strip, but she managed to throw the gun
out the window and escape.

Within days of the killing, while Sullivan was awaiting bail on charges
of second-degree murder, a new woman, his future wife, 'moved in on the
jailed widower before Maureen was cremated.' After Sullivan was found
not criminally responsible by reason of a mental disorder, Sandi left
Prince George, 'unable to stomach the lesbian rumours and the thought
of bumping into her friend's killer.'[163]

Sullivan was ordered to be 'confined in a secure mental facility,'[164] yet
four years later, he was seen working at the mill and shopping with his
new wife. An indignant reporter commented: 'All he got for his depraved
deeds was an extension last week on an order to ban the booze and

weapons and to pay periodic visits to the forensic psychiatric outpatient unit.'[165]

Theory 6: The 'Immature Adolescent' Theory

I analysed 117 Canadian incidents and discovered that 42 per cent of them involved at least one teenaged queer-basher – one was only thirteen.[166] Many researchers have observed that homophobic violence falls into two rough, overlapping categories. West believes that homosexuals face attacks not only from those 'with pathological obsessions with sexual non-conformity, but from ordinary young delinquents whose exuberant aggression finds an outlet in the sport of "queer bashing."'[167]

Franklin echoes this view, dividing queer-bashers into the 'Antigay Ideology' assailants, who feel they are enforcing violations of gender norms, and those motivated by 'adolescent developmental factors.'[168] According to Harry, 'the option of gay-bashing offers a nearly ideal solution to the status needs of the immature male.'[169]

Van de Ven interviewed several young male offenders about their anti-gay behaviour. Only one-third said they had never harrassed or bashed gays or lesbians; one-third 'unequivocally admitted to having bashed'; one-third 'were at least potential perpetrators of anti-gay and anti-lesbian victimization and violence.' Over half the young men expressed completely negative attitudes toward gays and lesbians.[170] Here are some of the 'defensive positions'[171] the young men took, cross-referenced with actual cases from my data set. Not all the following examples involve adolescent assailants; the 'scripts' are utilized by gay-bashers of all ages.

- **Homosexuals are too visible in public.** In 1996, three men approached a gay man in a park in London, Ont. and said: 'We don't want people like you in this park.'[172] The same year, a Hamilton man with HIV found the words 'Fag we will kill u before human rights' stencilled on his apartment door.[173]
- **Homosexuality is sick and unnatural.** In Toronto, a two-hundred-pound bodybuilder beat on a man, calling him a 'faggot' and a 'fucking freak of nature.'[174] Another basher asked his victim: 'Why did God make you?'[175]
- **Homosexuals have particular mannerisms and modes of dress, speech, and appearance.** In Vancouver, a gay-bashing victim who complained to police was told: 'Well, what do you expect, wearing that scarf?'[176]
- **Homosexuals are coercive in areas of sexuality.** In Ottawa, a man

claimed he hadn't realized he was in a gay bar. He punched two men after being 'grabbed in a sexual way.' In Nanaimo, a seventeen-year-old claimed an older man came on to him; he used a tree branch to smash the man's jaw, which was wired shut for six weeks.[177]

• **Homosexuals are responsible for the spread of AIDS.**[178] In 1995 an Ottawa man seemed shocked to discover he had walked into a gay video store. He called the clerk an 'AIDS-infested homosexual' and a 'faggot,' then punched him in the head and spat in his face.[179]

• **Older gay men are a particular concern.** A fifteen-year-old boy, accompanied by his father, turned himself in to the police and explained that he had killed Robert Lemay, a fifty-five-year-old television newscaster in Shawinigan. The victim's nude body, stabbed repeatedly, was recovered from a snowbank outside his riverfront home.[180] The boy claimed that he had been fending off an unwanted sexual advance. However, one activist described the boy as a 'prostitute' and complained that the media were portraying Lemay as a dirty old man.[181] The police dismissed the possibility of hate motivation. A Quebec Provincial Police officer told me that although 'the crime scene didn't fit with the young man's version of events,' it wasn't a gay-bashing.[182]

• **Homosexuals try to seduce children.** In 1999, a fifty-nine-year-old man hired six men, ranging from seventeen to thirty-four, and drove them to a remote area of Vancouver Island near Duncan. William Davis asked them to act out a masochistic scenario: he wanted to be punished for being a 'pedophile.' He supplied drugs and alcohol and spelled out the rules. He was not to be killed: no stabbing or hitting in the face or other visible parts of the body. After it was over he wanted to be driven home. In the aftermath, four men were charged with manslaughter and a teenager was tried for aggravated assault:

Things spiralled out of control, the court heard. The youth initiated the scenario by kicking Davis in the chest and admitted to punching him repeatedly in the head and leg. The other men, drunk and stoned, allegedly continued the beating over several hours.

Davis was allegedly punched, kicked and sexually assaulted, his lung was pierced with needles and his body was burned by logs from a camp fire. At one point, he pleaded with his assailants to kill him, saying he couldn't take it any more, the youth said. The group took a vote and returned the injured man to his home.

Five days later, police were led to Davis' home, where he was found dead.[183]

Was this a victim-precipitated suicide? No, because the victim apparently said he didn't want to die. Did he choose to die rather than go to the hospital? We don't know if he was even capable of picking up the phone to call an ambulance when he got back to his house. Was the victim actually a pedophile? We're not sure. Perhaps he was troubled by his own fantasies and wanted to expiate them in this crude fashion. Did the men cause his death because they knew he *was* a pedophile – or because the victim himself implied it?

It is possible that the homophobic motive in this killing was downplayed or overlooked. At some point the men crossed a threshold – from the fantasy of hurting a pedophile to the killing of an older, vulnerable man who was quite possibly a closeted, self-hating homosexual. The homophobic discourses common in our society – that we are all 'child molesters' – may have provided these men with sufficient justification to do him in. B.C.'s queer community did not rush to 'own' this case, probably because of the association with pedophilia and masochism. Many will no doubt claim that this gruesome killing had nothing to do with the queer community. But I think homophobic violence disguises itself in multiple ways.

Teenage Killers

Out of thirty-one 'gay-hate killings' in Australia, twelve were attacks on complete strangers who were perceived to be homosexual. The perpetrators were young men and teenage boys who killed in groups. I analysed fifty-two homicides in my data set and found that 17 per cent involved teenage killers.[184]

Although most youths acted alone or in pairs, in Toronto a gang of youths knifed Jim Bwabwa to death in 1998.[185] Another gang-related death – one of the most shocking I came across – received little press coverage. In 1991, nineteen-year-old Eric Samuelson was convicted of manslaughter in the death of a visually impaired man in Sackville, New Brunswick. Robert Read was chased through the streets by six young men yelling 'faggot,' while bystanders yelled, 'Get him, Eric!' The mob 'knocked him unconscious and left him lying on the street, where a truck ran over and killed him.'[186]

The following Toronto murders reveal a different pattern. A fourteen-year-old boy said he regularly visited the home of John Somerton, a forty-two-year-old man who gave him beer and cigarettes. The boy claimed that Somerton made a sexual advance; he said he warned Somerton he would kill him if he did it again. The boy smashed a three-foot iron bar into the man's skull ten times – the apartment walls were spattered with blood. Although the boy claimed he didn't intend to kill the victim, one psychiatrist wrote: 'In relating this tale, the accused seemed calm and happy about what he had done.' The boy also assaulted a homosexual inmate while in detention.

At sixteen, the youth pleaded guilty to second-degree murder and said sorry at the sentencing hearing – 'the first scintilla of remorse,' said the judge, who feared the boy was a dangerous psychopath. The judge ordered the maximum sentence: three years in custody and two in the community. The victim's sister was disgusted with the sentence: 'You drink and drive – you get more.'[187]

In 1991, two teenagers – Adam Harris and 'AJR' – escaped from a youth facility and went to visit an actor named Michael Vadeboncoeur, 'a single male homosexual who had a history of picking up younger males in various gay "pick-up" areas.' Harris said Vadeboncoeur had paid him for sex before. The youths bought two knives, went to Vadeboncoeur's house, stabbed him in the neck, and robbed him of various gear. After they were arrested, Harris claimed he was defending himself because the victim had ordered him to perform fellatio. AJR was convicted of manslaughter and sentenced to the maximum three years. Harris, who was sixteen at the time of the murder, was sentenced to life.[188]

Adolescent Homophobia

Mark Totten's powerful book, *Guys, Gangs and Girlfriend Abuse*, points to disturbing links between misogynist and homophobic violence. Screening interviews were conducted with ninety marginalized male youths in the Ottawa area; out of this group, sixty had physically and/or sexually abused their girlfriends.[189] Out of this group of sixty, almost all 'reported that the ideal man needs to be tough, aggressive, and muscular; heterosexual,' and most approved of hitting their girlfriends.[190]

Only one of these sixty teenagers admitted he was gay; two others were unsure of their sexual orientation. All three were in the closet and 'feared being beaten up by their male peers if they disclosed their sexual orientation to them.' The youths felt they 'were making a clear break from their father's abusive behaviour' by choosing a different sexual orientation.[191] Thirty teenagers were chosen for in-depth interviews. Almost without exception, 'heterosexuality was presented as "natural" and moral, and gays and males with feminine characteristics were described as being immoral and therefore deserving physical punishment.'[192] One of his research subjects equated his poverty with masculinity; conversely, he categorized men who went to university and got middle-class jobs as 'rich faggots ... They're pussies. They probably get rammed up the ass every night by their boss ... You gotta be a fuckin' faggot – kissing some guy's ass – to get a job like that.'[193]

A native youth revelled in the fact that he was *not* gay: 'The only thing going my way as a guy is that I'm not queer. Can you imagine a queer unemployed Indian? You might as well kill yourself. You'd be nothing. Zero. Cut off your cock and flush it.'

Many of the youths expressed anxieties about sexuality, speaking proudly of their penises and 'beating up anyone with effeminate features. It was as if a male with any hint of femininity posed a direct threat to their masculinity.' For example, Bob asked rhetorically. 'Would you like to be called a faggot and a pussy all the time? I gotta show that I can fuck, and fuck a lot. I'm no queer.'[194]

Eight of the thirty participants said they 'routinely' beat up gays, yet Totten observed that they 'were over four times as likely than non-bashers to be gay, bisexual, or have serious questions about their sexual orientation.' Totten analysed the youths' 'defensive posturing ... These participants indicated that they faced a daily risk of being raped by gays, and that the only way to protect themselves from this constant threat was to beat up anyone they thought was gay.'

Watney has noted that even the possibility of anal sex creates anxiety in many males: 'The male rectum is the most thoroughly policed part of the male anatomy.'[195] Echoing this sentiment, one of Totten's fourteen-year-old subjects warned: 'You gotta watch out for them. Bend over and they'll ram their cock up your ass.' However, a seventeen-year-old reflected: 'If you want the truth I think a lot of it's about a guy being paranoid that his friends will think he's a faggot. So if you beat on faggots and get into a different pussy every night, no fucker in their right mind would ever think you were queer ... Even when I was really young – like around 8 or 9 – I can remember beating ... faggots.'[196]

In one heart-breaking interview, seventeen-year-old Nick explained that when he was twelve, he began to feel attracted to men and told his father he might be gay. Nick said his father, who was a biker, 'kicked the living shit outta me ... was screaming at me "No son of mine's gonna be a fuckin' queer!" Then he put his hands around my throat and held me up against wall and screamed in my face "Don't you ever, ever tell anyone ... You're gonna get fucked every night by a cunt even it costs me a million dollars."'

After the attack, even though Nick was taken out of the home, his father and uncle still gave him money every week to visit prostitutes. Despite his homosexual desires, Nick 'routinely beat up gays on the street with his gang.'

Have you ever had sex with a guy?
Fuck no. I'm too scared. All I can think of is my Dad's hands around my throat. I'll never do that. He'd kill me.
Do you want to sleep with another guy?
Kind of. But it's not worth it. I think I've got it under control now.

Most of the youths came from homes in which 'sexual objectification of women and homophobia was commonplace.' The youths believed that the abusive behaviour of their biological fathers was justifiable and 'an appropriate way to resolve conflict and ensure the appropriate behaviour of other family members.'[197]

Totten's observations shed some light on the motives of the following murder, carried out by a man who said he was raised in a homophobic environment. Jason Mason lived in a trailer near Salmo, B.C. In 1991, Mason's old friend Charles Stewart stayed with Mason for several days after Stewart had a fight with his wife. Stewart said he woke up one day and discovered Mason stroking his penis. Stewart said he was disgusted but remained silent for three days. 'As he was about to leave, Mason told him that 'man with man' sex was alright, at which point Stewart said he 'lost it.' He had a strong aversion to homosexuality, stemming from his childhood, during which his father had repeatedly cautioned him and his brothers against such practices and urged them to do violence to any man who attempted to seduce them. He grabbed a knife from the workbench ...'

Mason's body was found in the woodshed, stabbed six times. Stewart was convicted of first-degree murder. On appeal, a conviction of second-degree murder was substituted.[198]

Summary

Theories from various disciplines help explain the construction of homosexual identity; the labelling, stigmatization, regulation, and targeting of homosexuals; and the queer movement's rise and resistance to these oppressive practices.

Individuals associated with a broad cross-section of religious, cultural, political, and social institutions engage in heterosexist and homophobic behaviour. Hopkins believes that the former is a precondition of the latter. Various theories about why males queer-bash focus on sexual repression; ignorance; political backlash; the revenge of abuse victims; adolescent developmental factors; and the tendency of some heterosexual men to feel rejected by women who prefer their own sex.

CHAPTER 3

The Horror of Homophobic Violence

In this chapter I explore the various ways that homophobic violence affects individuals, subgroups, and society as a whole, citing Canadian cases that can only be described as acts of shocking brutality. First, I examine the 'extreme violence' thesis, which posits that violence against queers is more intense than 'regular' violence. Second, I analyse the following characteristics: the number and sex of the victims; the number and sex of the suspects; drug and alcohol issues; temporal and geographical considerations; and other techniques predators use to ensnare their victims. Finally, I examine the impact of homophobic violence on vulnerable subgroups, including teenagers, college and university students, the transgendered, prostitutes, prisoners, and queer refugees.

The following 1995 case demonstrates how queer-bashers can strike without warning and with relative impunity – even in spaces the community tries to keep safe. 'Miriam,' an activist in Victoria's women's community, got more than she bargained for the night she decided to visit her first gay bar, Rumours. She worked up the courage to dance with a twenty-one-year-old woman who had just moved to Vancouver Island. But a man kept getting in Miriam's way, cutting in and insisting that her dance partner dance with him instead. The younger woman said no several times. He drew close and pulled out a knife. The first thrust was so quick nobody knew what was happening. Miriam recalls:

> After he stabbed her once – we both never saw the knife and thought he had pushed her – I went up to him and told him to leave this woman alone. He approached her again on the dance floor and I danced into his personal space, forcing him off the dance floor and again told him to leave her alone ... and that's when he stabbed her in the back ... He didn't make a move to leave (perhaps waiting to finish her off) till I looked him in the eye.

He then walked quickly towards the doors. I intercepted him, told him he couldn't leave, he shoved me aside, I chased him yelling at the bouncers to stop him and finally as he was going up the steps to leave the bouncers grabbed him.[1]

Two weeks later, the man was released on bail, which sparked a demonstration by thirty women at the Victoria courthouse. The victim said the bail decision 'really blows my mind.' But a police officer said the young man didn't belong in jail because he had no previous record.[2]

Seven months later, the victim, whose ribs and bowels were still damaged, stated: 'I don't believe this was any sort of gay issue ... This can happen to anyone and it doesn't matter if you're homosexual or heterosexual.'[3] Miriam was enraged that the crime wasn't considered a premeditated hate crime: 'I don't buy that. I saw him stalk her, watched him staring at her as she collapsed in my arms and lay bleeding on the dance floor ... I don't agree ... about it not being related to being a lesbian. Would it have been different if she was dancing with a man? I think so, it wouldn't have been as much a wound to his machismo, but to get rejected for a woman, well that's worth killing over I guess.'[4]

The man defended his actions: 'I've never been able to handle rejection ... This girl kept rejecting me.'

Consequences to Victims

Sometimes it's easier to calculate the financial impact of homophobic violence. Queer-bashers can inflict thousands of dollars of damage and permanently disable victims, depriving them of their livelihoods.[5] But how can we measure the emotional costs?

According to Stermac and Sheridan, queer-bashing victims experience depression, anxiety, 'headaches, nightmares, crying, agitation and restlessness, weight loss, increased use of drugs and alcohol, and deterioration of personal relationships.' Queer-bashing victims live 'in continuous fear of future aggression'[6] and 'may experience a resurfacing of critical issues in their identity development, such as increased feelings of self-loathing, guilt, shame, alienation and isolation, and rejection of homosexuality. [They] may feel that they have been justifiably punished for being gay; they may be blamed by others for the assault and accused of inviting or deserving the attack ... Significant rage and anger at society, and even at the gay community, following a victimization is common.'[7] As a way of illustrating some of these symptoms, here is an Ottawa man's account of being gay-bashed on his way home from a bar:

> I also remember the watch of the person who was punching me. The watch
> finally broke and fell to the ground. I can remember that as I was being hit,
> the watch became covered with blood ... One of his friends, as they cheered
> him on, told him to watch it because he'd get AIDS from my blood. I was
> bleeding quite profusely and each time I was hit it would splatter quite a
> distance. At the mention of AIDS the person attacking me stopped ... My
> eyes were swollen shut. My ear was swollen shut and bleeding quite pro-
> fusely ... I realized what had happened to me: I had been beaten because I
> was gay. I went into shock. I went into uncontrollable shivers and convul-
> sions. I was sick to my stomach several times.[8]

Peterkin and Risdon have written an important clinical guide for the
care of queer patients. In the section on physical assault, doctors are
encouraged to do the following:

- Refer the patient for urgent care and rape tests, and make sure the
  injuries are photographed.
- Ensure the patient's safety in case of retaliation, and explore housing
  options.
- Report the incident to the police and to queer support networks.
- 'Actively challenge any assumptions of self-blame or the emergence of
  increased internalized homophobia.'
- Find out if the patient is vulnerable to post-traumatic stress disorder,
  and refer to gay-positive counselling if necessary.[9]

Queers who are closeted – or in their early stages of coming out – will
have less 'resilience and support' and may be afraid of 'double disclosure' – not only of the attack, but also of their own sexual orientation.
Unconsciously, they may believe 'that their homosexuality is the cause of
the victimization, and be plagued by feelings of vulnerability, helpless-
ness, depression and low self-esteem.'[10] For example, a gay man in
Edmonton who was kicked and stabbed in the face in 1994 said he heard
people laughing during the trial.[11]

The verbal abuse that often accompanies homophobic violence is especially damaging 'to a survivor's sense of self, as it provokes feelings of
self-hatred ... Clients may attempt to hide or even deny their sexual
orientation to avoid further victimization.'[12] A California study of queer
victims demonstrated that they had higher levels of anger, depression,

anxiety, and post-traumatic stress disorder. 'They also displayed less willingness to believe in the general benevolence of people and rated their own risk for future victimization somewhat higher than did others.'[13]

Extreme Violence and Abjection

An analysis of assaults in Toronto suggests that 'crimes of violence directed against gays and lesbians involve a greater degree than the average assault ... All respondents reported bruising of some kind, with almost one in five reporting a fracture ... Of the 22 cases of head injuries, one-third resulted in concussion.'[14] Here is a partial list of weapons used in the non-fatal incidents I analysed: tree branch,[15] baseball bat,[16] high-powered rifle,[17] broken beer bottle,[18] exacto knife,[19] stones,[20] fish club,[21] knife,[22] skateboard,[23] wooden board,[24] pepper spray,[25] 9-mm pistol,[26] rubber bullets,[27] stun gun,[28] steel pipe,[29] pellet gun,[30] mahogany paddle,[31] metal post[32]

A Toronto hate crimes officer reflected: 'Gays aren't like other victims. You can't just buy a lock. You can change your name but you just can't change who you are. I've seen gay people attacked with billiard balls. The hate crime perpetrator has hate in his heart. He goes overtime on the assault.'[33]

More to the point: *Why* do they go to such extremes? Wax and Haddox examined six dangerous youths and came up with three predictors of violent behaviour: fire setting, cruelty to animals, and bed wetting that continued on into adolescence. The youths all came from 'deprived' and 'disorganized' family backgrounds.[34] However, Langevin dismissed these findings, arguing that there were no control groups and that vague concepts – such as 'poor parenting' – might predict antisocial behaviour but did not necessarily predict extreme violence. That said, it has been established that many murderers have endured 'cruel and extremely violent parenting.'[35]

Many social theorists make sense of the senseless – this intense, extreme violence – by applying Kristeva's theory of *abjection*. Young describes abjection as 'the feeling of loathing and disgust the subject has in encountering certain matter, images, and fantasies – the horrible, to which it can only respond with aversion, with nausea and distraction.' At the same time, the abject fascinates: 'It draws the subject in order to repel it. The abject is meaningless, repulsive in an irrational, unrepresentable way.'[36]

Kristeva points out that the repulsion is caused by 'what disturbs identity, system, order. What does not respect borders, positions, rules. The in-between, the ambiguous, the composite.'[37] Young explains that the abject triggers 'fear and loathing because it exposes the border between self and other as constituted and fragile, and threatens to dissolve the subject by dissolving the border,' thus creating 'an irrational dread that latches onto a material to which it is drawn in horrified fascination.' A socially constructed link exists between abjection and 'racism, sexism, homophobia, ageism, and ableism': 'the theory of abjection describes how these associations lock into the subject's identities and anxieties. As they represent what lies just beyond the borders of the self, the subject reacts with fear, nervousness and aversion to members of these groups because they represent a threat to identity itself.'

Young believes that homophobia is a 'border anxiety' and is exacerbated by the fact that 'homosexuality has become increasingly deobjectified, no specific characteristics, no physical, genetic, mental, or moral "character" marks off homosexuals from heterosexuals.' Because of the increasing difficulty to 'assert any difference between homosexuals and heterosexuals,' homophobia is 'one of the deepest fears of difference precisely because the border between gay and straight is constructed as the most permeable; anyone at all can become gay, especially me, so the only way to defend my identity is to turn away with irrational disgust.'[38]

Sexual Homicide

Some researchers believe that homicides with a sexual element are generally more violent. One study demonstrated that sexual homicides are more likely to involve knives, premeditation, and overkill.[39] But is there an overabundance of queer sexual homicides? Swigert and colleagues examined 444 homicides in the United States and identified five as 'sexual homicides' – which they defined as any killing preceded by sexual activity between the killer and the victim. Four out of the five homicides occurred in the victim's house. 'The methods employed to produce death were strangulation and knifings.'

Out of these five cases of sexual homicide, two involved homosexual victims. In the first case, the killer demanded money. The victim refused and apparently threatened to tell the killer's family that the killer was a homosexual. In the second case, a man picked up the victim in a public toilet, went back to the victim's house, had sex with the victim, then plunged an ice pick into his head.[40]

It appears that forensic scientists are already aware of the extreme violence in homosexual homicides. Forty years ago, Kiel surveyed twenty pathologists. He sent each pathologist photographs of four murder victims, along with brief case descriptions. He asked them to speculate on each assailant's state of mind and modus operandi, in the hope that these insights would assist law enforcement personnel in investigating and prosecuting the crimes.

One of the four case studies involved a nude fifty-year-old man found kneeling beside his bed. He had been stabbed, punched, hit with a hammer, and strangled. Sixteen of the twenty pathologists suggested that the murder was linked to homosexuality. At trial, a seventeen-year-old boy claimed that he had had sex with the victim and then became enraged after the victim threatened to tell the boy's girlfriend he had engaged in homosexual activity.[41]

Measuring Extreme Violence in Queer Homicides

Reineke is fascinated with the 'trajectory of violence ... its apparently inexorable march toward brutality.' 'I find myself seeking a calculus that I might use to measure protracted violence ... I want to know, once a body is invoked by a perpetrator of violence, why does violence reach down ever deeper into it? Why does shoving give way to violation, to tearing and splitting open the body, to slow torture ending in death?'[42]

Anecdotally, there has been much to suggest that killers inflict higher levels of violence on queer homicide victims. But how does one measure the degree of violence? Bell and Vila came up with a list of 67 male 'homosexual' homicide victims and 195 male 'heterosexual' victims by interviewing police, medical examiners, alleged assailants, and the victims' friends and lovers. The control group was matched for age and race. The methodological conundrum is obvious: How could they be certain their control group was 'really' heterosexual? A man with a wife and children is not necessarily straight. Still, Bell and Vila's study has come closer than any other to unravelling the 'extreme violence' mystery. The cause of death for the two groups is outlined in table 3.1. When Bell and Vila did an analysis (using the Fisher two-tailed exact test), they found no statistical difference in the causes of death between the homosexual group and the control group.[43] The researchers also analysed the average number of injuries per case, as shown in table 3.2. Using the Mann-Whitney rank sum test, they found statistical differences regarding the mean number of blunt-force injuries, sharp-force injuries, and total injuries per case. Finally, the authors divided the body into various sectors

Table 3.1
Cause of death of homosexual and heterosexual male homicide victims

Cause of death	Percentage of homosexual victims ($n = 67$)	Percentage of control group ($n = 195$)
Sharp force injury	30	17
Gunshot	22	61
Mechanical asphyxiation	21	4
Blunt force	15	13
Multiple causes	12	5

Table 3.2
Number of injuries sustained by homosexual and heterosexual homicide victims

Mean number of	Homosexual	Control group
Sharp-force injuries per case	18.3+/–19.5 (range, 1–82)	10.8+/–12.8 (range, 1–51)
Gunshot wounds per case	1.7+/–1.1 (range, 1–5)	2.0+/–1.9 (range, 1–13)
Blunt-force injuries per case	9.0+/–8.0 (range, 1–36)	6.7+/–7.9 (range, 1–51)
Total injuries per case	14.5 +/–17.3 (range, 1–82)	6.5+/–10.0 (range, 1–58)

Table 3.3
Location of injuries sustained by homosexual and heterosexual homicide victims

Location of injury	Homosexual	Control group
face	54%	36%
head	63	46
neck	58	19
back	46	28
arms	48	35
legs	22	14
chest	42	42
abdomen	16	22
genitals	0	2

and measured the average number of body sites with injuries per case (see table 3.3).[44] Using this data, the authors found a statistical difference between the homosexual and control groups. For gay men the mean number of different body sites with injuries per case was 3.5 +/– 2.0 (range, 1–7). By contrast the number for the control group was 2.4 +/– 1.7 (range, 1–8). Bell and Vila concluded: 'Homosexual homicides are more violent than heterosexual homicides when one compares the mean number of injuries (fatal sharp, blunt, and total)/case and the extent of the injuries on the body. The mean number of gunshot wounds/case and the percentage of cases with multiple causes of death, however, were not statistically different between the two groups.'[45]

Extreme Violence in Canadian Queer Homicide Cases

My method of measuring extreme violence was much less scientific. First I determined how many of the homicides in my data set included a description of the actual violence inflicted. I found fifty-eight descriptions. In 60 per cent of these cases, I found that at least one of the victims

- had had his throat slashed
- had been strangled
- had been subjected to ten or more blows or stab wounds
- had experienced a severe impact that fatally smashed or crushed the victim
- had experienced an execution-style shooting
- had experienced a prolonged, agonizing death

However, my system raises troubling questions. For example, who suffered more – a multiple stabbing victim, or Gerrard Morin, the Toronto man who was beaten and then fell nineteen storeys to his death?[46]

In the following two cases, the corpses suffered further indignities, which compels us to ask: Does desecration of the body 'count' as 'extreme violence,' since the victim (it is hoped) may not have felt this pain? Certainly, it is an act of symbolic violence. In his analysis of 'righteous slaughter,' Katz states: 'It is not incidental that the marks of sacrifice are signs of the body penetrated and its normally hidden elements revealed.'[47]

In 1996, the partially burned body of Jean Chenier, forty, was discovered at his home near Hull. The police said the victim had been robbed and stabbed to death; also, a fire had been set in his apartment. Chenier's brother said the victim 'lived an active gay nightlife, had a boyfriend, and sometimes brought male hustlers into the home.' Maurice Pilon, twenty-two, was charged with first-degree murder.[48]

The same year, just before Christmas, a burnt corpse was discovered in Toronto. Paul Armstrong disappeared after a car picked him up at his house. Armstrong's roommates never saw who was in the driver's seat.

Armstrong's friends became concerned when he didn't return for his own Christmas party that night. Two days later, a body was found smouldering in a dumpster: it took three days to determine the victim's age and sex.[49] Dental records eventually identified Armstrong. His twin sister explained to reporters that their thirty-eighth birthday would have taken place that Christmas Eve.

Armstrong's brother said: 'Paul was a very good brother and always thought of other people first. We just can't believe he was found this way in a dumpster after the good he had done.' In contrast to some parents – who were ashamed of their children or discouraged the queer community from attending the funeral – Armstrong's father said his son 'never burdened us and was always a joy. Paul was well-liked by everyone.' Many Toronto people attended the Belleville service: 'We figured we should let his friends say goodbye.'[50] The 519 Community Centre was asked to consider the killing a hate crime but decided against it.[51] But it makes me wonder: How much more hateful could a crime get?

By any measure, the most violent death in my data set was the frenzied killing of David Curnick. In 1994, the fifty-year-old gay high school teacher was found dead in his Vancouver apartment, stabbed 146 times with his own kitchen knife.[52] I interviewed one of Curnick's friends, who said the victim 'was short, balding, and didn't fit into the club scene.' Apparently, Curnick had had hundreds of sexual encounters and had even secretly videotaped some of them. Curnick 'was rarely in relationships and would always fall for gorgeous straight guys. He would have a lot of casual sex, and had a unique system ... He started with personal ads in magazines. He would offer massage for straight and bi-curious guys. He had a great set-up going. On his computer he had a checklist which sorted out everyone, and he was able to screen out calls.'[53]

The investigation into Curnick's death took a dramatic turn when the police released a grainy video image of the tattooed killer to the press.[54] Darren Young had met Curnick six or seven years earlier. He was 'fresh out of jail' and had gotten together with Curnick again a few days before the murder. Young was quickly arrested and pleaded guilty to second-degree murder.[55] At the sentencing hearing, the judge seemed confused. At first he thought Curnick had been running some sort of brothel. Young received the standard sentence – 'life,' but eligible to apply for parole after ten years.

However, the victim's friends felt the sentence might have been longer if the Crown had tried harder to challenge Young's claim of being a 'victim.' The defence lawyer apparently implied that Curnick had 'sexually abused'

Young, suggesting that Young had been underage at the time of their first sexual encounter. His friends argued that this was not mathematically possible, since Young was twenty-six at the time of the killing. Moreover, Curnick's friends felt the Crown should have pushed harder to demonstrate a pattern of homophobic violence. On two occasions, they claimed, Young had stabbed a transsexual woman.[56] Again, any homophobic dimensions of this hideous crime were pushed to the side.

Characteristics of Homophobic Violence

The Number, Sex, and Sexual Orientation of Victims

Table I.1 showed the cases I analysed in which the exact number and sex of the victims was known. As can be seen in that table, more than three-quarters of the incidents involved single – as opposed to multiple – victims.[57] The majority of these incidents appeared to involve homosexuals. However, in several cases the victim claimed to be heterosexual or denied being queer, or, from all appearances, *was* heterosexual but in the wrong place at the wrong time.'[58] In a letter to the editor, a straight man bashed in Vancouver's West End expressed his gratitude. 'To the man who handed me his phone so that the police could talk to me, and didn't mind when I returned it covered with blood ... To the father and son who pursued at least one of the assailants while maintaining contact with the police ... To the police ... you caught all three of them ... To the numerous people who called 911 when I was attacked: thank you for not just turning away.'[59]

The Number and Sex of Suspects

As can be seen in table 3.4, the difference between male and female participation in these crimes is dramatic. In the few cases involving female perpetrators, the woman was usually the lookout, the driver, or a basher's girlfriend who turned a blind eye.[60] One of the most horrific cases in my data set involved two men and a woman who assaulted and humiliated three men in a Moncton rooming house. Sarah McMillan got two years; the men got between three and four. McMillan said she wanted to see the 'queers' suck each other's penis: 'She ordered them all to pull down their pants, which they did out of fear of the continued beatings. [She] was saying "that's what you cocksuckers deserve." She then went into the kitchen to fetch her curling iron and returned into the

Table 3.4
Number and sex of suspects in queer-bashing incidents

No. of suspects in an incident	No. of cases	Percentage of cases
1 male	136	53.9
2 male	56	22.2
3 male	27	10.7
4 male	13	5.2
5–15 male	12	4.8
1 female	2	.8
Both male and female suspects	6	2.4
Total	252	100

bedroom. She had Mr. Chaisson and Mr. Bindas hold down [Victim A] ... The curling iron was then inserted in the rectums of [Victim B] and [Victim C].'[61]

More commonly, women acted as accomplices for their basher-boyfriends. In Saskatoon, a lesbian couple had just left an alternative bar when two men and two women yelled obscenities at them from a truck. According to a local activist who recounted the story, the two men then grabbed tire irons and rusty chains and 'hung a licking on the girls,' knocking out teeth.[62] Their girlfriends did not participate in the beatings.

Forty-five per cent of the incidents in my data set were perpetrated by multiple attackers.[63] With swarming incidents, it is difficult to know how many in the crowd were perpetrators, and what percentage were male.[64] On Halloween in 1991, for example, about fifty thugs came into Toronto's queer neighbourhood, 'taunting, threatening and attacking gay men.' A man whose nose was broken said he had been kicked and punched by several in the crowd. 'It was like a pack of jackals,' one witness said. 'You know, big tough guys travelling in packs of thirty.'[65] Xtra noted that 'the gang seemed well organized, adept at dispersing and then reassembling once police had left the scene.'[66]

Sex, Drugs, and Booze

In many cases, the violence occurred after the victim and the suspect had picked each other up, usually at a bar or in a cruising area.[67] For example, in 1999, two men met in Montreal's Gay Village. After having sex, the man who was visiting fell asleep. He woke up when his 'host' began smashing his skull with an object and making homophobic insults. The basher was tried for attempted murder.[68]

In other cases, drugs and/or alcohol were involved, either on the part of the assailant or on the part of the victim – or both.[69] In several homicides, the victim and/or the suspect had either consumed excessive amounts of drugs or alcohol or had some connection with the drug trade. For example, in 1991, a coke dealer named Normand Gareau was killed in his Montreal apartment and then dumped outside the city.[70]

In Vancouver, François Bolton, fifty-seven, was strangled by a twenty-nine-year-old man on a two-day cocaine binge. The *Vancouver Sun* portrayed this as a domestic killing, yet the victim shared his home not only with Marc Poirier, but also with Poirier's girlfriend and her children. Bolton had befriended Poirier while Poirier was 'working the streets' and had tried to control Poirier's drug use. Poirier pleaded guilty to manslaughter and got four years. The judge called the killing 'irrational, terrible violence caused by cocaine psychosis.' His nephew said Bolton 'hated what drugs did to people and look what happened to him – he got killed by a drug addict.'[71]

Temporal and Geographical Considerations

Queer-bashing, like many other crimes, can intensify during public events and celebrations. Halloween brings out both queers and their bashers.[72] Gay and Lesbian Pride events also attract homophobes. On Pride weekend in 1991, a Toronto man confronted three men making homophobic comments on Church Street. As events escalated, two hundred people came to his aid. The three men were charged with uttering threats and assault.[73] Before Toronto Pride Day religious services in 1994, a letter warned: 'We know about Maple Leaf Gardens. If you go ahead, a lot of blood will spill and a lot of faggots will die.'[74] In 1998, London's HALO club received a bomb threat on the day of the Toronto Pride parade.[75]

In most cases, I was able to pinpoint the actual locations of the incidents in my data set. As shown in table 3.5, almost 16 per cent of the queer-bashing incidents in my data set – and 11.5 per cent of the homicides – took place in or near parks and/or cruising areas. In 1995, a Winnipeg man was found barely conscious, 'savagely beaten, stripped nude and left for dead on a riverbank walkway notorious for gay-bashing.'[79]

Gay men's sexual activity in public spaces is a controversial topic. Some gay men consider cruising areas to be 'safe havens,' despite the physical dangers. Tewksbury interviewed eleven gay men who frequented cruising areas. They portrayed the danger as a pleasurable element in pursuit of their goals, which were *conquest* and *survival*.[80] Gay therapist

Table 3.5
Location of queer-bashing incidents

Location	No.	%
Inside or just outside a queer establishment[76]	65	21.2
In a neighbourhood or on a street where queers are visible[77]	61	19.9
Cruising areas, including parks and prostitution strolls	48	15.6
In or near the victim's residence[78]	50	16.3
In custody: police station, prison, prison hospital, youth detention centre, jail, or drunk tank	13	4.2
In or near the suspect's residence	5	1.6
Other locations	65	21.2
Total	307	100

Doug Arey contends that certain men who have anonymous, public sex are sex addicts[81] or abuse survivors; for some of them, 'frequenting cruising areas is frightening and a deep source of shame and humiliation.'[82] However, one patient explained that such areas were the only ones where 'his world was not falling apart ... He belonged to a community of men ... without concern that his self-identity as a good (i.e., heterosexual) Catholic family man would collapse.'[83]

A Vancouver man was interviewed about his sexual habits in the wake of the brutal killing of Aaron Webster. He said the killing had no impact on his practice of picking up two or three men a week in the heavily wooded area. He said he preferred park sex to meeting men at bars or on phonelines. He estimated that up to twenty people a night had sex there on the weekends, adding that some of them engaged in group sex.[84]

Two unsolved park murders took place in Montreal in 1991. The bloody corpse of Marc Bellerive, thirty-three, was found beside his bicycle in Parc Maisonneuve, the site of three other queer-bashings around that same time period. His throat had been slashed and he had been stabbed forty times. Less than three weeks later, Pierre-Yvon Croft, forty-eight, was stabbed fifteen times in Parc Jarry. Neither victim had been robbed.[85]

In 1993, Michel Comeau, who had AIDS, was beaten by at least two assailants in a park in Fredericton. He never reported the beating, waited several weeks before going to the hospital, and died about seven weeks after the assault. His brother went public, urging the bashers to get an AIDS test: 'When they hit him, they bled and so did he.'[86]

In an interview, a Saskatoon activist described a nasty attack in Kinsman Park in 1997: 'The victim thinks there were four perpetrators. He was hospitalized and off work for a while ... To his credit, he's now back

Table 3.6
Location of queer-related homicides in data set

Location	No. of cases	%
Victim shot or beaten inside or in front of a queer establishment	8	8.3
Victim killed in or near park or cruising area	11	11.5
Victim killed in or near his/her own residence	62	64.6
Victim killed in suspect's residence (if different from victim's)	7	7.3
Other locations	8	8.3
Total	96	100

cruising the park.'[87] The activist's stance of 'cheering on' the victim – to continue cruising in a dangerous park – raises complex questions about sexual activity and violence in public settings.

Victims Killed at Home

In a few cases, it was not possible to deduce from the source material exactly where the victim was killed. However, in ninety-six homicides I was able to ascertain where the killing took place. By far the largest percentage of the victims in my study were killed at home or very close to home (see table 3.6). In Toronto, at least four men were killed in their own residence in 1999 and 2000.[88] Table 3.7 lists some Montreal men who were killed inside their own home, with no signs of forced entry.[89]

Victims Killed in Bathhouses and Bars

In 2003, rumours spread quickly throughout Toronto after a man died in a bathhouse. Although it was later determined that the man died of a heart attack, Global Television offered live coverage about 'the possibility of the city's 62nd murder this year.' Citytv commented that 'all sorts of activities go on in those places, including SM.'[90]

When I interviewed a police officer about homophobic violence in Quebec City, he said didn't know of any cases. Then I asked about homicides. After much prodding, he finally said: 'Well, there was a double homicide in a gay bathhouse a few years ago. Does that count?'

In 1990, Ghislain Girard, thirty-four, went to a gay bar and pulled out a gun. Later, he went to a gay bathhouse and opened fire. He shot two strangers dead:[91] a thirty-one-year-old clerk, Mario Fortin, and a twenty-

Table 3.7
Homosexual men murdered in their homes in Montreal

Year	Name	Age	Circumstances
1990	Edward Yong Sua Mok	26	doctor; bound, stabbed, and beaten[a,b]
1991	Garfield Walker	30	killed in Gay Village; three years later, Stephan Corbeil, 25, was charged[c]
1992	Michel Hogue	42	met Jean-Pierre L'Abbé, a reported prostitute, at a gay bar in the Village. They went to Hogue's home, where he was later found stabbed to death[d,e]
1992	Robert Panchaud	36	ten days after Hogue was killed, Panchaud went to the same gay bar where Hogue met his killer; beaten and stabbed to death in his home; killer was never found[d,e]
1993	Rolland Gagné	70	reported to be a retired priest; bound body found in his home; police arrested two men, one of whom was 17[a,e]
1995	André Lafleur	54	public servant; strangled in his bed; Nadir Ikhleff, 19, charged with first-degree murder[f]
1996	Normand Trudel	45	owner of gay bar; killer never found
1996	Réal Halde	53	found on bed with throat slashed; André Lortie, 28, charged with second-degree murder[a,g,h]
1997	Walter Bourbonnais	70	killer never found[a]

Sources: [a]Letter from Dire Enfin la Violence, 11 May 1999; [b]André Picard, 'Montreal Gays Fear Serial Killer,' *Globe and Mail*, 12 February 1993, A1; [c]Canadian Press, 'Man to Be Arraigned for 1991 Slaying,' *Montreal Gazette*, 6 November 1994, A3; [d]Eddie Collister, 'Murder Suspect Arrested in Gay Village,' *Montreal Gazette*, 23 June 1993, 3; [e]*Climate for Murder*, prod. Arnie Gelbart, dir. Albert Nerenberg, 1994; [f]'Youth Arraigned in Gay Slaying,' *Montreal Gazette*, 21 July 1995, A4; [g]'Neuvième meutre homophone en 18 mois,' *RG*, 17 September 1996; [h]Andy Riga, 'Killing Was a Hate Crime: Gay Activists,' *Montreal Gazette*, 22 August 1996, A6.

three-year-old patron, Michel Landry.[92] Girard was arrested at his home, where he lived with his wife and child.[93] During interrogation, Girard didn't want to admit he was gay, although his wife said later he had gone to gay bars in the past. He committed suicide in custody about three months after the killings.[94] The Laval University gay group immediately announced that the crime 'had nothing to do with the sexual orientation of the individuals.'[95]

Another man was shot in Quebec City in 2000 at the gay bar La Malette. As usual, the police said the killing had 'nothing to do' with the victim's sexual orientation.[96] Similarly, in Toronto, it's difficult to determine what hate motivation, if any, lies behind the many victims killed in the city's nightclubs. Some of these killings were published in *Xtra* because the homosexuality of the victim was common knowledge. Others were published in *Xtra* because the killings occurred in clubs with a primarily queer clientele. Then there were the homicides mentioned in *Xtra* that happened in clubs with a straight or mixed clientele. It is possible that some of these deaths actually had 'nothing to do' with the victim's sexual orientation; even so, the violence can't help but have an insidious effect on the community as a whole.[97]

Fishing for Trouble: Phone Lines, Classifieds, and the Internet

Singer believes that fear of AIDS, instead of reducing demand for sexual services, has actually developed new markets that reach out and touch consumers in the privacy of the home. This growth industry is producing 'new and enlarged mechanisms for commodifying the sexual body, erotic and reproductive, and for profit by the fact that in catastrophic conditions which place the sexual body in question, value is intensified.'[98] She points out that 'telephonic promiscuity' is a safer bet 'in an age where other forms of sexual contact are ... far more risky.'[99]

These days, strangers meet one another through personal messages in newpapers, on phonelines, and on the Internet. In eastern Ontario, these types of meetings have been quite dangerous. In 1996, one man complained after the *Perth Courier* refused his ad, which simply said he was a gay father looking for a relationship. The resultant publicity led to obscene phone calls – and a visit from a car full of teenagers who yelled: 'We're gonna fuck you with a broomstick.'[100]

Closer to Ottawa, a thirty-five-year-old man received one hundred responses after taking out an ad for 'males seeking males.' He was looking for 'an older gentleman, more sincere and honest to maybe show me a few things I don't know yet in life.' He claimed that a sixty-three-year-old man responded to his ad and then shot him in the chest, saying: 'You're going down, sonny.' The victim protested that he had only placed the personal ad to find a 'fishing buddy,' not a gay lover.[101]

Classified Killings

At least five of the homicides in my data set had some link to classified ads. In 1995, Dennis Colby, who met men through the personals, was found in his Toronto apartment with his head beaten in. The *Sun* reported that 'Metro homicide detectives will be delving into the world of tele-phone gay-sex contact lines.'[102] An officer commented that the victim allowed 'street-type' people to stay at his place. The *Sun* claimed that the investigation was 'hampered by the fact that Colby was sexually aggres-sive and had numerous sexual partners on a weekly basis.'[103]

But the danger cuts both ways: assailants don't just answer ads from unsuspecting victims. Predators actively seek out victims by taking out their own ads. In 1991, Ronald Cooney took out an ad in Toronto's *Now* magazine:[104] he described himself as an 'extremely attractive' young male seeking an 'older professional.' Norman Cardwell, fifty-one, apparently responded to the ad. He was found dead in his own house, handcuffed and shot in the head point-blank four times, 'probably from a .22 calibre rifle with a sawed off barrel.' Sex had taken place, and the victim's bank card was missing.[105]

Although Cooney owned both handcuffs and a .22 calibre AR-7 rifle, he blamed the death on his friend Darrel Marsh.[106] He and Marsh used the bank card at eight different locations. After the *Sun* published photos of Cooney taken by bank surveillance cameras, he fled Toronto. A third man testified that during a barroom conversation, Cooney bragged that he and Marsh had lured a homosexual victim by putting an ad in a 'fag' magazine; that he had taken the man's bank card and 'scared the shit out of him' to get the PIN number; and that he had shot the man four times in the head and thrown the sawed-off gun into Lake Ontario.

Soon afterwards, Cooney's buddy Marsh mysteriously disappeared. Two months later, Marsh's body was found at the foot of the Scarborough Bluffs.[107] Although it appeared he had died of an overdose,[108] the 'au-topsy could not precisely determine the cause of the man's death.'[109] By the time Marsh's body was discovered, Cooney was already in custody, pinning the blame on Marsh. At trial, Cooney denied everything. He claimed he had been home when the killing took place and that he had given the gun to Marsh before the killing.[110]

The jury deliberated for two days and found Cooney guilty of man-slaughter. The judge sentenced him to twelve years, disturbed by 'the random way in which the victim was selected,'[111] noting that Cooney 'knowingly participated in the scheme both before and after the kill-ing.'[112] His sentence was reduced to eight years upon appeal; however, the judge noted that the crime 'obviously involved obtaining access to Mr. Cardwell's home. He was probably subjected to force so that he would disclose his PIN. His killing appears to have been a virtual execution. It was simply a terrible crime. The appellant is criminally responsible for the death of a completely innocent victim.'[113]

The Targeting of Specific Subgroups

The Victimization of Teenagers

Many of the media reports I analysed did not mention the victims' ages. In fact, the age of the victim was only reported in about one-third of the cases, making it difficult to draw any conclusions about the targeting of specific age groups.

Because of the proliferation of literature on hate crimes against youth,[114] I decided to examine teenager victimization. Out of the 121 cases in which the victim's age was known, 16 per cent involved teenaged victims. D'Augelli believes that queer teenagers are especially vulnerable to homophobic violence, for the following reasons: teenagers generally experience more violence; queer teenagers frequent neighbourhoods where queer-bashing is more common; and there is a backlash resulting from increased queer visibility in our society.[115]

It's encouraging that more and more initiatives, from phonelines to theatre productions to support groups, are now educating teenagers about homophobic violence.[116] In London, support is provided by a volunteer organization called PAYSO, Positivity About Youth's Sexual Orientation. In 2000 this group released a comprehensive report on homophobic violence, featuring interviews with sixty-two youths. This report noted the following:

- Young men reported more than twice as much physical assault as young women.
- Young men reported almost twice as much violence at home.
- Young men reported more than twice as much street violence as young women.
- Young women reported more than three times as much sexual assault.[117]

Here are some excerpts from the interviews:

- *Kerry (17):* 'I wrote something in my diary about a girl in my class who I thought was pretty and my stepfather found it. He took me out into the woods behind my house and told me he would shoot me in the head if he ever found out I was queer.'[118]
- *Lorie (15):* 'Some guy came up to us and started staring at our

breasts ... He began to punch me in the face and called me a 'fucking little dyke.'[119]
- *Tony (17):* 'These guys came up to me and asked if I was queer ... They shoved me in a phone booth and started kicking the phone booth really hard and yelling names.'[120]
- *Danny (21) and Steven (24):* 'We were walking home and all of a sudden these guys were right in front of us calling us "queer" and "fag" ... My friend lost his front tooth and his face looked pretty bad ... Now my head hurts all the time. I have really bad headaches.'[121]
- *Julia (21):* 'I was in high school and I was walking down a hallway and this girl got in my face cause I was a lesbian ... A crowd of other students gathered around us and they started yelling, "Kill the dyke, kill the dyke."'[122]

In an American survey of 350 queer high school students, 11 per cent said they had been physically assaulted because of their sexual orientation.[123] A teenager in London confirmed that he did not feel safe in his own high school and was constantly being called 'queer boy' or 'fag.' He finally confronted one bully who told him he would break his face if he ever talked back again.[124] A Winnipeg hate crimes officer told me he usually gets three queer-bashing reports a year from high schools: 'The parents call and say their kids have been shoved or assaulted. But the parents don't want to do a police report.'[125]

Coming home from school can also be dangerous. On an Edmonton bus, a gang of youths accused two straight teenagers of being gay. After the victims got off at the bus loop, they were assaulted in front of three or four bus drivers.[126] Attacks on high school students in Vancouver, Longueil, London, Trois-Rivières, and Ottawa have also been reported.[127] Many teachers' federations are now taking steps to raise awareness among educators about how to confront homophobic behaviour in classrooms.[128]

In 2004 the Lesbian Gay Bi Youth Line celebrated its tenth anniversary. Volunteers receive between three hundred and five hundred calls per month from young people across Ontario between the ages of twelve and twenty-six. Almost half of the $200,000 annual budget comes from donors and fundraising activities.[129] Toronto is also home to the Triangle program, Canada's only gay high school. Between 1996 and 2004 nearly 250 students went through the program, which includes both individual academic lessons and specialized queer studies in history, literature, and sociology. The program is a haven for queer youths fleeing discrimination and violence at home and at school.[130]

Queer Youths in Welfare Settings

Mallon surveyed fifty-four gay and lesbian youths and eighty-eight social service workers in Toronto, New York, and Los Angeles. He discovered that more than half the young people had been assaulted, and that many lived under the constant threat of violence.[131] In O'Brien's Toronto research, young gay men – who lived in residential settings and were forced to pass as heterosexuals – complained of constant homophobic language, including 'name-calling, gay-baiting and bragging about gay-bashings.' Ironically, this danger was used as an excuse to turn a young man away from one shelter. Because he was dressed in drag, he was told, 'We don't want you to get hurt.' A young lesbian resident was forbidden to dress in masculine attire. Another was outed by a worker at age fourteen: 'She would always call me a dyke. It was really wild. She told the other residents that I was a lesbian.'[132] A teenage boy said his 'foster father' suggested he go to a psychiatrist to change his sexual orientation, telling him: 'If you ever touch one of my sons, I'm going to kill you.'[133]

Homophobic Violence on Campus

In one American survey, university students were asked, 'Have you ever physically attacked lesbians or gay men?' Two per cent of the women and 16 per cent of the men said yes.[134] In another survey, 21 per cent of the gay and lesbian students reported having been assaulted, compared to 5 per cent of the total student body.[135] In response to the question, 'Have you ever been forced to have sex against your will?' another university survey revealed that the following groups had said 'yes': heterosexual men, 3.6 per cent; gay men, 11.8 per cent; heterosexual women, 17.8 per cent; lesbians, 30.6 per cent. The author concluded that campus rape prevention and education programs needed to target gay and lesbian students.[136]

Dowler surveyed 565 students at the University of Windsor about their attitudes toward homosexuals. Four admitted to some form of homophobic violence.[137] Students have been threatened and bashed at Red Deer College, York University, and Carleton University.[138] Queer professors are also at risk. In 2001, David Buller died of multiple stab wounds in his studio office at the University of Toronto. The fifty-year-old art professor, who had taught there for fifteen years, was described as an expert in homoerotic art, 'a passionate and sought-after teacher, a favourite among students and faculty.'[139] Some suggested the killer was 'one of the male prostitutes he was known to hire.'[140] In 2004 the David Buller Memorial Scholarship was awarded for graduate work in the Visual Studies program at the University of Toronto.[141] The same year, after Henry Durost, a seventy-eight-year-old psychiatrist, was strangled, the police said they were examining the links between the two killings.[142]

Transgender Issues: Discrimination and Violence

Out of 335 queer-bashing cases I analyzed, I was not able to find any involving FTM transsexuals. However, I did locate nine cases involving MTF transsexuals.

When Montreal police, investigating a complaint in 1990, stepped off the elevator of an apartment building, 'a shot rang out as they came face-to-face with a man brandishing a 20-centimetre-long knife and waving a 9-mm pistol.' Inside the apartment were another armed man and an unconscious transsexual woman in a pool of blood. One suspect was on probation; the other 'was on Christmas holidays from a Montreal detention centre.'[143]

A Toronto transsexual woman complained that police did not take her complaint seriously after a woman leapt out of a man's car and choked her, then repeatedly kicked her. The man accompanying the assailant told police that the victim and her friend 'were gay guys dressed up as women. 'The police started giggling,' the victim complained. 'If I was any normal woman, you can be damned sure she'd be locked up.'[144] In Hamilton in the summer of 1998, there were two reports of transsexual women being beaten. One of them worked as a bartender.[145] There were also several reports in Ottawa and Hull in the 1990s,[146] and in Toronto in 2003.[147]

The West Coast transgender community is strongly organized and outspoken.[148] Jamie-Lee Hamilton, a transsexual activist, was critical of the way police handled the unsolved 1994 murder of Kristine Kavanagh, who was killed in her own Vancouver apartment. The transsexual woman was not a prostitute 'and led a life removed from the street. She had been post-op for many years.' Hamilton said the police press release mentioned that Kavanagh used to be a man.[149] The *Province* interviewed the victim's neighbour, who said: 'I didn't really know her ... She had a nice figure, but her voice was always a little hoarse.'[150]

The Toronto transgender community has become increasingly vocal and is calling for an end to body searches of transsexuals by American immigration officers[151] and for a health/community centre that would cater to Ontario's trans community.[152]

Prostitution and Homophobic Violence

In this section, I consider prostitutes – as both perpetrators and victims of violence, and provide Canadian examples. Singer believes that prostitution, pornography, and 'addiction' are the three major ways sexuality is exploited in 'late capitalism': 'All three are strategies for maximizing and consolidating the socially useful, profitable excess produced as sexual energy, excess desire.'[153] She refers to the 'logic of specialized sexualities, each of which can then be fetishisized in its differences through a capital- and commodity-intensive erotic aesthetic.' This 'erotics of supply and demand' permits 'certain sexual practices to be preferred at premium prices, given their presumed relatively limited availability.' The 'multiplication of erotic possibility' leads to 'perpetual stimulation and incitement and also maximizes sites of profitability.'

In one study, 475 male, female, and transgendered prostitutes were interviewed in Thailand, Turkey, South Africa, Zambia, and the United States. Researchers found that 60 per cent had been raped and beaten since they entered prostitution, and 92 per cent said they wanted out. Two-thirds met the criteria for post-traumatic stress disorder.[154]

An analysis of Canadian incidents of violence against queer prostitutes is difficult, because these prostitutes self-identify in different ways – as straight, gay, lesbian, bisexual, and transgendered – and because they provide sexual services in a variety of forms and settings. I found scant literature on female prostitutes who are targeted because of their lesbianism. I noted in chapter 1 that two lesbian prostitutes were killed in Toronto in 1994. However, the motives behind these murders were unclear.

I interviewed a front-line social worker who works with prostitutes in Edmonton. Their drop-in centre serves about twenty clients per day. She estimates that one-third are lesbians, one-third are transgendered, and one-third are straight women. About twice a week, the centre receives a report about a violent attack against one of its clients. The centre distributes a bad date sheet, but faces a growing problem: girls not affiliated with a gang risk increased violence. Lesbian couples with children sometimes work in pairs: one engages in sex while the other spots for her. Three-quarters of the drop-in centre's clients are aboriginal.[155]

Table 3.8
Boles's categorization of male prostitutes

	% of male prostitutes (n = 224)	% that engages in receptive anal sex
Homosexual group	17.9	63.4
Bisexual group	35.7	23
Heterosexual group	46.4	5.6

Several studies have examined the self-perceptions of male prostitutes. In one article, fifteen hustlers reveal how they attempt to retain a 'heterosexual' label, hiding their same-sex activities from significant others.[156] Another describes the complex processes that male prostitutes and customers utilize in order to 'read' one another.[157] One research project divided ninety-eight male prostitutes into four different categories: full-time prostitutes who work in bars and on the streets; full-time escorts and 'kept boys'; part-time hustlers; and 'peer delinquents,' who engage in prostitution and same-sex activity in conjunction with crimes like assault and robbery.[158]

Other research has focused on sexual activity and exposure to HIV.[159] Boles studied 224 male prostitutes in Atlanta, examining the links between HIV infection, drug use, sexual behaviour, and 'sexual self-identity,' which Boles describes as a 'cognitive construct' that takes into account each hustler's self-identified sexual identity; clothing styles, mannerisms, and sexual role preferences (insertee–insertor); sexual acts (oral–anal); and friendships and associations.[160]

Boles divided the hustlers into three groups, shown in table 3.8. Surprisingly, relatively few male prostitutes identified as gay. One bisexual prostitute said in an interview: 'I guess I appeal to the gay guy who is afraid of the real rough trade and doesn't want a fem.' Men in the 'straight' group 'exhibited overt displays of stereotyped masculine traits through their stance, dress and mannerisms ... The men would assume a "threatening male posture" and glare at the potential customers driving past. Many wore studded belts; tattoos adorned their bare arms, and their jeans were very tight-fitting.' These men claimed they had

girlfriends or sexual relations with women. They showed the field team pictures of their girlfriends and recounted stories about their sexual conquests ... noting that those men who choose hypermasculine-appearing men wish to be dominated ... Most denied enjoying the sexual aspects of their work. They could calculate, almost to the minute, how long it took them to make an agreement with a customer, perform the agreed-upon sex act, and return to the street. Moreover, they often found intimate physical contact with paying partners unpleasant or, in some cases, disgusting.[161]

It is unclear what proportion of prostitutes in Canada are male. However, Allman quotes various experts, government reports, and sex workers themselves, and comes up with a figure of approximately 25 per cent: 'In a city like Toronto there may be approximately 200 male workers working indoors and 150 male sex workers working outdoors during any one season.'[162]

Female prostitutes tend to be beaten by pimps and johns; in contrast, 'for hustlers the greatest problem is created by homophobic onlookers who assault and/or rob them.'[163] Jamie-Lee Hamilton estimated that male or transgendered prostitutes in Vancouver 'can expect to have a knife pulled on them, or to be assaulted or raped ... I've heard of police officers who force prostitutes to perform oral sex on them. I've heard it happen to a male or transgendered prostitute about five times.'[161]

Does the public perceive violence against male prostitutes as different from violence against female prostitutes? Male prostitutes are sometimes described as being more 'independent' than female prostitutes, as having more 'choices' because they don't work for pimps; their sexual encounters are characterized as being more 'equal.' The implication here is that male prostitution is not necessarily something the boys *have* to do, but more of a lifestyle choice – a rebellious celebration of their sexuality.

On the cover of Allman's report, for example, a sexy young man sporting a cowboy hat poses for the camera. His pants are unzipped, and his penis protrudes through his underwear. If a government-funded report on female prostitution featured a cover photo of a saucy young woman with erect nipples protruding through her wet T-shirt, feminist groups and opposition parties would no doubt denounce it as objectifying women. So what is so different about hustlers? Why the erotic, romantic portrayal?

Part of the answer may lie in the numbers: hustlers are less likely to be killed than their female counterparts. Allman points to another federal study indicating that less than 5 per cent of the prostitutes murdered in Canada between 1991 and 1995 were male.[165] The 1993 killing of an Ottawa hustler raised some poignant observations in a letter to the *Citizen*:

I waited to hear of candlelight vigils or of flowers on the sidewalk in front of the house. I waited for statements from social activists about the tragedy of people trapped in a life of prostitution, about the violence they face. I waited in vain. Not a word was said about the sad life and meaningless death of Benoit Villeneuve. Only a short time earlier, when the body of a prostitute named Sophie Filion was found in a Westboro parking lot, the papers were filled with stories of her life and justifiably angry statements about the conditions she faced. Vigils were held and a reporter even covered her funeral. But Mr. Villeneuve was not so remembered. Was it because he was a man, and a homosexual?[166]

The Prostitute as Perpetrator

Of the hundred homicides I analysed, 21 per cent involved a killer who was reported to have either worked as a prostitute at some point in his life, or posed as a prostitute as a way of luring the victim into a vulnerable situation.

Two men – well known on the Canadian stage – were killed by men who fit in these two categories. John 'Bev' Wilson, stage manager for the Bayview Playhouse in Toronto, was found stabbed to death in 1994 in the laundry room of his own apartment building. Wilson worked with stars like Richard Monette and Brent Carver. Barbara Hamilton described him as a professional 'from the old school. He didn't put up with any nonsense.'

Wilson's personal life seemed less ordered: he was in a relationship with a prostitute and was in the process of kicking him out of the apartment.[167] Darren Mellish, twenty-nine, was charged with the killing. Police described Mellish as an 'aging street hustler.' Two years later, Mellish was declared unfit to stand trial. He believed someone was injecting Vaseline into his bloodstream – an indication, said one psychiatrist, of paranoid schizophrenia.[168]

The following year, the bloody, naked body of Richard Niquette was found on an east-end street in Montreal. The actor, known for his work on the series *Lance et compte*,[169] 'picked up two men he thought were prostitutes in the Gay Village.' He was stabbed to death and robbed of $350[170] in the apartment of Sylvain Jomphe, who pleaded guilty to second-degree murder.[171] In a dramatic flourish, a Montreal activist, criticizing federal policy on hate crimes, declared: 'The blood of Richard Niquette is on the hands of the Minister of Justice.'[172]

Violence against Transgendered Prostitutes

In 2002 and 2003, three transsexual prostitutes were killed in Canada: Faye Urry in Prince George,[173] Tracey Tom in Vancouver,[174] and Cassandra Do, strangled in her Toronto apartment. One hundred people attended her vigil.[175] There has been relatively little research on transgendered sex workers in North America. One European article estimates that more than 80 per cent of the transvestite prostitutes in France, Spain, Portugal, Belgium, Germany, and Italy are from South America and North Africa. The author, instead of examining the victimization of transvestite prostitutes, describes them as violent drug dealers who rob their clients.[176]

In 1996, Toronto social workers estimated there were 'about 40 "tranny" or "TV" hookers working Toronto streets. Most work in the "boys town" track.'[177] The conservative values of queer urban culture have been indirectly linked to violence against this group: Gary Kinsman has noted that transgendered sex workers are 'shunned and rejected' by the mainstream gay community – a situation that forces them to work in more dangerous neighbourhoods.[178] An activist said: 'The gay community has to take responsibility for pushing the stroll eastward.'[179]

In Vancouver, an activist complained about the violence inflicted on transgendered prostitutes by 'irate johns who have discovered their true sexual identities ... Street transsexuals need their own "safe house" or drop-in, so they can get counselling and health care from people who understand their special problems.'[180] In 1999 a transsexual prostitute was brutally beaten by a john who forced her to perform oral sex. She died of AIDS a short time later.[181]

In my data set, 5 per cent of the homicide victims were transsexual women. One, Grayce Baxter, a transsexual call girl in Toronto, was killed in 1992 by Patrick Johnson, a twenty-three-year-old part-time prison guard. Baxter, twenty-six, had changed her sex seven years earlier: 'She used her sturdy 6-foot 1-inch frame to her best advantage as a dominatrix.' Her home was a luxury waterfront condo and 'she lived the high life, wearing furs and driving a black 1989 BMW.' She was rumoured to have a hundred wealthy regulars.

She arrived at Johnson's apartment at 3:30 a.m. and charged him two hundred dollars for a forty-five-minute session. Johnson said afterwards he was having difficulty coming and that he became angry when she said his time was up. He strangled her, cut her body into several parts with a hacksaw, placed the remains in a dumpster, and pawned an expensive diamond ring and watch. Police spent eight weeks searching for the body in a dump, in vain. Sixteen months after the killing, Johnson pleaded guilty to second-degree murder, with no possibility of parole for ten years.[182]

One of the saddest stories I heard was the killing of Chantal – a Vancouver pre-op transsexual prostitute last seen getting into a black pickup in 1995.[183] Her body, wrapped in a blood-soaked tarpaulin, was thrown into an alley behind the Richards Street hooker stroll. Her family would not claim her body at the morgue.[184] Jamie-Lee Hamilton complained that the police released a mugshot of Chantal as a man, 'focusing on her previous criminal record.'[185] Perhaps the police had pangs of guilt: they attended a moving vigil for her, along with many members of the community and the media.

Sex, Rape, and Violence in Prisons

Violence is a concern for gay, lesbian, bisexual, effeminate, and transgendered prisoners. American gay and lesbian organizations have received letters from prisoners describing 'widespread beatings, rapes, verbal harassment, and other abuse of those who are gay or HIV-positive, or perceived to be so.'[186] Four per cent of the queer-bashing incidents in my data set occurred in custody: in prisons, prison hospitals, youth detention centres, police stations, jails, or drunk tanks.

Few of the prison incidents I analysed involved purely physical violence;[187] rather, there was usually a sexual element, ranging from coercion to rape. In 1995, for example, a sobbing teen begged a judge not to send him back to the Edmonton Young Offenders Centre, where, he said, he had been brutally raped by other kids: 'They had perceived he was a homosexual,' the judge said. Unfortunately, he added, he had no choice but to return the youth to the centre.[188] MacDougall points out that judges sometimes sympathize with the victim but then claim that nothing can be done: 'Superficial empathy and sympathy without substantive help is arguably the worst of the possible responses because it communicates a message of inevitability of homophobia.'[189]

An acquaintance of mine who was an inmate in a B.C. penitentiary gave me an example of non-consensual prison sex that he considered abusive. The victim, twenty-three, was 5'5" and weighed 120 pounds. They put him in a cell in a maximum security institution with a man fifteen years older than him – six feet tall, 240 lbs, and muscular. 'He was raped repeatedly, forced to submit to subservient acts in the middle of the night. He was in there for eight months until they eventually put him in the hole.'[190] At Kingston Penitentiary, several inmates alleged that they 'had been raped or used as sex slaves' by an inmate who sold drugs in prison. 'Because of his "muscle" both inside and outside KP, he was able to command silence and co-operation from his victims.'[191]

Prison research in this area is slowly changing. Lockwood cites prison experts from the 1980s who recommended that gay inmates should avoid '"feminine" hairstyles, gestures and clothing,' and that they should 'not be allowed to refer to other men by female referents' or engage in 'consensual homosexual activity.'[192] However, preventing all prisoners from having sex is a rather naive and heterocentric approach to a complex issue. In the guise of 'protecting' gay prisoners, these approaches regulated homosexuality in prison even more.

An expert on prison rape contends that researchers using an essentialist framework categorize male prisoners as either 'homosexual' or 'heterosexual.' This creates the paradox of 'normal' heterosexual prisoners who engage in 'situational' homosexuality. Eigenberg believes that prisoners need to construct their own sexuality.[193] Terminology can also be confusing: the terms *homosexuality* and *rape* can sometimes become conflated. For example, Marron refers to 'predatory homosexual prisoners, or "wolves."'[194] A sex offender who targets women is almost never described as a 'heterosexual rapist' – so why is a man who targets other men called a 'homosexual predator?'

To confuse matters even more, Eigenberg notes that 'researchers and inmates re-define acts of rape as consensual homosexual behaviour.' Rape reporting rates vary from 0.3 per cent to 14 per cent; this divergence may be the result of prisoners wishing to avoid being stigmatized.[195] At Toronto's Centre for Addiction and Mental Health, Dr Paul Federoff said, 'I don't think [rape is] nearly as common as people think,' even though he was working with sex offenders both inside and outside jails. An AIDS activist argues that rape is less common because Canadian prisons are smaller, sentences are shorter, and sex offenders are kept segregated. *Xtra* was not able to get rape statistics from the Correctional Service of Canada (CSC); however, Ontario Correctional Services offered the following statistics: out of 411 assault reports between January and March 1999, 'eight were allegations of sexual assault (those could involve everything from inappropriate touching to rape.)'[196]

Eigenberg's survey of correctional officers found that they 'were slightly more willing to prevent rape than to deter homosexuality, which is especially problematic if some rape is being committed under the guise of consenting homosexual acts.' Also troubling was that officers said 'they were more willing to protect heterosexual inmates from rape'; thus, they were equating 'bisexuality and homosexuality with voluntary participation.'[197] Eigenberg discovered that nearly one-half of the officers believed that 'some victims deserve to be raped'; one-third thought these victims were weak; and one-sixth thought that rape victims were gay.[198] Incredibly, none of the American training modules for federal or state prisons actually covered issues of male rape or homosexuality.[199]

Consensual vs Non-Consensual Sex in Prison

Lockwood believes that reports of widespread prison rape are exaggerated; a more realistic term is 'sexual harassment.' In his survey of American prisons, 28 per cent of the inmates reported having been 'the targets of aggressively perceived approaches at some point' in their incarceration.[200] Marron describes how predators operate: 'In the sick dynamics of these relationships, the predator usually passes himself off to others as a normal heterosexual man, while exploiting the shame that the victim feels and threatening to expose him as a "faggot." [The inmate] maintains that such relationships are usually initiated without violence, but "once things are behind closed doors, intimidation can be used both to perpetuate and deepen the intimacy and to keep outsiders away."'[201]

The question of consensual sex is controversial. A 1994 article stated that consensual sex in federal prisons is technically forbidden, 'punishable by 30 days in segregation or a move to a higher security institution.'[202] A 1996 report on HIV/AIDS in federal prisons criticized CSC for failing to 'remove prohibitions against consensual sexual activity between inmates.'[203] When I contacted CSC, a legal advisor said he could not find any specific regulations prohibiting consensual sex between prisoners in federal prisons. However, he suggested that individual wardens have some discretion when it comes to regulating various behaviours in their respective prisons.[204]

One gay prisoner estimated that 40 per cent of the men at Kingston Pen have sex with other men: 'Gay inmates refer to these prisoners as "institutional gays," men who have sex with men only because they're in jail.'[205] In 1995, CSC randomly sampled more than four thousand male prisoners in federal institutions.[206] Three per cent reported having been sexually assaulted by fellow prisoners in their current institution; twice that number reported having been 'pressured for sex.'[207] Six per cent said they had had sex with another male inmate since entering their current institution. The study found that 4 per cent of all the prisoners surveyed had had sex without condoms.[208]

In this charged atmosphere, why not consider more proactive approaches? In 1998, *Xtra* reported on Kingston Penitentiary's gay support group, Discovery, whose members lobbied for same-sex conjugal visits and for same-sex commitment ceremonies, to be performed by a gay and lesbian church. It took Discovery more than two years to get the government to provide prisoners with safe-sex information. Unfortunately, although *Xtra* did a good job reporting on queer prisoners, the paper also objectified them by including a crude homo-erotic cartoon of two prisoners having sex.[209]

Female Prisoners and Female Prison Guards

An American study of forty-one female prisoners suggested that lesbians are treated more harshly. It found that lesbians are incarcerated for longer periods of time, even when their crimes are less violent than those of their heterosexual fellow prisoners.[210] Robson has concerns about the criteria used to 'theorize' female offenders as lesbian. She questions the methodology of an article which claims that out of forty-one women on death row in the United States, seventeen have been 'implicated' as lesbians. Robson points out that few of these women have consistently maintained their lesbian identities on death row.[211] Another researcher studied the media portrayals of thirty-five women on death row and found that five lesbians were depicted as manly, man-hating women.[212]

Lesbian relationships in prison have also been a source of tension. Two lesbian partners, convicted of killing a Toronto police officer, were attacked in the media for wanting to bunk together in prison.[213] In 1996, female prisoners in Truro, Nova Scotia, went on a rampage, 'claiming they were being discriminated against because they were gay ... Inmates articulated a concern relating to the level of antagonism and violence surrounding same-sex relationships.' A board of inquiry concluded that although staff were not homophobic, the rules governing lesbian relationships were unclear. A male Conservative MLA demanded to know 'what in the heck is going on ... There's been some allegations of open lesbianism.'[214]

This statement is either naive or intolerant – or both. Was he suggesting that it was inappropriate for lesbian prisoners to come out, but 'closed lesbianism' would be tolerated? Or was he saying, 'The existence of openly lesbian prisoners is truly frightening'? A male CSC spokesman said that although lesbianism is tolerated, authorities 'will intervene if the sexual activity is coercive or predatory, offensive to others or against community standards.'[215] But which community is he referring to? And whose standards?

Female prison guards also face 'accusations' of being lesbian. At one Quebec prison in 1992, male guards subjected a female colleague to insults and claimed she was sexually involved with another female guard. 'She was also threatened with assault and rape.' The woman received $143,000 from the Quebec Human Rights Commission.[216]

Another Quebec case involving a queer prison guard made headlines. A woman – who legally changed her name from Hélène to Claude-Marc – began taking hormones. She also underwent a double mastectomy and grew facial hair; however, she retained her female genitalia. Claude-Marc managed to find work as a part-time male prison guard without anyone finding out. He was arrested after giving the names and addresses of his co-workers to a motorcycle gang. His bizarre plot involved terrorizing the guards and their families through beatings and intimidation; he hoped they would quit so that he could then get the full-time job he was hoping for. Only after the guard's arrest did his transgendered identity become known. The judge recommended that he serve his sentence in a women's prison. His lawyer argued that he risked being raped in a men's prison.[217]

Issues Affecting Transgendered Prisoners

Marron interviewed Joe, a man who had been a drag queen at a prison in New Brunswick. Joe said that while he was inside, there had been fifteen queens, and that each of them had had a 'formidable partner.' If any of the other 'men' bothered the queens, 'you'd be lucky if you made it out of the prison alive.' An inmate who was a former minister performed 'wedding ceremonies'; these were followed by wedding dances in the gym: 'It was the only time that the husbands let the girls dance with the other guys.' Joe was shielded from 'conflicts with other prisoners as long as his husband and friends protected him.' However, whenever he got too close to other prisoners, his husband would threaten to kill him.[218]

Violence affecting transgendered prisoners was confirmed by my source in a B.C. penetentiary. In the mid-1990s a pre-op MTF transsexual was raped in a prison hospital. The suspect was charged, but there was insufficient evidence to proceed to trial.[219] In Ontario, however, a prisoner at Maplehurst Institution took his rapist to court and won. The defendant's lawyer blamed the victim, suggesting that he had invited the defendant into his cell for consensual sex. The lawyer said that other prisoners considered the victim a 'bisexual' and a 'drag queen.' The victim objected: 'Even if I was gay or bisexual, it doesn't mean I deserve to be raped.' The rapist was sentenced to six years and scheduled for deportation to Colombia.

A transsexual police officer in Vancouver told me about a transsexual woman who, upset because her surgery was postponed, robbed a store. 'Because she's pre-op and still has a penis, she'll probably have to go to a men's prison.'[220] Although CSC now has guidelines in place for trans-sexual prisoners, Katherine Johnson's previous requests for a sex change were not taken seriously. In her book, *Prisoner of Gender*, she discussed her suicide attempts in bloody detail, as well as a brutal self-castration: 'I did the deed with the aid of a suitable tourniquet ... carefully cut through the scrotum from bottom to top ... flushed the two testicles down the toilet.'[221] On another occasion she tried to gain entry to a women's lockup but was turned away: 'The keeper ... asked if I had a penis. When I told him yes, he ordered me to the men's lockup ... I ... tied a tourniqet very tightly against the pubic bone and I made a deep strong cut. My penis was now connected by a thread of skin ... Later I remember saying, "No penis now, put me in with the women" ... Later they stitched the member back on.'[222] Johnson added that beatings, rape, and harassment were commonplace and noted that one transsexual woman, Crystal Morgan Furry, was murdered at Joyceville Penitentiary.[223]

Johnson recounted being locked inside a bathroom, held down, and raped by two prisoners: 'If I had yelled I would have been killed.' A young prisoner smashed her with his fists thirty or forty times 'for no specific reason ... As usual there were no repercussions.' A steady relationship offered protection but also subjected her to more violence. Her abusive lover kicked her repeatedly in the back: 'This and other abuses while in prison have left me with three injured vertebrae.'[224] Fortunately, the Elizabeth Fry Society accepted her with open arms after she moved to a women's halfway house.

In 1999 the Canadian Human Rights Tribunal heard a complaint from Synthia Kavanagh, a male-to-female pre-op transsexual. The case re-ceived widespread coverage; unfortunately, the *National Post* insisted on calling the prisoner 'Mr. Kavanagh.'[225] She was serving a life sentence at Kent Institution, a B.C. maximum-security prison, for the killing of her best friend, also a transsexual woman. Kavanagh said she was 'routinely taunted, harassed and sexually assaulted by the male prisoners.'[226] She claimed that many of her requests were constantly denied – for hormone therapy, for gender reassignment surgery, for transfer to a women's prison, and so on. Corrections officials said she couldn't be housed in a female prison without female genitalia, so she was caught in a vicious circle.

In 1991, while serving at Millhaven Penitentiary, she tried to cut off her penis. Eventually she received hormone therapy;[227] a few months after her case made national headlines, she received breast augmentation and signed a confidential agreement with CSC, one that allowed for surgery and a transfer to a women's prison.[228] A rape crisis official dismissed Kavanagh's complaint and expressed concern that a convicted murderer was going to a women's prison: 'If I was in a male prison I would be willing to transform into pretty much anything to get out of there.' In 2003, a court ruling forced CSC to revise its regulations and to pay for the reassignment of 'less than a dozen transsexuals.'[229]

'An Innocent, Honest Misunderstanding'

Queer-bashing can even occur in temporary lockups. One night in 1993, Brian Nolan left a gay bar in St John's by himself just after midnight. He recalled: 'I turned to go up this alley. I noticed there were two or three police cars, and some kind of commotion. I turned to see if there was an accident.' Later, he learned he had stumbled into the wrong place at the wrong time: 'Some greasy guy had been barred from the gay bar because he'd caused fights. Apparently he'd come back and was causing trouble.' He continued:

> A policewoman grabbed me by the collar and said, 'What's the matter, faggot, got nowhere to go?' She and her partner pushed me into the back of the cruiser and drove me to the lock-up and during the drive were verbally abusing me: 'We got a place for you fags. We'll give you a place to stay, you fucking faggot.'[230]

In a later statement, Nolan noted the following: that he hadn't been staggering or acting in any improper manner; that he hadn't struggled or fought with the police constables; and that he had done nothing to provoke them, and in fact had not even spoken because he was totally overwhelmed by the situation.[231] He was placed in the local drunk tank for the night:

> At 6 or 6:30, they banged on the cell and got everyone to get up. I happened to be the last one in the line to pick up my money and my wallet. They asked me to sign this paper. I said, 'Before I sign this, could I please have the name

of the woman who brought me in ... The burly prison guard who was behind me grabbed my left arm and wrenched it up behind my back. He comes around and while still holding my arm, knees me and then punches me in the stomach.

Brian was 5'10", 175 pounds; the guard was about the same height but weighed about 230:

There were four men and a woman in the room ... The woman picks up a book and sticks it in front of her face [so she can claim that she hasn't seen anything]. I'm bent over in pain and meanwhile he's continuing to wrench my arm and kicking me and pushing me up against the wall. He pushed me back to my cell, and said, 'You'll sign, you fucking faggot' ... Then he jumped on me and was kneeling on me and continued to wrench my arm even more forcefully when I said, 'I'll sign!' He pulled me up, using that same arm, pushed me back down the hallway in front of me. They gave me my things, I signed and then he threw me out ... I came into Lynn's apartment about 6:30 or 7 a.m. sobbing and in shock.[232]

In his statement, Nolan reflected on the guard's actions:

The ferocity of his attack and the lack of any interference by his co-workers made me feel that my life was threatened. Thus I was willing to agree to anything they wanted and therefore I told him as best as I could through the pain that I would sign.[233]

The guard was eventually charged with assault but acquitted. The Crown appealed to the summary conviction appeal court, but lost. The Crown also lost at the provincial Court of Appeal, whose judges noted:

The accused's honest belief he was authorized by law to physically detain the complainant was reasonably held and he acted rationally in the circumstances ... The accused acted in good faith, and was justified in executing the performance of his duties as he perceived them ... Nothing more than an innocent, honest misunderstanding by a correctional officer in the carrying out of his duties.[234]

Queer International Issues

For some people in Canada's queer community, it's difficult to see the links between a gay-bashing on Yonge Street and the murder of a transsexual in Turkey. However, both these violent acts target people who violate gender norms – and both challenge the justice system to acknowledge and punish these crimes. Canadians can engage these issues in two ways: by becoming aware of Canadian policies that affect queers fleeing repressive violence abroad, and by linking up with domestic and international organizations.

Gays and lesbians have successfully lobbied for changes to Canadian immigration policy so as to allow more same-sex partners of Canadians to immigrate legally. The Lesbian and Gay Immigration Task Force (LEGIT) provides support to queer Canadians with immigration-related concerns.[235] However, some queers who immigrate to Canada do not have Canadian partners. In 1992, a Dutch gay man's application for landed immigrant status was denied because, during the Second World War, the Nazi occupiers of the Netherlands convicted the man of "homosexual offences." Lahey notes that if prospective queer immigrants 'disclose prior criminalization before entry, even if those laws are unconstitutional in Canada, they can be denied entry as "undesirable aliens" without right of appeal. If they do not disclose prior criminalization, they can be deported for non-disclosure of that prior record even if the prior record would be invalid here.'[236]

Amnesty International has published some excellent books on queer human rights issues.[237] As of 1998, sex between men was illegal in seventy-six countries, including India, Burma, and Armenia; sex between women was illegal in fifty-one countries, including Romania, Cuba, Nicaragua, Taiwan, and the Philippines. The International Lesbian and Gay Association (ILGA) and the International Gay and Lesbian Human Rights Commission (IGLHRC) monitor oppressive laws and repressive practices affecting queer populations around the world.[238]

Canadians are involved in the international struggle for queer human rights in various ways. Giuliani, for example, explores the ability of human rights workers to advocate on behalf of lesbians.[239] The Amnesty International Members for Lesbian and Gay Concerns (AIMLGC) has a core group of Canadians, many based in Toronto, who are electronically linked to other activists around the world.[240] Members in Montreal organized a vigil in front of the Egyptian Consulate after fifty-two men were arrested in Cairo in 2002.[241] In Kingston and Toronto, PEN Canada – a human rights group that supports persecuted writers around the world – sponsored a series of readings that included lesbian author Deb Ellis.[242]

In 1998, EGALE supported my application to attend, along with a few other Canadians, a series of gay and lesbian human rights workshops sponsored by Amnesty International. The event coincided with the Gay Games, during which hundreds of thousands of queers poured into Amsterdam for an international celebration. Queer delegates from five continents and the Pacific identified two common concerns – a lack of protection *by* the criminal justice system, and a lack of protection *from* the criminal justice system. Latin Americans and Asians registered alarm over the homophobic discourse of Catholicism, Islam, and increasingly popular Protestant fundamentalist groups.

A São Paulo activist stated that a Brazilian homosexual is killed every three days. A lesbian from a former Soviet republic spoke of police carrying out rapes. A transsexual from an Islamic republic in Central Asia said: 'There is a lot of brutal violence and murders. We don't know where to start. We need support.' This emotional gathering led me to conclude that the queer-bashing described in this book is part of a much broader global phenomenon.[243] In 2001, EGALE's president attended a UN conference on discrimination in Johannesburg, where queer human rights were discussed on the world stage.

Queer Refugees

In April 2004, the *Globe and Mail* reported that since 2001, 2,500 people from seventy-five countries had claimed refugee status in Canada on the basis of sexual orientation.[244] I first became sensitized to refugee issues in 1996 while working as a Spanish-language facilitator at the International AIDS conference in Vancouver. One young delegate – a gay man from South America who couldn't speak a word of English – told me he had been targeted in his city after organizing Gay Pride celebrations and conducting AIDS education.

He decided to stay behind and apply for refugee status. After the plane left, he slept fitfully on my sofa, traumatized by the past and terrified about what the future might hold. But some Canadians were sceptical. One gay man told me: 'Very clever. Some gays will say anything to get into our country.' My young friend's claim was eventually accepted. He now speaks English fluently, holds down a good job, and is grateful to be in Canada.

Many refugees must confront issues like bureaucratic delay, public indifference, and post-traumatic stress disorder. A queer refugee workshop I attended pointed to other barriers besides:

• Some queer refugees are reluctant to discuss sensitive questions of sexuality with lawyers from their own national, religious, or cultural

background, since the immigrant communities they have landed in are sometimes as homophobic as the societies they have just fled.
- Their applications may be linked to the claims made by other family members, who are unaware of their sexual orientation.
- Some Canadian lawyers are unwilling, or lack the necessary background, to file claims based on sexual orientation.
- Claimants often rely on interpreters at every stage of the process. If the interpreter is unwilling to use language that provides crucial details of the claimant's sexual orientation – including sexually explicit terms like 'anal rape' – the application may be doomed.
- Immigration officials expect queer refugees to 'prove' that their persecution derives from their sexual orientation. This is almost impossible, when it relates to countries where lesbianism is invisible and where queer clubs and networks operate underground or simply do not exist.[245]

Since 1991, Canada's Immigration and Refugee Board (IRB) has been granting refugee status on the basis of sexual orientation.[246] In 1993, *(A.G.) v. Ward*[247] 'confirmed that sexual orientation establishes the cognizability of a "particular social group."'[248] Because the IRB is only required to give written decisions if the outcome is negative, many positive decisions go unheard of. In 1997, one IRB official estimated there had already been two hundred queer refugee claimants. A Vancouver lawyer worked on fifty such cases between 1992 and 1999. Lawyers in Montreal and Toronto have experienced similar caseloads. Vancouver seems to receive more Asian applications, especially from Malaysia.[249]

In 1999 a University of Ottawa law professor analysed ninety-four Canadian queer refugee cases. Fifty-four were successful, and five more were successful upon appeal. Of the ninety-four cases, fourteen involved lesbians and five involved transgendered applicants. Over half the claimants were from Latin America; the rest came from Eastern Europe, the Middle East, Asia, and Africa.

Although acceptance rates have generally been quite high, many queer Mexican claimants began to be turned down in the late 1990s because they were unable to prove a systematic pattern of persecution. Laviolette believes 'the concept of "persecution" is applied narrowly.' For example, a gay man was sent back to Moldovia although homosexuality was illegal in that country. The IRB reasoned that the offence was no longer being enforced and was slated for repeal.[250]

Millbank compared Canada's and Australia's approaches toward queer refugees. She studied 331 decisions from the two countries. Her research

Table 3.9
Frequency and success of queer refugee claimants

	Gay male	Lesbian	Transgendered	Total number/ overall success rate
Cases studied (no.)				
Canada	104	18	5	127
Australia	161	42	1	204
Success rate (%)				
Canada	52	66	60	54
Australia	26	7	0	22

Source: Jenni Millbank, 'Imagining Otherness: Refugee Claims on the Basis of Sexuality in Canada and Australia,' Melbourne University Law Review 26, 1 (2002): 148–9.

suggests that queers had a better chance to secure refugee status in Canada than in Australia (see table 3.9). However, Millbank cautions that the results are somewhat misleading because the two countries' refugee determination systems are different. The IRB is a 'first instance' tribunal – that is, all refugee cases land on its doorstep. In contrast, Australia's Refugee Review Tribunal (RRT) hears appeals from first-instance decisions. Consequently, the success rate of Australian queer cases at the lower level is unknown.[251]

Millbank found evidence that decision makers in both countries 'were often unable to see that abuse of lesbians and gay men was bad enough to constitute persecution and they often denied that the abuse was because of the claimant's sexual identity.' She notes that the RRT made 'false analogies' by conflating torture and other human rights abuses against queers in countries like China with the situation of Australian queers. Callous statements – implying that intolerance against gays 'is common in other countries, including Australia' – demonstrate 'a terrible failure of empathy.'[252]

Millbank states that the RRT is harsher than the IRB 'both in the reasoning and discourse employed in the decisions and in the trend of outcomes.' She criticizes Australia's repetitive cut-and-paste, boilerplate method of writing decisions compared to Canada's concise personalized method.[253] She also points to general trends: lesbians' cases fail because their sexuality in their home countries is too private, whereas gay men's cases fail because their sexuality is too public. Lesbians suffer 'at the hands of family members, former male partners, or current female partners' families, in contrast to the gay men's cases where the agent of persecution was more often a state actor such as a police officer or other official.'

The IRB appeared to be more sympathetic to lesbian concerns, taking sexual abuse and the 'private' nature of lesbian sexuality into account.[254] Millbank praises the IRB's use of gender guidelines to sensitize decision makers to women's concerns. However, she questions the way evidence is gathered about queer lifestyles in the countries being placed under the microscope. For example, the RRB ruled that Beirut had a fairly open gay scene, based on the fact that there was a gay porn movie theatre. 'These claims about public space were completely irrelevant to lesbians in those locales, yet worked to discredit their stories and disadvantage their applications.'[255]

Similarly, Michael Battista, a Toronto lawyer representing a gay Mexican refugee claimant, complained about the documentation the IRB was using to evaluate his client's claim – information from gay tourist destinations like Puerto Vallerta, which created the impression 'that somehow these little pockets of Mexico are representative of what's going on in the whole country.'[256] One Australian official went so far as to say a Nepali could avoid persecution in his country by getting married and then having a 'secret gay life' – a theme that arose in 33 per cent of Australian cases, but in only 8 per cent of Canadian cases. Lesbian sexuality was constructed as 'passive and readily suppressed': one Australian decision suggested that a lesbian could always go back to China and lead a celibate life.[257]

Canada rejected a Colombian gay man because he didn't seem 'overtly gay,'[258] as well as a Mexican who was not 'visibly effeminate.'[259] A Venezuelan was deported after submitting to a rectal exam to 'prove' his homosexuality. He said that on his return to Venezuela, he was attacked with rocks. He finally received a permit to return to Canada on compassionate grounds; this prompted a federal official to observe that 'the system does work when applied properly.'[260] Over the past ten years, queer refugees have come to Canada from many countries, including Jordan,[261] Venezuela,[262] Trinidad,[263] Mexico,[264] Colombia, Argentina,[265] and El Salvador.[266]

Queer refugees to Canada also face violence here. A Costa Rican named Gerson Acuna Ugalde visited Montreal in 2001 and requested information on applying for refugee status. He was found dead in a swimming pool before he could submit his application.[267] 'Diego,' a refugee from Mexico, who was beaten and robbed by police there, explained to me that in Vancouver, 'four or five times I've been called faggot or queer on the street, and I constantly feel unsafe on the street or buses. I feel paranoid ... I feel intimidated when I see heterosexuals on the street.'

This young man was gay-bashed in Canada, further compounding his distress. 'Somebody beat me up at a work party ... There was a drunk Latino. He wasn't invited, but he was hanging around. There was a lot of booze ... He called me *maricon* and split my lip.' After four years, Diego's refugee claim was finally accepted. Now he has a job and a nice apartment overlooking English Bay. Looking back on his process of leaving Mexico and integrating into Canadian society, he talked about himself in the third person: 'It's a great opportunity to discover who Diego is. I'm not just a faggot. I'm Diego.'[268]

Vancouver's Rainbow Refugee Committee is Canada's first organization to offer support to queer refugees. Since 1999 this group has been educating immigration officials on queer issues and encouraging queer churches and other community organizations to sponsor refugees who are still trapped overseas. The volunteer-run committee, which organizes a drop-in once a month, receives almost no funding but responds to around two hundred e-mails a month from around the world.[269]

Summary

A small amount of preliminary research indicates that queer victims face more extreme violence compared to other victims, but more research is needed to validate this hypothesis. Queer-bashing victims are not just attacked physically – their sense of who they are and how they fit into society is assaulted as well. The majority of queer-bashing cases in my data set involved men who were alone at the time of the attack. Over half the attacks occurred in queer-identified spaces, and 40 per cent involved multiple perpetrators. Almost two-thirds of the homicide victims I studied were killed in the home. Contacts through the Internet, phone lines, and classified ads have led to robberies, assaults, and/or death.

MTF transsexual women appear to be assaulted and killed in disproportionate numbers. Queer prostitutes are targeted; that said, a significant proportion of the killers I studied were also associated with this vocation. There are reports of queer and more vulnerable prisoners being targeted for physical assaults, sexual assaults, and sexual coercion in Canadian prisons. As awareness in our community increases around global human-rights abuses, thousands of refugees have come to Canada and have sought asylum on the basis of sexual orientation.

CHAPTER 4

Law, Homophobia, and Violence: Legislating against Hate

Sociological and psychological theories do not tell the full story about homophobic violence. The missing link is the way homophobia is reproduced in law. It is bad enough that people form hateful thoughts about homosexuals and proceed to beat on them, but the real horror lies in the legal practices that tend to downplay or excuse this violence. This chapter examines the way homophobia saturates the legal system; the system's limited ability to address homophobic violence; the movement to develop hate crime legislation; and legal remedies for victims of queer-bashing.

If a group of punks went on a rampage at a restaurant in Vancouver's Chinatown – yelling 'Chinks,' beating up patrons, and provoking a riot that shut down Pender Street – it would probably make the front page of the *Vancouver Sun,* and police would probably call a press conference to denounce the crime. But in 1994, when a group of thugs yelling 'faggots' beat up customers at a crowded gay cafe on Davie Street, the story landed squarely on page two – and the police never mentioned it at their weekly press briefing.[1]

A minor quibble? I don't think so. The attack was an affront to the queer community, and the pathetic outcome – to which the mainstream media paid scant notice – was even worse: not one of the bashers served any jail time. I was in the courtroom the day the plea bargain was announced; there was no public outrage when the legal process sputtered to a halt. Perhaps Vancouverites had become inured – not just to the violence, but to its inevitable 'resolution.' I adduced many hidden facts about this case by interviewing 'Brian,' one of the victims.

Late One Night at the Edge Café

On 5 May 1994, five drunk men leaving a Davie Street restaurant – located next door to the Edge Café, a gay nightspot – began screaming homophobic abuse at Brian, who was on his way home from a gay bar at 2:30 a.m. The men slammed him into the wall beside the cafe, which had a hundred patrons inside.[2] Brian estimated that one of the assailants weighed three hundred pounds.[3] The gang burst into the cafe and began attacking patrons and yelling anti-gay slogans.[4] 'The thugs were grabbing hot coffees and throwing them in people's faces, shouting "fucking faggots, we'll kill all of you."'[5] One of the co-owners of the cafe was hit over the head with a wrought-iron stool; eleven stitches were required to close the wound. The customers inside fought back bravely, and two men – who managed to tackle and hold down two men trying to escape – suffered cracked ribs and a broken wrist.[6]

But Brian was the most unfortunate: one thug caught him in a bear hug, then smashed him against the sidewalk at full force. His thorax and two vertebrae were shattered, and his body was bruised for six months. Despite the severity of his injuries – and after arriving at the hospital in an ambulance – he was given a Demerol shot and told to either walk home by himself or pay for his own taxi. A year and a half later, Brian was on welfare, suffering from depression, and living in a rooming house on $285 a month after his rent was paid. Although he had received $6,500 in victim compensation, it had mainly gone toward debts accumulated during his ordeal. He was also suffering sinal pilonitis, an intestinal infection, and a skin infection – side effects from his daily medication: ASA, tetracycline, clonazepam, trazodone, penicillin, cloxacillin, ibuprofen, and lithium.[7]

Only three of the five men were charged. It took a year for a preliminary hearing, which was remanded five times.[8] The defence lawyer asked Brian if he was a friend of any of the other witnesses. He said no. The defence went on to describe the Edge Café as a 'last-chance pick-up joint' for gays coming out of the bars at two a.m. The defence asked Brian three more times if he knew any of the witnesses. He said no. Then the defence asked him if he had ever *slept* with any of the witnesses. Brian yelled: 'I object to this. You've asked me four times if I knew any of them, and I told you, "No." Now you're asking me if I slept with any of them? I told you: No!'

It was only at this point that the Crown objected. Later, the prosecutor was asked if it was normal for victims to be asked whether they had had sex with bystanders. The Crown replied: 'Brian was asked questions that other witnesses would not have been asked because of his homosexuality.' Dennis Dahl, a Vancouver lawyer, sees a double-standard at work: 'We limit cross-examination of female victims about their sexual history, but most judges say that it's very relevant to talk about gay men's sexual history. The Crown definitely showed a lack of sensitivity.'[9]

Three months later, Brian complained to Victim Services about the continued delays. (The trial, remanded three times, finally got going almost two years after the actual attack.) Apparently in the belief that Brian was going to commit suicide, a dozen police officers arrived with an ambulance. Brian said a policeman stormed into his apartment, swore at him, then slammed his back into a table and handcuffed him so tightly he had blue marks on his wrists for a week. Then they left him, unattended, at the office of a psychiatrist who had wandered off for lunch. 'If I was such a threat to myself,' Brian said later, 'why did they leave me in an unlocked office?' After waiting for an hour, Brian gave up and walked home by himself.[10]

Two weeks into the trial – after seventeen witnesses had been called – a plea bargain was struck: only one man pleaded guilty to assault causing bodily harm. He received a suspended sentence.[11] He was ordered to publish an apology to one of the victims in *Angles*, a queer Vancouver newspaper that folded in the mid-1990s.[12]

Legal Scholarship on Homosexuality

The Edge Café incident and its shameful aftermath exposed homophobic violence on three fronts: the actual physical violence inflicted on queer victims, the secondary victimization doled out by the criminal justice system, and the symbolic violence suffered by the entire community when such acts appear to go unpunished.

Some legal scholars have attempted to explain this mysterious and sometimes debilitating process. In discussing 'the legal construction of heterosexual privilege,' Ryder notes that the law is mainly silent on gay and lesbian existences, except when gay men are presented as 'powerful victimizers, deserving weak victims, or as the perpetrators of unmentionable indecent acts.' This silencing normalizes heterosexuality and discourages queers from expecting recognition and support.[13] According to Robson, 'lesbian legal theory must put lesbians in the centre of its theoretical perspective,' allowing lesbians to become 'the centrifugal force around which all else is problematized.'[14]

Stychin contends that students of common law are routinely taught to slot legal problems within specific, essentialized categories; 'however, queer theory underscores the contingency and contestability of categories – that there is nothing natural about them.'[15] He analyses the infamous

British case *R. v. Brown*. In 1993, five gay male adults involved in consensual sadomasochist acts in a private home were convicted of assault causing bodily harm, even though there had been no complaints to police and no permanent injuries had been suffered. The gay men's 'uncontrolled and unregulated need for sexualised violence'[16] came out in the appeal. One judge referred to 'legalised buggery, now a well-known vehicle for the transmission of AIDS.'[17]

Stychin explains how Canada's Charter of Rights and Freedoms, when 'viewed through the lens of postmodernism,' allows new legal, political and cultural identities to broaden and deepen 'along sexual lines.' In contrast, in the United States, 'distinctions in law based on sexual orientation in general have been upheld as "rational" and not subjected to rigorous judicial examination.'[18] Backer notes that in 1996 there were more than two hundred constitutional challenges to sodomy statutes in the United States. Twenty-three states continued to criminalize sodomy[19] until 2003, when the laws forbidding it were finally struck down by the U.S. Supreme Court.[20] *Bowers*[21] – an unsuccessful 1986 Supreme Court challenge of American sodomy laws – was supposed to be a cut-and-dried test case involving two adult men who had consensual sex in a private home. Instead, the Court was confronted with 'images of predators and pedophiles, of whores and defilers.'[22]

By 2003, Canadian queer activists were celebrating their recently won right to marry; however, many were unaware of the multitude of Canadian statutes that regulate homosexuality. Kinsman points out that Pierre Trudeau's famous line – 'the state has no place in the bedrooms of the nation' – was 'widely misunderstood as legalizing homosexual sex.' The reforms of 1969 simply allowed two consenting adults over the age of twenty-one to have sex in private. In fact, gay sex actually began to be targeted more intensively, using some of the laws described by Kinsman and Cossman:

- Anal sex (Section 159 of the Criminal Code) is technically illegal in Canada for people under eighteen, even though the age of consent for penis–vagina sex is fourteen in most circumstances.[23] It's legal for three or more people to get together and have sex, 'as long as there is no anal penetration.' Although this discriminatory law was challenged in Ontario, 'the law is still on the books and remains enforceable in other provinces.'
- Indecent acts (Section 173 of the Code) are never defined, although courts have agreed that they are linked to a 'community standard of

tolerance.' Cossman explains that this section has been used to control many different sex acts, including oral sex, anal sex, masturbation, exhibitionism, lap dancing, and sexual touching. These activities are not usually regulated in private homes, but what about strip clubs? In this grey zone, there is more ambiguity: owners and performers 'are at risk of being charged with indecent acts or indecent theatrical performances,' and bathhouse owners risk charges 'if there's any hint of sex occurring outside of a locked cubicle.'

- Owners of these clubs and bathhouses – where police have deemed that indecent acts occur on a regular basis – can be charged with running a common bawdy house (Sections 197 and 210 of the Code). Patrons can be charged with being found in a common bawdy house.[24]

Some heterosexuals believe there is a double-standard at work. Perhaps they are unaware of the extent to which queers have been regulated by these laws. In the late 1990s, Montreal undercover police, equipped with a hidden camera, arrested heterosexuals at a swingers' club. After his conviction, a club owner grumbled: 'The gays, they do whatever they want. But hetero people, they can't do what they want? It's a joke.'[25]

Homophobic Legal Practices in Canada

In the courtroom, queer issues can ruffle feathers. In Milton, Ontario, potential jurors were questioned about homosexuality prior to one trial; around 20 per cent admitted they wouldn't be able to view the case fairly.[26] An American survey of 1,012 potential jurors found that 'gays and lesbians who are parties in a trial are at least three times as likely to face a biased jury as a person who is white, African-American, Hispanic or Asian.'[27] During a California civil trial, a gay defendant's lawyers set up a mock trial that included jurors whose demographics matched the local jury pool. The mock jurors' deep-seated homophobia was rampant: they found against the defendant. Later, so did the trial jury.[28]

In 1993, an Ottawa jury consisting of one man and eleven women acquitted a man accused of killing Benoit Villeneuve, a male prostitute.[29] The *Ottawa Citizen* said the trial 'provided a glimpse into the sordid subculture of homelessness, drug addiction and gay prostitution.'[30] Villeneuve's body was found four months after his death, buried in a steamer trunk under his house.[31] The defence lawyer, congratulating himself after the victory, said he had tried for an all-woman jury: 'Nothing is scientific,' he said, 'but because of the homosexual overtones in this case, women are less likely to be homophobic than men.'[32]

Canadian queers face subtle forms of discrimination in the courtroom. Casswell points out that nearly twenty years ago, it was decided that evidence of the accused's homosexuality should only be raised if it has sufficient similarity to the circumstances of the evidence alleged.[33] However, lawyers have found other ways of labelling the defendant: Have you ever been married? Do you live with men? Do you think this boy is handsome?[34]

In Canada, judges and prosecutors have been known to downplay the homophobia inherent in some hate crimes. MacDougall notes that 'the judge might even blame the target for his homosexuality causing the "natural" reaction of a "normal" person.'[35] A classic case of blaming the victim occurred in 1997 at the Vancouver Pride celebrations. 'Sister C' – a beloved drag queen (alias Mr Johnson), who wears a nun's habit – was assaulted on Denman Street. A group of gay men surrounded the suspect, named 'Mr Jolicoeur,' until police arrived. The judge dismissed the charges, noting that

> there's also a misunderstanding perhaps on Mr. Johnson's part as to what Mr. Jolicoeur intended with his homophobic comments ... Mr. Jolicoeur was simply speaking in frustration ... It's clear that Mr. Johnson, in wearing a nun's robe, upset Mr. Jolicoeur ... so without any intention of doing that ... Mr. Johnson upset Mr. Jolicoeur and, I would guess probably upset a lot of other people ... I would have to say that Mr. Johnson was perhaps insensitive of the sexual proclivities of others and perhaps Mr. Jolicoeur was hypersensitive about that.[36]

The courts exhibit lenience in other ways. For example, a teenager who knifed three men in Ottawa was charged with attempted murder. The judge chose not to raise the youth to adult court, saying that he came from a good home – even though, as MacDougall notes, he had been 'exposed to and participated in a variety of street crime and activities such as ... "rolling queers" ... The profundity of the homophobia was ignored.'[37]

In Toronto, Hugh Conroy, who was HIV-positive, brought Robert Moyer home from a pub. Moyer beat and robbed him. Conroy's sister said the victim 'never regained his spirit and his health rapidly deteriorated.' He died a year after the attack. The Crown seemed surprised: 'We didn't know he wouldn't be around for the trial, so we did not ask him all the things we might have.' Since there was nobody to contradict Moyer's version, the Crown agreed to a sixty-day sentence, to be served on weekends.[38]

If a wife-beater were sentenced to work at a battered women's shelter, a hue and cry would be heard from coast to coast. But in Saskatoon, when a man on the dance floor of a gay nightclub punched a man whom he claimed had come onto him, his sentence was thirty hours of community work at the local gay and lesbian centre.[39] The activist I interviewed waxed philosophical. Instead of emphasizing the importance of maintaining spaces that are safe from queer-bashers, she felt the basher should be exposed to the queer community – so that his attitude toward us would change.

The question of community service also surfaced after a Ryerson student bashed a gay man on Church Street in 1991. Judge Harris wrote a thirty-nine-page judgment that compared gay-bashers to Nazis and Ku Klux Klan members. He also asked one of the victims what he thought the sentence should be. The victim said the basher should serve at the 519 Community Centre 'to force him to see that gay men and lesbians aren't the great evil other the basher believed them to be.' However, the policy of making bashers to work at the centre was eventually reversed.[40]

In this vein, an activist for the 519 Community Centre said that jail time was not 'going to teach people not to hate. We need a more creative restorative justice for queer-bashing.'[41] In Port Dover, Ontario, a basher was fined $1,000, payable to 'Family and Friends of Gays and Lesbians.'[42] One Toronto basher was banned from living in the city.[43] However, restorative justice is sometimes ineffective. In 1996, a gay Toronto man was punched; the wound took sixteen stitches to close. The judge called the assault a 'vicious and cowardly act' motivated by homophobia, but felt the two assailants were not 'looking for gays to beat up.' The two convicted bashers received an 'alternative' sentence instead of jail time. Besides being fined more than $1,000, one was ordered to write an essay on a 'famous homosexual,' while the other was ordered to write about 'a homosexual persecuted for his beliefs.'[44]

In September 1993, three gay-bashings on a single night terrified Winnipeg residents. One of the accused incurred the wrath of the judge, who declared, 'This is how Nazi Germany got started.'[45] The assailant was sentenced to two years. However, Judge Huband reduced the term to seven months on appeal, writing that the accused was sorry and had dissociated himself from the others. MacDougall notes: 'This is the school-of-quick-change-of-heart-on-homosexuality-come-time-for-sentencing.'[46]

Queer Criticisms of the Criminal Justice System

In several cases, what first looks like lenience may simply reflect the inability of our system to address this type of violence. In one Vancouver incident, a gay man was assaulted. His friend said the police 'basically told me to shut up ... I was to understand that someone could chase you down the street yelling "fucking faggot" and as long as they did not touch you or say "I am going to physically harm you," they were not guilty of a crime.'[47] The suspect was fingerprinted and released, but failed to appear in court.[48] When asked why the basher had been released, the Crown replied: 'People with eight-page records are being released from this location every day.'[49] One officer noted that if a separate hate-crime statute existed for hate-motivated assault, 'and if we had seen that the offender had recently gay-bashed someone else, then we'd be able to keep him in.'[50]

In 1994, a high-profile Toronto bashing ended in an acquittal. Ross Mulhearon and his partner Steve were outside the Second Cup cafe when a van containing six young men pulled up, followed by another car containing friends. Mulhearon said one passenger began yelling 'fucking queers' from the van, and smashed a beer bottle on the road. Mulhearon reacted: 'What's your problem?' Four men jumped out and attacked the couple. Another man trying to defend them was smashed over the head with a beer bottle, and required twenty stitches. A week after the attack, 250 people gathered at the Second Cup, then marched down Yonge Street in protest.[51]

At trial, one of the accused suggested that Mulhearon had spat on the van, inciting the violence. With so many conflicting versions of the event, the accused was acquitted – which gave rise to cheering in the court-room.[52] Mulhearon complained: 'They were laughing and having fun – to them it was nothing.' He wrote a play, described as 'a gaybashing victim's revenge fantasy ... The attacker is kidnapped and restrained in a chair.' He proposed putting on the play to raise funds for the 519, but the community group balked at the play's premise and chose not to participate.[53]

Police bend over backwards to warn communities when pedophiles arrive in town. Should the gay community be warned when a convicted basher is in their midst? Don Gunn was convicted of manslaughter for killing a gay man in 1986. In Hamilton in 1993, he assaulted another gay man at a donut shop. In a second Hamilton example, police noted that another basher, released in 1998, had 'accosted and robbed a 72 year old male. Smith has 7 prior convictions for robbery, some of which were related to gay bashing type robberies.'[54] In 2004, Toronto police issued a warning after a twenty-seven-year-old man failed to return to a Toronto halfway house. He was described as a predator known to frequent the Church–Wellesley area.[55]

A man with fifty convictions to his name used classified ads as his modus operandi. After moving in with gay men, he would rob them. He held a knife to the throat of a Toronto businessman, demanding cash. After his arrest, the man bragged to police about his victim. The judge commented: 'He takes pride and justifies his criminal activities by replying ... that [the victim is] "just a fag" ... and that type of thinking has to stop.'[56] But what, if anything, did the criminal justice system do to prevent this violence from recurring?

Killers Who Get Off Easy

In certain trials, procedural issues emerged – either during the investigation or in court – that possibly allowed killers to either go free or plead down. In 1990, James Gee was charged with killing his apartment building manager, Gerald May, in a Vancouver suburb. Gee claimed that May had come onto him. The charges were stayed after the police breached Gee's rights. His girlfriend told an undercover officer she helped cover up Gee's involvement after Gee beat, stabbed, and robbed the victim.[57]

A killer in Ottawa also beat a murder charge. This killing occurred after Garth Balderston met Ian Anderson in a bar. Apparently they walked to a nearby park, where Balderston was beaten to death and robbed of his ring. Some friends said that Anderson bragged about beating a gay man in a park and showed them a stolen ring.[58] In all, Anderson hired and fired six lawyers. One lawyer told the judge that 'the accused is admitting his acts caused the death,' but this comment – which the jury never heard – was stricken from the record. Anderson was convicted of manslaughter.[59]

Did a procedural error allow a twenty-three-year-old man in a Calgary restaurant to 'get away with murder'? In 1994, Robert Carolan, who was extremely drunk, went to the washroom, where he claimed that a fifty-three-year-old man made a pass at him. The audio track on the in-store camera at the front of the restaurant recorded thirty-two blows being struck. The victim went into a coma. Carolan was later arrested on the street with blood on his boots.[60] When the Crown tried to introduce the videotape as evidence, the judge refused, stating that 'any attempt to

colour the events and inflame the court in this fashion is totally improper.'
I noticed in the case headnote that the victim had 'subsequently died of
respiratory failure.'[61]

When I called the Crown's office to see whether the victim had indeed
died, I was assured that the victim could *not* have died; otherwise, they
would have raised the charge to manslaughter or murder. I then called the
Calgary police to see whether anyone on the force was responsible for
following up to see whether crime victims had died from their injuries. A
deputy chief told me there was no particular person responsible for this
task. This means that some assailants – and not just queer-bashers – may
only face aggravated assault charges even after their victims die.[62] In a
sad, ironic twist, Carolan's eight-year sentence for aggravated assault was
probably more severe than he would have received for manslaughter.

A series of administrative errors may have actually caused the murder
of Mario Desrosiers, who met Gregory Hanson in Montreal in the
summer of 1994. 'They were always together,' a detective said afterwards.[63] Police seemed unaware that Hanson was wanted for violent
crimes in California and British Columbia. One report said Hanson
'engineered a daring escape from a BC prison on the back of a garbage
truck' in May 1994.[64] He was arrested in Montreal two months later for
assaulting a policewoman and possessing a gun used in a robbery. Montreal
police apparently didn't realize they were dealing with an escaped convict
– they let him out on $500 bail with an order to appear in court 23
August, 1994. By then, Hanson had met and killed Desrosiers.[65]

The two were in Gatineau, apparently planning an armed robbery.
Hanson, afraid that Desrosiers would inform police, strangled him with a
belt.[66] Hanson was arrested at Ottawa's airport on 18 August with
Desrosiers's ID and possessions and a one-way ticket to Fiji. However,
Hanson was in jail for two months before police eventually made a
connection between him and Desrosiers. That was because friends didn't
report Desrosiers missing for a few weeks. The victim's body was finally
discovered, months later, buried behind the Hull police station.[67] Hanson
pleaded guilty to second-degree murder, with no possibility of parole for
thirteen years.[68]

Killers on Parole

Many gay men have been killed by men who drifted into the gay community after being released from prison. In 1992, Terry Fitzsimmons married
a Kingston woman while still in prison for killing a fellow prisoner.

Within days of being released, he moved in with another woman, stole $10,000 in jewellery. and disappeared into Toronto's gay scene. He teamed up with 'travel agent and sometime prostitute' Don Hebert, who became smitten. During a six-day crime spree in 1993 that spanned three cities, Fitzsimmons, twenty-nine, killed three men – including two gay men.

Hebert, who was HIV-positive, fancied himself and Fitzsimmons as the 'first gay Bonnie and Clyde' – even though Fitzsimmons denied being gay. Both were coke addicts, and they held up the same Toronto bank twice to support their habit. The pair met up with Norman Rasky, sixty-two, a dentist with a crack habit,[69] who moved in with them[70] after being evicted for not paying rent.[71] While Fitzsimmons was high, he stabbed and bludgeoned Rasky repeatedly, with Hebert looking on. They left the body in the basement of the apartment building and fled to Montreal. They ran out of money, killed a taxi driver, then headed for Ottawa.[72]

After Rasky's body was found in Toronto, a homicide detective insisted that the killing of Rasky 'had nothing to do with his sexual orientation. It wasn't gay bashing.'[73] Toronto police appealed to the gay community to help them find the pair: 'Mr. Fitzsimmons is described as 5-feet-7, 153 pounds, with numerous tattoos on both arms and chest. Mr. Hebert is 5-feet-10 with a dark mustache, a three-inch scar on the right side of his neck, and a tattoo of the Canadian flag on his right shoulder. Police believe the two men have shaved their heads to disguise their identity.'[74]

On their last night of freedom, the two were seen wearing identical Blue Jays shirts at an Ottawa gay bar.[75] They ended up in an abandoned restaurant on Bank Street. Fitzsimmons said Hebert told him he couldn't bear the thought of going jail for the previous murders. Fitzgerald then strangled Hebert with a T-shirt, 'injected two vials of his friend's tainted blood into his own veins,' and 'plunged a butcher blade through Hebert's heart.' After calling 911, Fitzsimmons injected cocaine, then walked into a police station and told the receptionist: 'It's got to stop. I'm tired of killing people.'

Fitzsimmons claimed that he and Hebert had made a suicide pact: he didn't want Hebert 'to rot away because of AIDS. It was almost like a brotherhood of the doomed.'[76] Fitzsimmons said he wanted to die by Hebert's blood and spoke glowingly of 'the best friend I ever had.'[77] However, he wanted to correct 'erroneous news reports about his relationship with Hebert' because 'it makes a difference in the way you're treated in prison.'[78] At sentencing, Fitzsimmons's lawyer argued that the death was the result of 'spontaneous combustion, brought on by drugs, years of sensory deprivation in prison and an unsympathetic parole officer.' The judge said the murder resulted from a 'depraved mind' and sentenced him to sixteen years before the possibility of parole.[79] Fitzsimmons killed himself in 1995.[80]

Another killer on parole was Michael McGray, who grabbed headlines in 2000 after claiming to be Canada's worst serial killer. In 1991, he spent a homicidal weekend in Montreal while on a three-day Easter pass from a Quebec minimum-security prison. McGray said he was one of his father's 'favorites' when it came to beatings, and that guards had sexually abused him at a boy's home in Nova Scotia.[81] He described 'how hard it is to strangle a person, how he liked to kill when he was not drinking or using drugs, "so he could enjoy it."' He said he was not gay, but he observed: 'It was just unbelievable how easy they tried to take you home, a total stranger.'[82]

Police in Saint John linked McGray to the 1986 stabbing of a gay man, James Lloyd Beyea, nicknamed 'Fluff.'[83] He also pleaded guilty to first-degree murder in the 1991 killings of Robert Assaly, fifty-nine – a retired schoolteacher from the Lebanese Christian community – and Gaetan Ethier, forty-five, an unemployed salesman. In McGray's version of events, he met Assaly in the Gay Village over a few drinks and went back to Assaly's condo. McGray bludgeoned him with a lamp, stabbed him sixteen times, then left to find his next victim. Assaly's brother discovered the body a week later.

Back in the village, McGray then met Ethier, who also invited the killer back to his place. McGray recounted that after Ethier was asleep, he smashed a beer bottle over his head and stabbed him. McGray left Montreal and was arrested three weeks later – but only for further parole violations, not murder. It was nine years before he was linked to the Montreal murders. Robert Assaly's brother insisted that Robert was not gay, but simply working as a bartender in the village.[84] His perspective was understandable: I met a straight couple – close friends of Robert's, who taught with him – who went on lengthy overseas trips with him. They said there was never a hint that Robert was gay. And if he was, it saddened them to think that his sexual orientation was not something he felt comfortable sharing with them.

The Social Construction of Hate Crime

Jenness points out that 'legal reform is a dominant response to bias-motivated violence.'[85] So far, I have demonstrated how the justice system's application of some laws – and its reluctance or failure to apply other laws – have created an environment in which homophobic violence can flourish. In this section, I focus on the movement that has constructed the term 'hate crime' and created hate crime laws.

For Mason, hate crime is 'a physical expression of the emotion of hate,' which is 'directed towards a person or persons on the basis, even if only in part, of a perceived group characteristic of that person.' She recounts the story of an activist who shied away from queer-bashing because it was 'not our kind of hate crime' – perhaps because the activist was not comfortable working with 'queers, trannies and sex workers.'[86]

Rosga deconstructs an infamous 'hate crime' in Maryland known as the 'burnt woman' case. She conducted interviews with the police to get the 'media' version, then spoke to one of the 'racist' and 'misogynist' men who had committed 'savagery' and 'lynching.' The man claimed he had many black friends and did not even realize his victim was black or a woman. He said he had been unfairly labelled a 'hate-monger' by a Jewish judge whose wife had pushed through a state hate-crime law.[87]

Jacobs and Potter question the precept that hate crime is an 'epidemic' in America, a precept that is 'expressed over and over again by politicians, journalists, scholars.' Gay and lesbian groups 'have been among the most vocal proponents of the hate crime epidemic theory.'[88] The authors heap scorn on Levin and McDevitt's overreliance on data obtained from advocacy groups[89] and question their central theory – that hate crimes are increasing due to 'economic decline and attendant social-psychological malaise.' Jacobs and Potter cite the lack of empirical evidence, 'a theory in search of a problem.'[90]

Jenness has authored and co-authored several analyses of hate crime legislation and the hate crime movement in the United States. She examines the Congressional hearings in the 1980s and 1990s that led to the passage of three federal hate-crime laws in the 1990s. She observes the ways in which social movement organizations 'interact with policymakers' interpretive and discursive practices to give meaning to statutes as they develop and stabilize over time.' Part of this process involves developing socially constructed definitions 'that result in assigning victim status to some individuals and groups, but not to others.'[91] The author delineates the following:

- The 'claimsmakers' of each bill – 'activists, politicians, social movement representatives, victims/survivors of violence.'
- The 'claims put forth in favor of and in opposition to' these bills.
- The way race, religion, ethnicity, sexual orientation, and gender are 'characterized, described, implicated and negotiated in the process of making federal hate crime law.'[92]

In the beginning, claims for race, religion, and ethnicity were made. But then 'the domain of hate crime law began to expand,' extending 'the boundaries of the phenomenon deemed problematic.' Gay and lesbian groups were 'crucial in evoking and sustaining the expansion of the law.' In part, they succeeded in this by comparing their violence with the hate violence that already enjoyed a certain legitimacy. Meanwhile, opponents dismissed the 'militant homosexual agenda,' refusing to equate homophobic violence with violence against other minorities.[93]

In another article, Jenness points out that before the term hate crime became popular, discrete minority movements politicized their own violence, albeit on a smaller scale. At the same time, an ever-growing crime victim's movement was beginning to demand 'special assistance, support and rights *as crime victims.*' The conditions became ripe for the creation of an American anti–hate crime movement, which 'invented the term hate crime, defined its initial properties, and demanded that lawmakers and other public policy officials recognize bias-motivated violence as a significant social problem.'[94]

Three federal hate-crime laws have been passed by the U.S. Congress,[95] but these only cover hate crimes that occur on federal lands and properties:

- 1990: The Hate Crime Statistics Act.
- 1994: The Violence Against Women Act, which, although it has since been ruled unconstitutional, allocated over $1 billion for 'education, rape crisis hotlines, training of justice personnel, victim services and police units.'
- 1994: The Hate Crimes Sentencing Enhancement Act, which allowed judges to enhance penalties 'of not less than three offence levels' for a list of eight specific offences, ranging from vandalism to murder.[96]

Jenness co-authored a book with Ryken Grattet, in which the two reflected on hate crime as 'an age-old problem approached with a new conceptual lens and sense of urgency.' What was once considered 'ordinary crime has been parsed out, redefined, and condemned more harshly than before.' Underlying this new trend is the desire to 'transmit the symbolic message to society that criminal acts based on hatred will not be tolerated.'[97]

The authors analyse hate crime as a 'policy domain.' Their focus, therefore, is less on the problem of hate crime itself, and more on the socially constructed 'definitional and classification schemes.' The first question of a policy domain is this: Which social actors, 'for example, politicians, experts, agency officials, and interest groups ... have gained sufficient legitimacy to speak about or act upon a particular issue?' The second question: Which 'cultural logics, theories, frameworks, and ideologies' are used to construct the problem and to determine the appropriate policy response?

The authors stress that policymaking is about more than just creating laws. Rather, policy 'is renegotiated and redefined at multiple points.' The policy domain can be traced through four overlapping phases:

- *Issue creation*, when the social problem 'is recognized, named and deemed in need of a solution.'
- *Solution choice*, which involves 'the adoption of a particular policy solution from a range of alternatives.'
- *Rule making*, at which time the exact meaning of the policy is 'fleshed out.'
- '*Real world*,' when the rules are specified and applied by enforcement agencies.

In other words, the authors trace 'how social movements constructed the problem of hate motivated violence, how politicians ... passed legislation defining the parameters of hate crime, how courts have elaborated the meaning of hate crime, and how law enforcement officials classify, investigate, and prosecute that behavior which is defined by statute as criminal.'[98]

Note that the making of laws is not the final step: 'Much of what constitutes a hate crime is determined by judges in the process of applying statutes to particular "real world" situations. Over time ... they clarify precisely what the laws cover.' Appellate courts play an especially crucial role; appellate judges 'can elaborate or complicate the meaning of a statute, delimit its meaning and application, reject the language of particular statutes, validate or valorize others, work out deeper justifications ... and decide whether to widen the scope to include new actions.' The authors analysed thirty-six constitutional challenges to hate crimes law and found that five main issues were disputed: vagueness; punishment of speech; overbreadth; speech regulation; denial of equal protection before the law.[99]

Jenness has argued elsewhere that in the courts, 'equal' treatment tends to translate into 'sameness'; the law cannot afford protection to one particular group without affording it to others. This is why hate crime laws do not spell out categories such as, 'violence against blacks' or 'violence against Jews,' but instead use general terms like race and religion. As a result, a hate crime against a white person or a heterosexual is deemed to be just as serious as a crime against a Sikh or a transsexual. Although this appears to be the 'right thing to do,' the historical basis and meaning of hate crime is elided 'by translating specific categories of persons ... into all-encompassing and seemingly neutral categories.'

By clustering different varieties of hate crimes into one category, hate crime laws ensure 'across-category sameness,' so that 'hate crimes against persons with disabilities are rendered equivalent to hate crimes against Muslims.' Jenness contends that the social movements that originally galvanized these debates have been 'muted.' In fact, a 'clear disconnect' has developed 'between the origins of hate crime politics, the development of hate crime policy (i.e. the law), and the implementation of policy (i.e. law enforcement).'[100]

Jenness and Grattet found that through the processes of judicial scrutiny, the 'substantive meaning' of hate crime has evolved in two ways. The legal definition has become more nuanced, and courts 'have consistently argued that states have a "compelling interest" in curbing hate crime.'[101] Moreover, the courts have elaborated on the extent to which the crime must be motivated by hate in order to be considered a hate crime. The tendency has been to consider bias as *a substantial factor* instead of *the sole factor.*[102]

To what extent have officials succeeded in prosecuting these crimes? The authors note that no statistics have been published because of 'the newness of the criminal category.' However, one way of measuring the 'success' of a law is by measuring the total number of incidents reported that were actually prosecuted. Preliminary research in California indicates that the prosecution rates for hate crimes do not appear to vary wildly from overall prosecution rates.

The authors suggest another way to analyze prosecutorial success: 'the proportion of hate crime filings that have led to convictions.' In California, now that the system has successfully labelled certain incidents as hate crimes, the preliminary data suggest that 'obtaining a conviction is no more difficult than in other crimes': 'California prosecutors have increased the frequency with which they file hate crime complaints. Conviction rates and guilty pleas are increasing, which suggests that prosecutors are becoming more comfortable invoking and enforcing hate crime laws and criminal defense attorneys are less likely to effectively interfere with their doing so.'[103]

Hate Crime Legislation at Home and Abroad

As I mentioned earlier, there has been an increasing tendency in the United States to criminalize hate. In Canada, however, there is still no law that makes hate-motivated violence a crime. In 2003, EGALE and other queer groups appealed to the community to support Svend Robinson's 'hate-crime bill' in the House of Commons. There were several references to gay-bashing victims, leaving the public with the impression that the law would address homophobic violence. In fact, Robinson's private member's bill – Bill C-250 – was created to rectify the hate propaganda law. As Roberts notes: 'Some writers make no distinction between hate-motivated crime and hate propaganda.'[104] Yet, the two issues are quite distinct.

Up until 2004, Sections 318 and 319 of the Criminal Code prohibited genocide and the spread of hatred toward other groups on the basis of their colour, race, religion, or ethnic origin – but not on the basis of their sexual orientation. For example, in 1995 a pamphlet was circulated in Winnipeg that called for the killing of homosexuals.[105] In 1997, an e-mail proclaimed: 'Death to homosexuals; It's prescribed in the Bible! Better watch out next Gay Pride Week!!!' This one was signed, 'Winnipeg's newly formed gay bashing patrol.' The police were unable to press charges in these cases.[106]

In 1999, Robinson asked the justice minister to include sexual orientation. She said she would look into it. Two years later, she said she was still considering it. The proposed change was supported by the justice departments of all the provinces as well as by the Canadian Association of Police Boards. After Robinson introduced the bill, he complained that the religious right 'flooded MPs with messages predicting apocalyptic results.' He said one Alliance MP complained that 'the bill could outlaw the Bible and Catholic catechism.'[107] On 29 April 2004, the bill received Royal Assent.[108]

As a result of this debate, some Canadians have been left with the impression that the Criminal Code includes a specific statute that prohibits hate-motivated violence. In fact, it does not. The only place where the code addresses this issue is Section 718.2(a)(i), the sentencing-enhancement provisions, which give judges the option of making the penalty harsher when hate motivation can be proved beyond a reasonable doubt. There has been little discussion of the fact that these provisions are largely cosmetic and ineffective.

In his review of hate crime legislation in three countries, Roberts notes that there are three models for enhancing penalties for hate-motivated crimes. Mandatory sentencing statutes clearly spell out 'a higher range, or minimum penalty for this kind of offending.' Then there is appellate decision making, where appeal courts eventually determine appropriate sentences. Finally, there is the 'statutory aggravating factor' model, adopted by Canada, which leaves the matter to the discretion of judges.[109] Generally speaking, the 'most popular legislative response to hate crime involves ... increasing the severity of the penalties imposed on offenders.'[110]

In the United Kingdom, the Crime and Disorder Act (CDA) sets out a very narrow definition of hate crime. In defining racially motivated acts, for example, the CDA has created a whole new set of offences, such as racially aggravated assault and racially aggravated harassment. The CDA also 'sets out a test for the court to apply.' An offence is considered to be racially aggravated if 'at the time of committing the offence, or immediately before or after doing so, the offender demonstrates towards the victim of the offence hostility based on the victim's membership (or presumed membership) of a racial group.'

Roberts points out the advantages of this approach: the term 'racially aggravated' is more nuanced than the term 'racially motivated.' In addition, the word '"immediately" ... establishes a temporal relationship' that 'expands the scope of legislation beyond that which exists in other countries where the hatred must precede and precipitate the attack.'[111]

The CDA clearly states that 'any offence is to be punished more severely if it is found to have been racially motivated.' In other words, discretion is taken out of the judges' hands. Once racial aggravation has been established beyond a reasonable doubt, the judge must factor this into his or her sentence, and furthermore, 'shall state in open court that the offence is so aggravated.' The CDA also spells out higher maximum penalties for racially aggravated crimes. For example, normally the maximum penalty for assault is six months. A racially motivated assault, on the other hand, could be punished by up to two years in prison.[112]

In the United States, the federal Hate Crime Statistics Act (HCSA) of 1990 had the advantage of establishing clear guidelines for the U.S. Attorney General regarding what does and does not constitute a hate crime. The HCSA's definition of a hate crime is broad; motivation can be 'in whole' or 'in part.' As well, the HCSA sets out 'a list of predicate or primary offences, including murder, non-negligent manslaughter; forcible rape; aggravated assault; simple assault; intimidation; arson; and destruction, damage or vandalism of property.'[113]

The Hate Crime Sentencing Enhancement Act of 1994 specifies that 'offenders convicted of hate crimes will have their offence categories "bumped up" at least three levels.' These 'significantly harsher sentence lengths' are determined using a grid 'in which the seriousness of the crime and the criminal history of the offender' are factored in.[114]

By 1999, more than forty American states had passed some form of hate crime legislation. Several states dole out more severe penalties by reclassifying hate-motivated crime; for example, 'a felony of the second degree is punishable as if it were a felony of the first degree.' In several states, hate motivation is considered 'one of the aggravating circumstances which can result in the imposition of the death penalty instead of life imprisonment without parole.'[115] For example, one Texas murderer was sentenced to death – instead of life in prison – after admitting that he killed his victim because he was gay.[116]

The Canadian Debate on Hate Crime Legislation

During the 1995 debate on Bill C-41 – which introduced Section 718's sentencing enhancement provisions – Giese opined that 'it doesn't actually do much to fight hate. It doesn't attack the root causes of prejudice, and it might even cause new human-rights abuses.' She was alarmed at the queer community's call for blood during the trial of a basher: 'Revenge – and punishment – provide a quick solution and temporary comfort to highly complex problems.' Moreover, 'joining the hate-crimes bandwagon has allowed the government to pretend that it's doing a lot more for minority rights than it really is.'[117]

According to Jeffrey, although the media and activist groups depicted Bill C-41 as a sea change, in reality the provisions do 'nothing to impair the wide discretion of judges to decide the weight to be attached to each factor when deciding sentencing.' Whether the provisions have any impact whatsoever is unclear 'since judges are not even obliged to cite the new provision when pronouncing sentence.'[118]

There is surprisingly little academic debate in Canada about this issue. Shaffer wrote an article on the inadequacy of Bill C-41 just as it was being enacted. She argues forcefully for a separate hate-crime statute to recognize 'that such violence constitutes a specific form of harm,'[119] since certain criminal laws play 'a normative or symbolic role in instructing citizens about the types of conduct that give rise to social disapprobation.' This separate hate-crime statute would allow for a more accurate statistical mapping of hate crimes since, at present, 'in the course of plea bargaining the Crown and the defence sometimes agree to omit motive from the attention of the trial judge.'[120]

Shaffer also asks why some governments are eager to adopt hate crime laws, an 'easy way for the government to claim that it is addressing a social problem.' Such a tack is relatively inexpensive and generates 'considerable media attention, as do trials conducted under hate-crime provisions. The publicity provides the government with free political mileage' – in a way that less glamorous, grassroots education does not.[121]

Since criminal law reform does not usually create genuine social change, Shaffer believes the powers of the sentencing provisions are largely 'illusory.' Judges are under no obligation use the sentencing guidelines. And even if they do, they do not have to explain the degree to which the sentence was increased because of aggravating hate factors.[122] On the whole, Shaffer feels that Canada would be better off adopting specific American-style hate crime laws.[123]

In my research, I analysed well over one hundred queer-basing cases that had occurred since Canada's sentencing enhancement bill was enacted in 1995. None of the media reports describing these cases ever indicated that the enhancement guidelines had been applied.

Relative to the United States and Britain, Canada's sentencing enhancement provisions are quite vague: Section 718 specifies that the sentence should 'reflect' the aggravating hate factors, but Roberts asks: 'How much should this aggravate the severity of the sentence imposed? No direction is given, and the maximum penalty remains the same. The maximum penalty for assault (s. 266) is five years in prison, regardless of whether there was a component of hate motivation or not,'[124] Roberts concludes that Section 718 reflects 'a rather muted response from Canada ... There is no evidence' that the section 'has changed the way judges respond to persons convicted of hate-motivated crime.'[125]

Does Enhanced Sentencing Really Work?

The head of the Toronto Police Service Hate Crime Unit seems to corroborate Roberts's assessment: he told me that in his experience, no gay-bashers had ever been handed a more severe sentence under Section 718. The only hate crime on his watch that garnered an enhanced sentence involved a skinhead who attacked a black victim on a streetcar, shouting, 'White power!' He was arrested with a racist manifesto in his pocket; police discovered he was involved with hate websites. Instead of getting a conditional sentence, he got five months.[126]

In one woeful Toronto incident – the assaults on dentist Ed Pollak and his partner – the judge refused to call it a gay-bashing. In 1993, a car bore down on the couple in the gay ghetto; after they jumped out of the way, four men bailed out of the car. Pollak's lip was split in four places, requiring stitches. He also lost a tooth and required two root canals.[127] His partner was kicked in the head fifteen times with boots.[128] Witnesses got the car's licence number, but police took forty-five minutes to arrive. They didn't ask whether it was a hate crime, and didn't even ask them if they needed an ambulance. 'They couldn't wait to get out of there,' Pollak said.[129]

Three young men from the Hamilton area eventually went on trial. One admitted to asking the victims what they were looking at, but he and another defendant said they were acting in 'self-defence,' while the third said he was trying to break things up. An independent witness testified he heard someone yell 'Fags!' Yet the accused denied it was a gay-bashing.[130] Another independent witness was walking his dogs and 'saw a man being punched and kicked, while huddled against a wall, protecting himself.'[131]

Although the judge felt that 'hate played a role' in the assault, he declined to call it a 'gay bashing.'[132] Only two of the men were convicted; each was sentenced to six months and two years' probation. However, the pair served only ten days in jail before being released on $10,000 bail. Both the Crown and the defence appealed the sentences. The Ontario Court of Appeal agreed that the assault was not motivated by the victim's sexual orientation. The sententecs of the accused were reduced to six months conditional, with no probation.[133]

Pollak killed himself three months before the appeal was held. Shortly before his death, he admitted that 'a portion of my freedom has been taken away for life ... By speaking out about what happened, it's given me power.'[134] But a former coordinator of Toronto's Anti-Violence Program complained: 'Increased sentencing provisions don't work. The judges don't want to use it. I don't think the criminal justice system in any way meets the needs of bashing victims – they are not heard or acknowledged.'[135]

Legal Remedies for Victims

There are many different paths that queer-bashing victims can take in the pursuit of justice. Jeffery has written an important handbook that spells out clearly the many ways Canadian hate-crime victims can seek legal redress. For example, under section 737(3) of the Criminal Code, judges may order the offender to pay restitution as a parole condition, even though one survey showed that restitution was ordered only six times out of 4,294 appearances by offenders – that is, less than 0.1 per cent of the time.[136] Besides the more obvious charges (assault, sexual assault, attempted murder, and so on), there may be other applicable statutes:

- The *torture* provisions (s. 269.1) provide a penalty of up to fourteen years to persons 'acting under the authority of a public official' who intentionally inflict 'severe physical or mental pain or suffering, for the purposes of intimidating, coercing, punishing or extracting information from the victim or a third person.'[137]
- Gangs who swarm their victims can be charged with *criminal harassment* (s. 264), *intimidation*, or *watching and besetting* (s. 423).
- Threats over the phone can result in charges involving *indecent or harassing phone calls* (s. 372) or *uttering threats* (s. 264.1).
- Harassing phone calls can also be pursued under Section 13 of the *Canadian Human Rights Act.*[138]
- Queer-bashers who demonstrate 'a persistent pattern of sexually or physically violent behaviour' and who are 'likely to cause death, physical injury or to inflict severe psychological damage on other persons in the future' may also be declared *dangerous offenders.*[139]

Unfortunately, queer victims cannot always rely on the state to investigate and prosecute these crimes. As I describe in the next chapter, dozens of Montreal police were recorded on camera beating queer protestors – but apparently nobody was convicted under the Criminal Code.

In some cases, private prosecutions may be the only way to achieve justice. Although the procedures require considerable legal expertise, time, and financial resources, they can have a huge impact, by bolstering subsequent litigation and creating public outrage.[140] For example, Jewish groups spearheaded a private prosecution against Ernest Zundel for 'wilfully spreading false news.' The state eventually took over the case and appealed it all the way to the Supreme Court of Canada. This generated a broad public debate about anti-Semitism in Canada.

Queer-bashing victims are eligible for compensation, which is administered by the provinces. Although compensation is relatively easy to apply for, there are many disadvantages to it. In 1998, Jeffery noted that the average award in Ontario was only $5,000. Lump sums were capped at $25,000, and at $1,000 for periodic payments. Applications had to be filed within a year of the crime, and the whole procedure could take up to three years to conclude. In addition, the payments affected welfare, insurance payouts, and disability pensions.[141]

Victims can file with quasi-independent police complaints commissions. In some provinces, including Ontario, these commissions have been abolished; police chiefs are now responsible for handling these complaints. In Brian Nolan's case, detailed in the previous chapter, the Newfoundland officers were eventually charged. However, all the police got was 'a slap on the wrist ... One got a 14-day suspension, while one got a ten-day suspension. But they wouldn't even offer an apology.'[142]

Compensation handed out by human rights commissions generally has a low ceiling: 'Often, defendants who recognize that there is little likelihood of being subject to a formal tribunal hearing will not make any genuine attempts at settlement in the hopes that the commission will simply abandon the case.[143] Provincial human rights commissions and their federal counterpart encourage both sides to resolve their disputes through mediation. Only a fraction of complaints are referred to a tribunal – the mechanism that has the power to order financial awards and other measures. The Canadian Human Rights Tribunal can order the respondent to pay a maximum of $20,000 for pain and suffering – although that respondent may also be ordered to pay for expenses incurred.[144]

Brian Nolan noted with some bitterness that the Newfoundland and Labrador Human Rights Commission Commission is 'very officious and bureaucratic, and decided that I had no case ... Seven months after the incident, they phoned and said I hadn't filed the claim in time and so my claim was cancelled, even though I had walked in the door the Monday after the incident and gave them the information ... It went back and forth and back and forth; after two years I was so frustrated. I thought, 'Why am I going through all this when they can't enforce anything?' ... By this time I was exhausted by the whole thing. You can only do it for so long.'[145]

According to Jeffery, litigation is 'expensive, time-consuming and stressful to plaintiffs.' Although many perpetrators of hate crimes are youths with limited financial resources, successful lawsuits can financially cripple or bankrupt perpetrators and organizations that would otherwise be untouched by the law. Since these are intentional torts, it is not necessary to prove physical harm: 'The mere threat of harm is sufficient to constitute assault.' These actions 'empower the victim to direct and define the issues, the burden of proof is less onerous, and the plaintiff can receive compensatory damages and possibly punitive damages.'[146]

In cases of assault, swarming, sexual assault, intimidation, and harassing phone calls, recognized grounds for civil action include the following: negligence, assault, battery, tresspass to person, intentional infliction of mental suffering, and wrongful imprisonment.[147] However, substantial punitive-damage awards – in the event of harsh, vindictive, reprehensible, and malicious behaviour – are rare. As of 1996, there had only been four in excess of $100,000 in Canadian legal history.[148] Moreover, to avoid the principle of double-punishment, punitive damages are not awarded when offenders have been sentenced in criminal court. However, this rule has been held not to apply where the defendant has received a conditional discharge.

Another option for queer-bashing victims is a class action, which is 'a legal suit initiated by a representative on behalf of herself and other people who have suffered similar harm due to the same act or omission ... They allow for a large number of victims to obtain redress in situations where no single individual could afford to sue on his or her own.'[149]

Jeffery notes: 'Class actions remain poorly understood and under-used tools for achieving group restitution under appropriate circumstances.' They are essentially 'an alternative means of law enforcement and private compensation' because they promote deterrence. In addition, they level an economic penalty on people or organizations that would normally escape the law. Since preliminary procedures are costly and very time-consuming, only people with ready access to lawyers can consider this option. However, most provinces provide an advance to cover initial costs.

The legal remedies listed above provide all the more more reason for a national organization to be established that would help victims take a stand against queer-bashers – and the laws, policies, and institutions that fail to protect us from them.[150]

Summary

Homophobia is reproduced in a myriad of legal practices that minimize, rationalize, and even negate homophobic violence. Sometimes, in the case of procedural or administrative errors, the homophobia appears to be 'unintentional.' However, these errors have led to situations in which queers have been killed; killers have also gone free or had their charges reduced.

'Hate crime' is a relatively new social construct that reframes an ages-old problem. According to Jenness, hate crime legislation develops through a process whereby victim status is assigned to certain groups but not to others. Recent research examines which social actors 'speak for' queer victims, and which discourses they use to frame the issues and develop policy positions.

Despite the proliferation of American hate-crime legislation and academic research, Canadian debate has been mainly limited to questions about the hate crime sentencing provisions and hate crime propaganda. Little evidence has emerged to indicate that the provisions have been effective. This book includes hundreds of examples of assaults and murders that occurred in Canada after 1995 – the year the hate crime sentencing provisions came into effect. Yet I have found almost no reports confirming that judges have increased sentences for queer-bashers. This would seem to corroborate Shaffer's contention in 1995 that these provisions are ineffective and that a separate hate-crime statute is needed.

CHAPTER 5

Homo-cide:
Getting Away with It?

In his book *The Celluloid Closet*, Russo includes a 'necrology' that lists the ways queer characters in films have met their untimely ends: execution by electric chair, suicide by straight razor, death by poison and falling trees, and murder by bludgeoning, cannibalism, and even a stake through the heart. During the 1980s, Russo would do speaking engagements around the world, ending his presentation with a barrage of short clips. Decades of queer deaths were condensed into a tightly edited and dizzying two-minute collage of stabbings and strangulations. As the lights came up, audience members, laughing nervously, would be visibly shaken.[1]

This chapter is an inquiry into queer homicide. It examines the widespread perception that men who kill queers 'get away with murder.' For years, men who killed other men have justified their actions by claiming that the victims wanted to have sex with them – that is, they had made 'sexual advances' or a 'homosexual advances.' A psychiatric theory called 'homosexual panic' – which originally focused on young men confused and threatened by their own latent homosexuality – gradually became a tenable legal defence. Legal and psychiatric discourses that blamed and vilified homosexual behaviour became increasingly interwoven.

The hundred homicide incidents analysed in this book, involving 107 victims, have occurred in the following provinces since 1990: British Columbia, 16; Alberta, 5; Saskatchewan, 2; Manitoba, 2; Ontario, 43; Quebec, 25; New Brunswick, 2; Nova Scotia, 4; Prince Edward Island, 1. None of the homicides took place in Newfoundland. 'Homo-cide' in Canada is very much an urban phenomenon. Nearly half of the homicides occurred in either Toronto (30 per cent) or Montreal (18 per cent). The homicides in my data set involve victims who were known to be queer; who were perceived to be queer by the community; who were perceived to be queer by the killer; who were killed in gay cruising areas; who violated gender norms and/or who were alleged to have made a homosexual advance.

Just to be clear: this is not a list of 107 'hate crime' victims. In fact, in almost all the cases, the police have refused to classify them as such. Let's say Al meets Bob in a bar. Al invites Bob home an hour later. Two hours later Bob kills Al. Generally, as soon as the police find out that Al voluntarily invited Bob home, it is no longer a 'hate crime.' The criminal justice system frames these killings as robberies or crimes of passion or attempted sexual assaults. However, although Al was imprudent for having invited Bob home, his killing is no less saturated with homophobia, which creeps into many aspects of these cases – if not in the execution of the crime, then in the way the crime is investigated, or in the way the killing is framed by the media, the defence lawyer, the Crown, or the suspect himself.

Let's say Al is openly gay, but Bob is not. Al and Bob have a surreptitious relationship until Al, impatient, starts telling others that Bob is his boyfriend. Does Bob kill Al because of a 'lover's quarrel' or because of his own internalized homophobia – his desperate need to ensure that nobody discovers that he actually has sex with other men? Instead of assuming that these are *not* hate-motivated killings, I am proposing that we consider the *degree* to which homophobia – both internal and external – motivates these homicides. Tomsen and George describe such killings in this way: 'A personal dispute between two men, possibly over sexual activity or an alleged sexual advance, leads to fatal violence between parties who are generally friends or acquaintances. These offences usually occur in private settings. The prosecutions and criminal trials that follow from these killings often lead to the controversial use of pleas of self-defence and provocation.'[2] Tomsen and George found that homosexual advances or assaults were alleged in thirteen of the sixteen Australian 'gay hate killings' they analyzed. They concluded that these claims 'have been effective in reducing sentences and appear to be growing in frequency.' This is 'reflected in the two full acquittals and six findings of manslaughter in completed trials which have occurred so far ... In the majority of instances where these allegations about sexual assault are raised (eight of 13 killings) they have demonstrably served the defence of offenders. Furthermore ... these claims may still be worth making even if they do not counter a charge of murder but raise factors that are taken into consideration when sentencing is determined.'[3]

Halifax Bloodbath

In the following 'homosexual panic' case in Halifax, the killer was found not guilty by reason of insanity. In 1990, William Munroe met a gay couple who lived in his apartment building. He was invited to a gay party at their place a few days later. At the end of the party, Munroe and one of the gay men in the couple, Lucien Bertin, went back to Munroe's apartment.[4] Munroe said Bertin, who weighed only 105 pounds,[5] made a pass. Munroe said he threw him out and went to sleep.

Munroe said he then woke up to find Bertin touching his penis.[6] He responded by stabbing Bertin forty times over the course of an hour. Three knives and a bent pair of scissors were seized by police.[7] 'A bloody trail traced a dying man's search for help ... down a stairwell to the second floor with bloodstains on floors, walls and doors.'[8]

The Crown vigorously challenged Munroe's claim of being a 'victim.' Munroe admitted in court that he attended the gay party with a 'mixture of curiosity and fear' and that he even danced briefly with the gay men. He also changed his story: first he told a psychiatrist that the victim's mouth had touched his penis, then he denied it. First he told police he stabbed the victim while sitting at a table, then he stated the killing occurred only after he fell asleep and was then wakened by the victim.[9]

The Crown suggested that Munroe was fabricating evidence 'and could possibly be a latent homosexual who made advances and was spurned.'[10] If Munroe was doing that, he certainly took great pains to hide it: Munroe fired his first lawyer, fearing he was gay. Two defence psychiatrists said the accused was suffering from 'paranoid delusions of persecution and homosexual panic.' The Crown's psychiatrist agreed with the defence that Munroe was insane, probably owing to 'cocaine psychosis' resulting from drug abuse a few years before.[11] The defence claimed that a 'real or imagined homosexual advance' triggered the killing.[12] The accused was found not guilty by reason of insanity.[13]

When I asked the Crown prosecutor why the verdict was not appealed, she said: 'There was no error ... by the judge to the jury.' She also felt the 'actions after the crime [were] more in keeping with the insanity defence than a "hate crime"' because Munroe was at his home 'waiting there covered in blood when the police arrived [and] never tried to wash himself up.'[14] This case raises certain questions:

- What difference did it make that Munroe never tried to clean himself up? Is it not possible to hatefully kill somebody and then pretend that you were defending yourself?

- A 'real or imagined' homosexual advance: what does that mean? Couldn't anything under the sun be considered that?

In a bizarre twist, 'outside the courtroom, Munroe's family and his girlfriend hugged and shook hands with Bertin's family and friends.' Tension between the two camps melted 'when Munroe presented a sympathy card to Bertin's family. That gesture brought the family to tears.' Joel Pink, the defence lawyer, said: 'I have a lot of sympathy for the family of the deceased.'[15]

The Origins of Homosexual Panic

The hallmarks of Lucien Bertin's horrible death were described fifteen years earlier by D.J. West in his definition of the term 'homosexual panic':

> Violent crimes in which a powerful young man, after allowing himself to be solicited or perhaps seduced by an older male, suddenly turns upon the homosexual in a blind rage and batters him to death. The unnecessary fury of these attacks, the absence of material gain, and the reckless disregard of consequences, reflect the assailants' disturbed state of mind at the time, which cannot be reasonably put down to ordinary feelings of disgust, but which could be a reaction to the intolerable pain caused by the threatened collapse of a heterosexual self-image.[16]

Edward Kempf, in 1920, was the first to coin the term homosexual panic. He devoted an entire chapter of *Psychopathology* to this topic. He defined it as 'panic due to the pressure of uncontrollable perverse sexual cravings ... wherever men or women must be grouped alone for prolonged periods, as in army camps, aboard ships, on exploring expeditions, in prisons, monasteries, schools and asylums.'

The chapter offers seventeen case studies, mainly about soldiers who were institutionalized after they returned home from the First World War. For example, one patient felt he was being 'teased and goaded' and developed feelings of inferiority. These feelings morphed into feelings of persecution which led to panic. Such panic can last 'from a few hours to several months.'[17] According to Kempf, homosexual panic is characterized by three symptoms: panic; the defensive compensation against the compulsion to seek or submit to assault; and erotic symbols and 'disturbances of sensation' (e.g., visions, voices, hypnotic trance states, and fears of poisoned food).[18]

Kempf felt that uncontrollable homosexual cravings caused patients to disown their feelings; they treated these feelings like 'foreign influences.' As a consequence, 'the patient feels he is being "hypnotized." Often such men and women attack the innocent person or yield to the hallucinated assault; or even do both.'[19]

Many of Kempf's patients complained of auditory hallucinations; one patient believed his companions were accusing him of being a fellator. Another patient, who was effeminate, with a 'pink girlish complexion,' complained that his shipmates had made advances; he was observed in the hospital kissing another man: 'His panic was clearly terror at his own homosexual eroticism which he could no longer control or understand.'[20]

One patient feared rectal gonorrhea and fantasized 'about the Major giving him salt enemas and eggnogs (seminal equivalents).' Case PD-19 was an 'unmarried, rather slender man' whose facial bones, 'while not small enough to be distinctly effeminate, were not as heavy as the average male.' He was certain that semen was being put in his bread. Another patient admitted 'numerous anal perversions with adult males ... but denied oral-erotic acts,' after experiencing accusations of 'going down on different fellows.'[21]

A slender sailor 'with scanty facial hair' said he went ashore one night, drank heavily, and spent the night in the same bed as another sailor. He thought he later overheard his friend calling him a queen. He believed his friend had drugged him; he was afraid his penis and testicles had shrunk. Kempf observed: 'The fear of the shrinking penis becoming invaginated into the abdomen was apparently due to an uncontrollable effeminate attachment to his companion.'[22] Case PD-26 was a 'mama's boy, seriously pampered, effeminate, dainty in manners, generally submissive in his make-up,' who was afraid that men were plotting to sexually assault him.[23]

Kempf stressed that men who suffer from homosexual panic are afraid of heterosexual relations: 'The amorous approach of the female ... like the serpent-headed Medusa, freezes his soul. Her sexuality horrifies instead of fascinates.' Kempf believed that women were also capable of these 'irrespressible erotic cravings.' One female patient was 'attracted to her neighbor, who she feared was telling everyone that she was going to masturbate.' This fear 'revealed the disguised interest of her eroticism, a masturbatory sexual interest in the woman neighbor and its attending feeling of being inferior to her.'[24]

Kempf noted that 'in a series of several hundred cases which have been recognized in the past six years, most of the cases recovered.' Recurrence resulted directly 'from inability to control the tendency to become perverse, i.e. biologically abnormal.'[25]

Mid-century Psychiatric Literature on Homosexual Panic

Kempf's cases did not offer many examples of patients who inflicted extreme violence on others. By 1941, however, Cassity had analysed the personalities of two hundred murderers. The killings were classified in different ways, including murders that occurred during an episode of homosexual panic.[26] That same year, another report analyzed five thousand cases of schizophrenia at a veterans' hospital. The authors observed that some latent homosexual men who experienced homosexual panic had attempted suicide.[27] In 1943, Karpman defined homosexual panic as 'latent homosexuality that is pressing strongly to the surface for open expression but is held in check by the dictates of the super-ego with its sense of guilt. Finding himself between these two conflicting trends which he is unable to reconcile satisfactorily, the patient is thrown into an acute conflict.'[28]

Glick was one of the first scholars to question Kempf's research, almost forty years after it was published: 'Acute homosexual panic is an acute schizophrenic reaction, usually temporary in duration, displaying the full panoply of schizophrenic symptoms accompanied by sensations of intense terror manifesting themselves in wild excitement or catatonic paralysis. It is based upon the patient's fear of loss of control of unconscious wishes to offer himself as a homosexual object which he feels will result in the most dire consequences.'[29]

Glick notes that although the term is widespread, homosexual panic has various meanings, 'ranging from vague feelings of discomfort to truly horrifying fright accompanied by disordered thought and behavior.' He points to two conflicting definitions. One dictionary says that homosexual panic does *not* appear in those whose homosexuality is conscious; the other calls the condition 'an acute and severe attack of anxiety based upon unconscious conflicts involving homosexuality.' The first definition describes psychosis and panic; the second describes a non-psychotic, but acute, anxiety attack. He emphasizes the difference between the two conditions: with panic, 'the terror reaches such massive proportions that the individual is unable to function *at all*.'

Glick argues that 'by definition,' latent homosexuality must be present in the condition of homosexual panic.[30] He wonders why some of Kempf's original seventeen cases had no homosexual content whatsoever. He also questions Kempf's assertion that no 'aggressive homosexuals' were observed in a homosexual panic state. Glick speculates that Kempf meant either 'overt homosexuals' or 'masculine homosexuals.' In either case, he believes that all homosexuals, not just one type of homosexual, are capable of developing 'acute paranoid reactions.'

Glick feels that homosexual panic is simply 'acute aggression panic.' The problem with diagnosing homosexual panic is that 'making the diagnosis ... is as much an interpretation as it is a diagnosis.' The symptoms Kempf described as homosexual panic differed 'in no way from any other acute schizophrenic state except perhaps content-wise in the predominance of sexual material.'[31]

Shapiro's literature review reveals that 'overt' homosexuals are generally less violent; 'latent' homosexuals – or heterosexuals who cannot accept homosexuality – are more likely to be aggressive, as a result of 'homosexual panic' and conflict. These men attack overt homosexuals as a way to prove their masculine toughness.[32] In another article, a patient attended sixty psychoanalytic sessions, because he was haunted by fantasies of being attacked by men from behind. The man had never had homosexual relations; in fact, he was revolted whenever the possibility arose.[33]

Sherwyn Woods uses the term 'pseudohomosexual panic' to describe a condition suffered by 'those heterosexual men for whom violence represents an ego defense against the intolerable psychic pain associated with a crisis of self-esteem.' The patient, perceiving his failure as a 'man,' begins to fear that he is gay, 'which the patient desperately attempts to ward off through acts of violence.' Woods recommends that the patient 'engage therapeutically with the feared homosexuality ... Failure to distinguish homosexual from pseudohomosexual conflict' could lead to 'an escalation of anxiety and acting out.'[34]

Ovesey and Woods expand on the idea of pseudohomosexuality. Many men who fantasize about having sex with men are not 'really' homosexual at all, and should not even be assumed to be latent. One 'exclusively heterosexual' patient was afraid of 'becoming gay' and being 'attacked from the rear.' These fears began to merge with fantasies of discovering, to his horror, that he enjoyed it. Apparently this had nothing at all to do with homosexuality, but rather with 'issues of dependency and power derived from unresolved oedipal rivalry with his father, who was a physician. His fears disguised a wish' that he could 'magically incorporate his father's powerful penis.'[35]

The authors conclude that the ultimate goal is 'to reverse the homosexual pattern, and to establish pleasurable heterosexual relations.' This is achieved by encouraging the homosexual patient to 'make the necessary attempts to have heterosexual intercourse ... until he is capable of sustained erection, penetration, and pleasurable intravaginal orgasm.' The patient must be shown that unhealthy fantasies have converted 'the vagina into a source of danger ... The patient must become more "masculine" by learning appropriate patterns of assertion.'[36]

Homosexual Panic's Gradual Association with Killing

The term 'homosexual panic' eventually became linked with homophobic violence. In 1965, Kiel described two young men who had stabbed and strangled an older man. One doctor speculated that 'the assault was the result of homosexual panic provoked by the victim's threat to disclose the younger boy's acquiescence to a homosexual act, setting off conflict between homosexuality and a conscious attempt to achieve heterosexual integrity.'[37]

Chuang and Addington observed in 1988 that homosexual panic 'can be used to describe a neurotic or anxiety state as well as a psychotic episode of brief duration.'[38] They noted that in the *Comprehensive Textbook of Psychiatry–II*, severely anxious people were described as 'fearful that their drives or impulses might lead them into performing prohibited or unacceptable actions which may be aggressive (such as murder) or sexual (such as homosexual behavior),' leading to 'castration anxiety ... often associated with homosexual panic.' This occurred in young men with unstable male identities, which, 'when exposed to close physical contact with other men, may arouse their underlying unconscious homosexual impulses, which in turn threaten their masculine ego, resulting in sudden eruption of violence.'[39]

A debate emerged in the textbook about whether homosexual panic was even linked to latent homosexuality: 'More often than not, the presence of such fears in cases of homosexual panic and in men in general is not related to any repressed homoerotic tendencies but to profound feelings of masculine inadequacy.'[40] Homosexual panic is characterized by delusions and hallucinations in 'patients with schizoid personality disorders ... Breakdown occurs in settings of enforced intimacy, such as a college dormitory or a military barracks. There may be a history of alcohol or drug use preceding the acute episode ... Treatment first involves rescuing the patient from the traumatic situation by hospitalization. Failure to do so may result in homicidal or suicidal acting out.'[41]

Comstock points out that Kempf's patients were not generally violent toward others. He found only two physical incidents in the original nineteen cases, and both involved teasing, not sexual advances. The violence tended to be more suicidal or self-inflictive. Comstock notes Kempf's patients were generally portrayed as helpless and passive; their behaviour was described using words like *whimpering, whining, weeping, moaning,* and *tremulous.*[42]

Walter discusses the links between homosexual panic and 'lust murder,' noting that 'the sudden recognition of the emergent repressed needs can cause ... a hostile transference onto an external scapegoat.' In one case study, the killer denied he had done anything to encourage a homosexual advance, even though 'he had conversed and drank with an alleged homosexual for 8–10 hours, negotiated a free meal from him, and accompanied the stranger/victim to a hotel room.' After the victim groped him, the accused strangled the victim with his bare hands, cut up the victim's scrotum and ejaculated on him.

The 'defence mechanisms' the killer utilized included 'escapism, projection, scapegoating, reaction formation, and avoidance.' The defendant blamed his drunkenness and mentioned that 'the two groups of people he dislikes the most are homosexuals and child molesters.' Walter believes the killer reacted 'in homosexual panic and projected onto the victim his undesirable traits that he feared within himself.' He believes the perpetrator could kill again, basing this on the killer's sexual gratification, his victim-blaming stance, and his 'assumption of a self-justification for the murder.'[43]

Gonsoriek describes three different scenarios in which psychiatrists use the term homosexual panic:

- The 'client may appear to be coming out or having a sexual identity crisis when, in reality, these behaviors or concerns are part of serious psychopathology.'
- The 'coming-out process itself' is capable of producing symptoms that appear pathological when really 'the individual is having a particularly difficult time coming to terms with his or her sexuality.'
- Coming out may also serve as a trigger for people with 'severe underlying problems.'

Using the term homosexual panic to describe such a broad range of situations simply creates more confusion. Gonsoriek suggests that homosexual panic 'be permanently assigned to the junkyard of obsolete psychiatric terminology.'[44]

The Merging of Psychiatric and Legal Discourses

Comstock feels that lawyers have misrepresented Kempf's original psychiatric theory by implying that extreme violence is caused by homosexual panic: 'A legal defense, perhaps, has more credibility if it can attach itself to a disorder.'[45] In 1967 in California, in the first judicial mention of homosexual panic, a defendant said he was urinating in an alley when he was grabbed from behind. He killed the victim because of 'acute homosexual panic brought on him by the fear that the victim was molesting him sexually.'[46]

Bagnall and colleagues were the first researchers to gather case law on homosexual panic. They noted in 1984 that 'no court has barred the defense, either as a matter of law, or because it rests on an untenable psychological theory, or because it is an unwarranted extension of the insanity defense.'[47] The legal debate centres on two questions: 'Whether the defendant who raises it must be a latent homosexual' and 'Whether homosexual panic is a "mental disease or defect" akin to insanity or a mere psychological disturbance that does not give rise to a level of legal insanity.'[48]

The following terms have been employed by expert psychiatrists to describe the personalities of defendants accused of homosexual panic killings:

- schizophrenic disorder or reaction
- acute psychotic process
- character neurosis
- a violent emotional reaction to a homosexual situation stemming from a person's conscious, or subconscious, awareness of his own homosexual tendencies
- paranoid personality
- dissociative reaction
- mental disease or defect
- highly delusional paranoid schizophrenic
- highly latent homosexual[49]

Bagnall and colleagues recommend that 'a threshold level of proof of a defendant's latent homosexuality' be required – otherwise, the defence could be invoked virtually every time a homosexual has been murdered. Given the 'rampant homophobia in our culture,' the defence risks being overused and supplying 'legal sanction to homophobia and to murder as a legitimate homophobic response.'[50] Ostensibly, someone could go into a homosexual panic 'whenever anyone becomes *aware* that someone else is gay.'[51] Comstock lists several objections to the use of homosexual panic in the courtroom:

- Only men have been driven to use it: 'Why have female patients not been driven to kill?'
- 'Uncontrollable latent homosexuality' has been replaced with '"fear," "disgust," or "aversion" to other people's homosexuality, which are not part of the psychiatric definition.'
- Why is there no emphasis on the 'aversion to heterosexuality' that Kempf observes in his patients?
- Some accused have used the defence even after they admitted that they had voluntarily had sex with their victims. 'Only those who have severe problems with *latent, not practiced, homosexuality* fit the disorder; recognizing or acting upon those feelings is understood in the psychiatric literature as the way in which the panic is relieved, not precipitated.'
- Homosexual panic is not something that lasts a few minutes or hours; rather it is a stage at the beginning or in the middle of a schizophrenic condition, one that necessitates 'on-going counseling and sexual adjustment during and subsequent to the panic state.'
- It is inappropriate to link homosexual panic with self-defence. In many of these homicides, defendants used excessive force, planned their attacks in advance, sexually propositioned victims, and robbed them.
- The *victim* is placed on trial. Self-defence 'is argued on the basis of the victim's sexual history and the testimony of the defendant, who in murder cases is usually the only witness.'[52]

Homosexual Advance versus Homosexual Panic

Many similar cases have emerged, even when the term homosexual panic is not actually employed. The common denominator in almost all of these cases is the allegation of a 'homosexual advance,' resulting 'in reductions of sentences for convicted defendants, mitigation in the degree of offence for which a defendant is convicted, and acquittals.'[53]

Homosexual advance allegations have been around a long time. In 1948, one controversial killing made the front page of the *New York*

Times. A Canadian businessman was killed at the Waldorf-Astoria by a nineteen-year-old 'delinquent,' Ralph Edward Barrows, who complained the victim had made 'improper advances.'[54]

Back in 1941, McHenry wrote about a Canadian boxer in New York who attended fights with an older gentleman, received money from him, went to dinner with him, then spent the night at his place on two consecutive nights. On the second night, the boxer claimed the man made an improper advance. McHenry argues that it is hard to believe that the defendant 'was unaware after one visit to the consular official's home that he was homosexual. Yet the fury of the assault, in which the face of the sleeping man was battered beyond identification, betrayed a towering emotional force of rage or disappointment or indignation behind it.'[55]

Mison distinguishes between the *homosexual panic* defence and the *homosexual advance* defence. The former is an insanity defence or a diminished-capacity defence, causing 'the defendant temporarily to lose the capacity to distinguish right from wrong, thereby absolving the defendant of criminal responsibility.'[56] Mison turns his attention to the latter: 'Should a nonviolent sexual advance in and of itself constitute sufficient provocation to incite a reasonable man to lose his self-control and kill in the heat of passion? If so, the defendant will be guilty of voluntary manslaughter, not murder.'[57]

Mison feels that if 'the reasonable man is the embodiment of both rational behavior and the idealized citizen, a killing based simply on a homosexual advance reflects neither rational nor exemplary behavior ... A reasonable person *should not* be provoked to kill by such an advance.'[58] The homosexual advance defence 'is a misguided application of provocation theory and a judicial insitutionalization of homophobia.' In a typical trial, the defence 'argues that a reasonable jury could find the victim's homosexual advance sufficient provocation for the defendant's acts and request the judge to instruct the jury on the lesser included offense of voluntary manslaughter. The prosecution does not object.' This practice 'sends a message to juries and the public that if someone makes a homosexual overture, such an advance may be sufficient provocation to kill that person.'[59]

Mison contends that defendants abuse this defence by raising it 'either as an alternative theory to self-defense or alone as a theory of voluntary manslaughter.'[60] For example, in *Doucette*, the defendant first stated that he killed for revenge and that it had nothing to do with homosexuality. By the end of the evening, he was claiming that the victim had made a homosexual advance. 'Although the jury ultimately convicted the defen-

dant of first-degree murder, the judge still instructed the jury on provocation' – even though semen was found in the rectum and throat of the
victim.[61]

These trials can also lead to the 'introduction of highly prejudicial and
often irrelevant evidence,' such as 'homosexual paraphernalia.'[62] The
Harvard Law Review points out that in cases where the accused claims to
have been raped by the defendant, evidence of the victim's homosexuality
'does not demonstrate his propensity to rape another man any more than
evidence of a man's heterosexuality demonstrates his propensity to rape a
woman.' The authors argue that the victim's orientation should only be
brought up if the victim had sexually assaulted somebody in the past.[63]

Recent Scholarship on 'Homo-cide'

Legal scholarship on homosexual panic and homosexual advance – especially from Australia – has proliferated since 1997.[64] Many of the articles
deconstruct the heterosexist assumptions of the courts, pointing to the
sheer absurdity of the defence. However, these articles tend to repeat
many points made by Mison and the *Harvard Law Review*. The most
engaging scholarship places the issues within the larger framework of
heterosexism and homophobia.

Green was a case that caused widespread alarm in Australia.[65] Two
close friends, Malcolm Green and Donald Gillies, ate and drank at
Gillies's home. Green stayed overnight and claimed that Gillies slipped
into his bed and began touching him. When he would not desist, Green
stabbed him ten times with scissors. What set this case apart was Green's
contention that Gillies' alleged advance triggered 'memories' of his own
father sexually assaulting his sisters. The kicker was the fact that Green
never actually saw his father abuse his sisters; his sisters had only told him
about it later. In other words, A touches B, and B kills A because it
somehow reminds him of C sexually assaulting D – even though B never
saw C do such a thing.

At trial, the judge – perhaps sensing a ruse – instructed the jury that
Green's pre-existing sensitivity to issues of sexual abuse was irrelevant
to the question of provocation. Green was convicted, but his appeal was
successful, and a new trial was ordered. The High Court focused largely
on the appropriateness of including details of Green's family's sexual
abuse, and did not really consider whether a non-violent homosexual
advance should warrant a provocation defence. However, Bradfield

notes that one judge characterized the victim as a 'revolting' sexual predator.[66]

De Pasquale: 'The Deployment of Culture'

According to De Pasquale, Green's successful appeal 'serves as a stark reminder of the resilience of homophobia in the law,' in that 'astute defence lawyers' will always be able to find loopholes.[67] He points to the 'dominant cultural assumptions' of the judges deciding these controversial cases, and he compares these debates to cases involving Aboriginal, Greek, and Muslim men who kill their wives. For example, a sociology professor testified that 'Muslims view marital infidelity as a sin and crime, preserving a code of honour.' Yet the views of Islamic women were ignored. It is men who 'have decided that adultery constitutes sufficient provocation.'[68]

As a parallel, De Pasquale cites cases featuring 'experts' who problematize homosexuality: 'These appeals to psychiatry are the latest manifestation of heterosexism in provocation law ... Any accusation of heterosexism is repudiated by judicial resort to a "credible" and "neutral" psychiatric discourse.' As a result, homosexual advance has evolved to mean almost anything. In New Zealand, a homosexual who touched the killer's thigh wore a smile that reminded the killer of abuse he had experienced as a child; the killer said the resultant flashback caused him to lose control.[69]

Some killers do not even have to prove they were reacting to the homosexual advance in the heat of passion. A Tasmanian man whose thigh had been touched by a homosexual said he had 'sexual child abuse accommodation syndrome' – which he used to explain why he waited thirty minutes after the touching incident before returning to rob and kill the victim. 'Remarkably ... the mere touching of the thigh, was *sufficient* evidence to call for a direction on provocation.' However, the author wonders why the 'courts are reluctant to introduce syndrome evidence in child sexual abuse cases while freely admitting similar evidence' in homosexual advance cases.

The Crown sometimes challenges these killers' stories more agressively. The provocation defence was denied when one killer falsely claimed 'that he was an innocent youth of heterosexual inclinations, who was the unwitting victim of unexpected and unwelcome homosexual advances from a much older man.' The Crown presented evidence that the killer was a 'practising homosexual.' The author notes: 'When the accused is labelled "homosexual," courts are reluctant to uphold a provocation defence' and may even hand out a more severe sentence.[70]

Chen's Analysis: 'Provocation's privileged desire'

Chen uses the infamous Matthew Shepard case in Wyoming as a starting point for her examination of homosexual advance. One killer claimed that Matthew Shepard touched his genitals, triggering memories of childhood abuse and 'five minutes of rage and chaos.' His strategy was 'to shift focus away' from his culpability 'by introducing elements of homosexual panic. This type of 'heat-of-passion' defense would negate the premeditation *mens rea* element required for first-degree murder ... mitigating the conviction to second-degree murder or voluntary manslaughter.'

Unlike other scholars, who present homosexual panic and homosexual advance as two distinct entities, Chen's approach is invaluable because she demonstrates, in plain language, the clear link between homosexual panic and homosexual advance. Her approach 'contextualizes homosexual panic as an insanity defense and explains its shift into homosexual advance as a provocation defense.' This defence 'creates a disparate legal impact on sexual minorities ... which reveals a specificity of privilege favoring heterosexual male defendants.'[71]

Instead of focusing on the fine points that distinguish one legal argument from another, she paints a broad picture of how homophobia works in the courtroom. As an insanity defense, 'homosexual panic was invoked by defendants with hopes of murder charge acquittals, and goals of complete exoneration from criminal responsibility and punishment.' Jurisdictions that recognized diminished capacity as a partial defence 'began accepting homosexual panic as negation of the mens rea element.' Medical–scientific discourse resorted to both the insanity approach and the diminished capacity approach to explain a psychotic, homicidal reaction, 'premised upon the latent homosexual's mental disorder of repressed sexual perversion.'

Even though a homosexual advance or other stimuli supposedly triggered this reactive panic, the underlying cause was always 'the defendant's larger psychiatric illness of homosexuality.' This stance became more problematic once homosexuality was 'demedicalized' in 1973, 'thus stripping homosexual panic of its medical-scientific legitimacy as a defense and as an illness premised upon homosexual latency.'

Chen contends that in the earlier formulation, the 'external stimulus' (that is, the homosexual advance) caused the panic, which led to psychosis and temporary insanity, which in turn 'caused the latent homosexual to kill.' In the current version, 'the homosexual advance itself provokes the understandable loss of normal self-control that incites uncontrollable homicidal rage in any reasonable person, regardless of homosexual tendencies.' In other words, whereas killers with 'homosexual panic' used to suffer 'an abnormal psychogenetic homicidal reaction, now the reasonable and ordinary person provoked by a homosexual advance kills because the solicitation itself causes an understandable loss of normal self-control.'[72]

Chen outlines the current debate on the subject. Opponents argue that a non-violent homosexual advance 'capitalizes upon society's heterosexist and homophobic disposition.' Proponents, meanwhile, 'refute that view as an unsupported assumptive proposition, but then point myopically to doctrinal principles validating Unwanted Sexual Advance as a provocation defense.' In the end, the two camps 'talk past each other.'[73] Chen bridges the gap by focusing on which social group benefits most from unwanted sexual advance (USA) defences:

> As victims, male heterosexuals are not burdened with the possibility that their non-violent unwanted sexual advance may partially excuse their killers because first, women rarely kill at all even when provoked. Second, male heterosexuals do not make sexual advances upon males ... It is a situational impossibility. Thus, under the USA defense, male heterosexuals become an insulated class accruing all the benefits attached with no burdens because they are protected by the defense's very definition.

In a 'perverse dynamic,' male homosexuals

> are extremely burdened with a high likelihood that their non-violent unwanted sexual advance will partially excuse their male killers because (1) the USA defense is premised upon the very notion that a sexual advance is adequate provocation; and (2) not only is homicide an overwhelmingly male act, the provocation is wholly skewed to favor homicidal male rage by mitigating the predominantly male reaction of retaliating for affronts and other 'injustices.'[74]

The Canadian Debate

Throughout North America, lawyers, journalists, and academics have created some confusion by using the generic term homosexual panic to refer to all cases that involved a homosexual advance. These cases have tended to the same outcome – the perception that a queer-basher 'got away with it'; even so, the loose terminology obscures the fact that few recent Canadian cases have actually used the term homosexual panic. In fact, although I found references to more than twenty homosexual advance homicides since 1990, I found only two homosexual panic homicides, both in Nova Scotia: the Halifax case described at the beginning of this chapter, and the Wolfville case described in chapter 1.

MacDougall observes that in Canada there is no 'homosexual panic defence per se. It is an American legal term; in this country, such a defence is subsumed under the guise of provocation or sometimes the defence of automatism, where it can be used to reduce the charge of murder to a conviction of manslaughter.'[75] Self-defence is also posited. The Crown considers provocation 'a justification for accepting an accused's guilty plea to a charge of manslaughter, rather than pursuing a conviction on a charge of murder.' Casswell reminds us that provocation is not a true defence per se, unlike 'self-defence or automatism which, if established, entitle the accused to an acquittal.' With provocation, 'the accused is acquitted of murder but convicted of the lesser offence of manslaughter.'

In Canada, a second-degree murder conviction carries an automatic sentence of life imprisonment, with no eligibility of parole for at least ten years; however, sentences for manslaughter vary wildly because 'while a person convicted of manslaughter is liable to imprisonment for life, there is no minimum sentence required.' Casswell reviews the provocation provisions[76] of the Criminal Code, which allow murder to be reduced to manslaughter:

- (Section 232[1]): 'If the person who committed it did so in the heat of passion caused by sudden provocation.' The first provision is an objective test: the question as to 'whether the wrongful act or insult was of such a nature as to be sufficient to deprive an ordinary person, not the individual accused, of the power of self control.'
- (Section 232[2]): 'If a wrongful act or an insult that is of such a   . nature as to be sufficient to deprive an ordinary person of the power of self-control ... if the accused acted on it on the sudden and before there was time for his passion to cool.' The second provision is a subjective test, in which 'the character, background, temperament, and idiosyncracies of the individual accused are now relevant.'[77]

Canadian Homosexual Advance Homicides

In twenty-seven of the hundred homicide incidents I analyzed, the suspect alleged that a homosexual advance had occurred. These suspects usually claimed to be shocked or disgusted by the victim's homosexual behaviour, and claimed that their motives for killing were not predatory.

Sometimes there were hints that a homosexual advance had been alleged. In 1994, Gerald Cuerrier, a gay drug dealer in Eastern Ontario, was found in his home, shot in the head. A teenager was accused in the killing. Two Crown witnesses said they 'regularly rebuffed [the victim's] sexual overtures while getting their drugs ... He never forced the issue or offered drugs in return for sex.'[78] All of the Canadian homosexual advance cases that I analysed featured one or more of the following characteristics:

- The victim was openly gay.
- The defendant had already had some previous contact with the queer community.
- The defendant had already had an intimate, long-term relationship with the victim.
- The defendant had met the victim through a classified ad catering to gay men.
- The defendant had already had sex with the victim.
- The defendant met or killed the victim in or near a gay establishment or cruising area.
- The defendant robbed the victim.

Even when killers meet their victims at gay bars, the claim of a homosexual advance remains a good option. For example, on 'Welfare Wednesday' – 28 September 1994 – Gary Gilroy met his victim, Dave Gaspard, at Vancouver's Dufferin Hotel. Gilroy said later he had 'ingested large quantities of alcohol, marijuana and Valium' that day.[79] Gilroy was in a hurry to leave the bar: the Dufferin's manager had called police after seeing Gilroy wearing brass knuckles. Some customers complained he was being rude and obnoxious. Gilroy ended up going back to Gaspard's apartment. Gilroy claimed he took a shower and that after he came out, Gaspard threatened to rape him. Gilroy defended himself vigorously: he stabbed and slashed the victim sixty times. Two-thirds of the wounds were inflicted after the victim was already dead.

The victim's friends said afterwards that 'a bloody hand-print on the door proves Gaspard was trying to escape.' A frantic neighbour in the downstairs apartment told the manager that 'pink water' was dripping from her ceiling. Six bloody knives were found;[80] three of them were broken.[81] Running water in the apartment triggered a fire alarm at three a.m. The manager opened the apartment and found Gilroy, who told him casually, 'He tried to rape me.' The 'pink water' flowed out into the hallway: 'a five-foot circle of floor had to be cut out ... because blood had soaked through the wood.'[82]

Gilroy pleaded guilty to manslaughter and received a five-year sentence. He said he had been physically abused as a child and sexually abused by an uncle. The Crown felt the term was appropriate because he 'couldn't disprove Gilroy's claim that he was provoked into killing the victim.'[83] The victim's aunt said that 'because my nephew was gay and Native he was expendable ... The public sees his death as no great loss.'[84]

What shocked Vancouver's queer community was the venue where Gilroy met his victim: the Dufferin is a gay landmark on the West Coast – a raucous mix of drag queens, hustlers, and working-class gay men. It's hard to believe Gilroy could go home with anyone from the Dufferin and be surprised about the possibility of gay sex. Even if the sexual advance did occur, the courts overlooked the obvious: Why didn't Gilroy just leave? Why didn't he just stab him once? Gilroy finished his sentence in July 2000 and was released.[85]

In the mid-1990s, another dangerous setting was the Playground in Toronto, where men and women, gay and straight, cruised for sex partners.[86] Rendell Gillette, twenty-one, was already a repeat offender[87] when he walked into the club in 1994.[88] He said that Stephen Kirby, forty-five, 'made a pass at him and grabbed his buttocks.' In front of the club, Gillette punched and spat on Kirby after kicking him repeatedly.'[89] Kirby bled to death.

Within forty-eight hours of the attack, the police had concluded that 'Although homosexuals are known to frequent the club, the beating was not a gay-bashing.'[90] Their stance would lead some to ask what right the police have to decide what does and does not constitute a crime against the queer community. Gillette pleaded guilty to manslaughter and got a five-year sentence.[91]

The Crown chose not to take the case to trial, and even signed a victim-blaming joint statement with the defence agreeing that Gillette never intended to kill the victim, who 'by his words and conduct, provoked a fight.' Kirby was described as a bisexual and 'an obnoxious drunk who often caused problems for other patrons and, on occasion, had to be asked to leave.'[92] The subtext here is that the victim was asking for it. Moreover, the Crown's hurry to strike a deal with a killer may have placed the queer community at even greater risk: Gillette skipped parole after serving four years.[93]

'He Tried to Put It in My Bum'

In some homosexual advance cases, the suspect and the victim were already in an intimate relationship – yet the killer still claimed to be horrified at the possibility of gay sex. About four months before his death, Guy Robert, fifty-five, met Steven Gilling and invited him to live in his Ottawa apartment. The court heard that Gilling, twenty-six, would have a few beers and get rough with Robert, who was described as a small, frail schizophrenic on welfare.[94]

The last time Robert was seen alive was Monday, 20 March 1995. A witness said he saw Gilling and Robert arguing that night.[95] After Gilling went back to his parents' home in Brampton, neighbours discovered Robert's nude body. His throat had been slashed from ear to ear;[96] the cut was 25 cm long and 5 cm deep, 'with enough force to nick his spinal cord.'[97] Pathologists estimated that Robert died sometime on Tuesday, 21 March. 'At trial, both parents testified [Gilling] arrived in Brampton on Monday, March 20. However, ... on March 25, 1995, [Gilling's] father stated that his son had returned home either on Monday or Tuesday of that week. Several witnesses called by the Crown reported seeing [Gilling] outside the deceased's apartment building on Tuesday, March 21.'[98]

Gilling's father told police his son fought with a man in Ottawa who had tried to rape him: his son defended himself with a knife, and the man got cut. At the beginning of Gilling's police interview, Gilling even blurted out: 'The knife, I still have it.'[99] He told Officer Neilsen what happened:

Accused: He tried to have sex with me, he tried to put it in my bum.
Neilsen: Did that make you angry?
Accused: (nods head, up and down)
Neilsen: Is that when you stabbed him?
Accused: Yeah.[100]

At trial, the Crown attempted to show a pattern of increased violence: Gilling had already committed two previous knife-related offences.[101] He was convicted of second-degree murder. The jury took forty-nine hours to reach the verdict.[102] Gilling's lawyer said nine of the jurors did not want to recommend a sentence; two others recommended that he serve fifteen years, and another felt he should serve twenty-five years.[103] He was sentenced to life with no chance of parole for fifteen years. Gilling told the court: 'It is not like I am a killer or anything like that. But he was a gay pimp and anything could have happened to him.'[104]

Gilling successfully appealed in 1997. During his new trial in 1998, the defence vilified the victim, saying that Robert would bring different men back to his apartment to drink. The Crown argued that the rape attempt 'simply could not have happened,' since there were no signs of struggle. This time the jurors took twenty hours; Gilling was found guilty of manslaughter[105] and sentenced to six-and-a-half years in prison.[106]

Sometimes homosexual advance cases involve two men who meet by chance. In 1999, the body of James Bewick, fifty-eight, was found near Swift Current. Michael Fiedler, seventeen, said he was hitchhiking from Medicine Hat when Bewick picked him up.[107] He said Bewick forced him to have sex by threatening him with a knife. However, the Crown's theory was that 'Fiedler overpowered Bewick after they had sex, strangled him and stepped on his neck.' Then Fiedler stole the car and picked up a couple of hitchhikers from Quebec, who later testified how strange Fiedler looked: he showed the couple his 'vampire teeth,' and boasted that he resembled the Devil.[108]

Let's Make a Deal

In homosexual advance cases, defendants often plead guilty to manslaughter.[109] In the following case, the killer got only three years. In 1991, John Russ, twenty-three, met two men in Edmonton who were also heading to the West Coast. They all went camping near Hinton, where Russ 'went totally berserk' after Yvon Parent tried to kiss him. 'I just said: "I'm not that way." I told him I was normal.'

Russ took a hatchet and struck the victim on the head and chest with the blunt side. 'For some reason I just could not stop. It seemed like I had no control over it.' He then forced the third man, Charles Martin, to help him bury the body, concealing the grave with broken branches and leaves. Martin escaped and later appeared at the door of a house near the campsite, bleeding from the head and trying to make himself understood in French. The next day, police arrested Russ about four miles from the campsite. His lawyer said Russ tried to commit suicide several times.[110] After he pleaded guilty to manslaughter, the Crown called for a lenient sentence: 'He said if he could trade places with the victim he would in a minute. He was definitely pretty tortured about it.'[111]

When the Crown refuses to accept a manslaughter plea, the results can be disastrous. Jim Detzler, fifty-four, was a gay, epileptic cross-dresser living on a disability pension in Toronto. Nicknamed Gracie, he had done a stint in prison for a non-fatal stabbing. A former inmate told the *Toronto Sun* that Detzler and twenty-six-year-old Steven Craig had been lovers in Kingston Pen. In 1997, Craig had been out of prison for only three weeks when Detzler was found, beaten and drowned in a bathtub.[112]

Craig offered to plead guilty to manslaughter. The Crown refused to accept the plea and charged him with first-degree murder. At trial, the jury was told of 'pornographic letters found at Detzler's home written by Craig indicating sexual encounters between the two.' Semen matching Craig's was found inside the victim. In a disturbing excerpt from the police interview, Craig referred to the victim as 'it' and a 'thing': 'Well thing's coming on to me. I am, y'know, I am not that way y'know. Just pissed me off, and I just started hittin' it ... He's a homosexual and started coming to me, so I pushed away.'[113]

Craig had admitted to police that he assaulted Detzler while the victim was handcuffed, but the evidence was ruled inadmissible. The jury heard nothing about Craig's criminal past – yet the defence was able to put the victim on trial.[114] Psychiatric reports stated that Detzler had a 'sexual identity problem' and 'antisocial personality disorder' and was violent when 'denied sexual favours.'[115]

In the end, Judge Keenan 'directed an acquittal on the first-degree murder charge' and Craig pleaded guilty to manslaughter. The judge called Craig 'a danger to society,' adding that Detzler's death was not accidental. The man who had spent his entire adult life on parole or in prison was sentenced to ten years. While Craig was being led out, he spotted the homicide detective who arrested him and shouted, 'You're next, you — pig!'[116]

Boastful Bashers

In the following homosexual advance case, the killer also got manslaughter, even though he bragged about his deed. In 1994, Christopher Sessions, twenty-two, was charged in the killing of a Calgary man, Elexer Martinez, who was twenty years older. Sessions, who said he was heterosexual but had gay friends and was not homophobic, had known the victim for a while. In fact, a social worker testified that six months before the killing, Sessions had admitted whacking Martinez on the head with a frying pan. Sessions denied having had this conversation.

Immediately after the killing, Sessions bragged to some friends about it, then left a note for his friend Anita: 'Wow, I can't believe I did it. I'm a murderer now. Something inside me tells me I should turn myself in.' The next day, Sessions was questioned by police, but made no mention of the homosexual advance allegation that would eventually reduce his charge from second-degree murder to manslaughter.[117]

In court a year later, Sessions's story – which the Crown declared he concocted – went like this: After several drinks, he dozed off on Martinez's couch and woke to find his pants down and the victim fondling him: 'He just wouldn't stop.' He said Martinez threatened him with a knife and he had to defend himself: 'I grabbed his arm and we started to struggle.' He kicked Martinez in the head ten times with combat boots, then left.[118]

After a dispute about the social worker's testimony, the Alberta Court of Appeal overturned Sessions's second-degree murder conviction and ordered a new trial.[119] Sessions pleaded guilty to manslaughter and asked for leniency because he had been abused by his father and raised in foster homes.[120] However, a psychiatrist stated that 'Sessions showed no remorse for the killing and that he occasionally "glorified" the incident.' He was sentenced to seven years; the judge said he could apply for parole after three-and-a-half. The judge 'urged prison authorities to offer anger management courses' to him in prison.[121]

The Case of the Missing Penis

Although many homosexual advance killings were spontaneous, others involved careful planning. In 1993, Carl Moore invited Henry Drosdevech to his apartment in Abbotsford, B.C., and stabbed him sixty-eight times. The victim, a gay man, was Moore's immediate supervisor at a restaurant. Moore was about to be laid off and told several people he planned to take over the victim's job. The Crown said the murder preparations were meticulous: Moore got the victim 'undressed and had him laying on a sofa bed to watch a pornographic movie when he was repeatedly stabbed from behind.'[122]

- A deboning knife, 'virtually identical to the one that had gone missing' from the restaurant a couple of days before the murder, was used to stab the victim.

- On the night of the murder, Moore brought garbage bags and a vacuum cleaner home from the restaurant, even though his apartment was filthy and he had been quoted as saying that cleaning his apartment was not important to him.
- Moore parked his car in the loading area of his parkade just before the killing.
- The victim's clothes 'had been removed and neatly folded before the attack commenced.[123]

Moore was found naked in the bathroom, splashing cold water on the body, 'whose penis and testicles had been cut off. The testicles were in the dead man's mouth. His penis was never recovered.'[124] Moore claimed he could not recall killing the victim because he was drunk: he said he would drink vodka every night until he passed out.

Moore also claimed he was defending himself from a homosexual advance. When asked if he had ever had sex with the victim, Moore said, 'Never ... I'm heterosexual.'[125] Moore said Drosdevech – described in court as a 'practicing but not aggressive homosexual'[126] – would occasionally pat his bum, but it didn't bother him.[127] Moore was convicted of first-degree murder. His appeal was dismissed. The judges discounted the sexual advance theory as 'circumstantial and tenuous.'[128]

Getting Away with It

Did the killers on these pages 'get away with murder?' To get a sense of the severity of sanctions against these killers, I divided the 100 homicide incidents – with 107 victims – into cases with 'clear' outcomes and 'unclear' outcomes. 'Unclear' cases included the following scenarios:

- Suspect was charged for murder, but killed himself before trial.
- Suspect killed himself before he could be arrested.
- Suspect was wanted in connection with a killing, but was killed before he could be arrested.
- Media reports were missing details about what exactly the defendants were charged with and/or convicted of.

I focused on fifty-one cases with clear outcomes. Because some homicides involved multiple killers, I divided the cases even further, as shown in table 5.1. I also wanted to know exactly what these defendants had been convicted of. This was sometimes difficult to ascertain because of

Table 5.1
Number of killers involved in queer homicides

Number of killers in each murder	No. of cases	%	Total killers
1 male killer	47	92	47
2 male killers	3	6	6
4 male killers	1	2	4
Total	51	100	57

Table 5.2
Judicial outcome of queer homicides

Outcome	No. of cases	No. of killers	% of killers
1 male killed the victim, but the charges were stayed	1	1	1.9
1 male killed the victim, but was acquitted by reason of insanity	2	2	3.8
1 male was convicted of manslaughter	25	25	47.2
1 male was convicted of 2nd-degree murder	17	17	32.1
4 males were convicted 2nd-degree murder	1	4	7.5
1 male was convicted of 1st-degree murder	4	4	7.5
Total	50	53	100

conflicting or incomplete media reports. I managed to find the final judicial outcomes for fifty-three of the fifty-seven killers (see table 5.2).

Measuring the Severity of Punishment

The above data are still somewhat misleading. For example, in the Montreal 'skinhead case,' four males were convicted of second-degree murder, but because they were all under eighteen, they got only three years in prison. Thus, I wanted to find a way to measure the severity of the punishment. In six cases, the killer was either convicted or pleaded guilty, yet there were no reports concerning the sentencing. However, the severity of the punishment was evident for forty-seven of the killers, who got anywhere from zero to twenty-five years in prison.

How can severity of punishment be analysed? In Canada, a first-degree murder conviction is for 'life,' with an obligatory twenty-five-year term before the inmate is eligible to apply for parole. A second-degree murder

Table 5.3
Sentences served by killers convicted of queer homicide

Sentence served	No.	%
Served no time in prison	3	6.4
Allowed to apply for parole within less than 2 years	9	19.1
Allowed to apply for parole at 2 years but before 5 years	14	29.8
Allowed to apply for parole at 5 years but before 10 years	3	6.4
Allowed to apply for parole at 10 years but before 25 years	14	29.8
Sentenced to at least 25 years before parole eligibility	4	8.5
Total	47	100

conviction is also for 'life,' but carries a minimum ten-year sentence before the inmate is eligible to apply for parole. Prisoners convicted of manslaughter may apply for parole after serving one-third of their sentence – unless the judge states otherwise.

It would be misleading to compare X, sentenced to 'ten years' for manslaughter, with Y, who is sentenced to 'ten years' for second-degree murder. In reality, X will be eligible to apply for parole in three years, four months, whereas Y will be allowed only to apply for parole after ten years. This does not mean that X will be free after three-and-a-half years. It means that if X follows the rules, he may be able to enjoy a certain measure of freedom. Y, on the other hand, has to wait three times as long for the same privilege. Instead of averaging their original sentences, I calculated the amount of time the killers would have to serve in a Canadian prison before being eligible to apply for parole.

For the killer whose charges were stayed because of police bungling, I put '0' years in prison. For the two men who were acquitted by reason of insanity, I also put '0' years. (Although spending time in a psychiatric hospital is indeed a punishment, it's not prison. As noted, Sullivan – the Prince George killer who shot his wife – was no longer hospitalized four years later. A reporter observed him going off to work and shopping with his new wife: 'All he got ... was an extension last week on an order to ban the booze and weapons and to pay periodic visits to the forensic psychiatric outpatient unit.'[129])

To summarize, more the half the fifty-three killers I analysed went free, were declared insane, or got manslaughter convictions. Regarding punishment, out of forty-seven killers, more than half were either eligible to apply for parole within five years or did not go to prison at all. Those who served no prison time either went free because of police bungling or served a period of time in a hospital (see table 5.3).

'Open Season on Homosexuals'

In a few homosexual advance cases, judges have become more sceptical. In one bizarre Saskatchewan case, the judge was refreshingly frank in his outrage over the killing of sixty-seven-year-old Stacey Clarke – a man who was 5'6" and weighed 138 pounds. In contrast, James Tomlinson was 6', 170 pounds, and twenty-nine years old. In 1997, Clarke – a cross-dresser living on a farm near Melfort – advertised for part-time farm help on a local cable channel. When Tomlinson called, Clarke pretended to be a widow in need. What Tomlinson thought when he arrived at Clarke's farm and discovered a man is anyone's guess. Clarke had apparently approached another farmhand in the same fashion.

One morning, Tomlinson was drinking heavily and asked Clarke to pick him up in Melfort. Back at the farm, an argument erupted, causing Tomlinson to punch Clarke, 'evidenced by droplets of his blood in the kitchen and dining room area.' Tomlinson claimed that Clarke pursued him out of the house 'and made inappropriate comments and gestures, including grabbing Tomlinson's testes and squeezing them' until he 'saw stars.' When Tomlinson retaliated, 'The force applied to Clarke's chest was extreme – of a nature equivalent to what one might expect in a high velocity collision between two motor vehicles, or where a bull rams the victim. The choking of Clarke to the extent a bone was broken in his larynx was something that neither pathologist had previously seen.'

Then Tomlinson dumped the body near a golf course, about an hour away. According to a psychiatrist, Tomlinson was addicted to drugs and alcohol and had a disorder that 'exhibits prominent features of an anti-social personality, a paranoid personality and a schizophrenic personality.' Tomlinson was convicted of second-degree murder with no possibility of parole for ten years. The judge simply did not believe Tomlinson's version of the events: 'In my view the defence of provocation is not intended to create an 'open season' on homosexuals who act unlawfully ... Tomlinson knew that Clarke was a cross dresser and had ... a strong desire for homosexual contact. He was not caught off guard.'[130]

Summary

The homicides analyzed in this book cannot be described simply as 'hate killings.' The victims were not all queer, but many were perceived to be. Although many killings took place in large urban centres, they occurred in every province except Newfoundland – and in a range of settings, including farms, small towns, and isolated areas.

Kempf introduced the term homosexual panic in 1920. He believed that his patients' uncontrollable homosexual cravings led to feelings of persecution and panic. By the 1950s, two conflicting definitions of the term had appeared: one described the condition as a psychosis, the other as an acute anxiety attack, the result of unconscious conflicts about homosexuality. Before long, the term was being applied to situations in which killers alleged that their victims had made a homosexual advance.

Psychiatric and legal discourses merged, and the homosexual panic defence was born. Scholars have debated the extent to which it actually differs from the homosexual advance defence. Researchers have highlighted the heterosexist and homophobic assumptions of judges, jurors, and criminal justice officials in many of these cases. This raises the possibility that many acts of brutal homophobia have been disguised as incidents in which the killers claim they were shocked by homosexual behaviour and forced to defend themselves from attack. The killers also often claim they were abused while growing up.

More than one-quarter of the Canadian homicides I analysed involved allegations of a homosexual advance. Judicial outcomes varied, ranging from first-degree murder convictions to the staying of charges as a result of police bungling. My research lends some credence to the perception that certain killers are 'getting away with murder.'

CHAPTER 6

Homophobia, Violence, and Policing in Canada

An American survey of victims of homophobic violence revealed that 73 per cent never reported the crime to the police.[1] In a similar survey, 67 per cent 'experienced or perceived the police to be anti-gay; fourteen percent feared abuse from the police; and forty percent feared public disclosure of their sexual orientation.'[2] In the early 1990s, sixty people – fifty-nine of whom were men – complained to Toronto's 519 Community Centre about negative police treatment; 5 per cent said they had been threatened by police with a gun.[3]

Although these figures are not necessarily representative of Canada's queer community, they do indicate a shaky relationship. In this chapter, I discuss a range of negative behaviours: the RCMP's homophobic legacy; the homophobia that police direct toward their fellow officers; the basic presumptions some police make about queer victims; and the ways that queers are targeted by the police. Homophobic violence by on-duty and off-duty officers is documented, as well as incidents in which police have been criticized for 'dropping the ball.'

In the second part of this chapter, I examine how various federal, provincial, and municipal law enforcement agencies and institutions are, with varying degrees of success, measuring and responding to homophobic violence. I look at the difficulties inherent in the collecting of hate crime statistics, and I demonstrate the extent to which twenty of Canada's largest police departments are recording this violence. I close the chapter with a case study of a double gay-bashing in rural British Columbia – a botched investigation that does much to explain why police departments need to be more accountable to victims.

Queer Perceptions of Policing and Public Space

Despite the Criminal Code reforms of 1969, the RCMP strictly enforced an anti-homosexual hiring policy until 1986. The Mounties considered homosexuality a 'character weakness.' As recently as 1985, RCMP documents described queers as a 'security risk,' an 'operational impediment,' and 'in conflict with "accepted moral standards."' The RCMP also strongly endorsed the federal decision to exclude sexual orientation from the Canadian Human Rights Act.[4] After the Vancouver APEC riots in 1998, Toronto's *Now Magazine* discovered that the RCMP had been tracking the demonstrators' sexual orientation and HIV status; files included notes like 'HIV-positive AIDS activist' and 'Lesbian activist.'[5]

To understand how institutions like the police interact with marginalized groups such as gays, lesbians, and people with AIDS, Kinsman examines 'the organization of normalizing and responsibilizing practices and the regulation and construction of social and personal "risk."' Stigmatized groups that are 'constructed as "responsible"' are managed through forms of self-regulation and professional forms of governance of their lives.' Those labelled 'irresponsible' are regulated by 'forms of criminal law, policing and public health governance.'

For example, during the 1980s AIDS crisis, public health groups and the media designated certain groups as 'high-risk' – instead of naming 'high-risk behaviours' that all people were theoretically capable of practising. Kinsman asks 'whose "risk" was being focused on here, and from what social standpoints was (and is) "risk" being defined?'[6] He notes that by the 1990s, the gay male community had been cleaved into '"respectable" and "responsible" gay men and the "rough" and "irresponsible" queers – those who are seen to be "promiscuous," "anti-family" or pro-sex activists.'

The Canadian gay and lesbian movement has focused increasingly on same-sex spousal benefits and relationship recognition. Kinsman believes that the community is split 'between "responsibilizing" those involved in family relations and "irresponsibilizing" those who are not.' For queers who do not fit into 'familial' or 'spousal' categories, 'there is continued policing and oppressive regulation in areas regarding sexuality and social life outside familial contexts. These practices remain "deviant" and possibly "criminal."'[7]

Warner expands on this idea. The ways that queers relate to the police – and the degree to which they resist sexual regulation – fall along a continuum: 'Sharp divisions have emerged, and vituperative discourse has been launched, between conservatives and assimilationists on one side and liberationists and sex radicals on the other.'[8] Lunny explores the concept of queer victimization: 'There is a sustained negotiation, slippage and contestation around sexual and gendered miniorities' inclusion under the sign "victims of hate crime."' Within the queer community, there is much division regarding the advantages of this 'victim status.' Lunny observes the process that allows certain queers to be labelled as 'undeserving' victims of hate crime, and feels that this status is contingent on the management of specific sexual behaviours.[9]

According to Warner, queer conservatives are fond of claiming 'that police homophobia and harassment are largely things of the past, that police repression of lesbian and gay sexuality has not been a significant issue since the early 1980s.' Arrests 'in bars, bathhouses, and public places are dismissed as not being gay issues,' because heterosexuals could theoretically be charged with engaging in similar offences:

> And there is little questioning by conservatives and assimilationists of the moral values that underlie the laws, particularly that sexual conduct must be restricted to places that are 'private,' or that homophobia still motivates the actions of police in the vigilant seeking out of queer sexuality. Liberationists, on the other hand, have sought to address such issues and have continued to call for the repeal of oppressive sex laws that criminalize consensual sexual activity, whether same-sex or heterosexual, under the guise of enforcing morality.[10]

Warner has observed the emergence of a 'growing element' of queers

> who see themselves as 'respectable' professionals and business people living in upscale neighborhoods. These upstanding citizens don't go to (or don't publicly admit going to) sex clubs or bathhouses or engage in sex in public places, which are presumed to be frequented by gays and lesbians who are not respectable, whose behaviour 'gives gays and lesbians a bad name.' These so-called respectable gays want the police to do things for them ... In exchange, they support police actions against the bars, bathhouses, and other establishments, even if, on occasion, police conduct may be excessive or targeted.[11]

On the other side, liberationists have been slowly asserting 'the right to have sex and/or be nude in certain places determined by the state to be public.'[12] With such a sharp divergence of opinions, it's not surprising that there is little consensus within the queer community about how it should be policed.

Homophobia towards Queer Police Officers

One way to gauge the homophobia of the police is to observe how they treat their own queer colleagues. Marc Burke, a gay man and former police officer, interviewed British gay male police officers about their 'two primary identities.' When colleagues made homophobic remarks, queer officers sometimes remained silent; this led to alienation, shame and resentment.[13]

Queer officers also felt awkward when arresting men engaging in public sex: One said, 'I understand what forces a man to go out and look for sex in a park or wherever.' The purpose of park raids late at night was mainly to harass and verbally abuse gay men, 'but on a couple of occasions I saw people physically abused as well ... The whole exercise was one of "Let's go and have a bit of fun with the poofs."'[14] One officer complained bitterly that they don't 'put out units to deal with all the heterosexual bonking that also takes place in the cars.'[15]

One officer described how gay men were entrapped by the 'pretty police,' who were 'sent as bait to the local public toilet.'[16] Another said citizens would be shocked at the amount of police resources devoted to these patrols. Many of the complaints used to justify these raids were phony; furthermore, 'in many cases, the police evidence is also fabricated ... The men plead guilty at court as they are too afraid to challenge the police lies.'[17]

A gay undercover officer described being bashed while on duty: two youths pounced on him before he could identify himself, yelling, 'Queer fucking faggot!' They broke his shoulder and ribs and punctured a lung with a wooden stick. Bitterly, he recalled: 'Blood was coming from my mouth ... Little did my attackers know ... they had scored a hole-in-one. Not only had they bashed a cop, but a queer one, too. They would have been very proud.'[18] However, one officer felt that gay men were being hypocritical, making 'such a fuss about our presence that we aren't supposed to patrol that area any more. They want to have their cake and eat it. What they actually want is for you to patrol the area in order to protect them whilst they have sex – but they don't want to get nicked if you catch them bonking in the bushes.'[19]

This echoes the view of an activist who was concerned about a police crackdown in Stanley Park after the murder of Aaron Webster: 'I don't want to hear [them] tell us to stay out of the parks. I want them to tell us how they're going to protect us when we go into the parks.'[20]

Discrimination against Canadian Queer Police Officers

In many Canadian police forces, queer officers may be out to their colleagues and their bosses but not necessarily to the public; alternatively, they may be out to their friends but not to their colleagues. Researchers or journalists can always phone the communications department of a police department and ask to interview a black or an Asian or an aboriginal officer. But don't try asking for a gay or lesbian officer. Generally, you won't be put through because of 'privacy concerns.'

A Vancouver recruiting officer underlined this double-standard when he admitted that 'gays fight an uphill battle in the Vancouver Police Department because there are many prejudiced officers on the force.' The VPD claims to be proactive in its hiring policies. Even so, a queer newspaper once asked why gay and lesbian recruits would not receive a warm public welcome like newly recuited people of colour. The recruiting officer's response: 'Sexual preference is a private matter.'[21]

Queer officers are sometimes discouraged from being too overt. In 1999, a gay male RCMP officer from Vancouver asked his superiors if he could march in the Pride Parade and was told he couldn't – and that if he did, there would be repercussions.[22] One closeted VPD officer – well-known in the community – on being contacted by the Vancouver Sun, 'denied he was gay and declined to be interviewed, even without his name being used.'[23]

There have been various Canadian reports of queer officers being ill-treated by their employers,[24] and of attempts by them to organize. In 1989, six gay officers in Toronto formed the Law Enforcement Gay Alliance (LEGAL) to fight harassment and discrimination.[25] In 1993, the editor of Blue Line, a national police magazine, refused to run an ad for Toronto's Gay Cops United Foundation, explaining that he didn't want to promote a 'deviant lifestyle.'[26] By 1995, forty officers had 'sought support from the group, including two from Vancouver.' One of the co-founders said the gay officers were afraid of losing their jobs or careers: 'Some are suicidal and they are very, very afraid of being gay in the police force.' In response, a police spokesman complained that these officers 'bring gay perspectives into work, making it an issue in confrontational ways. The self-declared are taking political positions.'[27]

In 1999, queer officers marched in the 1999 Montreal Pride parade and organized a Quebec association for gay police officers and firefighters, which soon had thirty members.[28] An anti-violence activist I interviewed dismissed this group, explaining that she had tried to work with them and had found them to be extremely conservative; furthermore, they neither criticized nor questioned their department's treatment of queers. She said they went out of their way to 'look and act straight' and to gain acceptance by their colleagues.[29] Some of these officers might fit Warner's definition of 'assimilationist': 'Desperate for accommodation within the mainstream, assimilationists denounce various activities, even when occurring in queer spaces, as giving gays, lesbians, and bisexuals 'a bad image,' and support their curtailment, including by means of police action.'[30]

Some lesbian and transgendered officers have been recognized. Lesbian officer Judy Nosworthy received praise for her contributions to the Toronto queer community in 2001 and 2002. After she received a promotion,[31] a straight officer was assigned to the position. In 2003, Jackie O'Keefe, an out lesbian and twenty-year veteran, was appointed. She soon announced that TPS would have a table at a Pride celebration in the hope of recruiting more officers from the queer community.'[32]

Fiona Weller, an out VPD officer, is a regular at Vancouver's Gay and Lesbian Pride parades. She helped head up the province wide B.C. Hate Crimes Unit in 2000 and 2001. Ros Shakespeare, a veteran VPD officer, went public about her gender-reassignment surgery in 1999. However, transsexual activist Jamie-Lee Hamilton was unimpressed – because of the violence inflicted on transsexuals while Shakespeare remained in the closet: 'Big deal. This person silently stood by when all these acts happened. I wish her the best, but just because someone in the police department is now taking on a new identity doesn't make her part of the family.'[33]

Police Perceptions of Queer Victimhood

Praat and Tuffin conducted in-depth interviews with police officers in New Zealand about their attitudes toward gay men. Distinct discourses emerged, including the stereotype of effeminacy and the equation of homosexual behaviour with deviance, promiscuity, and pedophilia. The officers had 'conditional acceptance' of gay men, but made a point of denouncing what they felt were the distasteful, intolerable aspects of homosexuality.[34]

Relations between police and the queer community are complicated by police perceptions of what constitutes a 'victim.' Richardson and May argue that 'lesbians and gay men are unlikely to be construed as "innocent" victims' because they are stigmatized. The queer victim's status is mediated by two variables: 'behavioural responsibility for risk' and 'the social characteristics of the victim.'[35]

In 1993, two straight men found out what it was like to be labelled 'gay victims.' The professors were attending an academic conference in London, Ontario, and made the mistake of walking back to their hotel through a small, wooded park. Two men beat them repeatedly with a lead pipe, knocking them out. When the first victim regained consciousness, he ran for help. He found an OPP officer, whose first words were: 'Sorry, I cannot help you. This is not my jurisdiction.' It took twenty minutes for an ambulance to arrive, and thirty before the police came.

The victims said the police – who suspected them of being gay – were arrogant and aloof. The police said they would meet them at the hospital, but they never showed up. The ambulance attendants wouldn't touch either of them, instructing them to 'get into the back.' The attendant gave one of the victims some gauze and said, 'Control the bleeding yourself.' After receiving the ambulance bill, the victims concluded they would have been better off taking a taxi to the hospital.[36]

Negative attitudes toward gay male victims may explain, at least in part, the reluctance of many officers to acknowledge gay-bashing – and the reluctance of certain departments to fund more patrols to deal with these crimes. In some cases, police have been criticized for showing up late or not showing up at all. In 1991, Glen Murray – who went on to become Winnipeg's openly gay mayor – was a city councillor. While walking near the Legislature, which is close to a gay cruising area, a man assaulted and threatened to kill him. The police refused to attend, 'then claimed to have lost any record of his complaint. It was only later, when he told police he was a city councillor, that he got any action from the department.'[37]

In this vein, Moran critiques 'the limits of the State's capacity to provide safety and security' for gays and lesbians. The safety literature distributed by police departments as a crime prevention tool 'works with the assumption that most homophobic crime is violence performed in public by strangers.' A British police pamphlet implores gays and lesbians: 'Don't be a Target.' Moran objects to the slogan's 'assumption that lesbians and gay men can choose to be and can choose not to be a victim of homophobic violence.' Moreover, the 'emphasis on stranger danger ... is reinforced by the catalogue of locations of danger, which makes no reference to the workplace, the local neighborhood or the family home, as places of danger.'[38]

In many of the cases I analysed, police minimized or negated the homophobic aspects of the crime. For example, after a car veered toward three men – including Duncan Wilson, a openly gay Vancouver politician – one of these men, out of anger, thumped the car as it brushed past. At least three teenagers jumped out with a weapon, striking Wilson in the face and yelling, 'Homo.'[39] Because one of the victims had thumped the car, the police immediately reframed the incident as a 'traffic dispute.' At a press conference, VPD's Anne Drennan downplayed the attack, while at the same time claiming to take it seriously. At the time, a reporter noted: 'The assault doesn't fit the pattern of most gay-bashings. Police were investigating both the hate crime angle as well as the possibility the attack was motivated by a traffic dispute ... She said most attacks usually involve a large group of 'good ol' boys' looking for just one or two homosexuals to assault. She noted this case is unusual because it started with a traffic dispute, Wilson was just hit once, and his friends weren't attacked. Drennan denied police are dodging the gay-bashing description.'[40]

Police Who Charge Queer-Bashing Victims

Nearly one-quarter of the sixty gays and lesbians who complained to the 519 Church Street Community Centre about police treatment claimed that they – rather than the perpetrators – had been charged with assault.[41] This trend was reflected in my own data set.

For example, in 1993, the owner of a gay bar in Windsor was questioned by police, who wanted to enter his bar at 4:30 a.m. After answering their questions, he tried to close the door to get his identification, at which point the officers pepper-sprayed him. Then they followed him in, punched and kicked him, beat him on the head with a flashlight, and threatened to shoot him.[42] He was found guilty of resisting arrest and assaulting a police officer. He said: 'In other cities, there is a definite rapport between the gay and lesbian community and the police. This does not exist in Windsor.'[43]

In 1998, according to London's HALO group, a university student at Western complained that after he told police he was gay-bashed, the assailants told police he had made a pass at them – and the police believed them. Another man phoned HALO to find a lawyer after he was gay-bashed and then charged with sexual assault.[44] In 1999, a Toronto man said four strangers began rocking his parked van. He drove away, but later on Church Street the same men – who turned out to be police officers – called him a 'cocksucker,' hit him, and arrested him. He was charged with 'dangerous operation' of a vehicle and 'resisting or obstructing a public or peace officer.'[45]

In 2002, an Ottawa man was attacked and robbed in his apartment. A week later, a friend of the victim inadvertently let the assailant back into the apartment. The assailant claimed to be a delivery man and burst in, knocking down the victim's friend. The friend called 911, grabbed a knife, and chased the man out of the apartment. The police apparently arrested the good Samaritan, detained him for twenty-four hours, and charged him with various weapons offences.[46]

Police Who Target Queers

George Smith contends that 'our interest in the police did not arise as a theoretical or legal issue ... Rather, it arose out of our generalized, everyday experience as gay people of having our sexuality denied and our lives overrun and sometimes destroyed by the police.'[47]

Over the past century, Canadian police have targeted thousands of men – and some women – in washrooms, bars, bathhouses, parks, and other places where same-sex social and sexual activity takes place. Maynard examined Ontario court documents and crime reports between 1890 and 1940, and found that they depicted 'an elaborate underground of public gay sex.'[48] In the 1960s, Toronto police would routinely create peepholes in the ceilings of men's washrooms. According to Kinsman, 'a man died in police custody after two cops spied on him through a ventilation grill in the washroom of a Toronto gay bar.'[49]

Police relations with urban queer communities have thawed in recent decades, since hitting a low point in 1981. An example of a moral crusade was the Toronto bathhouse raids of that year. Fleming analyzes 'Toronto's largest arrest quota since the War Measures Act was invoked in 1970, and the largest mass arrest in the city's history.'[50] He looks at three interwoven themes: police procedures, media constructions of deviance, and gay resistance to this criminalizing process. The images of police smashing through bathhouse doors with hammers and axes hearken back to images of raids on illicit bootleggers. Such raids can also be seen as 'a form of political protest by enforcement authorities against what they may construe as overly liberal laws.'[51]

The 1981 operation was extremely costly, requiring six months of investigation. Four bathhouses were raided simultaneously, and three hundred officers were involved.[52] The police used prostitution, organized crime, and youth involvement as a justification for the raids – charges that went almost completely unsubstantiated.[53] Media coverage of the bathhouse raids was juxtaposed with an article about a police officer who died during a bar robbery, raising the rhetorical question: 'Who shall we support, gays who engage in bizarre sexual activities, or the police who die to protect us against unscrupulous criminals?'[54]

Smith uses the same sequence of events to focus on 'the secret penetration of gay men's lives by the police.' He teases out some of the competing 'explanations' of homophobic police activity that analysts and activists routinely employ:

- A case of 'homophobia simple.'
- The 'clean-up campaign' explanation, whereby gays are described as pawns in a broader political scenario.
- 'The rule of sergeants' – that is, oppressive force is instigated by specific local officers with a grudge.
- A conspiracy involving the entire criminal justice system: 'a rather self-serving arrangement whereby judges have an easy day of it handling guilty pleas ... the police their clearance quotas ... and the lawyers, their sometimes extravagant fees.'

Smith questions whether these actions can be explained away as 'homophobic.' Oversimplified accounts of police oppression conveniently fail 'to provide a concrete description of how the various critical sites of ruling involved in regulating sex are articulated to each other.'[55]

In the 1980s, the Ontario Provincial Police (OPP) would lend a video surveillance system to small police forces across the province. This enabled the latter to make mass arrests in public washrooms. These arrests would be followed by press releases 'naming the names of the men charged. In St. Catherines in 1985, one of the thirty-two men charged committed suicide on the day his name was printed in the local paper.' Another technique is to use an undercover officer, who stands 'at a urinal, pretending to play with his cock, until another man signals interest. Sometimes that interest can be as little as eye contact or the nod of a head. According to some reports, the really zealous cops even flash their own hard-ons. It's a simple arrest, the cop's word against the man's in court.'[56]

Desroches interviewed fifteen detectives in five different urban areas, where 190 men had been arrested for committing indecent acts. He would prefer to see preventive measures, including the redesign and relocation of washrooms, as well as signs warning that the premises are under surveillance. He also suggests that private security guards, rather than police officers, be assigned to this type of duty.[57]

Gay-bashing does occur in public toilets, but is almost never reported.[58] In the early 1990s, teenagers used to harass gay men in a washroom at a highway rest stop near Joliette, Quebec. Daniel Lacombe – whose family claimed he was straight – stopped at the washroom one night and was beaten and killed by a teenaged gang. Afterwards, they went out and bought French fries with the $15 they stole.[59] One was sentenced to two years for manslaughter.[60] Another teenager – who got eighteen months for aggravated assault – complained that his sentence was 'too harsh.'[61]

Police suspected the youths were responsible for sixty other assaults in the Joliette area,[62] yet their main response was to place the rest stop under surveillance – and arrest a dozen men on sex-related charges. A police spokesman said two undercover police officers were looking for cruisers, not bashers, and felt the operation was a 'great success.'[63]

The Decoy and the Sitting Duck

Police use many methods to target and intimidate queers. In 1993, a gay Anglican priest from Cambridge was arrested in Kitchener's Homer Watson Park.[64] Daniel Webb met an attractive man, shirtless and in shorts, and invited him into the bushes. Webb said that after the man voluntarily followed him in, he asked the man if he was a police officer. The man apparently replied, 'No, I can't even get a job.' As soon as Webb touched his groin, the man arrested him for sexual assault.

The next day, Webb's name appeared in an article in the local paper about police attempts to 'clean up homosexual behaviour in the park.'[65] After twenty-seven years of service, Webb talked to the archbishop and faxed him a brief letter of resignation. Until that point, neither the community nor his family – an ex-wife and two teenage sons – had any inkling of his homosexuality. The charge was later withdrawn; his arresting officer didn't even appear in court. But the damage was done: Webb sued the Waterloo Regional Police for $4 million.[66]

In court, Webb's lawyer argued that, unlike undercover campaigns that target drug dealers, consensual sex is legal: 'Touching someone is only illegal if the other party ... does not consent to the touching.' But the police service denied it had acted maliciously: 'The plaintiff has caused his own loss of income claim by voluntarily resigning his employment.'[67] A surprisingly liberal National Post editorial pointed out the hypocrisy inherent in the state inviting consensual sex and then portraying the response as a criminal act: 'And if the authorities wish to prevent public indecency, they should place uniformed police officers in 'cruising' areas to deter it – rather than inviting crimes in order to punish them. Exactly what cause is served when cops dress up like the Village People, set a trap, make an arrest, release the information to the media and ultimately withdraw the charges?'[68]

Webb's lawyer believed the goal of the police operation was to 'bring social or communal scorn and humiliation and hatred through the media.' But Judge Borkovich refused to allow expert testimony, stating that his role was limited to 'whether there was consent or a lack of consent.'[69] Seven years after the sting, Webb lost and was forced to pay the police force's legal costs. 'The plaintiff knew that he was engaged in a very risky situation when he went to the park to engage in sex,' the judge wrote.[70]

The vast majority of these actions go unreported. As table 6.1 indicates, the settings can range from a nudist beach to a washroom in a strip club. We know a lot about Webb's case because he chose to fight.

Police Who Humiliate Gay Men in the Media

Kinsman notes that after the Toronto bathhouse raids of the early 1980s, police switched tactics: 'Surveillance, entrapment and the arrest of men allegedly engaged in sexual acts in washrooms and parks increased significantly.' In 1982 and 1983, 'more than 600 men were arrested in washrooms'; in 1985, 'more than 600 "indecent act" arrests took place in Toronto.' Especially in small towns, washroom arrests 'are hard to fight ... because of the social stigma attached to the offence [and] the difficulty in mounting a legal defence,' and because so many men who have sex acts with men are in the closet.[71]

A community relations coordinator for the Hamilton police noted that a 1996 raid 'reflected "old-style" policing involving an undercover operation ... rather than the newer approach of being highly visible in the community and dialoguing and partnering with community representatives.' Although 'it is not normal police practice to issue a pro-active media release naming names every time charges are laid,' the officers 'listed the names, ages and addresses of twenty men' whose 'sexual assault' charges were all eventually withdrawn by the Crown. 'At least one person lost his job because of the police action.'[72]

The issue erupted again in Belleville, Ontario, in 2002. Two undercover

Table 6.1

Police raids, arrests, and intimidation in Canada since 1990 targeting queer social and/or sexual activity

Year	Location	Description	Source
Early 1990s	Quebec City	Mounties arrest gay men in cruising areas at the citadel and the zoo	Commission des droits de la personne et des droits de la jeunesse, *De l'illegalité à l'égalité*, May 1994, 61–2.
Early 1990s	Oka, PQ	QPP officers arrest gay men at a nudist beach	Letter from Dire enfin la violence, 14 July 1999.
1992	Ottawa	Undercover police arrests in Ottawa washrooms. Eight criminal charges laid	Ottawa Police Service Liaison Committee. *Heard for the First Time*, June 2002.
1992–3	Sydney, NS	1,000 people questioned regarding the killing of a gay man. See this chapter	Canadian Press. 'Halifax man charged in 1992 Sydney stabbing.' *Halifax Daily News*, 31 May 1995, 4.
1993	Oakville	In Shell Park, 49 men were arrested for sex; one who had AIDS killed himself soon after his arrest.	'Shell Park,' *Xtra!* 3 Sept. 1993, 11.
1993	Joliette, PQ	12 men were arrested at a public washroom at a highway rest stop. See this chapter.	André Picard. 'Gays target of police, activist alleges.' *Globe and Mail*, 13 May 1993, A2B.
1993	St John's	Police installed video cameras in washrooms and caught 60 men having sex. They arrested 33 men, whose names were published on the front page: 'Police deny reports that some men have subsequently committed suicide.'	'St. John's arrests.' *Xtra!* 11 June 1993, 15.
1993	Kitchener	Undercover police arrested men for sex in Homer Watson Park. See this chapter.	'Ontario: Ex-priest loses gay sting suit,' *National Post*, 1 July 2000, A4.
1993	London	60 men were arrested as a result of 'Project Guardian.' Police conducted nearly 2,000 interviews. See Chapter 7.	Shannon Bell and Joseph Couture, 'Justice and Law: Passion, Power, Prejudice and So-Called Pedophilia,' in Dorothy Chunn and Dany Lacombe, eds., *Law as a Gendering Practice* (Toronto: Oxford University Press 2000), 40–59.
Mid-1990s	London	In the aftermath of Project Guardian, police instituted 'massive' washroom arrests.	Letter from HALO activist, 6 May 1999.

Table 6.1 (Continued)

Year	Location	Description	Source
1995	Toronto	Two gay men were arrested in the washroom of the Wilson subway station in two separate incidents. The first man complained of entrapment by a tag team of undercover TTC officers. He said the younger of the two men kept staring at his crotch and followed him to a stall – but as soon as he touched the younger man's crotch, he was charged with sexual assault. In the second incident, a man – charged with sexual assault and committing an indecent act – said an undercover officer stared at him for five minutes before identifying himself. The defence lawyer noted the officer has been involved 'in many similar cases.' The judge dropped the charges because of contradictory versions.	Matthew Guerin 'Subway washroom bust,' Xtra! 24 Nov. 1995, 1, 'TTC testimony "not consistent."' Xtra! 29 Aug. 1996, 20.
1996	Longueuil, PQ	Police patrolled Parc Marie-Victorin on a regular basis. A gay man was charged with 'sexual assault' there after an undercover operation in August 1996. The police claimed that the gay man approached the policeman and grabbed him by the crotch; the accused said the policeman never identified himself, wore very tight pants, spent six or seven minutes staring at the accused and even licked his lips. The court found that the man had no intention of sexually assaulting the officer; he was looking for consensual sex and was therefore acquitted.	'Plaintes et accusations en chute,' RG, 22–23 Sept., 1996, and 'La police déboutée une fois de plus,' RG, May 1997, 10–11.
1996	Toronto	A gay man was approached by a man in Mary Curtis Park. After talking about the weather, the man asked him three times, 'What do you like?' When the gay man finally responded that he liked to get fucked, the undercover agent arrested him and charged him with counselling to commit an indecent act. He pleaded guilty to get it over with – but the judge, smelling entrapment, ordered him to return with a lawyer.	'Park Arrest,' (1996) Xtra! 12 Sept. 1996, 19.
1996	Hamilton	'Project Rosebud' was an undercover operation at Royal Botannical Gardens, which resulted in 20 men being arrested. See chapter 7.	Jane Mulkewich 'The Hamilton Wentworth Regional Police Gay/Lesbian/Bisexual/Transgendered Task Force: A Public Relations Success Story.' Report prepared by the Community Relations Coordinator, Hamilton-Wentworth Regional Police, 31 March 1998, 3.

Table 6.1 (*Continued*)

Year	Location	Description	Source
1998	Bradner, BC	Undercover officers were reportedly arresting men at a rest-stop washroom on the TransCanada.	'Cruising Alerts,' *Xtra!* 27 Aug. 1998, 19.
1998	Kitchener	Police reportedly harassed single men in Victoria Park.	'Sex alerts,' *Xtra!* 9 April 1998, 20.
1998	Montreal	Police reportedly arrested several men in the washroom of the Queen Elizabeth Hotel.	'Sex alerts,' *Xtra!* 9 April 1998, 20.
1998	Montreal	Dire Enfin la Violence reported that police were entrapping men in Angrignon Park.	Claudine Metcalfe 'Attention c'est chaud!' *Fugues*, June 1999, 38.
1998	Calgary	Police reportedly installed a surveillance camera to observe sexual activity at the Zoo.	'... And around Canada,' *Xtra!* 2 July 1998, 20.
1999	Quebec City	According to one report, someone falsely complained that gay men were masturbating and having anal sex in front of children along the St Charles River, a Quebec City cruising area. The complaint apparently led to a crackdown.	Serge Gauthier, 'Un autre tabassage homophobe,' *RG.* 8 January 2000.
1999	Toronto	Police raided the Bijou Porno Palace.	Brenda Cossman, 'Sex law,' *Capital Xtra,* 19 June 2003, 15.
1999	Montreal	Police made 24 sex-related arrests at the Botanical Gardens, where plain-clothes officers were posted around the clock during the summer.	Claudine Metcalfe, 'Attention c'est chaud!,' *Fugues,* June 1999, 38.
1999	Calgary	A three-man police team were reported to have arrested men in Bottomlands Park on the pretext of a prostitution sweep.	'Cruising alerts,' *Xtra!* 27 Aug. 1998, 19.
1999	Sudbury	Gay men were arrested in a prostitution sweep.	Interview with Gary Kinsman, 27 April 1999.
2000	St-Jérôme, PQ	In St-Jérôme, the local newspaper featured a front-page article, complete with photos, complaining that a local waterfall had been taken over by 'sexual deviants.' Two undercover QPP officers complained of being 'attacked.' However, one of the cops was caught with his pants down (literally), and was arrested for public sex as well.	'Les chutes Wilson: Un repère pour les déviants sexuels,' *L'Écho du Nord,* 14 June 2000, quoted in Messier, Eric in 'Plaintes et accusations en chute,' *RG,* 22 September, 2000.
2000	Toronto	A complaint circulated that police had Sunnyside Beach under helicopter surveillance at night after 11 p.m. Undercover cops were also reported to be posing as truckers in the washrooms of a truck stop, the 5th Wheel.	'Cruising warnings,' *Xtra!* 19 Oct. 2000, 15.

Table 6.1 (Concluded)

Year	Location	Description	Source
2000	Toronto	300 women were in attendance at the 'Pussy Palace' bathhouse event when it was raided by police. See chapter 7.	Eleanor Brown 'Male cops at the Pussy Palace,' Xtra! 21 Sept. 2000, 11. 'Naked dance victory,' Xtra! 11 July 2002, 11.
2000	Toronto	'The Barn faced Liquor Licence Act charges of permitting disorderly conduct because police officers found patrons drinking, talking and playing pool while naked at a private party.' After two years, a judge dismissed the charges. 370 men subsequently attended an all-nude dance without police interference.	
2000	Toronto	Police raided the Toolbox during a 'Naked Night' and laid liquor charges.	Paul Gallant, 'Toolbox charged,' Xtra! 2 Nov. 2000.
2000	London	Four undercover officers reportedly stripped, cuffed,and threatened to expose a gay man in Gibbons Park. See chapter 7.	'London alert,' Xtra! 11 Jan. 2001, 20.
2002	Windsor	Police were reported to have washrooms at the University of Windsor under surveillance.	'Cruising warning,' Xtra! 7 Mar. 2002, 15.
2002	Toronto	Police were reported to be patrolling sexual activity at The Bay washroom at Yonge and Bloor.	'Cruising warning,' Xtra! 4 April 2002, 14.
2002	Calgary	Thirteen bathhouse patrons were arrested for being 'found in a bawdy house.' Two co-owners and four staff were charged with keeping a bawdy house. See chapter 7.	Robin Perelle, 'Bathhouse on trial,' Capital Xtra, 13 March 2003, 10.
2002	Belleville, ON	Nine men were arrested at a park in Belleville. See this chapter.	Steven Maynard, 'Park cruisers feel slap of sex sting,' Xtra! 16 May 2002, 4.
2003	Edmonton	Police raided a bathhouse.	Gary Kinsman, (2003) 'History,' Capital Xtra, 17 July, 13.
2003	Montreal	Police raided the gay strip club Taboo. There were 34 arrests: 23 dancers were charged with being found in a common bawdy house. Seven staff were charged with operating a common bawdy house. Four senior citizens were charged with committing indecent acts. Police said the club had been under surveillance for several months. They claimed that oral sex and oral-anal sex was taking place.	Paul Gallant, (2003) 'Strippers busted in Montreal.' Capital Xtra! 22 May 13.
2004	Hamilton	Two people were charged with indecent acts following a raid at The Warehouse, a gay bathhouse. One person was charged at Show World, 'a peep show often patronized by gay men.'	Tanya Gulliver, Capital Xtra. 12 August 2004, 7

officers spent several afternoons in a park and arrested nine men. One officer complained that a man – a senior citizen – 'walked right up to my window, asked me how I was and grabbed me by the balls.' The senior was charged with sexual assault,[73] and pleaded guilty.[74] Some single men in the park were subsequently pulled over and interrogated. Other cruisers complained that men having sex in their cars during the daytime 'broke the implicit code of discretion and careful use that governs public sex.'[75]

The queer media noted that the coverage in the *Belleville Intelligencer* 'had all the makings of a media-driven moral panic.' A television newscast went 'live on location,' catching a heterosexual couple in the act, but police let the couple off 'with a warning.' The newspaper also interviewed a police officer 'on condition of anonymity': 'It's an odd policy for a newspaper to print the names of accused men – effectively no longer innocent until proven guilty, but grant anonymity to a police officer who is presumably accountable to the public.'[76]

Shortly after the arrests, prosecutors decided to drop charges against one gay man, who asked: 'Do the newspapers and the police walk away smiling after this legal gay-bashing?' He explained that an undercover cop engaged him in a 'sexually explicit conversation.' He said he never exposed himself or touched the officer but was arrested anyway. The officer told him their conversation had been recorded. The man said his small local business had suffered as a result of his arrest.

Although the editors at the *Intelligencer* insisted their coverage was 'standard procedure,' the announcement of the court date of each of the nine men was 'followed by a story in which the complete list of men's names, ages and residences' was reported.[77] Charges were dropped against six of the original nine.[78] A rural newspaper in the area questioned the policy: 'We don't run charges for anything, only convictions, because we don't have enough reporters to sit in court all day.' A police spokesman claimed that if a heterosexual couple had been caught in a similar situation, they would have been treated the same way in the media.[79]

Police Who Gay-Bash

Although it is more common to humiliate queers by dragging them through the criminal justice process, police have also resorted to more overt violence. Out of sixty gays and lesbians surveyed in Toronto, 17 per cent claimed to have been physically assaulted by the police.[80] In my own analysis of 344 cases of homophobic violence, more than 4 per cent involved on-duty or off-duty police officers – or other officers working in prisons, jails, and drunk tanks. These incidents, all of which occurred between 1990 and 1999, are listed in table 6.2.

One convicted gay-basher continued working for the Peel Regional Police, west of Toronto. In 1991, two off-duty constables, Daniel Johnstone and Charles Morden, were at a talent night, drinking in a Mississauga bar. After one man – described in the media as 'a 130-pound make-up artist' – came off the stage, one of the cops loudly asked him 'as a homosexual, whether he preferred anal or oral sex.' The artist's friend defended him, and a row ensued. The two cops were asked to leave, but apparently lay in wait. They showed up outside the men's apartment building just as they were about to enter for the night. One victim was punched in the eye; the other was punched 'several times in the face, causing his head to bounce off the pavement.'

The judge found the cops' versions of the events were 'outright lies,' but only fined them $1,500 each – with no jail time, since they would be facing 'disciplinary action' from their employer. Although their lawyer lamented that their future as police officers was 'in jeopardy,' their commanding officers still filed letters of commendation.[81] I called Peel Regional and was informed by Inspector Cryderman that Morden was no longer working for Peel, but Johnstone was. Cryderman said he could not describe the 'internal discipline' the officers received because all files pertaining to their hearings had been 'purged.'

Police Violence in Montreal

The most atrocious Canadian example of police homophobia in recent memory hit the Montreal headlines in 1990, then quickly faded from the public eye. On 15 July of that year, squadrons of police descended on a private gay and lesbian warehouse party. The police claimed the organizers had asked them to break it up – a charge that was vehemently denied. Fifty people were injured and nine were arrested.[82]

> Having removed their badges, and armed with nightsticks, 'peace officers,' standing in formation, provoked the party-goers as they poured out of the single entry to the empty loft-factory. With verbal insults ('maudites tapettes,' etc.) then with mock masturbation (using their nightsticks), and limp wristed gestures, the motive for the raid was evident to those present ... One of the

Table 6.2

Complaints of brutality against the queer community perpetrated by on-duty and off-duty police officers in Canada since 1990

Year	Location	Description	Source
1990	Montreal	At least 50 – and possibly more than 100 – members of the queer community were beaten by police during raids and demonstrations. See this chapter.	Commission des droits de la personne et des droits de la jeunesse, *De l'illegalité à l'égalité*, 1994.
1991	Ottawa	A gay man complained that an Ottawa police officer tried to hit him with a police cruiser. See chapter 7.	'Charges against Ottawa officer withdrawn,' *Ottawa Citizen*, 9 Nov. 1994, B8.
1991	Mississauga	Two off-duty Peel Regional Police officers were convicted of beating a gay man. See this chapter.	Farrell Crook 'Two Off-Duty Peel Police officers fined for beatings outside bar,' *Toronto Star*. 28 Nov. 1992, A22.
1992	Vancouver	A Vancouver AIDS activist complained he was pepper-sprayed by police while attending a demonstration against gay-bashing. A few months later, he was arrested for being intoxicated in a public place. Witnesses said he threw himself on the floor and spat at a police officer; his nose was broken when he was pushed into a wall inside the police station.	Kevin Griffin 'No appeal planned by AIDS activist.' *Vancouver Sun*, 15 Apr. 1994, B4.
1993	St John's	A gay man was roughed up by St John's police officers. See chapter 3.	*R. v Devereaux* (1996), 112 CCC (3d) 243 (Nfld. CA).
1993	Windsor	The owner of a gay bar said he was pepper-sprayed, punched, kicked, beaten on the head with a flashlight, and threatened with a gun. See this chapter.	'Bar owner guilty of assault,' *Xtra!* 3 March 1995, 1.
1994	Montreal	A depressed gay man with AIDS, living on welfare, used a pay phone in Montreal's Gay Village to call a suicide hotline. After ten minutes on the phone, the police showed up, handcuffed him, and took him to the police station, where one officer asked him twice if he was a 'faggot.' After Collins finally responded with a derogatory comment, 'That's when they all started punching me ... One was hitting me on my rear and asking if I liked it.' Then, Collins said he was 'dragged, still handcuffed, into a cell where he was punched some more ...' In 1995, after turning down several out-of-court settlements, he sued the police for $350,000. He said that eleven gay men with similar concerns were filing a lawsuit, 'but he couldn't comment specifically on their cases.'	Mike King, and Katherine Wilton, 'I Was Roughed Up by cops after call to suicide line, teen says,' *Montreal Gazette*, 16 Dec. 1994, A3. 'Maybe he thought he was an unemployed taxi driver,' *Montreal Mirror*. 20 Apr. 1995, 7.
1995	Vancouver	A police officer slammed a gay man's back into a table at his apartment. See chapter 4.	Douglas Victor Janoff, 'Gay-Bashing in Vancouver: A Case Study' (unpublished ms).

Table 6.2 (*Concluded*)

Year	Location	Description	Source
1996	London	A pre-op transsexual woman complained to the community group HALO that the police were after her.	Letter from HALO activist, 6 May 1999.
1997	Vancouver	A gay man said he witnessed police throwing a gay man into the wall of the Dufferin Hotel, then smacking him on the back of the head. The eight police officers attending the scene prevented the witness from getting the badge number of the alleged assailant.	Gareth Kirkby 'Police actions questioned,' *Xtra West*, 26 June 1997, 7.
1998	Winnipeg	A woman complained to the Winnipeg Gay and Lesbian Resource Centre that a female police officer beat her up. The victim had mentioned to the officer that she was bisexual.	Letter from the coordinator of the Winnipeg Rainbow Resource Centre, 9 August 1999.
1998	Vancouver	A Vancouver police officer ticketing cars downtown denied he called a gay man a 'wiseguy faggot' and took him down. The man said he had had three beers over three hours at the Royal, but the officer said the man was drunk, screamed obscenities at him, then stuck a finger in his face. In the struggle, the complainant was knocked to the ground, then charged with causing a disturbance and resisting arrest.	Tom Yeung, 'What caused Allan's injuries?' *Xtra West*, 4 Mar. 1999, 7.
1999	Toronto	A gay man complained that four police officers on Church Street hit him and called him a 'cocksucker.' See this chapter.	'Schisler in court,' *Xtra!* 5 Oct. 2000, 15.
1999	Toronto	A straight man delivering the *Toronto Sun* near a gay cruising area said he was pummeled by an off-duty Toronto police officer who stank of beer, called him a 'fucking queer,' and threatened to kill him. Although Daren Arsenault was arrested the next day, the police never issued a press release, 'which is done routinely whenever an officer is charged criminally.' Six months later, it was the *Toronto Star* that informed the Toronto Police Service's public affairs department about the incident. Even though a prosecutor had assured the victim that the matter was being treated as a 'hate crime,' the Hate Crime Unit didn't seem to be aware of the incident either. Arsenault turned around and sued the victim. Then he filed a private prosecution, accusing the victim of assault with a weapon. The officer was convicted of assault in 2000. His sentence: eighteen months' probation, a $500 fine and a letter of apology. However, the judge said Arsenault's actions were not motivated by hatred.	Rosie DiManno, 'Assault case against officer heads quietly to court,' *Toronto Star*, 16 Aug. 1999.

victims of the beating, a well-known Montreal photographer, photographed the police attack ... [She] was tripped and thrown to the ground and her camera was smashed.'[83]

One man was 'treated like an animal' after trying to help a friend who had been shoved to the ground by police. 'They pushed me face down on the pavement and told me they would break my arm if I moved ... Then they put handcuffs on me and threw me into a car.'[84] The photographer wrote later:

> I was beaten twice by the police in two days, lost equipment, was subject to arrest in two separate incidents (including a false arrest during which I was 'charged' with 'Conspiracy to commit armed robbery' by the MUC), threatened, followed and intimidated and finally after all this, compelled to pay a fine.[85]

Two days after the raid, about two hundred angry demonstrators gathered in front of Station 25. Sixty officers in riot gear – again, with name badges removed –

> formed a wall on three sides of the demonstrators sitting in the street. On signal, they attacked ... The TV cameras recorded the brutality ... It took about 20 minutes to beat the 200 or so gays and lesbians sitting on the street. 48 were arrested, taken into Station 25 and beaten again inside the station. One man had a ruptured testicle from being beaten with a nightstick in the groin while in Station 25; he lay screaming on the floor for 30 minutes (until the journalists had left the scene) before the Police would call an ambulance for him.[86]

One of the most unforgettable scenes from the documentary *We're Here, We're Queer* shows a policeman dragging a young woman along the street by the hair. Later, a television reporter interviewed the man clubbed in the groin from his hospital bed. The police were denying they had hit him. 'They're lying,' the victim said.[87] Five years later, there still was no formal apology to the queer community.[88]

One activist who gathered information to submit to a human rights commission report told me: 'The police had an "internal" investigation which produced confidential internal reports and we were told that disciplinary action was taken in unnamed cases.'[89] Although I repeatedly requested details from the communications section of the Montreal police, they refused to specify what sort of disciplinary action was taken. They also refused to confirm or deny a report that gay men assaulted by the Montreal police had received out-of-court settlements (see table 6.2).

Police Response in Queer Homicide Cases

According to Tomsen and George, police sometimes portray queer homicide victims as promiscuous or predatory: 'Police may also unintentionally produce material that may have a prejudicial effect on the outcome of any future trial if it should be entered as evidence.'[90] For example, in Kitchener, police were criticized after Joseph Gligor and his wife were found hacked to death in their home in 1991. Police told the media that Gligor led a 'promiscuous double life'; they quarantined the axe and knife for several weeks as a 'precaution against AIDS.' Critics said police were delaying the investigation unnecessarily.[91]

In Cape Breton, gay men complained that police applied themselves a bit too vigorously while investigating a homicide. Roderick MacLeod, a music teacher in Sydney, was stabbed to death in 1992; his camera was stolen. The victim's family put up a $23,000 reward; the police spent thirty months on the case. More than a thousand people were interviewed over a year and a half;[92] one activist said it began to resemble a witch hunt. Closeted men who cruised Sydney's north end were quizzed about the men they had had sex with.[93] The police profile 'indicated two people may have been involved and that one – if not both – would be known within Sydney's gay community.'[94]

In 1992, police stated they would not be pursuing a second suspect after arresting Bernard Whiffen, who was eighteen at the time of the killing.[95] Whiffen, described as a male prostitute, pleaded guilty to manslaughter and was sentenced to two years less a day. He claimed the victim 'tried to rape him,' and that he responded by beating and stabbing the victim, then leaving his body in the bathtub with the water running.[96] A couple of years later, Whiffen was accused of killing a Sydney woman around the same time he killed MacLeod. These charges were eventually dropped.[97]

A source in the Halifax gay community wondered why the police stopped looking for the second suspect: 'I've known Bernie a long time. I don't believe Bernie did it all by himself. The murder was supposed to take place downstairs, but how could he have dragged that body all the way upstairs and put it in the bathtub? He's only a little guy – 5'5" with a small frame. Someone else was involved.'[98]

The Power of Suggestion

In the following two homicides, there were suggestions that police actually invented homosexual advance theories and planted them in the heads of murder suspects. For example, in 1993, Cameron Friesen and his best friend Richard Gerlitz, both in their early twenties, went on a three-day drinking binge in Calgary. Friesen went to the garage and got an air-powered nail gun and pumped twenty-three nails into his friend's head.[99] When Friesen was questioned, police suggested that perhaps the victim had made a pass at him. 'Friesen denied the suggestion and "was, in fact, laughing" when detectives offered it as a possible provocation.'[100]

By the time the trial came around, however, Friesen's lawyer and psychologist were portraying him as the victim of a rape that 'unleashed the uncontrollable rage he harbored.'[101] The victim's family vehemently denied that the victim was gay; Gerlitz's aunt said he had had many girlfriends and 'always had a photo of a pretty girl in his wallet.'[102] At trial, the Crown said: 'And every time a nail went into him there was the same sound, kathunk, kathunk, kathunk ... It felt good to you at the time, didn't it?'[103] Friesen was convicted of first-degree murder, ineligible to apply for parole for twenty-five years. 'Emotions were so charged in Courtroom 504 that some of the jurors wept as they walked past Gerlitz's weeping family members.'[104]

Police in Charlottetown used a similar tactic. According to one source, Gary Gormley had a reputation for rolling gay men. In 1995, he went to the house of Clifford McIver, who frequented cruising areas and had a penchant for rough trade.[105] Gormley said he went to see McIver to buy drugs; McIver was found beaten and strangled with a telephone cord. Gormley claimed that McIver opened his bathrobe 'and said what are you going to do for me ... What do you think happened? I lost it.'[106] Gormley stole bank cards, pills, and the dead man's car, and arrived at his friend's place in a panic. His friend explained Gormley's actions to police: 'Gary's not gay ... he's not a fag. He took offence.'[107]

On the way to his sentencing hearing, Gormley escaped from the prison van. A week later he was brought back to court and sentenced to life for second-degree murder, with no possibility of parole for twelve years.[108] He apologized to the victim's family for their loss, but insisted he was not guilty.[109] On appeal, the videotape of the police interview was played: 'The police seen on the tape tell Gormley that if he says nothing, rumour will spread that he was a homosexual and was at the victim's home because they were 'fruiting buddies.' Hornby said the officers hear that Gormley strongly denies being homosexual and they encourage him to confess to beating McIvor as a sort of manly response to being propositioned.'[110]

'Officers Quinn and MacQuarrie encouraged Gormley to come clean. Otherwise, his girlfriend and all her workmates would think he was gay. 'She's got to listen to everybody else at Zeller's coffee break saying "I didn't know that guy was a fruit,"' MacQuarrie said.[111]

'Above and Beyond': When Police Go That Extra Mile

While I was conducting this research, the negative police incidents invariably prevailed. However, I also found examples of police going undercover to catch gay-bashers – sometimes at great personal risk. These types of operations, although which admittedly are not very common, expose police to the dangers faced by some gay men on a daily basis. Unfortunately, we hear few stories like this. We hear more about police mounting undercover operations that target gay men themselves, instead of the criminals that prey on them.

In 1990, an officer overheard four teenagers planning to 'roll some gays' on a Calgary stroll. The officer drove to a Calgary park and invited a young man into his car. After the youth began to negotiate for sex, he grabbed the officer's wallet, punched him, and ran. The officer suffered bruised ribs, but three teenagers were arrested. There is also a report of Winnipeg officers working undercover to detect gay-bashers.[112]

Police have even gone into prison to catch gay-bashers. Rodney Glode, twenty-five, was described as a 'one-man wrecking crew in the homosexual community.' In 1990, he went on a rampage, terrorizing seven men over a four-week period that culminated in the death of Michael Boley, fifty-six. His first victim, who had invited Glode home for drinks, was struck on the head, bound and gagged, then hospitalized for six weeks with serious head injuries. In the following five robberies, 'the victims agreed to having their hands tied and then found themselves being gagged and securely bound hand and foot.' Boley, his final victim, died of asphyxiation after Glode gagged him over both nose and mouth.

A day after the murder, Glode was arrested for failing to pay a taxi fare. Eventually, he was linked to the murder. In prison, he told an undercover officer that his 'beef' was having 'robbed a faggot and he died. It was my luck he had a bad heart.' He bragged about his success in picking up homosexuals: 'I guess I've got a pretty face the faggots like.'[113] The judge called him 'an extremely dangerous 25-year-old man' and gave him a life sentence, with no possibility of parole for seventeen years.[114]

Police Hate Crime Reporting, Data Collection, and Statistics

This section demonstrates how vague and arbitrary Canadian police hate-crime policies and statistics can be. In the United States, Balboni and McDevitt surveyed 705 law enforcement officers and concluded that only one-third of them were working in departments with official hate-crime policies. The authors found that two key factors encouraged officers to implement these policies: 'overt departmental influences,' and adherence to the philosophy that investigating and reporting hate crimes was the 'right thing to do.'[115]

Haider surveyed 152 local police chiefs in the United States to determine what hate crime policies, if any, were being implemented. He found that success depended on whether the state had hate crime policies in place, and whether individual police leaders and the public were lobbying for this type of reporting.[116] Jenness and Grattet quote a 1999 report from the U.S. Department of Justice stating that 40 per cent of American cities with more than half a million people have police departments with bias crime units employing full-time staff.[117] Bell observed the inner workings of one of these big-city bias crime units.[118]

Stanko offers an in-depth analysis of police hate-crime investigation and reporting in the United Kingdom. Every month, London's Metropolitan Police Service (MPS) records more than nine thousand incidents of hate crime, defined as 'crime where the perpetrator's prejudice against any identifiable group of people is a factor in determining who is victimised.' The three main groups of hate crime that have emerged are 'domestic, racist and homophobic incidents.'[119]

So how do MPS officers determine which incidents should be counted as hate crimes? Some officers use straightforward evidence, like racial or homophobic epithets. Other officers may check the hate crime box simply '*because* the victim is black, gay or otherwise socially vulnerable.' Although all three targeted groups are technically included in the definition of hate crime, the MPS makes 'distinctions between hate crime and domestic violence,' which is 'not defined as a hate crime against women.' For example, two handbooks have been published: one addresses hate crimes, the other domestic violence.[120] The author recommends reconceptualizing these broad definitions of hate crime as *targeted violence,* which 'allows for a more complex commentary about where the borders of "other" lie.'[121] She envisions that this more 'nuanced approach' would require victim statements and evidence of 'the special vulnerability of the victim' as well as an analysis of how police constructed the incident.

According to Stanko, 'many of those who experience "hate" violence do so at the hands of neighbours, clients, and co-workers – those who live in close quarters with the "objects/recipients" of their prejudice.' Of all the racist and homophobic incidents reported by MPS, 'by far the top category of assailant reported by victims of race and homophobic violence is that of neighbour, followed by business associates and other acquaintances or relatives.' The image of the violent stranger 'obscures our ability to understand the ordinariness of hate crime.'[122] She argues that many of the MPS hate crimes actually involve 'people who are "already" known to one another.'[123]

Tracking Hate Crimes Nationally and Consistently

Some Canadian police departments document hate crime based on sexual orientation. However, Faulkner notes that 'this data is limited because there is no nationally recognized definition of hate crime and not all police forces collect such data.'[124] Roberts advocates a uniform definition that would include both members and 'perceived' members of the group being targeted. Jeffery feels that crimes partially motivated by hate must be included: 'The definition should be conceptual and should avoid limiting its scope to closed categories of victim characteristics.'[125] One suggested definition was: 'Behaviours which flow from or give rise to hatred and which target persons by reason of their real or perceived membership in an identifiable group or which target a group as a whole.'[126]

Roberts defines hate crimes as 'crimes in which the offender is motivated by a characteristic of the victim that identifies the victim as a member of a group towards which the offender feels some animosity.'[127]

Consistency of reporting is also a key issue. Researchers in Baltimore County discovered that hate crime statistics quadrupled between 1987 and 1989. However, despite the addition of sexual orientation as a hate crime category, and a growing number and proportion of Asian and Hispanic residents in Baltimore, these groups' numbers were not noticeably reflected in the burgeoning statistics.[128]

Similarly, Roberts compared the number of hate crimes reported in 1993 in Ottawa (176) to the number reported in Toronto (155). Since

Toronto had approximately triple Ottawa's population at the time, it would appear that Ottawa was using a different threshold 'to define a hate crime ... *It is clear then, that a standard definition of hate crime as well as uniform criteria for application need to be developed.*'[129]

At present, Canada's Uniform Reporting System cannot rise to this challenge because it does not keep track of data related to offender motivation.[130] New legislation could solve this conundrum. Roberts points out that in 1993, the Hate Crime Statistics Act received first reading in Parliament. Bill C-455 'would have required federal, provincial and municipal agencies to record the 'number of incidents investigated by a police force in that year that are classified as bias incidents by that force and that identify which identifiable group was the target of bias in each such incident.'

However, this bill, like many private member's bills, 'did not get very far in the Parliamentary review process.'[131] In contrast, in the United States, the Hate Crimes Statistics Act of 1990 mandated the FBI 'to collect and analyse the statistics from local and state-level law enforcement agencies.'[132] At least twenty-four states have adopted laws mandating the collection of hate crime statistics:[133] In one study, more police departments were found to report hate crimes in states where hate crime reporting was mandatory. Conversely, states that did not require police departments to report hate crimes had much lower compliance rates.[134]

Roberts sees many advantages to resuscitating Canada's Hate Crimes Statistics Act. Federal legislation would make sure all police services were committed to a uniform definition, and thus make 'it more likely to produce uniform data.' The collection of these statistics by a federal agency would 'serve to sensitize the community in general to the importance of the issue.'[135]

Canadian Federal Anti-Hate Initiatives

There have been three federally sponsored gatherings on hate and bias activity. An initial meeting in 1997 brought together several experts. In early 2000, the Hate and Bias Activity Roundtable followed up by inviting thirty-seven participants – from police agencies, government departments, and non-governmental organizations – to create an anti-hate action plan, consisting of five specific areas: research and data collection;[136] legislation;[137] enforcement;[138] 'new media'; and public education and community action.[139]

Later that year, an even larger group came together and broke into working groups devoted to the five main areas. The legislation group identified the need to enumerate various hate/bias legislation provisions; analyze the effectiveness of sentencing enhancement provisions; and evaluate the feasibility of a hate crime statistics act.[140] The new-media working group wanted to develop an all-inclusive definition of hate/bias activity; educate Internet providers about on-line hate; integrate Internet issues into national anti-hate campaigns; and use the Internet as a tool 'for receiving, processing, verifying, evaluating and acting upon complaints regarding content on the Internet.'[141]

The public education/community working group advocated the development of anti-hate curricula and teacher training; the creation of an anti-hate youth awareness week; support for community-based youth organizations; and the inclusion of youth in future hate-related discussions: 'Celebrities and sport stars should be asked to speak out against racism and hate.'[142]

The law enforcement group lamented the lack of hate crime training for Crown prosecutors and the delays by provincial justice departments in giving their assent to prosecute – assent that is required before certain hate-related charges can be laid. The 'lack of coordination and cooperation between and within provinces in sharing' hate-related data was also noted, as well as the tendency for police to gather intelligence data on hate groups, 'even though individual random acts of hate are a much larger problem.'[143]

The research and data collection group was concerned about the absence of a standard definition of hate crime – and the chasm between the community's definition and that of most police. The group called on the Canadian Association of Chiefs of Police (CACP) to bring their hate crime definition into line with the 'in whole or in part' definition used by other large urban departments in Canada and by the OPP.[144]

In 1999, the Canadian Centre for Justice Statistics (CCJS) embarked on a four-year project to study hate crime in Canada. The first phase culminated in the release of a preliminary report that provided historical background and reviewed data collection strategies in the United States and Britain, the data collection efforts of community agencies in Canada, and the hate crime policies of thirty-four police departments.[145]

The CCJS also analyzed the 1999 General Social Survey,[146] which randomly sampled crime patterns in 26,000 households across Canada. One-quarter of those interviewed said they had been victims of a crime; 4 per cent of those interviewed said they had been victims of a hate crime.

Over 40 per cent of the hate crime victims interviewed said they believed they had been targeted because of their race or ethnicity. Thirty-seven per cent of hate crime victims chose the next category, 'other' – which included age, sexual orientation, religion, language, and disability.[147]

However, Faulkner dismissed these findings, because homophobic violence was 'placed in an "other" category and marginalized, making the data virtually meaningless.' She felt that thousands of tax dollars would have been more effective had they been diverted toward underfunded victim-assistance programs.[148]

The RCMP and Hate Crime Policy

There is no particular office or committee that oversees queer-related issues at the RCMP. One officer told me: 'The victim's sexual orientation is none of our business. We'll get in trouble if we ask the victim's sexual orientation because of the human rights code.' When I explained that there were many queer victims who were willing to tell the police their sexual orientation, he became agitated and ended the conversation.

With more persistence, I reached a younger, more politically correct officer, who was responsible for crime prevention programs, policy development, and victims' issues. That officer told me: 'Are we actively studying anti-gay violence or monitoring it? Not to my knowledge. Why not? A good question. There isn't a real movement to do this.' Then he echoed the first officer: because of human rights legislation, the RCMP was 'not allowed' to track crimes affecting minorities. When I asked why the RCMP was 'allowed' to track crimes affecting aboriginals, he explained that the RCMP had an agreement with the Assembly of First Nations. He speculated that a national gay and lesbian organization could be mandated to capture queer-bashing data.[149]

I also learned about the Operational Statistics Reporting (OSR) System. An RCMP officer's paperwork is two-tiered. The officer must first provide all the details of the offence. The second and more time-consuming part involves filling in codes that track more detailed trends. Of the five hundred internal codes, only one, Code DK29, refers to hate crimes – directed towards any one of several marginalized groups. 'Filling in the internal codes is not supposed to be optional,' explained the manager. In reality, many hate crimes are simply not captured through this cumbersome process. Table 6.3 shows the only statistics that exist in the RCMP database for all hate crimes against all target groups.

Thus, 1998 was the year the RCMP registered the most hate crimes

Table 6.3
Number of hate crimes in Canada according to RCMP database

Year	Number of crimes
1995	7
1996	28
1997	31
1998	75
1999	67
2000	37[a]
2001	121[b]
2002	95
2003	90
2004 (until 18/06)	60[c]

Sources: [a]Letter from RCMP National Information Services Manager – OSR, 2 Feb. 2001; [b]Letter from RCMP National Information Services Manager – OSR, 2 Dec. 2002; [c]Interview with RCMP officer, 18 June 2004.

across Canada – a total of seventy-five. Meanwhile, Toronto recorded ninety-two over a six-month period in 1998, using the 'in whole or in part' definition. The RCMP has chosen to take a narrow approach to hate crimes. In the past, if a driver got out of his car, yelled 'faggot,' and beat up the other driver, it would be recorded as a traffic incident, since hate was not the 'sole' motivating factor. In the 1990s, the OPP and police forces in Edmonton, Calgary, Winnipeg, Hamilton, Ottawa, Toronto, and Vancouver came to the realize the difficulties of gathering evidence of crimes 'solely' motivated by hate. These forces adjusted their policies to take into account crimes motivated 'in whole or in part' by hatred or bias.

However, in 1998, the Canadian Association of Chiefs of Police (CACP) turned back the clock by bucking this trend and eliminating the 'in part' provision of their hate crime definition, thereby making hate motivation much harder to prove in court.[150] Whenever I have challenged the RCMP on this point, they have responded defensively and tautologically: this is the 'official' definition, they 'must' use it, and they are morally justified in doing so. (However, even though this narrow and outdated hate-crime definition has been 'officially' accepted by the CACP, in reality, the RCMP is the only large police force in Canada that uses it.)

Hate crime officers in Vancouver, Toronto and Ottawa have developed an expertise in the area of homophobic violence through their constant exposure to the problem. The RCMP does not appear to have experts in this area. Still, any national hate-crime strategy will have to take the RCMP into account, since crimes in their jurisdiction account for more than one-quarter of Canada's annual crime statistics.

The Quebec Provincial Police (QPP) and the Ontario Provincial Police (OPP)

The QPP also does not have a hate crimes unit and does not keep track of hate crimes.[151] Spokespeople assured me that queer-bashing cases are pursued on an 'ongoing basis,' but could offer no examples from their jurisdiction. When pressed, three QPP spokespeople claimed there was no real problem because their jurisdiction falls outside Montreal's large queer community. I spoke to a QPP officer who in the mid-1990s coordinated a gay and lesbian liaison committee (which has since been disbanded): 'We've taken a step back because it's not a priority from the community point of view.'[152] By 2003, the focus had changed slightly. The QPP set up an anti-terrorism unit with five mandates; one included the responsibility to investigate hate crimes. In 2004, I asked the unit's inspector if he knew of any hate crimes against the queer community. He said he didn't: 'This is relatively new for us.'[153]

Queer culture in Ontario has changed dramatically in the past decade: today, smaller cities have their own queer bars and thriving communities. This has led to higher visibility – and more reports of victimization. The OPP has a hate crimes unit with three officers on staff. The coordinator explained that their role is not to investigate specific hate-crimes, but to ensure that proper hate-crimes procedures are being followed. When I asked him how many queer-bashing cases in Ontario he had heard of, he said, 'zero,' explaining that 'we go by the Criminal Code definition of crimes.' In other words, since hate-motivated assault is not listed in the Criminal Code, they have no record of it – even though large urban departments across Canada routinely keep track of these offences.[154]

The Crown cannot recommend enhanced sentencing without police evidence demonstrating that the crime was motivated by hate. This would appear to be impossible if the OPP's hate crimes unit has not recorded a single case of homophobic violence. In a later interview, the coordinator said his unit has no idea how many hate crimes – of any kind – have occurred in their jurisdiction because they do not collect statistics for *any* group, gay or otherwise. He reiterated that not one case of homophobic violence had ever come to his attention.[155] In 2002, the new coordinator also said he had no hate crime statistics for any group in

Ontario. He mentioned that he had heard of some anti-gay crimes in the Orillia area that year, but he had no details.[156] In 2004, he reiterated that the OPP's hate crimes unit still does not track cases of homophobic violence. Their new system tracks hate propaganda and promotion of hate, but this does not capture actual cases of homophobic assault. He explained that this is because the unit is 'purely intelligence-based.' This police terminology means that they focus on organized hate activity – not on random acts of hate-motivated violence.[157]

Cooperation between the RCMP, British Columbia, and Vancouver Police

British Columbia is the first province to develop a provincewide, universal definition of hate crimes, a provincewide enforcement policy, a provincial toll-free information line, and a provincewide database 'to track details of hate crimes across BC.' In 1996, under the provincial NDP government, an RCMP officer and an officer from the Vancouver Police Department (VPD) were brought together under the auspices of the B.C. Attorney General to coordinate the provincial Hate Crimes Unit.[158] The mandate of the unit is to:

- attain consistency in police investigation and reporting,
- coordinate enforcement,
- develop a data-tracking system,
- strengthen linkages with provincial, federal, and international agencies,
- respond to victim needs,
- identify required legislative changes, and
- provide training for police and other personnel.

Out of 7,000 police officers in the province, at least 1,200 had been trained to investigate hate crimes by 1999.[159] Investigating officers are expected take the following issues into account: the suspect's statement and comments; the use of symbols or gestures associated with hate; the timing of the event (for example, a specific holiday); the perception of the victim or the victim's community; the perception of witnesses; the location of the crime; and the suspect's past involvement in similar crimes.[160]

There are also new guidelines for prosecutors: 'The Crown is supposed to oppose release and isn't supposed to go to alternative measures without express permission of the victim. The Crown must put the accused before court, and isn't supposed to plea-bargain,' one of the unit coordinators said. Unfortunately, not all prosecutors have received training on these new guidelines, which means that many hate crimes are still being prosecuted the old way. 'We find we're having to motivate the Crown to implement the new policies.'[161]

The unit's ability to cooperate with the RCMP in rural B.C. appears to refute the old-school stance that the RCMP is 'not allowed' to track queer-bashing cases because they'll 'get in trouble' by asking the victim's sexual orientation. The RCMP detachment in Mission contacted the unit after a man using homophobic language uttered a threat.[162] Unfortunately, RCMP budget cuts have affected the unit's capacity to investigate outside Greater Vancouver.[163] In 2004, VPD's dedicated hate-crimes officer explained that owing to a limited budget, he was unable to analyze the unit's hate crime statistics dating back from 2004. However, he said a full report was due out later in the year.[164]

Urban Police Departments: The Problem of Inconsistency

Police initiatives across the country vis-à-vis the queer community have ranged from proactive outreach to reactive violence and 'old-style' policing strategies. Even within a given police department, it is impossible to generalize. A program that received a lot of media coverage one year could be dead the next. The negative or stupid comments of one officer could be at complete variance with the insightful, lucid perspective of a colleague.

- Many police departments claim that they 'keep track' of hate crimes, but when you ask them a specific question like, 'How many lesbians were assaulted last year?' they are unable to reply.
- Other departments say they don't have a 'separate category' for hate crimes, but they 'keep track' on a 'case-by-case' basis. But when you ask them to describe certain gay-bashing cases over the past five years (even when they've been reported on by the local media), again they are silent.
- Some departments sent me statistics for 'hate crimes' without explaining how many involved queer victims.
- Others sent me 'sexual orientation' statistics, but these did not distinguish between hate-motivated assaults, domestic assaults, and less serious offences such as mischief or vandalism.

It is precisely this lack of uniformity that has been criticized by experts.[165] But it should be remembered that even when police cannot furnish statistics, it doesn't mean they haven't done a good job investigating homophobic violence. The inability of many police departments to access, manage, and disseminate this information does not make them 'homophobic'; it just means they have not been able to keep up with community demands for increasingly complex data. Generating these statistics requires specially trained analysts and community relations officers. Many police departments are either unable or unwilling to hire these people.

In my view, police departments should adopt the approach of the Toronto Police Service, which posts its hate crime statistics on its website, broken down into specific, easy-to-understand categories. Instead of placing the onus on researchers to repeatedly cajole investigating officers – who are understandably taken up with more urgent duties – police departments should make this data available on a regular basis to the public. Table 6.4 shows how hard it is to make sense of many police statistics.

Hate Grips a Small Town

A terrifying home invasion in the South Okanagan town of Osoyoos illustrates the inability of small-town police detachments to recognize queer-bashing, let alone deal with it. In the worst parody of small-town justice, cops fumbled and a judge let three men walk. The incident is not reflected on any of the previous charts, since B.C.'s hate crime data from outside Vancouver only began to be recorded in 1996.

On 7 October 1995, a gay couple – Randall Lampreau and Brian Coutts – went to a bar with their straight friend Ian and were taunted by a rough crowd sitting at the next table. The group included a tall blonde, according to pub staff. The men said 'faggots should be killed' and 'anyone sitting at the table must be a homo lover.' Ian reacted, driving an elbow into the blonde's nose, and a scuffle ensued.[166] Afterwards, Ian attempted to apologize, but the others were enraged and 'warned that things were not over.'[167]

Later that night, it was Brian and Randall who suffered the fallout. The young, struggling couple were living in a tiny, one-bedroom cabin with no telephone. At two a.m., after they were asleep, three men smashed their way through the cabin door with a tire iron. The same tall blonde from the bar was there in the cabin, along with two men of Asian descent. The

Table 6.4

Statistics relating to homophobic violence: urban police services

	Victoria	Vancouver	Calgary
1994		26 gay-bashing incidents from August 1992 to February 1994 (Janet Smith, 'Police Report Progress in Fight Against Gay Bashing,' *Westender*, 10 Feb. 1994, 2)	
1995		13 assaults, 3 threats based on sexual orientation (Doug Ward, 'Attackers Were Targeting Gays, Park Board Chair Says,' *Vancouver Sun*, 11 Dec. 1996, A1)	
1996		25 offences based on sexual orientation including 16 assaults (Tom Yeung, 'Victoria Forms "Hate Crime Unit,"' *Xtra West*, 6 Feb. 1997, 7)	8 assaults related to sexual orientation, 1 mischief, 1 threat and 3 robbery/roll jobs (Calgary Police Service, 'Year End Summary – 1997 to September 2000,' hate/bias crime statistics, sent 23 Oct. 2000)
1997		59 offences based on sexual orientation: 23 assaults, 5 assaults with a weapon, 1 sexual assault, 9 threats of violence, 3 domestic assaults (Tom Yeung, 'Tracking the Bashers,' *Xtra West*, 2 Oct. 1997, 9)	2 assaults related to sexual orientation, 1 break and enter, 2 harassment, 4 mischief, 1 threat and 1 robbery/roll job (Ibid.)
1998		34 offences based on sexual orientation: 23 level 1 and 2 assaults, 1 robbery, involving 20 male victims, 2 female victims and 2 transgendered victims (Letter from head of B.C. Hate Crimes Unit, 23 Sept. 1999)	18 assaults related to sexual orientation, 2 break and enters, 2 thefts, 1 robbery/roll job and 3 threats (Calgary Police Service, 'Year End Summary – 1997 to September 2000,' hate/bias crime statistics, sent 14 Feb. 2001)
1999	0 hate crimes (Interview with Victoria Police Department spokesman, 28 April 1999)	33 offences involving sexual orientation (Letter from Hate Crime Community Coordinator, British Columbia Attorney General, 30 Nov. 2000)	10 assaults related to sexual orientation, 1 harassment, 5 mischief, 1 threat and 1 theft (Ibid.)
2000	3 hate crimes (Letter from Victoria Police Department spokesman, 31 Oct. 2000)		4 assaults related to sexual orientation, 1 break and enter, 1 robbery, 1 threat (Calgary Police Service, 'Year End Summary 2001, hate/bias crime statistics,' sent 27 Nov. 2002)
2001			13 crimes related to sexual orientation (Calgary Police Service, 'Year to Date Stats 2002,' hate/bias crime statistics, sent 27 Nov. 2002)
2002	4 hate crimes since June 2001 (Interview with Victoria Police Department spokesman, 2 Dec. 2002)		15 crimes related to sexual orientation, including 8 assaults, 5 mischief, 1 robbery and 1 threat (Calgary Police Service, 'Year End 2003,' hate/bias statistics, sent 14 June 2004)
2003			

Table 6.4 (*Continued*)

	Edmonton	Winnipeg	London
1994	5 hate crimes (Edmonton Police Service, 'City of Edmonton: Bias Crimes Four-Year Statistics, 1994–1997,' statistics from EPS Annual Statistical Reports)	4 gay bashings (Letter from Hate Crimes Coordinator, Winnipeg Police Service, 24 Oct. 2000)	
1995	6 hate crimes (Ibid.)	6 gay bashings (Ibid.)	
1996	5 hate crimes (Ibid.)	3 assaults in the gay community (Ibid.)	
1997	7 hate crimes (Ibid.)	5 assaults in the gay community (Ibid.)	2 non-violent homophobic crimes (Letter from London former hate crimes officer, 31 Aug. 1999)
1998		3 assaults, 2 threats and 2 robbery/mugging incidents in the gay community (Ibid.)	1 non-violent homophobic crime (Interview with London former hate crimes officer, 10 May 1999)
1999	3 hate/bias crimes (Letter from Edmonton Police Service, 12 Dec. 2002)	7 assaults in the gay community and 1 charge of arson (Ibid.)	
2000	5 hate/bias crimes (Ibid.)	1 property damage incident, 3 incidents of uttering threats, and three assaults (Interview with Hate Crimes Coordinator, Winnipeg Police Service, 25 Nov. 2002)	2 hate crimes involving homosexuals: 1 threat and 1 assault (Letter from London former hate crimes officer, 23 Nov. 2000)
2001	11 hate/bias crimes (Ibid.)	1 gay man assaulted; 1 attempted robbery of a gay man, and 2 incidents of 'hate correspondence (Ibid.)	39 hate crimes against all groups (Letter from London Police Service, 15 June 2004)
2002	4 hate/bias crimes (Ibid.)	8 crimes against the GLBT community: 1 property damage, 2 assaults, 1 assault with a weapon and 4 hate correspondence. (Interview with diversity coordinator, Winnipeg Police Service, 16 June 2004)	45 hate crimes against all groups
2003	21 incidents against the GLBT community, including 7 criminal code offences.	3 crimes against the GLBT community: 1 property damage, 1 threat, 1 hate correspondence. (Ibid.)	40 hate crimes against all groups (Ibid.) (Interview with Edmonton hate crimes officer, 3 Nov. 2004)

Table 6.4 (*Continued*)

	Hamilton	Ottawa	Toronto
1994		1993 and 1994 crimes against gay, 43; lesbians, 3 (Ottawa-Carleton Regional Police Hate Crime Section 'Case Summary,' summary of hate crimes from 1 Jan. 1993 to 20 Nov. 1998)	11 crimes based on sexual orientation (Metropolitan Toronto Police Service, 'Annual Hate Motivated Crimes 1996,' Statistical Report, 2–7)
1995		crimes against gays, 24; lesbians, 4; bisexuals, 3; transgender, 2 (Ibid.)	22 crimes based on sexual orientation (Ibid.)
1996	hate crimes against 4 gay men, 1 lesbian, 1 trans-gender (Hamilton-Wentworth Regional Police, 'Hate-Bias Incidents 1996')	crimes against gays, 33; lesbians, 18; bisexuals, 7; transgender, 7 (Ibid.)	14 homophobic assaults (including 2 lesbian victims) and 2 threats (Ibid.)
1997	hate crimes against 6 gay men, 2 lesbians (Hamilton-Wentworth Regional Police, 'Hate/Bias Incidents 1997')	crimes against gays, 42; lesbians, 12; transgender, 1 (Ibid.)	9 assaults against gay men, 1 against lesbian (Metropolitan Toronto Police Service, 'Intelligence Services Hate Crime Report,' 1998, 4–8)
1998	sexual orientation: 5 hate crimes / 4 bias (Jane Mulkewich, 'History: Violence against the Gay/Lesbian/ Transgendered Community,' report prepared by the Community Relations Coordinator, Hamilton-Wentworth Regional Police, 28 May 1999)	crimes against gays, 38; lesbians, 7; bisexuals, 1; transgender, 4 (Ibid.)	6 homophobic crimes (Eleanor Brown 'Queer Fear,' *Globe and Mail*, 24 Oct. 1998, D1)
1999		cases with a sexual orientation bias: 1 hate mail/ propaganda; 3 graffiti; 3 intimidation/ threats; 11 harassment/stalking; 5 assaults (level 1) (Ottawa-Carleton Regional Police Hate Crime Section, 'Case Summary,' Summary of hate crimes from 1 Jan. 1999 to 30 Sept. 2000)	44 crimes motivated by sexual orientation (Heather Ross 'Homos Are Hot Targets,' *Xtra!*, 23 March 2000)

Table 6.4 (*Concluded*)

	Hamilton	Ottawa	Toronto
2000		cases with a sexual orientation bias: 2 hate mail/propaganda, 3 intimidation/threats, 2 assaults (Ibid.)	Crimes against gay men: 15 assaults, 9 threats, 2 criminal harassment, 3 robbery; lesbians: 2 assaults, 1 criminal harassment, 1 theft, 1 threat, 2 assaults against transgendered. (Telephone report from police officer in Toronto's Hate Crimes Unit, 13 Oct. 2000)
2001		17 anti-gay, 1 anti-lesbian, 1 anti-heterosexual, 1 anti-bisexual, 1 anti-transgender acts	24 crimes related to sexual orientation ('Hate Crimes' *Xtra!*, 3 April 2003 13)
2002		9 anti-gay, 2 anti-lesbian acts	4 assaults against gay men, 1 assault against a lesbian, 5 threats against gay men. (Toronto Police Service '2002 Hate Bias Crime Statistical Report' (2003).)
2003		11 anti-gay, 1 anti-lesbian, 1 anti-transgender act	14 crimes related to sexual orientation: 5 assaults, 1 criminal harassment, 6 mischief, 2 robberies (Ibid.)
2004		6 anti-gay, 2 anti-lesbian, 2 anti-transgender acts	(Telephone report from police officer in Ottawa's Hate Crimes Section, 10 Jan. 2005).

cabin was dark: the couple didn't even have time to turn on the lights. The two Asian men grabbed Randall's arms, then the blond man smashed Randall over the head with a metal bar, yelling, 'I'm going to kill you, you fucking faggot!' When Brian tried to defend him, he was knocked on the head with the bar.

In desperation, Randall grabbed a large pepper mill from the counter – the type used in fancy restaurants – and smashed one of the Asian men on the head with it. Then he grabbed a bread knife and said: 'Get the fuck out of my house!' The attackers ran out screaming Randall's name and declaring: 'You're fuckin' dead. We're going to kill you, this is not over – we will be back.' Then the trio picked up several empty bottles and a chunk of concrete and hurled them inside, breaking every window in the cabin as the terrified couple dove for cover.[168]

Once the assailants were gone, Randall wrapped a towel around his bleeding head. They called on their neighbours for help, but no one would respond. The couple drove a few blocks to Ian's house, where they called the police and the ambulance. Even though the blood spattered throughout the cabin would probably have incriminated the assailants, the police did not guard the crime scene, which meant that the site became 'contaminated.' Randall was treated for a minor concussion and then released. The next morning they returned to the cabin, which was a complete mess.[169] Later, the couple listed the damage to their personal possessions for victims' compensation: '1 large bath towel (burgundy) soiled with blood ... 1 pair kitchen curtains, soiled with blood and torn.' Bloodied items also included a tea towel, jacket, rug, shorts, socks, tie, bathrobes, jeans, and T-shirts.[170]

Across the street from the laundromat, the couple was horrified to discover one of the Asian men who had attacked them the previous night. Since there were only a handful of Asians in Osoyoos, he wasn't hard to identify. He was sitting outside his parents' Asian restaurant, where he worked, nursing the cut on his head where Randall had whacked him with the pepper mill. The couple had to go back to the police and beg them to arrest the men.[171] All three men had criminal records: one was on probation for armed robbery, one had been convicted of aggravated assault, and one had been convicted for assault with a weapon.[172]

The police couldn't understand why the couple kept claiming they had been gay-bashed. Brian said bitterly: 'The cops were calling it a break and enter the first day ... The police didn't go after the case like an aggravated assault ... They didn't take pictures of us.'[173] At the trial it was noted that 'blood-stained objects and clothing were not analyzed and no line-up was conducted.'[174] Brian recalled: 'Our Crown attorney was homophobic so we got rid of him ... He said he couldn't understand why we wouldn't call it a break and enter.'[175]

In court, the defence lawyer cross-examined Brian: 'You pushed him. I'm going to suggest to you that any conflict between the two of you was a result of you pushing him and attacking him and he did not, in fact, attack you, did he?' The defence lawyer also pounced on another detail: shortly after the attack, Brian had written in his statement that the non-Asian assailant was tall, with blond hair and blue eyes. It turned out that he was tall and blond, but didn't have blue eyes. In the end, the judge dismissed the charges against the men, citing insufficient evidence.[176]

On a balance of probabilities, the victims felt they might get something for their pain and suffering at a civil trial. They had no money, but contacted a gay lawyer in Vancouver, who claimed he was sympathetic to their plight and who agreed to take the case on a contingency basis. But the lawyer dropped out of contact, missed a deadline for filing the writ, then tried dropping their case. Brian had to take out a bank loan to hire a second lawyer to threaten the first one with a lawsuit for breach of contract: 'Meanwhile, the assailants are driving a $30,000 car and living in a half-million dollar home.'

Brian was diagnosed with neurological damage resulting from the blow to his head and stated that he was 'unable to sleep at night ... suffering from recurring dreams ... depression ... loss of home and having to relocate ... fears of returning home.' Randall recalled: 'I had stitches ... No cash settlement through WCB. I didn't get anything for losing my job. I lost four months of wages, I had to move, it took a month to fix the windows and doors, but we still had to pay the rent. My hip still bothers me ... Severe headaches for six months. I was popping Tylenol 3 like it was candy. I got $300 for work-related injuries from WCB, and $950 for criminal injuries.'[177]

They relocated to a larger centre, where they have organized a gay and lesbian social group. They are embittered, not just by their experience, but by the indifference of B.C.'s large and vocal queer community. They pleaded for financial, legal, and moral support, but to no avail. Five years after the attack, a civil court finally awarded them approximately $40,000 each plus legal costs.[178]

If anything, this crime bolsters the case for a national watchdog organization that would monitor homophobic violence, publicize cases of police incompetence, and offer legal, financial, and emotional support to victims battling not just queer-bashers but an indifferent criminal justice system. It is sad to think that queer victims may have to turn to private prosecutions, litigation, and class action lawsuits to force police agencies and prosecutors to protect us from this violence.

On the plus side, if a similar attack were to occur again in the B.C. Interior, it would come to the attention of a provincewide unit rather than a small RCMP detachment. If other provinces followed B.C.'s lead, queer victims in small towns and rural areas across Canada would be much better served.

Summary

There has been a history of tension and mistrust between police and the queer community in Canada. Police engage in homophobic behaviour by discriminating against their queer colleagues and by adhering to traditional notions about what constitutes a 'legitimate' hate crime. Since 1990, Canadian police have arrested hundreds of men and some women for being found in locations associated with same-sex sexual activity: public toilets, bathhouses, parks, and gay nightclubs. Police sometimes entrap men and then humiliate them by releasing their names to the press; by not following through on the charges, police engage in a very effective form of social control. My research also yielded fourteen reports of homophobic violence by police officers. Although officers from some police forces have beaten homosexuals, there are indications that their punishment was relatively light. There is also an unconfirmed report that the Montreal police have settled out of court with up to a dozen male gay-bashing victims.

Police data systems at present make it impossible to know how many hate crimes have been committed; the record-keeping systems surveyed in this book vary dramatically from one jurisdiction to another. The QPP has new responsibilities to investigate hate crime, but still no statistics; the OPP has a hate crime unit that does not investigate or keep track of homophobic violence. The RCMP uses an outdated system to define and classify hate crimes; its database captures only a fraction of these crimes, with no specific mention of homophobic violence. The RCMP has no dialogue with Canada's queer movement, although there is no reason why this could not be established. Despite recent cutbacks, B.C.'s Hate Crimes Unit demonstrates that it is possible for disparate police departments to coordinate provincewide strategies regarding investigation and data collection. An activist-oriented 'safety net' is needed to monitor cases when the justice system fails to protect queer-bashing victims.

CHAPTER 7

Urban Cowboys and Rural Rednecks: Community Resistance to Homophobic Violence

In 1998, a gay man in Burlington who was called 'fag' by a group of ten teenagers 'picked up a rock and threw it at one of the youths, hitting him squarely in the head.' Police took the man away in handcuffs, but he was later released. He told *Xtra* he wasn't sorry: 'We put up with it every day, and the laws are not working for us ... If the police aren't going to do anything about it, then gay people should take it into their own hands and deal out their own punishments.'[1]

As I demonstrated in the previous chapter, many queers are not happy with the way police treat them and investigate violence against their communities. In the United States, a queer gun club called the Pink Pistols had thirty-seven chapters as of 2003.[2] Although queer anti-violence activists in Canada aren't exactly taking the law into their own hands, they are becoming increasingly organized. Faulkner explains that while community responses to homophobic violence have existed in Toronto since the early 1990s, 'disorganized responses' are more the norm in the rest of country: 'While American lesbian and gay organizations have documented anti-gay/lesbian violence since the early eighties, Canadians have either not recognized the importance of documenting such attacks or have lacked the resources and funds to do so.'[3]

This chapter has three parts. First, I examine the approaches to homophobic violence in Canada's three largest urban areas. I place these community programs on a continuum: Montreal's activists have worked at arm's length from the police; Toronto's program is a 'mixed model'; Vancouver has tried both approaches. Then I examine programs in medium-sized cities like Ottawa and Calgary. Finally, I look at the challenges facing queers in small cities and small towns, as well as rural, remote, and northern regions.

Each part of Canada has its own strategy. In less populated areas, there are relatively few reports, so victims must seek support through existing Victim Services agencies and informal queer networks. Programs that address this violence are underfunded – they are limited in terms of the services they can provide, and furthermore, 'lack of funding for educational training means that experts are isolated in large urban centres.'[4] These programs require not only committed volunteers but also long-term core funding to pay office rent, salaries, and communication expenses such as for pagers, cell phones, and toll-free hotlines. Many initiatives create a big splash when first announced, but then become underfunded or underutilized and die a quiet, gradual death.

Faulkner describes anti-violence programs in New York and San Francisco. The programs in these cities have annual budgets of over $250,000 and several paid staff positions. In contrast, the 1998 budget of Toronto's 519 Anti-Violence Program totalled less than $35,000.[5] The New York group published profiles, licence plate numbers, and even photos of gay bashers in a local newspaper.[6] The National Coalition of Anti-Violence Projects (NCAVP) compares statistics from various queer organizations across the United States; 'there is no comparable organization in Canada.'[7]

Police have been dismissive of or indifferent to some of these community initiatives. Community leaders, with the best of intentions, campaign to 'take back the streets' and develop anonymous phoneline reporting systems. However, from a law enforcement perspective, the idea of volunteers donning pink berets and armbands to protect queer citizens from bashers is daunting. It's not simply a question of bad PR; police are concerned that without the proper training, volunteers may be placing themselves at risk. Police generally want *less* anonymous reporting, not more. Unless witnesses and victims are willing to identify themselves, the likelihood of conviction is almost zero.

The degree to which individual police departments engage with the community is another bone of contention. Stanko and Curry argue that in the same way that women are told to 'behave' to avoid male violence, police-queer liaison committees have, in effect, created a class of 'respectable' queer citizens who negotiate police standards of same-sex behaviour for the broader queer community. A dichotomy has developed between the 'responsible' queer citizen – who avoids walking in certain public areas or behaving 'inappropriately' – and the 'irresponsible' queer, who engages in public sex or who fails to conform in public settings.

Moreover, commitments to the community ring hollow. Stanko and Curry note that police 'promises' amount to a 'declaration of intent to support "true victims" of homophobic violence. More generally, the

Table 7.1
Location of queer-bashing incidents in Canada, by province

Province/territory	No. of cases	%
Yukon/NWT/Nunavut	2	.58
British Columbia	73	21.22
Alberta	24	6.98
Saskatchewan	13	3.78
Manitoba	20	5.81
Ontario	156	45.35
Quebec	29	8.43
New Brunswick	10	2.91
Nova Scotia	9	2.62
Prince Edward Island	0	0
Newfoundland	7	2.03
Not specified	1	.29
Total	344	100

Table 7.2
Location of queer-bashing incidents in Canada, by city

Location	No. of cases	%
Toronto/Mississauga	70	20.35
Greater Vancouver	57	16.57
Montreal/Longueil	25	7.27
London	24	6.98
Other parts of Canada	168	48.83
Total	344	100

police promise of sensitive treatment when someone comes forward to the police *after* he or she has been assaulted is what is meant by protection.' These authors believe that almost the only thing the police offer the queer community is advice: the '"responsible" queer must consider himself or herself to be perpetually at risk.'[8]

Table 7.1 shows the provinces in which the 344 queer-bashing incidents I analysed occurred. More than half the incidents occurred in Toronto, Vancouver, Montreal, and London (see table 7.2).

The Mixed Model: Toronto's Approach to Homophobic Violence

Toronto's 519 Church Street Community Centre's Anti-Violence Program (AVP) is Canada's leader in the delivery of services to queer victims; this advocacy model reaches out. Community workers accompany victims to court, organize self-defence classes, and do public education during Pride celebrations. According to a former coordinator, 'a person calls in, leaves a message, and we try to get as much information as we can about the incident.'[9] Workers encourage people to report incidents to the police and lobby police on the victim's behalf. AVP began collecting queer-bashing statistics in June 1990.[10] According to Roberts, between 1 January 1990 and 1 April 1995, 'Over 90 percent of the calls to the Toronto hotline were made by gay men ... Almost half (46 percent) of the incidents involved some form of physical assault ... Less than 10 percent were hate-motivated cases of vandalism or theft ... Of the 239 reports recorded by the hotline, only 104 were reported to the police. Of these charges were laid in 8 cases, and convictions recorded in only 2 cases.'[11]

Faulkner also compared police statistics to AVP's statistics. The police recorded only 59 homophobic incidents, compared to AVP's 410 reports of violence, originating from 589 people, more than 83 per cent of whom were male. These included:

- 294 bashings involved one victim
- 94 bashings involved two victims
- 16 bashings involved three victims
- 4 bashings involved 4 victims
- 2 bashings involved more than 4 victims[12]

AVP's former coordinator told me that she and her colleagues were so overworked they did not have time to clip newspaper reports of bashings, let alone do sophisticated data analysis. Statistics are important for small non-profits like AVP. These figures are added to grant proposals, which guarantee future funding. Developing publicity campaigns year in and year out – directed toward schools, hospitals, government agencies, law enforcement personnel, and community groups – is an extremely costly and time-consuming process. Without this outreach, the well of potential clients runs dry. When that happens, programs have their funding cut or eliminated. Discouraged volunteers, who feel they have nothing to do, stop showing up. It's a vicious circle.

Still, over the years, a wide range of intitatives have sprung up in Toronto. Activities have ranged from marches down Yonge Street, to special youth programs, to joint projects with other minority communities and even theatre productions.[13] At Wellesley Central Hospital, emergency staff were trained 'how to ask more questions and be more sensitive when treating someone they suspect has been assaulted because they're gay or lesbian.'[14] The hospital surveyed 368 gays and lesbians and found that 50 per cent had been threatened with violence. During the three-month pilot program in 1996,[15] 'victims are referred to a hospital social worker who is an expert on victims of violence. Gay-positive volunteers and clergy are available for support. Patients are also referred to 519 Church for help, should they choose to pursue the assault in court ... Patients are followed up by telephone three or four days after their initial visit to hospital, and again after three to four weeks.'[16]

Not long afterwards, the program came to a halt after a series of provincial health-care cutbacks: Wellesley Central was amalgamated with another hospital, then closed down as a free-standing site.

The Toronto Model: A Critical Assessment

Faulkner's doctoral research on the 519's AVP combined 'survey research, participant observation, semi-structured interviews, and content analysis.'[17] The program had a more radical activist approach in the early 1990s; between 1993 and 1995, Faulkner participated in a variety of activities that exposed her to the 'cultural context of anti-gay/lesbian violence activism.' She attended criminal trials that allowed her 'to hear expert witness testimony, assess the political dynamics of court procedures, and observe the attitudes of alleged perpetrators and their supporters.'[18]

In the second half of the decade, a more 'grassroots' approach linked AVP with city, police, and hospital officials within 'institutions that had been previously considered unsympathetic to lesbian and gay concerns.' Faulkner explains how AVP evolved over the years: counselling and emergency response skills were honed, allowing for more one-on-one attention to victims. New support groups were developed. Domestic violence, once considered completely separate from homophobic violence, was gradually integrated. Advocates also fanned out into the broader community, creating alliances with women's groups, Jewish groups, and urban crime committees.[19] With this sort of approach, however, Faulkner questions 'whether the tactic of working from within organizations to challenge homophobia and heterosexism has worked, or whether institutional discourses of acceptance represent only a symbolic intention toward societal and institutional change. In whose interests do anti-violence programmes work and whom do they represent?'[20]

Faulkner was critical of some aspects of the 519's program: only after 1997 could the telephone line be accessed 'in any other way than a central switchboard which was only operative during the day and evenings until ten o'clock ... Callers may now leave a message and get information from an answering machine after hours.'[21] Because of communication problems, 'many complaints have gone undocumented ... Lack of funding for staff and ineffective use of volunteers have led to a focus on outreach and research rather than victim assistance ... Debating with police about police statistics is making a political statement that looks good in the media; however, the immediate needs of victims are more important.'[22] Perhaps as a result of some of this criticism, the 519 program's former coordinator told me: 'We do lots of follow-up. Our focus has shifted: it's more of a client focus.'[23]

Faulkner also observed 'the gendered and racialized face of the anti-gay/lesbian violence movement and its focus on Caucasian male victims.' This approach 'reproduces a white, ethnically homogenic, male, middle-class response to anti-gay/lesbian violence,' which 'conflates lesbian women's experience of crime with that of gay men.'[24] She points out 'how these services diminish an understanding of women's experience of violence ... Connections need to be made between anti-woman and anti-lesbian hate crime.' Her research indicates that 'since 1993, only five incidents of gender-based crime has been considered sufficiently hateful to be counted compared to 158 incidents of mostly anti-gay crime.'[25] She notes that 'misogynist' motivations 'are left unexamined in the present documentary process.'[26]

AVP's original feminist framework 'has been eroded in the interests of providing politically-neutral "social services."'[27] For example, in 1998, 1200 people showed up for a Matthew Shephard memorial vigil organized by AVP.[28] However, Kinsman questioned why a march was not organized: 'Victim culture: these are social work notions. You get a feeling that the 'victims' are being put into a category. They have to compile stats to justify their existence. They are not given funding. The 519 board was told that they were not allowed to organize a Matthew Shephard demonstration. This is self-control. We're not getting at the social roots of the problems, we just manage the problem.'[29]

The former coordinator argued that 'we're a city-funded agency. If people had wanted to organize a march, they could have, but ... we don't have the volunteer resources to do something like that. Our priority is to provide service to victims.'[30] To be fair, she was only paid to work twenty-five hours a week. However, Kinsman is making the point that AVP is a 'band-aid' solution to a complex problem that is all too prevalent in Toronto.

Repairing Police-Community Relations in Toronto

Compared to other cities, relations between Toronto police and the community are fairly good; AVP tries to maintain a critical stance. Although they do no independent investigations, they intervene if things get overlooked. In one case, a victim insisted he had been gay-bashed even though the police did not at first classify it as such. The crime was finally reclassified, but 'not all victims are willing to persist,' according to the former coordinator.

Out of forty-five queer-bashings in 1998, she disagreed with the police on only five cases: One involved a bomb threat to the 519 Community Centre; in two cases. the centre was shot at with BBs; in another case, excrement was smeared on the door; in the fifth case, a gay man was chased by a beggar. She criticized the 'narrow' approach the police use when they investigate. 'The Hate Crime Unit is part of Intelligence Services,' she noted. 'But what's happening is not through organized hate campaigns. Violence against gay men is random acts of crime.'[31]

The unit was set up in January 1993. From 1993 to 1997, a hate crime had to be 'solely motivated' by hate. Now it's 'in whole or in part.'[32] The unit has two police officers and a civilian analyst and is involved in investigative support, public education and outreach, police training, education, and crime analysis.[33] It has participated in hate crime training for hundreds of Crown attorneys.[34] The head of the unit explained that he is also TPS's in-house consultant for diversity issues. He said that when he did a presentation at the 519 in 2002, seven people showed up.[35]

Faulkner feels that despite TPS's efforts to reach out, the force excludes 'prostitutes, transvestites, homeless, youth, [and] the mentally ill.'[36] In 2000, AVP initiated a queer-community liaison committee with the police – a process that has been repeated across Canada since the early 1990s. George Smith feels that many activists are misguided when they try to establish these committees: 'The central mechanisms of organizing the policing of gays is the Criminal Code ... Getting the police off our backs is not ... a matter of developing better public relations with police departments, etc. but of changing the law.'[37]

Given the sheer size and complexity of Toronto's queer community, it was suggested that a two-tiered committee structure be developed. This would allow for broad community representation and for individuals to work on specific issues, like youth and public sex. In 2000, over a five-month period, thirty-nine groups came together to discuss similar committees in Ontario, the United States, and Australia.[38]

Table 7.3
Queer bashing figures in Toronto, AVP versus police

Year	AVP	TPS
1997	95	16
1998	98	31
1999	116	44
2000	64	18
2001	59	24
2002	65	11

One police officer insisted that committee members undergo a police check and said the condition was 'not negotiable.'[39] He elaborated his criteria: 'a wild and crazy youth' who had stayed out of trouble and now had 'good character' would be included; people who had been involved in violence or trafficking drugs would be excluded. Queer prostitutes would also be excluded, since the queer community had long been 'victimized' by prostitution.[40] The committee eventually convinced the police to withdraw this requirement. One of the co-chairs said they had 'no intention of being puppets' or 'public relations tools' for the police.[41]

At a national conference in 2003, AVP presented its statistics and compared the number of reports it had received with the number of queer-related reports received by TPS (see table 7.3). It acknowledged that comparisons were problematic, since the two organizations had different definitions and methodologies.

AVP said that although the numbers were going down, the violence was more intense, and was resulting in more overnight hospital stays. After 11 September, queers wearing gowns and/or skullcaps had been accused of 'looking like a terrorist' and targeted.[42]

What Do We Want? Pussy!!

In 1999, just before Julian Fantino was appointed Toronto's police chief, gay city councillor Kyle Rae complained that Fantino was 'arrogant and hostile,' citing his connection to the 'kiddie porn' operation in London, Ontario, which is described later in this chapter. In an article titled, 'Will Anti-Gay Cop Become Next Toronto Chief?' Rae said that Fantino's appointment 'would set back relations 20 years.'[43] In early 2000, the new chief addressed The Fraternity, an elite gay men's organization. He told the room: 'You can't ask for immunity. Do the right and lawful thing and you won't have any trouble from us.'[44] How wrong he was.

All hell broke loose in September 2000, when seven plainclothes officers raided Club Toronto, a gay men's bathhouse that occasionally sponsors an all-woman event called 'The Pussy Palace.' Around three hundred women were in attendance; some had waited up to two-and-a-half hours to get in. The police spent an hour checking for 'liquor license violations.'[45] A spokesperson objected: 'Women were topless ... feeling violated. Why couldn't they have sent female officers?'[46]

As it turned out, they did: two undercover female officers stripped and donned towels to check out what was going on. They needn't have bothered: five male cops followed them in, 'knocking on doors and chatting up patrons.'[47] Police reportedly questioned about a dozen women, writing down names, addresses, and telephone numbers.[48] One organizer complained that officers spent twenty minutes questioning two women in a private room, attempting to look through personal belongings.[49]

Police said an anonymous female caller had tipped them off, describing the bathhouse event an 'organized orgy' and a 'free-for-all sexorama.'[50] Police even hinted that the lesbian community *wanted* police to raid the event in order to generate publicity. 'What, so that we could have a big media frenzy? Oh for heaven's sake,' said one of the organizers, laughing.[51] Lawyers for the Pussy Palace refused to say whether the organizers had been warned in advance about the raid. According to *Xtra*, a *Globe and Mail* reporter confirmed she had been there for work reasons, but declined to say whether she had been tipped off.[52]

Two hundred angry people attended a community meeting, then spontaneously marched down Church Street to the College Street headquarters of the police service, chanting: 'Hey hey, ho ho, Julian Fantino has got to go.'[53] In October 2000 – late on a Friday afternoon – police announced the charges to be laid, which included three counts of disorderly conduct, one count of failing to provide sufficient security, and two liquor offences.[54] Three weeks later, demonstrators waving underwear showed up for a 'Panty Picket' in front of 52 Division, amid chants of 'Fuck you 52.'[55]

At trial, male officers in attendance attempted to rationalize their presence by arguing that some transsexuals had also been there. Since the transsexuals had been born with male genitals – and were at the event – what was wrong with male cops being there too? The judge pointed out that the event was advertised in advance for women and transgendered people. He threw out six liquor-related charges levelled at two of the women. He stated that the presence of male officers was a 'flagrant' abuse of power that 'went against common decency' and shocked the public. [56]

Shortly after the raid, Councillor Rae fumed: 'No crime; no victim; but an opportunity to cop a peek at topless women.'[57] Police were upset with Rae's references to 'rogue cops' on a 'panty raid' – and with his assertions that 'beat cops went into the Pussy Palace without an okay from a high-ranking superior officer.'[58] Before long, he was served with a $500,000 lawsuit by seven police officers, who claimed to have been 'subjected to harassment and ill treatment by members of the Toronto gay community as a result of the defamatory comments of the defendant.'[59] Rae said: 'It's an outrage that members of council are not free to criticize the police in defence of their community – yet the police union calls city councillors scumbags.' George Smitherman, whose provincial riding includes Toronto's gay ghetto, said: 'Julian Fantino empowers rogue cops by giving them a sense that he will protect them.'[60]

At Rae's trial, seven police officers portrayed themselves as victims: they claimed they had suffered professional, personal, and health problems as a result of his comments. They said they deserved between $50,000 and $80,000 each. One officer said he lost weight, experienced insomnia, and was denied promotions because of Kyle's comments. One lesbian officer claimed she was labelled a 'traitor,' split up with her partner, and quit the police force because of the affair.[61] The police were finally awarded $170,000. Athough Rae apologized, his lawyer noted that the police 'still insist they did nothing wrong – they said they would do it again.'[62]

Giese reflected on the effect the raid had on Toronto's queer community. The rallying cry at one demonstration was: 'What do we want? Pussy! When do we want it? Now!' The new rainbow coalition includes the 'young, rowdy crowd,' the 'Cabbagetown guppies,' sex workers, transgendered people, racial minorities, 'civil rights activists, mainstream politicians and veteran gay politicos.' Gay men who rioted and lobbied in the face of the 1981 bathhouse raids are teaching a whole new generation of queer activists: 'Combining the best of the activism of the past with their own distinct style, the bathhouse defence women have reinvigorated queer politics in Toronto.'[63]

Montreal: 'A Series of Killers'

Any discussion of homophobic violence in Quebec inevitably centres on Montreal. A Montreal police spokesman said officers don't keep track of hate crimes at all. He added, 'there are fewer hate crimes in Montreal than there are in Toronto or Vancouver.'[64] However, police do keep tabs on gay men, having arrested dozens on public sex charges.[65]

Since the infamous 1990 riots, relations between the community and the police have been on shaky ground. In 1992, Montreal police released a report claiming that crime in the Gay Village was lower than in surrounding areas.[66] The same year, however, an activist stated that he saw 'an average of two assault cases a week, ranging from punchings to knife cuts. And talk is rampant about late-night beatings outside bars in the Gay Village.'[67] Queer activists collected the names of twelve officers 'whose behaviours have been particularly offensive,' and threatened to make the names public if those officers were not 'taken off the street and assigned to desk duty.' In a gesture of reconciliation, the head of Station 33 announced that gay-bashing victims could file complaints at the Gay and Lesbian Community Centre.[68]

Between 1989 and 1993, more than a dozen gay men had been killed in Montreal. Activists claimed the police were 'homophobic' and were letting a 'serial killer' run rampant,[69] and faulted the police for waiting three weeks before announcing the killings of Michel Hogue and Robert Panchaud.[70] 'If these were thirteen teenage girls, heads would be rolling.'[71] Two magazines and two anonymous donors offered a $6,000 reward for information about the killings.[72] The police eventually invited community activists to review the evidence: although a serial killer might not exist, 'a series of killers' was terrifying Montreal's gay community.[73]

The media frenzy relating to the homicides perhaps hastened a decision by the Quebec Human Rights Commission to mount an inquiry. Montreal's large queer community had long been quite fragmented along linguistic and ideological lines; the hearings – which opened on 6 December 1993 – revitalized the movement. The timing could not have been more dramatic: early on 6 December, Harry Dolan, fifty-seven, was found in his apartment 'stabbed repeatedly in the face and chest with a knife, which was left in his body.' There were no signs of forced entry, and the murder was never solved.[74]

An anti-violence organization, Dire Enfin la Violence (DELV), was born in September 1995. (The name does not translate well into English – 'Finally Say Violence' – but the sense is, 'Take a stand against violence.') Within two years, the group had received almost six hundred calls – half of which involved queer-bashing – and had:

- established an 800 number,
- distributed complaint forms,
- produced and distributed flyers and press releases,
- attended court cases and other judicial procedures with victims,
- produced and presented audio-visual material,

Table 7.4
Location of gay-bashing incidents in Montreal

Locations	No. of incidents
park	33
street	99
business	69
victim's residence	246
accused's residence	9
at work	25

Source: Dire Enfin la Violence, 'Rapport des Activités, mars à octobre' (1998), 3–4.

- organized a 'Violence Week' and a vigil for murder victims,
- put up information booths in the Gay Village and distributed information in bars,
- educated police officers, and
- organized bashing and domestic violence support groups.[75]

DELV analysed more than four hundred reports dating from 22 September, 1995 to 31 May 1997. Most of these incidents had occurred around the Gay Village.[76] More than half of the 409 incidents occurred in the victim's home (see table 7.4). A picture emerges: most of the victims were anonymous men, who did not go to the police and who were victimized behind closed doors.

DELV posed the following questions when analysing their data: Were homophobic or sexist words used during the incident? (Yes, 128; No, 288). Did the victims identify themselves on the phone line? (Yes, 182; No, 327). Did the victims report to the police? (Yes, 186; No, 282).

In 1997, DELV closed for six months for restructuring. In 1998, three employees continued DELV's programs. Contacts with suburban police departments were expanded,[77] and an educational seminar was organized for police recruits, who were given a guided tour of the Gay Village. DELV also provided host families for queers fleeing abusive partners.[78] From March to October 1998, there were 441 phone calls from women and 658 phone calls from men. Four men complained about police treatment.[79]

Around the same period, DELV attacked an academic article on crime in the Gay Village. Its title, 'Rhetoric of Victimization,' indicates the article's basic thrust. The authors asserted that 'the risks of victimization are generally extremely over-estimated by the media and pressure groups that represent the "interests" of the gay community.'[80] In conducting their study, the researchers immediately excluded all crimes in which the victim and perpetrator knew each other.

The authors studied thirty-four crimes reported to police and thirty-one crimes reported to DELV.[81] They concluded that reporting rates in the Gay village were similar to those in other parts in Montreal.[82] In fact, the authors argued that crime in the Gay Village was probably lower than other areas because the neighbourhood is a 'microcosm that prevents and discourages crime.' They said that 'the pool of potential criminals' who exploit homosexuals is limited, since few heterosexuals are willing to work as street prostitutes. The authors also claimed that homosexuals are less predisposed to crime because they don't participate in violent sports and are less exposed to crime as teenagers.[83]

In an unusual move, the *Canadian Journal of Criminology* allowed DELV to denounce the authors in the same issue. The activists took their names off the study, complaining that the researchers had used them to gain access to the gay community. DELV noted that the authors had originally promised to 'establish the prevalance of predatory violence, motivations of the criminals and a bank of possible suspects that the police could question at the end of the research.' Instead, the authors 'provided a partial analysis of partial data.'[84]

DELV was the most outspoken of the Canadian organizations I studied; its *raison d'être* was to expose the roots of violence – sometimes with mixed results. For example, when victim support groups were not well attended, they were replaced with individual therapy sessions. The idea of providing support to violent lesbians also fizzled: DELV realized they did not have the expertise to address this issue. The former coordinator said: 'We had lesbians calling us, saying, "I'm the one doing the hitting. If it continues, I'm going to kill her."'[85]

In 1999, two thousand people turned to Dire Enfin la Violence for services over a six-month period. However, organizers wondered whether they were spending their resources wisely in 'demystifying homosexuality' in schools and training health and social workers.[86] Educating police officers throughout Quebec was an important goal for the group. However, DELV noted that it 'is an ongoing, and demanding process, which is why we are doing it gradually and only on demand.'[87]

DELV also participated on a provincewide committee on homophobic violence that included municipal, regional, and provincial government representatives, as well as the Quebec Human Rights Commission, the regional health board, the QPP, the Montreal police, and other gay and lesbian community representatives.[88] Despite all their efforts, the former coordinator said: 'Every two weeks, someone else comes in to say, "The police didn't want to take down my case."'[89]

The former coordinator pointed to some areas of concern. In 1999, six men, all in their fifties, were robbed at knifepoint by the same man over a two-month period.[90] In 2001, three violent incidents occurred along the Lachine Canal cruising area. One of these victims, a photographer for the gay magazine *Fugues*, was in a coma for ten days.[91] That same summer, two American tourists on their first visit to the city were assaulted and hospitalized.[92]

As queers become more visible, a growing problem is 'neighbour violence.' In 2000, a suburban gay couple complained that their neighbours had harassed them and and had tried to run one of them over.[93] The case snowballed, and the couple became a *cause célèbre* – 1,500 gathered in the suburbs to march in support of the two men. The couple lodged 'a series of complaints to public security, the police and the Quebec Human Rights Commission,' then sued a television station for defamation. However, their straight neighbours fought back. They claimed they had been unfairly typecast as homophobes and had been systematically harassed by the gay couple – who for years had kept a log of their neighbours' comings and goings. The couple also recorded the licence plate numbers of all their neighbours' visitors, and even followed their neighbours to work one day in their car.[94]

I had been contact with DELV's organizers since 1999, and I was struck by how the group had bogged down by 2002 – the year that Mario Joanette's body was found on rue Ste-Catherine in the Gay Village.[95] By then, DELV had only one employee, who was working ten hours a week. The former coordinator complained that the Quebec government had not followed through on its funding commitments. Because she was the only paid staff member, she was expected to do all public education and volunteer training and to answer phone calls. She felt it was unfortunate that the group couldn't hire a man to do outreach.[96] In an e-mail, the former coordinator reflected: 'Almost nothing is being done about hate crime in Montreal. Gay-bashing continues ... but the police do very little. Communication with the police has completely broken down. They've turned their backs on our community, refusing to take gay-bashing complaints. It's a nightmare! The head of the Village precinct said community groups like ours are only interested in getting government hand-outs. The gay police officer who was on our board has just quit. The situation has gotten very ugly.'[97]

The organization folded in 2003, after its only source of funding – a $25,000 crime prevention grant – was denied. The coordinator said she would be hanging on to the file boxes in the hope that 'someone some-where' might want to do statistical analyses of the data that DELV had collected.[98] Meanwhile, no other group was taking responsibility for the violence in Quebec City, Trois-Rivières, and Sherbrooke – all sizeable Canadian cities – and the rest of Quebec. The former coordinator of DELV said it did not even have a budget to make long-distance calls to other parts of the province. Fondation Émergence is a relatively new organization that addresses homophobia but does not directly assist victims of homophobic violence.

Vancouver

Despite a series of high-profile assaults and murders that have occurred in Vancouver since the Gay Games in 1990, community organizing around violence has lacked continuity. In 1992, a series of bashings – including the Stanley Park attack I described in the introduction to this book – prompted several hundred people to march down Davie Street. Two thousand names were collected on a petition 'demanding that police pay more attention to the rights of gays and lesbians.'[99] The chief of the VPD promised that officers would 'be given sensitivity training and instructed to record the sexual orientation of assault victims when responding to reports of gay-bashing' – although 'confidential notations on sexual orientation will be taken only if members of the gay community agree.'[100]

Four different anti-violence organizations have disbanded. In 1991, the Pride Foundation established Equal Justice, aimed at 'keeping track of gay-bashings, assisting people in pressing charges and helping them through the court process.' Self-defence courses were also planned. The group said it had 'fielded 21 complaints about verbal and physical attacks' from May to August 1991.[101] In 1994, the Q-Street Patrol, 'the first of its kind in Canada,' was introduced to keep the West End safe.[102] It folded due to lack of support in 1995.[103] The patrol attempted to reorganize in 1998, without success.[104] In 1997, the Violet Foundation was formed to provide self-defence classes and counselling. This group modelled itself after Toronto's 519 program.[105] It conducted a survey, but folded in 1998, again because of lack of community support.

In 1997, VPD became increasingly involved in queer-bashing issues. As part of the city's community policing initiative, the department opened an office just off Davie Street. The police also established drop-in hours at the The Centre, the queer community centre.[106] Bruce Chambers made headlines as the first Canadian police chief to march in a Pride parade. He was asked to establish 'a real committee where community members can have a real effect on the way policing is done,' but he refused, saying that the current civilian complaints process worked well.[107] By 1999, queer-sensitive 'diversity training courses' were being given to recruits, although veterans were not required to take them. This was seven years after the chief's initial promise.[108]

The Bashline Experiment

VPD set up a phone line, called the Bashline, in May 1997. It began with a lot of publicity and a $15,000 budget, mainly to publicize the new telephone number.[109] For all its good intentions, the Bashline ultimately failed. This is an interesting case study about what happens when police involve themselves too deeply in grassroots community work.

As a graduate student, I decided to volunteer with the Bashline – a disappointing but eye-opening experience. I filled out a standard police volunteer application form, which required me to pass a background check and be 'of good moral character.' Volunteer selection was 'at the sole discretion of the Neighborhood Patrol Officer.' A long list of rules for volunteers were spelled out, including a requirement to be 'neat and presentably attired while on duty.' Furthermore, 'As the mandate of the Bashline is strictly to assist callers through police and other referral resources, it is essential that volunteers display a professional, politically neutral demeanor. While volunteers may support the aims and objectives of various causes and organizations, these opinions shall not be expressed or recommended to people calling the Bashline, without prior consultation with the Neighborhood Patrol Officer.'[110]

Clearly, many queer volunteers would have difficulty adhering to these rules. Who decides what is 'good moral character'? And why? Queers who do not pass the 'background check' may actually have valuable insights into the criminal justice system – and may have even been victimized by the police. Why should they be excluded? Why should the selection of all volunteers be at the 'sole discretion' of one officer? If volunteers are simply talking on the phone, why does my appearance have to conform to what the police consider 'presentable'? When trying to be supportive of queer-bashing victims – essentially an oppressed group, with limited access to services – how do I remain 'politically neutral'?

After undergoing a two-weekend training session, I volunteered from September to November 1997, but there was really nothing to do. Unless someone happened to call during the few hours per week that I was actually in the Yaletown office, callers would be instructed to call a pager, which the officer carried almost the whole time. Several people had the access code to the voice mail, and messages were sometimes deleted without being logged. In a memo, I wrote that 'there needs to be a "Master List" that keeps track of every single call into the Bashline 24 hours a day, 7 days a week ... If we don't start doing this, the Bashline is going to become engulfed in problems ... which will erode our credibility.'[111]

One incident made me decide I could no longer work there. A victim called to explain that while walking down the sidewalk in front of the Orpheum Theatre, a few metres from the Dufferin Hotel, he had been bashed by a man who was part of a large crowd entering the theatre to attend an Indian music concert. The victim was knocked unconscious on the sidewalk. When he came to, two police officers were standing over him, asking if he was armed. After producing ID, he was frisked, cuffed, put in a paddywagon, and dropped off at his home – in plain view of his neighbours and landlord. He told me he was too intimidated to argue, but four days later called to see how to protest this treatment.[112]

I instructed him to write a letter to the chief. Yet when I asked the Bashline officer, he shrugged and said the victim's complaint would likely be ignored, and that the arresting officers would get, at most, a slap on the wrist. More and more complaints about the Bashline began to surface:

- A gay man, who claimed that he had been attacked by two Vancouver officers in 1998, said he called the Bashline but hung up after he heard the following message: 'If this is an emergency, phone the police.'[113] Another gay man, who said police threw him into a wall, also refused to call the Bashline.[114]
- The organizer of a Matthew Shephard memorial 'tried to get the Bashline involved but volunteers at the Pacific Street community police office only had a vague idea of how to get in touch with the line's organizers.' After another gay man was bashed, his friends said the Bashline did not return calls for a week.[115]
- One victim told me: 'I tried to follow up the whole matter with some constable from the Bashline and ran into nothing but bureaucratic walls. To this day I still am unclear as to what function that line is supposed to fill.'[116]

In a letter to the editor, a journalist complained: 'Not one of several phone calls to the Yaletown Community Police Office was returned.' Then he decided to call the Attorney General of British Columbia, who, ironically, was easier to contact than the Bashline: 'He referred me to the police, as they determine the use of their resources and the Bashline. I again made calls to the Yaletown Community Police Office; again not one was returned ... The community hasn't abandoned the Bashline as your headline suggests; I believe its outreach efforts were ineffective at best.'[117]

In 1999, I went back to the officer and asked him about the numerous complaints. He explained that they had stopped recruiting volunteers from the queer community because 'there wasn't enough to keep them busy or interested.' Instead, they began to use regular volunteers, who 'didn't want to do work on the Bashline. It was too intense for them. A couple of them are homophobic, and the majority of them are straight.'[118] (In other words, he didn't say to them, 'Part of your duty in this job is to work on the Bashline. If gays and lesbians make you uncomfortable, you can't work here.')

The officer deflected these problems back onto the queer community, complaining to *Xtra West* that the Bashline was barely getting by 'with virtually no support from gays' and with 'almost no volunteers from the gay community.'[119] This victim-blaming approach was then internalized by queers themselves. Instead of demanding an effective, community-based organization, one activist placed 'the blame squarely on gays, saying we've failed to keep the Bashline staffed with enough volunteers.'[120]

Despite the complaints, few criticized how the Bashline was actually organized. It had begun with a hand-picked 'advisory board,' which supposedly guided the officer's decisions. By 1999, however, the officer was saying, 'I don't have to report to anyone.' He carried the pager with him seven days a week, for which he was paid an extra twelve hours per month.[121] In 2000, Bashline officials said that all victims were being called back regularly. But they also noted that 'a significant number of callers don't want to involve the police at all, but do want to talk about incidents they find themselves victims to.'[122] In 2001, the Bashline registered 402 calls, but only eight of those calls involved reporting a criminal incident. The rest of the people just wanted information.[123]

However, since there were no specific Bashline staff who actually investigated queer-bashings – and since the B.C. Hate Crime Unit handled all hate crime investigations – people began to wonder what the Bashline's actual role was.

The Lessons of Aaron Webster

In 2001, a horrific killing led Vancouver's queer community to develop an alternative to the Bashline. A straight construction worker in Stanley Park claimed that four young men had gone after him with baseball bats on four different occasions over the previous year. During the last attack, he managed to get a licence plate number of a car belonging to one of the youths.[124] Two weeks later, a forty-two-year-old gay man named Aaron Webster was beaten to death in Stanley Park late at night. His best friend was driving through the parking lot near a gay cruising area and found Webster lying there. He died in his friend's arms.[125] Webster was naked except for his hiking boots; the rest of his clothes were found in his car.[126]

Over the next week, four witnesses stated they had seen a man, surrounded by a group of others, beating Webster with either a baseball bat or a pool cue.[127] VPD aired a re-enactment of the murder on television in an attempt to generate tips.[128] A month after the murder, the police board announced a $10,000 reward.[129] Detective Rob Faoro worked on the case full-time for fourteen months before announcing the arrest of a youth – who could not be named because he was seventeen at the time of the incident.[130] Although the police immediately described Webster's murder as a 'hate crime' and gave the impression that a severe punishment was in the works, the opposite occurred: one youth pleaded guilty to manslaughter and was given three years – the maximum possible sentence in youth court. According to Faoro, a group of four young men hid in the bushes clenching golf clubs and baseball bats.[131] Ryan Cran and Danny Rao, in their early twenties, were also charged with manslaughter, along with another young man who was a minor at the time of the killing. The men lived with their families in nearby Burnaby. Cran was convicted of manslaughter; the second youth eventually pleaded guilty to manslaughter. The courtroom erupted after Rao was found not guilty.[132]

The murder had a dramatic impact on Vancouver's queer community.[133] Almost two thousand people marched down Davie Street to English Bay,[134] where a local politician was heckled by people who felt the provincial government was not doing enough to fight hate crime.[135] The following week, more than one hundred people attended a community forum to discuss homophobic violence.[136] All of this soul searching led the community to reflect on the effectiveness of police programs. The only formal dialogue in place at the time was the VPD Diversity Advisory Committee, which had one gay male and one lesbian representative; however, many criticized this group for having no interaction with the community. A staff member at The Centre recalled that during a meeting with the police chief and the mayor, 'we had to explain to them the difference between sexual orientation and gender identity.'

Before long, an ad hoc Public Safety Committee was set up, which brought together The Centre, queer businesses, and the police. During their discussions, it became evident that the Bashline was not being utilized to its full potential; meanwhile, the Prideline – The Centre's toll-free provincewide information line – was duplicating some of its services. The committee decided to merge the two.[137] Jim Deva, a Vancouver activist and bookstore owner, described the committee as a working group: 'We're down to five members.' Although Webster's murder was a catalyst for change, 'we don't want it to be used as a public relations tool for VPD.' He noted that the concept of 'community safety' is something everyone can relate to: 'It's a slogan for our times.'[138]

In 2003, The Centre began a pilot project: a gay male Victim Services worker came on site one afternoon per week. In two months, he served eight clients. The Centre also received a substantial grant to develop a module to educate service providers on the 'queer experience of violence.' Detective Ros Shakespeare, the transsexual officer, has been active on the committee, playing a vital liaison role. In the 1990s, Vancouver's community had often been criticized as complacent; now, in the wake of Webster's murder, a staff member from The Centre remarked how unfortunate it was that it had taken this event for things to change: 'We've moved into a state of activism that we've never known before.'[139]

The Ottawa Experience

Ottawa's community organizing around homophobic violence demonstrates that in many ways it is easier to bring about change in medium-sized cities. In 1989, Alain Brousseau was accused of being gay and died after being thrown off a bridge between Ottawa and Hull. The killing spurred the creation of the Ottawa-Hull Lesbian and Gay Task Force on Violence.

The Ottawa experience demonstrates how communities can and should state clearly what they expect from their police force, which is supposed to be protecting them. The task force demanded that police document hate crimes; install a bashing hotline; make a public announcement warning of the violence; and increase police visibility, not only in dangerous areas but also at public events like Pride parades. The group demanded that the police chief take a more public profile and that the police attend conferences as well as visit police departments with hate crime units.

The police responded, developing a Hate Crime Section and participating in a liaison committee, which has been meeting regularly ever since. Unlike other police departments, the statistics distributed by the Ottawa Hate Crime Section include all reports of homophobic behaviour, 'from yelling to assault. A large number of the complaints recorded don't have a Criminal Code definition.'[140] Over the years, other issues have emerged, including a 'request that entrapment not be used' in the policing of washroom sex.[141] The police received their first homophobia training in 1992, around which time an Action Plan Project was developed.[142] The report, released in 1994:

- examined community-based policing, crime prevention, and bias crime units;
- described a series of community forums and meetings, outreach, speaking engagements, and information sharing; and
- discussed different outreach strategies, including posters, pamphlets, and campaigns.

This report, which was a blueprint for change, chronicled the growing pains of a police department attempting to become more queer-sensitive. One officer 'objected to being seen with gay-related material.' Queer volunteers were often 'excluded from taking an active role in information displays' – even though community workers from other programs were constantly visible.[143] One of the report's coauthors, David Pepper, organized events after Brousseau's killing and works as the Director of Community Development for the Ottawa Police Service.

However, there have also been complaints. In 1991, a gay man said that Constable Eric Fenato tried to hit him with his police car on Bank Street. Fenato – who said the man looked like a drug dealer he wanted to question – asked to speak to the gay man, who refused, gave him the finger, and blew him a kiss. Fenato was found guilty of the dangerous operation of a motor vehicle, but was acquitted of three more serious charges. A judge eventually handed the officer an absolute discharge: 'A conviction would have an effect on your future that is disproportionate to the crime itself.'[144] After an appeal, the Crown withdrew the charges altogether.[145]

In 1994, two gay men returning from a gay club in Hull said their car was followed by four men, who pulled up beside them, screaming: 'You fucking flaming faggots, we're going to kill you.' Then they rammed into the gay men's car in Byward Market. The victims were able to drive to a police station, but an officer ordered one of the victims back to his car and 'fined him $265 for careless driving and leaving the scene of an accident.' The police even gave the name, address, and phone number of one of the victims to the alleged assailants, who phoned him at home and threatened him.[146] One officer said the victim was looking for 'preferential treatment' and that his complaint was 'self-serving.' If he 'was expecting more because he is gay, he is mistaken.'[147]

One gay man had nothing but praise for Ottawa police officers after a man he picked up and brought home turned violent. He had met the man at the Remic Rapids cruising area, along the Ottawa River, which is patrolled by the RCMP.[148] A gay man walking his unleashed dog near the Rapids complained that – out of all the others walking their dogs off-leash in the same area – he was singled out by a Mountie, who ran toward him holding his gun and who referred to him as a 'fucking faggot' while speaking to his fellow officer.[149]

Criticizing Ottawa's Approach

In 2002, a string of assaults – all by one perpetrator – raised questions about the effectiveness of Ottawa's liaison committee. Typically, the robber/assailant would meet his victim on Cruiseline, a popular gay phoneline, then go to the victim's house. One victim said that after sex, the man demanded money and choked him, saying, 'I will kill you, cocksucker.' Some of the other victims were punched, and stabbed with scissors.[150] One victim was terrorized three times: the first time he paid the man to get rid of him, but the assailant came back a month later for more money. The third time he pretended to be a delivery man and barged into the victim's apartment.[151]

This series of assaults raised questions about the committee's ability to prevent such crimes. In December 2001, police had released a media advisory stating that 'at least five users of gay dating services had been assaulted and robbed ... at the hands of someone they met over the phone.' Yet, this information was not conveyed to the liaison committee or to *Capital Xtra* for nine months. By then, two more incidents had occurred.[152]

Cruiseline began warning first-time users and gave one detective access to the line so that he could try to catch the assailant.[153] Lawrence Pigeon, thirty-seven, was eventually arrested and entered into a plea agreement for thirty-eight criminal charges – relating to ten separate incidents – including assault causing bodily harm, forcible confinement, extortion, break and enter, and twelve counts of robbery.[154] However, the police refused to acknowledge any hate motivation whatsoever in Pigeon's crimes against the community. The committee chair heaped praise on the way the police dealt with it: 'Were they gay-bashing offences? ... The chief investigator and senior investigator determined through admissions by the accused and the facts of investigations, they were not. Mr. Pigeon admitted to police he was bisexual and as such, his motivations were not to gay-bash our LGBT community. Robbery was apparently his only motivation ... I expressed our deepest gratitude to the officers, investigators, and command staff of the Ottawa Police for their diligence in these matters.'[155]

Instead of questioning the way police and the assailant had framed the incident, one committee member told the *Ottawa Sun*: 'The guy is gay and he is preying on the gay community.'[156] Using this logic, after a violent robber commits dozens of crimes against the queer community, all he needs to do is claim he is gay or bisexual, and *voilà*: problem solved. Not only will the police ignore the hate motivation angle, but the committee that supposedly represents the community will applaud the police for doing it.

A few months later, two leather men were attacked in Ottawa. This time the hate crime section confirmed it would be treated as a hate crime because one of the assailants said, 'Fucking little faggots, I am going to bash your head in.'[157] How is this so different from a dangerous robber who puts his hands around your throat and says, 'Cocksucker, I will kill you'? According to the Ottawa police, one incident conforms to their definition of a hate crime whereas the other does not. Why is the queer community allowing the police to define what is and is not hateful toward their community?

A Tale of Two Victims

Ottawa police also refused to consider any hate motivation in the killing of Christopher Raynsford, which occurred around the same time that Pigeon was arrested. Raynsford had played in a local production of *The Laramie Project*, a play about the killing of Matthew Shepard in Wyoming.[158] The media coverage was remarkable: The *Ottawa Sun* ran page one stories about Raynsford's death three days in a row. A vigil attracted 150 people on a cold December night in front of the Human Rights Memorial on Elgin Street.[159]

A month before his death, the popular Centretown resident had met a man on gay.com.[160] He invited the man to his apartment; the man then robbed him. One report noted that the victim 'was a frequent user of Internet and telephone dating services, chat rooms, and often met other men once or twice a week.' The police began searching for a Quebec man who had been seen with Raynsford. Although the *Sun* initially splashed the possibility of a 'hate slaying' liberally through its pages, a hate crimes officer quickly stated: 'There is no evidence the victim was targeted because he was gay.'[161]

Within six weeks, Sebastien Roy had been arrested for killing Raynsford (as well as the victim's cat). Another officer reiterated: 'I'm quite comfortable saying that this is not a hate crime.'[162] Later, the Hate Crime Section explained to *Capital Xtra* the criteria they use when deciding whether a crime was a hate crime: 'Was there a relationship between the victim and the offender, did they both belong to different communities, was the victim part of a targeted group, were bias-related objects, items or symbols used or left at the crime scene? These are some of the specific things we look for when we conduct our investigation.[163]

In the paradigm of the police, two men who meet each other on gay.com are in a 'relationship.' And since they are in a 'relationship,' hate motivation is automatically discounted. This policy was applied again seven months later, after a stench emanating from the apartment of Bill Goodwin, a fifty-eight–year-old senior bureaucrat at the Canadian Nuclear Safety Commission, led to the discovery of his body. The only clue in the media that he was gay came in a brief mention about his relationship with a 'longtime roommate': 'Neighbours said the two men had been a couple about fifteen years ago but had an amicable breakup and remained close friends.'[164] Joshua Colpitts, twenty, was charged with first-degree murder and robbery 'in connection with items that were missing from Goodwin's upscale Metcalfe St. condo and the victim's stolen PT Cruiser.'[165]

Raynsford and Goodwin seem to have been targeted by killers using the same modus operandi, yet Goodwin's death barely registered in the queer community: this time there were no marches or page one denunciations of his death. This time the liaison committee made no public statements. I e-mailed the coordinator to find out why the committee had been so silent about the second death. She acknowledged receipt of my e-mail, but never responded. Raynsford had been portrayed as a saint; in contrast, Goodwin was assassinated by a page one headline in the *Ottawa Sun*:

Slain bureaucrat's secret life of crack, booze, male hookers
NUK EXEC'S TAWDRY END
Strangled, robbed, found with underwear down throat, court hears

Colpitts was drunk and stoned when he woke up and discovered 'that Mr. Goodwin was performing oral copulation on his private parts,' the

Crown prosecutor stated while reading an agreed-upon statement of facts. 'The accused panicked and wrapped his arm around Mr. Goodwin's neck and squeezed his neck as hard as he could until Mr. Goodwin stopped struggling and breathing.' After shoving a pair of underwear down the victim's throat, 'he sat in the corner and cried.' But then he stole Goodwin's TV, VCR, and car. Colpitts apologized to the victim's family and pleaded guilty to manslaughter. He was sentenced to twelve years, but will be allowed to apply for parole after five-and-a-half years.[166]

Ann Field, who has done doctoral research at Carleton on the topic of liaison committees, stated in an interview with *Capital Xtra* that Ottawa's committee is successful because high-ranking officers come to the table, 'compared to Vancouver or Toronto whose committees have only patrol constables present at meetings.' She said that relations between Ottawa community members and the police are more harmonious than, say, in Toronto.

In the same article, I argued that there was *too much* police presence at the committee meetings, based on the four that I sat in on in 2002. I questioned whether a city the size of Ottawa needed a committee that met for several hours every month. At some meetings there were more straight people than gay people – and more criminal justice personnel than community members, 'giving a real bureaucratic feel to it.'

> A liaison committee is more effective if it creates a core group of community activists that could fan out at the grassroots level ... All the strategy is taking place in the same room with the police. We need to meet in our own space and discuss issues important to the queer community, then go to the police and say, 'These are our issues' ... It's now time to re-consider how representative of the community these meetings are ... It's now difficult to separate the issues of the community from those of the police.

Despite the criticisms, the Ottawa police have been more consistently supportive of the queer community than any other force in Canada. One of the committee's most remarkable achievements is a sixty-page report – released on the tenth anniversary of the committee – that chronicles every single incident that was reported from 1992 to 2002. *Heard for the First Time* is a must-read for activists – proof that knowledge is power. It is clearly written, and it is accessible to the general public on the Ottawa police's own website.

The report lists queer-bashings, queer domestic incidents, and more general complaints about the homophobic behaviour of a disturbing number of ignorant people. It also describes several cases from Gatineau. On paper, Gatineau has the only police service in Quebec that keeps track of hate crimes. However, when I called its crime analyst and asked her for statistics on hate crimes, she was unable to provide me with any data.[167] Fortunately, the report provides some insight into homophobic violence in Gatineau. The worst incident occurred in 2001: a gay male victim of a pick-up crime was stabbed twenty times. The suspect was charged with attempted murder.[168]

Medium-Sized Cities: Victoria

In 1994, a spate of gay-bashings at Beacon Hill Park led to a public outcry. A gang of teenagers dragged one man to the ground, kicking him and yelling, 'Faggot.' A month later, another man was beaten. An activist complained that police were staying in their cars and avoiding the more secluded areas. He wanted them to add bike patrols. Around the same time, 'the Victoria Community Foot Patrol' started up. Sixteen volunteers wore fluorescent yellow arm bands and carried flashlights and whistles.[169] In 1995, queer-bashing incidents were chronicled 'on behalf of the Victoria Gay and Lesbian Anti-Violence Project.'[170]

Since then, police have reported sporadic attacks; two lesbians camping in Sooke were attacked, and the RCMP was called in to investigate.[171] Aaron Webster's killing also had an impact on Victoria's queer community: a vigil in 2001 led to a community safety forum, where more queer-bashing incidents were revealed. A self-defence class for the community was organized.[172] An officer who worked full-time on diversity issues retired in 2002; a part-time officer has taken over the position.[173]

Edmonton

In 1992, the Alberta Human Rights Commission released a report with concrete examples of queer-bashing in Edmonton and across the province.[174] In 1999, a researcher at the University of Alberta noted: 'To the best of my knowledge, no-one has ever attempted a rigorous survey of anti-gay violence in Edmonton.'[175] There have been few reported incidents; however, a university student said he was 'beaten and choked into unconsciousness by roommates' on two separate occasions in the early 1990s.[176] In 1998, Michael Phair, an openly gay city councillor, received a flood of homophobic messages after the Supreme Court rendered the *Vriend* decision,[177] which ruled that the Alberta government had discriminated against homosexuals: 'One caller threatened to shoot Phair; another threatened to mutilate his genitals.'[178]

The Edmonton Police Service established a gay and lesbian liaison committee in 1992, which a senior officer has chaired for several years; he has also spoken on queer radio shows and at the gay and lesbian community centre.[179] In 1997, an activist complained that despite support from the top brass, most officers did not take the committee seriously, 'and no significant commitment had been made to conducting education on sexual orientation issues.'[180] Although hate crime statistics have been generated since 1994, there is no indication what percentage, if any, involve the queer community. This lack of statistical evidence was gleefully noted by a right-wing magazine in Edmonton: 'Not a single "gay-bashing" assault has been reported to the police ... The homosexual political lobby seeks to promote itself by creating a mythical persecution.'[181]

One source of support is the Gay and Lesbian Community Centre. An activist said that several men have been harassed while entering bars over the past few years. A flamboyant gay man in his early twenties 'gets thumped from time to time, but I don't know the details.'[182] In 2000, a man left a message saying he was waiting for people to leave the centre so he could stab them and slit their throats. The following night he threatened to shoot them. The police traced the calls to a young man, who proudly confessed. Two months later, he was still reported to be in 'secure psychiatric care.'[183]

In 2002, the Edmonton police began using a dedicated cell phone number for community members to report violence. Six of the calls required follow-up, and two led to investigations: one was a domestic assault, the other an unprovoked assault. The same force developed its first dedicated hate crimes unit in 2003 with 'core funding for the next several years' and a full-time officer, who analyzes statistics and responds to requests for information. In response to complaints that the liaison committee was not meeting regularly enough, the officer has added new faces to the committee, which meets every four to six weeks.[184]

The Calgary Conundrum

One activist observed: 'Few gay men in Calgary seem interested in organizing to combat this phenomenon. Part of this is Calgary has historically never organized itself along political lines.' He recalled one victim who 'spent several weeks in hospital, some of it in a coma. He continues to suffer headaches and has some motor and memory problems. His attacker was ... linked to several other such attacks.'[185] In the late 1990s, there were two robberies in Centenary Park: both victims had to be hospitalized but denied being gay. A third man was lured to a truck stop, assaulted, and relieved of his wallet.[186]

Relations with the Calgary police have been spotty. A liaison committee was established, but officers were constantly assigned to it, only to be taken off it. Some activists requested an anonymous reporting system – a move strongly opposed by the police, who apparently threatened to throw people off the committee who opposed them.[187] For a few years, relations improved. An officer has been appointed hate/bias crime coordinator, and assists in investigations and provides the Crown with hate-related evidence. He co-chairs the gay and lesbian liaison committee – which meets once a month – and does community outreach. He participates in Calgary's Pride Parade, the AIDS walk, and the Gay Rodeo. He has distributed a victimization survey and works with youth and AIDS organizations.[188]

However, Calgary's proactive approach to hate crime has clashed with 'old-style' attitudes towards gay sex. In 1998, the Calgary police reportedly installed a camera in a washroom at the zoo[189] and arrested gay men at Bottomlands Park. One complainant said the police were 'part of a three man team which is investigating "male prostitution at many locations in Calgary." There is no prostitution at this spot.'[190]

In 2002, relations were set back considerably when Goliath's Sauna was raided by the vice unit. Thirteen patrons were charged with being 'found in a common bawdy-house,' and two employees were charged with 'keeping a common bawdy-house.'[191] Goliath's two owners, its manager, and a third staff member were charged later.[192] In 2004, the trial heard that Calgary police had mounted an undercover investigation based on two anonymous phone calls and an unrecorded conversation with a male prostitute. The police posed as gay customers; after seeing two clients masturbating, they decided to lay charges.[193]

EGALE's executive director called the laws 'Victorian': 'The State has no place in the bathhouses of the nation.' One activist noted bitterly: 'The police had other options available to them, but chose the one most destructive to community relations.' A liaison committee member was angry that 'the Vice Unit chose to not even consult the very body that is in place to facilitate communication between the queer community and the Police Service.'[194]

In 2003, thirty men waving white towels braved 20-below weather on the steps of the courthouse to support the accused, who were making their first appearance. Although their names were read out in court, no media outlets chose to publish them. Almost all the clients 'entered the equivalent of guilty pleas in order to access the court's alternative measure program and drop off the public radar as quickly as possible.' The owners and staff, however, all pleaded not guilty, then returned 'to the bathhouse to officially re-open it and host a defiant, jubilant celebration.'

One of the thirteen clients, Terry Haldane, refused to sign the alternative measures form 'accepting responsibility' for his criminal actions: 'I've done nothing wrong here.' He alone decided to plead not guilty. His lawyer contends that the bawdy house laws are obsolete, noting that 'a bawdy house is defined as a place where prostitution and/or indecent acts occur.' Since there was no prostitution taking place at Goliath's, 'they must think gay sex is indecent.'[195] Activists started 'Goliath's Defence Fund' and said they were willing to take the case all the way to the Supreme Court.[196]

Saskatoon

The Saskatoon police do not track hate crimes.[197] However, in 2002 the gay and lesbian community made inroads with the department: activists met with the new chief and his superintendants, 'who all seem willing to carry on a dialogue with our community.' The force hired a cultural affairs officer to work, in part, with the queer community: 'We have begun talks about training and some formal liaison committee.'[198]

Gay and Lesbian Health Services provides support with a newsletter, a phone line, a library, and various discussion groups. The newsletter sometimes describes the vehicles belonging to queer-bashing suspects. In 1996, a young man was chased after leaving a club. One activist recalled: 'This guy in a half-ton started following him and swearing at him from the truck. He ran and started going up the Broadway bridge ... They jumped out of the truck and tried to grab him. So he ran back to the club. By then they had two vehicles. They were cowboys. The woman in the club gave him a ride home. An hour later they were still waiting for him. This all happened sometime after 2. That is when all the assaults go on.'[199]

Another activist said he had had 'some close brushes' in Kinsmen Park. He estimated that there have been 'hundreds of bashings in the past ten years,' but that these are never publicized. Many men 'believe they have been bashed because they were cruising the park. They take the victim role. They don't report it to us, or to the police. For two people, it seems to be a recurring thing.'[200]

Regina

Regina is one of the most underreported cities for homophobic violence in Canada. The only media reference I found came from 1997, when assailants caused $1,700 damage to the car of one man. He was on his way home from a club 'when he was attacked by two men while a third one watched. [The victim] tried to drive away but the first man opened the door and started kicking him in the face ... The second person ... attempted to pull [the victim] out of the car but his seat belt prevented them ... "The two guys hung onto my door and were running with the car."'[201]

The victim said another man was gay-bashed a year or two later in Wascana Park 'by a group of kids ... I understand that they were quite startled when he ended up beating the crap out of them.'[202] The Regina police stated that hypothetically, they would 'keep track of crimes if they did occur. But it's not a policy to specifically classify those crimes.' The only hate-related incident they had on file was a homophobic letter sent to the mayor in 1998 after a Gay Pride event was announced.[203]

As of 2002, the Regina police still had no hate crimes reporting system.[204] However, the department organized a meeting attended by fifty or sixty people representing several community groups. An activist told me the queer delegation – which included lesbians and drag queens – made a presentation to discuss cruising and violence in Wascana Park. They were dissatisfied with the way the police treated a homicide in 2001. A young aboriginal man had been beaten to death; the victim 'was very obvious and open about his sexual orientation.' His family had apparently disowned him because he was gay, and made it clear they did not want any gay people at the funeral. The police said the only motive was robbery.[205]

Winnipeg

I was unable to find queer-bashing reports outside of Winnipeg – the prairie city with the most reports of homophobic violence. The Winnipeg police have had a hot-and-cold relationship with the queer community.

In 1992, the police were praised for taping a Crime Stoppers commercial that recreated the 1991 murder of Gordon Kuhtey, whose death heightened concerns about queer-bashing in the city.[206] However, a victim said police 'are more often scornful and uninterested when they respond to complaints of gay bashing.'[207] Meanwhile, an activist said he had heard 'of a minimum of three incidents a week.'[208] He knew '24 people who were assaulted and only two went to the police.'[209] On the banks of the Assiniboine west of the Osborne Bridge, 'packs of "gay bashers" have been known to brutally beat men ... almost every weekend at night between the middle of May and the middle of October.'[210]

A gay group distributed pamphlets with 'instructions on how to thwart an attacker by jabbing at his throat' and announced plans to distribute warning whistles in the cruising area.[211] In 1993, five officers were assigned 'to investigate gay-bashings near the Legislative Building ... Police will also step up the frequency of bike patrols in the area.'[212] In 1993, a man cruising at the Legislature was lured back to the apartment of two teenage brothers, who beat and sexually assaulted him.[213] After the older brother was listed on Manitoba's 'Ten Most Wanted,' a woman in Gimli complained that the RCMP wouldn't take her tip because the address she had given for the suspect was incomplete. Crimestoppers wouldn't take her tip because she had given her name. The Winnipeg police wouldn't accept collect calls.[214]

In 1994, an activist was criticized for trying to distribute safety kits with 'whistles, self-defence pamphlets and other information.' A columnist felt the community 'should think about putting the money to some more productive use. If 20 years of proselytizing hasn't convinced people to steer clear of the area, then nothing will.'[215] A Winnipegger launched a campaign, demanding that teenage queer-bashers be tried in adult court.[216]

Since 1993, the Winnipeg police have had officers trained in hate crimes.[217] One complained that he gets frustrated when police are criticized for not asking if the victim is gay: 'Get the bad guy first ... At 2 a.m., the cops are going to be brusque. Afterwards, they can go into detail.'[218] Winnipeg's queer community centre, the Rainbow Resource Centre, has set up an anonymous, alternative reporting system: it faxes descriptions of queer-bashers to the police, then destroys the form. However, it only does this two or three times a year. Some activists complained that an openly gay officer insists on doing all the police sensitivity training on his own, without consulting the community – and that he only facilitates discussions between the community and the police on his own terms.[219]

In 2000, after a gay man was threatened and chased out of a downtown McDonald's,[220] the centre spearheaded the Community Safety Project, which involved focus groups, 'safety audits' of various gathering places, and the distribution of 250 questionnaires. One respondent wrote that two people had been murdered, possibly by the Manitoba Warriors gang – but there was no indication as to whether the victims were gay, or whether the killings had been motivated by homophobia.[221]

The Winnipeg force's diversity coordinator is a police officer, who acts as a liaison between the police and various communities. He runs a liaison committee with the community, but one activist has complained that it meets rarely: 'For all his good intentions, I don't think he has a depth of understanding about how much our community is at risk. Two weeks will go by before he returns our calls. When we ask him about specific incidents, he says, "Nothing has come across my desk."' He's not proactive.[222]

For his part, the officer told me how difficult it is to build trust in the queer community. He said the police have a recruiting booth at Gay Pride events; once, at a community gala, a lesbian told him about a crime she had experienced but had been afraid to report. He also said he spent hours with a gay couple who were not happy with the way the police had handled their case.[223]

The community is dissatisfied with the way police have investigated murders in their community. Although one took place in October 2002,[224] it was the killing of Kelly Bouboire earlier that year that created tension. The twenty-four–year-old victim was described in the *Winnipeg Sun* as a former prostitute[225] – a fact not mentioned in the queer press. Bouboire, who was openly gay, attended a party with his boyfriend and was seen arguing about the issue of sexual orientation with somebody. Bouboire's boyfriend left before Bouboire did. At 7:30 the next morning, Bouboire was found near a bridge, bleeding from stab wounds; he died shortly afterwards.[226] A vigil at the Legislature attracted 150 people, including local politicians.[227]

There were rumours that the killer had been a client of the victim.[228] Although Joseph Cleeton was charged with first-degree murder, the police discounted hate motivation: 'Based on the evidence which I cannot share, this was not a hate crime,' a spokesman said. The victim's best friend objected: 'The only reason the police are not calling it a hate crime is because this guy is in the closet. They are asking themselves how this could be a hate crime if the murderer is gay.' An activist declared that 'internalized homophobia ... was one of the major causes of hate crimes.'[229]

Sudbury

Reports of queer-bashing in Northern Ontario are difficult to come by, except in Sudbury, which has an increasingly visible queer community. In 1994, one activist reported two queer-bashings and four 'attempted bashings' in Sudbury.[230] In 1999, a transsexual was attacked in a pizzeria, and there were complaints the that Sudbury police were arresting gay men in a 'prostitution sweep.'[231]

There have also been reports of assaults outside Zig's, the local gay bar.[232] According to a local activist, the police have begun to increase patrols in the area. In 2002, a gay man was brutally assaulted coming out of a bar; six months later, the victim was reported to be learning how to read again. Two men were convicted, and were handed relatively lengthy sentences – four years and two years less a day: 'The beating was apparently unprovoked and included homophobic slurs directed at the victim.'[233]

In 1999, the strangling of a Sudbury man raised eyebrows. Denis Villeneuve, thirty-four, was a regular at Zig's. His car was stolen; his body was found in the trunk of a second car. André Gervais and Carmen Bailey were charged with first-degree murder. Because Villeneuve knew the suspects and had been at the house of the accused just before he was killed, the police disavowed any hate motivation: 'As far as we know there is no relationship to his sexual orientation whatsoever.' Later, a friend of the family apparently approached a bartender at Zig's and said: 'Denis's funeral is coming up. Is there any way you can put the word out not to have anyone come to the funeral who is gay?'[234]

The Sudbury police claim that they introduced a hate crime policy in August 1995.[235] Yet they have produced no statistics since then, even though queer-bashing stories have appeared in the local media. For example, one man complained that a bouncer kicked him and his friends out of a straight bar because two of the women were kissing. The bar owner was painfully frank: 'They can call it discrimination ... Had they stayed another five minutes they'd be bleeding today ... We don't want any gays in our bar.'[236]

London

London now has an active gay scene, but in the 1990s, many activities centred around the Homophile Association of London, Ontario (HALO), which operated a community centre and had a committee that monitored violence and criminal justice issues. The committee's former chair wrote that during the 1990s, 'seven assaults or serious threats were reported to us. 14 assaults or serious threats outside HALO or other gay bars. Nine assaults in other areas of town that were reported as gay bashings.'[237]

In contrast, a London police officer I interviewed said: 'From an official and personal point of view, it's not much of a problem.' In the 1990s, he had worked both as a hate crimes investigator and as a vice squad investigator. He saw no contradiction between the two roles.[238] Yet the role of the London vice squad is an extremely sensitive one. Community relations were poisoned in 1993 when police discovered some videotapes and proceeded to institute 'Project Guardian,' a moral panic based on the premise of a 'kiddie porn ring.' This project eventually became a 'joint-forces operation' involving the Toronto police and the OPP. Journalist Joseph Couture began interviewing the 'victims' – young male prostitutes – who were then warned by police to stay away from Couture.[239]

At the time, the London police were headed by Julian Fantino, who went on to become Toronto's police chief in 2000. Police arrested two middle-aged men, using the controversial child pornography laws, which criminalize 'any material that shows people who are under 18 or appear to be under 18 in sexual situations.' On the same day as the arrests, 'Fantino held a press conference in London and announced that the London police had broken the largest porn ring in Canada.'

Gerald Hannon's scathing article observed that 'Project Guardian ... was based on several lies ... It is simply untrue that there was ever a child-pornography ring ... They continued to use that loaded term to barter for what they wanted.' The police seized 875 videotapes

> and though the police did not display them all, those mute stacks around Chief Fantino certainly conveyed the impression ... that it was out of control ... an alphabetical list, and the first title is Abbot and Costello Go to Mars ... The last ... Zorro. Every title in between is a mainstream American or European film ... They could, however, use them to window-dress a press conference, which they did.[240]

A total of sixty men were arrested. Although the *London Free Press* wrote more than a hundred articles about the 'child pornography ring,' Bell and Couture note that

> only one person was charged with making child pornography and only a handful of the 60 men arrested were charged with possession of child pornography, and none of the pornography was made for commercial purposes. The child pornography ring turned out to be a group of teenage boys who introduced one another to men. Very few of the men even knew each other. The most common charge was s. 212(4), obtaining sexual services of a person under 18 for consideration. This charge involved primarily gay men who were alleged to have had sex for money or gifts with teenage hustlers.[241]

Project Guardian conducted almost two thousand interviews and turned into 'a blitz of the gay community ... a witch-hunt, with the mere suggestion that someone might be involved in child pornography being enough for police to procure a search warrant.'[242] Bell and Couture also provide examples of a 'gendered double standard' whereby – during the same time frame in London – heterosexual clients who used the services of teenaged female prostitutes were never charged 'for their involvement with female "children."'[243]

Many at HALO actively opposed Project Guardian. Activists claim that this resistance triggered 'massive' washroom and park arrests. Meanwhile, the mayor bolstered anti-gay rhetoric by refusing to issue a Gay and Lesbian Pride proclamation and by claiming that there was no queer-bashing problem in the city. When victims did go to the police, they were told: 'You have HALO, why don't you go there?'[244] A HALO activist said he was targeted by Chief Fantino himself, who wrote him the following letter:

> Your conduct over the life of Project Guardian, attacking the integrity of our efforts to pursue a criminal investigation delving into the sexual exploitation of children, causes me and all members of the London Police to be suspicious and guarded about your motives. You have spearheaded a malicious campaign with what we know to be negligible support from the community at large ... We will continue to provide professional services and assistance to all citizens regardless of your skewed perception of reality.[245]

Alarmed, the activist took a back seat to another HALO member – who then received this letter from Fantino:

> It is, indeed, regrettable that proponents of adult/child sex have, in a very sinister way, brought disrepute to the integrity of the gay/lesbian community ... Under no circumstances will I engage and give credibility to the proponents of criminal activity (i.e. the sexual exploitation of children).[246]

Although London's queer community has left this traumatic episode behind, problems continue to surface. In 2000, four undercover officers in Gibbons Park threw a gay man to the ground

> to frisk and handcuff me. They told me they were going to notify my wife and names would be posted in the paper. Once I was on the ground they proceeded to pull my pants off for a 'search.' Once I was totally naked and humiliated they groped me. I won't go there again.[247]

In 2002, a multicommunity Hate Crimes Steering Committee, with the support of London City Hall, opened an office and received a federal grant to research the extent of hate crimes in the London area. The committee set up a hate crime hotline, which received from five to seven calls per week. Its next goal is to hire victim services workers who specialize in the needs of specific communities.[248] In 2002, the police said they were tracking hate crimes, but they were unable to provide any statistics.[249] The police now seem more proactive: by 2004, hate crime statistics from 2000 to 2003 had been collated and were being sent to researchers on request. Officers on the London force are now attending various queer community meetings and attending the local Pride parade.[250]

Hamilton

Grant analyses the political struggles over queer space in Hamilton:[251] until the late 1990s, the point of reference for the Hamilton police regarding queer issues was 'around public sex and not around bashing.'[252] In 1996, the police arrested twenty men on sex-related charges at the Royal Botanical Gardens. Seventy-five angry people gathered for a community forum, which quickly brought results: a liaison committee began meeting in 1997, attended regularly by the chief.[253]

An anti-bashing campaign was launched in 1998.[254] One gay man on the committee said he 'witnessed seven different incidents in 3 years. The victims didn't report them because they didn't trust the police.'[255] The hate crime statistics produced by the police have a category for 'sexual orientation,' but don't indicate how many of these involved violent crimes. However, the community relations coordinator and the liaison committee compiled an exhaustive report, which detailed dozens of queer-bashing incidents in the 1980s and 1990s.

In 2004, the owner of a local nightclub was slashed in the basement of a downtown bar. He required more than two hundred stitches 'after he was slashed repeatedly with a broken glass' by a man, apparently of Portuguese descent. More than one hundred people attended an emergency meeting, which was attended by the deputy chief.[256] Mayor Larry Di Ianni expressed his outrage in the *Hamilton Spectator*. However, the victim was reportedly upset that he was outed as a result of the media coverage – and he was displeased that *Xtra* had published a large photograph of him. One queer group was angry about 'perceived Portuguese-bashing by the mainstream community and homophobia within the Portuguese community.'[257]

Quebec City

The police service in Quebec City has no hate crime unit, no officers who specialize in hate crimes, no liaison committee, and no hate crime statistics of any kind. An officer there echoed the view of the Quebec Provincial Police, opining that queer-bashing is 'not important here. We don't have anti-gay violence. Maybe one or two cases out of thousands. Nothing major or organized, no movements against gays. To say that there are not specific crimes would be wrong. There are isolated incidents but no patterns. There's no problem for gays.'[258]

However, the former coordinator of Dire Enfin la Violence facilitated a workshop in Quebec City in 1998. She told me that at first, everyone was silent. 'But as the evening wore on, and when the cases started to come together, the stories were horrifying!' According to one report, two young men seriously bashed a man at the St Charles River cruising area in 1999. Although the bashers were charged with robbery and assault, there were complaints that hate motivation was not attributed.[259]

Halifax

In 1994, the Halifax police claimed they were beginning to collect hate crime statistics.[260] Five years later, however, a deputy chief told me: 'We don't keep track of hate crimes. Unless there is a separate violation put into the Criminal Code, we're not going to change [this policy].'[261] In 2002, a police spokesman said that the department had a special code for hate crimes. But then, he checked with an analyst and found there had been no reports of gay-bashings over the past five years.[262]

This doesn't mean there has been no violence.[263] For example, in 1991, three men screamed 'Fag!' at a drunken, twenty-year-old man. Robert Hogan kicked the victim in the head, which struck the pavement. When the victim tried to get up, 'Hogan struck him again with a jumping kick that smacked [the victim's] head back into the road ... Hogan smiled at [the victim]'s friends and walked away. [The victim], now 21, suffered a skull fracture and damage to cranial nerves that left him with a permanent hearing loss in his right ear that cannot be corrected by a hearing aid, and partial loss of his sense of smell.'[264]

The results of a 1994 victimization survey of three hundred queers in Nova Scotia are given in table 7.5.

A Halifax activist told me that in the early 1990s, a gay phone line 'gave out good advice on avoiding getting bashed.'[265] He explained: 'The

Table 7.5
Results of Nova Scotia Survey on homophobic violence, 1994

Offence	% lesbians	% bi women	% gay men	% bi men
Chased or followed	20	33	51	26
Threatened with violence	27	33	47	60
Pelted with objects	9.3	19.4	19	43
Punched or kicked	5	10	31	16
Assaulted with a weapon	1	0	6	13
Sexually assaulted	11	19	15	20
Harassed by police	5	9	24	26
Assaulted by police	0	0	1	6

Source: Carolyn Smith, *Proud But Cautious: Homophobic Abuse and Discrimination in Nova Scotia* (Halifax: Nova Scotia Public Interest Research Group, 1994), 16–18.

entire gay culture in Halifax was dominated – and this remains a big reality – by a level of closetedness that would shock people from larger cities ... police try very hard ... but they are definitely working with many uncooperative victims.' He estimated that about half the incidents involved men cruising for sex on Citadel Hill.[266] The following warning appeared in a queer newspaper: 'Don't go cruising with your judgement impaired by alcohol or drugs ... Keep your doors locked so that people can't jump in unexpectedly ... If you feel that you're being followed, drive carefully to the Police Department and park near the night entrance ... Cruising is a silent activity and, like hunting, a chance for you to use all of your senses to the utmost ... "The regulars" note styles and colours of cars and even licence numbers.'[267]

Citadel Hill does sound like a very dangerous place. In 2000, 'John,' one of the hill's regulars, told me that a friend of his was cruised by a man, who suddenly pulled out an icepick. One night, the police warned John to get off the hill immediately because someone had a gun. On another night, John witnessed a man – who had just administered oral sex – suddenly get up off his knees and beat up his sex partner, calling his victim a 'faggot.'[268]

In 2000, the Nova Scotia Rainbow Action Project (NSRAP) initiated meetings between the community, the RCMP, and the Halifax police, who said that software to effectively track hate crimes would be too expensive to purchase.[269] In almost the same breath, the police went on television to say that they were very concerned about queer-bashing and were taking all the necessary precautions. NSRAP also organized a community meeting on violence and policing that generated favourable media coverage. One activist took a reporter to NRG, a gay bar where a bashing had occurred a month earlier.[270] The community meeting – the first of its kind in Nova Scotia – generated even more examples of Halifax violence:

- In 1993, 'Bill,' who has a black belt in karate, was followed home from a bar by two men wielding a large stick. They split open Bill's head, which required twelve stitches. After Bill responded – by beating up both of the attackers – two police officers threw him to the ground. He was released – but only because he knew one of the officers.
- In 2000, a gay couple was attacked by four men yelling, 'Faggot' in front of the Horizons gay bar. The assailants ran away after three bar staff came to the victims' defence. It took police forty-five minutes to arrive at the scene.[271]

After several meetings with the Halifax police, NSRAP has put its anti-violence initiative on the back burner. It feels that the Halifax police and the RCMP are not really interested in queer issues. Still, NSRAP suppports individual victims who call NSRAP for help. For example, in 2000, 'Jeremy' went back to a man's house for 'rough sex.' The session spiralled out of control. Jeremy was severely beaten and then a knife came out. He fled. Two days later he called an NSRAP member, who went with Jeremy to file a report. The police took it seriously, arrested the man, and kept him in jail until the trial. But the assailant still went free.[272]

Smaller Cities

In Red Deer, the local newspaper interviewed Stockwell Day, who was the local MLA in 1996 before becoming leader of the Canadian Alliance:

> Day said in 10 years of government, he has never had a complaint, even anonymously, from anyone who was fired or evicted for being gay ...
>
> Day said anecdotes about people getting fired or evicted are pure fabrication.
>
> 'Stories are one thing. Facts are another. I'm so tired of dealing with a few scant, fabricated stories. It just is not happening.'[273]

Accompanying this piece was the story of Robert, who had been bashed in front of a popular Red Deer tavern by two men who called him a 'fucking faggot.' Some customers even came out of the bar to watch. One of the men 'kicked me really hard in the head. I started feeling my head bounce on the ground. They were using my head for a soccer ball.' A month later, his retina was still partially detached. One of the suspects, and the suspect's mother, begged Robert not to pursue charges 'because it would ruin the young man's plans to join the military.'[274] That same year, four chain-swinging skinheads stormed into Red Deer's only gay bar, smashing a glass door: 'Doug, the bar owner ... and a patron returned punches, sparking a brawl which put one attacker in the hospital and left Doug with a bleeding head. The fight ended after the slightly-built bar owner shot a fire extinguisher at the attackers, temporarily blinding them until police arrived.'[275]

In Fort McMurray, Richard Sneath was killed in 2002. He first met Chad Bath on a chatroom at Gay.com, and they had gotten together several times. They met on a park trail and had oral sex. Although Bath 'denied intentionally beating or killing Sneath,' he was found guilty of manslaughter and sentenced to seven years. A local activist noted that there are 10,000 to 15,000 men living in the camps at any given time. She said that Freedom Fort McMurray, a local queer group, receives many inquiries from people who are too scared to go to meetings.[276]

In Lloydminster, a gay man living with another man was attacked on his front lawn in 1995. That same night, two men tried to firebomb their house and were charged with causing a disturbance.[277]

The same year, Alexander Turner, a Windsor man, was found suffocated in his home. 'Initial reports also stated that Turner's hands were bound.' Robert Griffin Antone, Jr, nineteen, was charged with second-degree murder.[279] In 1998, a gay graduate student at the University of Windsor was kicked by a man – claiming to be an engineering student – who called him a 'faggot.' The victim's arm was set with six pins and a permanent metal plate.[279]

In 1994 in Sarnia, 150 people attended a rally by 'People Against Queering Canada,' a group that distributed brochures demanding that homosexuals be 'treated no differently than any other sex offender, rapist or child molester.' Around the same time, two gay men and their female roommate were attacked with two-by-fours after talking to the media about queer rights. Two men wearing Ronald Reagan masks broke into their home in broad daylight.[280]

At Barracuda, an alternative bar in Peterborough, five men assaulted a man and a woman in 1993. The woman 'was choked and punched and a man was held down and kicked repeatedly in the face and body.' Only one man was charged, and police did not classify it as a hate crime. The assistant manager said gay patrons shouldn't be too 'flamboyant' and should 'understand if they're going to start kissing each other there's going to be trouble.'[281] In 1994, a Peterborough artist received homophobic death threats after he opened a controversial show on queer-bashing.[282] In 2003, Peterborough held its first Pride festivities, attracting almost four hundred people.[283]

John Fisher, EGALE's former executive director, said he was 'name-called and spat at and shoved around while leaving a gay bar in Kingston' when he was a graduate student there in the early 1990s.[284] In 2000, two bashings were recorded in Kingston: an altercation with a cyclist and an attack outside an alternative bar.[285] In 2002, Robert LeClair, a local waiter, was beaten and stabbed in his apartment. Two men – at least one of whom was known to the victim – were charged with first-degree murder. Police denied there was any hate motivation.[286]

In Charlottetown, the police randomly receive reports of queer-bashing. They are unable to provide any numbers. A spokesman said this policy is unlikely to change unless a separate statute for hate-motivated assault is created.[287] An activist observed: 'There's a very closeted mentality here. I only know five or six openly gay men, but I know fifty closeted men.' Since the opening of the Confederation Bridge, 'a quarter of the people in the Moncton gay bars are from P.E.I.' He said there are some 'incredibly dangerous' cruising areas in Charlottetown.[288] In early 2001, a workshop was organized, 'Homophobia and Crime Prevention on Prince Edward Island.' David Pepper, from the Ottawa Police Service, was the guest speaker.[289]

In New Brunswick, queer bars and organizations are found in each of the province's three main cities. In Moncton, Safe Spaces – a program funded by Health Canada in 2000 – focused on queer youth under twenty-five and offered workshops and support groups dealing with safe sex, homophobia, and violence.[290] During one discussion, a teenage boy revealed that in 1996 he had been beaten up for being gay at a junior high school. The coordinator noted that young gay men tend to be much more at risk of violence than young lesbians.[291] On the streets surrounding Moncton's only gay bar, there are periodic reports of assaults.

Two gay men from Maine visiting Saint John were attacked at their hotel in 1998. One of them was sent to hospital with serious injuries. A few months later, a gay bar owner had his nose broken by a man who said he wanted to 'kill all the queer people in the world.'[292] In 2000, two men assaulted and slashed a gay man in the cemetery near an alternative bar in Saint John. The following week, 'a man entered the bar, threatened the bartender and said basically, "I'll do to you what I did to the guy last week."' The man was ejected, but the police made no arrests.[293]

In Fredericton, a few well-publicized queer-bashing incidents have raised awareness.[294] After a gay man and his straight friend left a gay bar in Fredericton, three men – seventeen, nineteen, and twenty-one[295] – came out of a car yelling 'faggot' and assaulted them. The victims were hospitalized, then released the next day. Fredericton's mayor refused to call it a hate crime: 'I'm not a judge. I haven't heard the other side of the story yet. As mayor, I can't go jumping to those conclusions.'[296] A police representative said the Fredericton force had 'an extremely sophisticated system' for capturing hate crimes, yet she was able to identify only one queer-bashing case in recent years.[297] In 2003, Andy Scott, a Liberal MP in Fredericton, was assaulted in his office by a bipolar man who was angry at Scott's support for same-sex marriage.[298]

Newfoundland Gays and Lesbians for Equality (NGALE) provides community support with a phone line and newsletter. I was unable to find any reports of homophobic violence outside of St John's. However, one activist said NGALE sometimes receives calls about queer-bashing in the city. The violence occurs in a small area of downtown and in one park: 'Information is sketchy at times and provides little to work with.'[299]

In 1998, a man was lured up a lane at 3:30 in the morning, where 'a couple of other guys were waiting for him ... This incident was pretty severe.' In 1998, another man was beaten up at the back entrance of a gay bar. In 1999, a man who frequents a cruising area said he saw four people in a van, two of whom were hiding under a blanket, ready to pounce.[300] NGALE believes police should be more visible in these areas and complained that 'police and media do not perceive a problem.'[301]

The Royal Newfoundland Constabulary (RNC) said it does not track hate crimes and has no formal dialogue with the queer community. However, it is the only police force I observed that practised 'shaming' when dealing with gay-bashers. One gay man I interviewed was harassed by four youths in a cruising area. He got the licence number of the youths' car and reported it to the police, who traced the licence and went to the home of one of the boys late at night. They woke his father up and informed him the boy had been harassing gay men – even though the boy denied it.[302]

Smaller Towns and Rural Areas

Riordon offers accounts of rural queers who have succeeded in creating unique lives outside the urban gay ghettos.[303] Harry's research revealed that urban gay-bashers have more 'available targets' than 'bashers in smaller places,' where the violence 'is probably more geographically diffuse and opportunistic in nature.' Queer-bashing rates are lower in smaller areas because (1) there are fewer 'gay-defined places' that bashers can target, and (2) 'the more conservative cultures typical of most smaller communities may induce homosexuals to go to greater lengths to conceal their sexual identity.'[304]

In 1994, Planned Parenthood in Nova Scotia developed a phone line that 'offered peer counselling to people 25 and younger who are struggling to accept their sexuality.' It was soon overwhelmed: 'The organization racked up hundreds of dollars in long-distance phone bills, all from rural kids calling collect because they were too scared to let their parents know they might be gay – and too isolated to talk to anyone else.'[305]

In 1994, two lesbians in Hubbards, Nova Scotia – after having graffiti spray-painted on their car – received an anonymous letter that said: 'AIDS KILLS FRUITS.' When the women showed the letter to an RCMP officer in neighbouring Tantallon, they were told the letter was not hate mail because technically, it was true: AIDS *does* kill fruits.[306]

In 2000, sixty-four–year-old Tim Barrett was killed in Renfrew, Ontario. Rodney Flegel was seen going home in a taxi with the victim. The driver overheard Flegel asking whether there was any beer in the house. Later, the driver picked up only Flegel, who was carrying a case of beer. A week later, the victim's naked, bound body was discovered, beaten to death with a dresser drawer. Flegel was charged with second-degree murder. As a way of showing that Flegel enjoyed homosexual contact, the Crown introduced a witness who testified that he had performed oral sex on the accused.[307]

A young man from a small town in northern Saskatchewan described his experience on the dance floor of a local bar: 'A group of guys sitting at the next table from us kept staring and swearing. We thought it was because we were Native and didn't think much of it ... They came up to us and started pushing me around and calling me a 'dirty fag' ... That night I ended up at the hospital with multiple fractures to my face, two of my ribs got broken, and a broken arm. That's my story of being gay in a small northern Saskatchewan town.'[308]

In British Columbia, most anti-violence programs, queer-bashing reports, and complaints about police originate in Vancouver.[309] In the late 1990s, an organization called Rainbow BC developed a provincewide network of queer organizations and organized conferences. A toll-free information line funded by the provincial government connected callers with The Centre, Vancouver's queer community centre.

Northern Canada: Yukon, Northwest Territories, and Nunavut

It was difficult to get information from Canada's North. GALA North, Yukon's queer group, is well organized, holds regularly scheduled dances, and maintains a phone line. On a visit to Whitehorse in 2000, I left a message on GALA's answering machine that was returned within hours. An openly gay man who had lived in Whitehorse for several years told me that taunting related to sexual orientation 'occurs regularly in bars and their proximity.' He mentioned a couple of unreported cases. In 1995, an eighteen-year-old gay youth was beaten by five youths. In 1997, a thirty-three–year-old gay male made eye contact with a man outside a bar. He was pushed against a wall and hit several times. The victim did not report it and declined counselling.[310]

I interviewed an openly gay man who had lived in Yellowknife for thirteen years and who had travelled extensively throughout N.W.T. and Nunavut. He knew everyone who was out in the region and had never heard any reports of queer-bashing. A gay and lesbian organization in Yellowknife holds regular social events and appears to provide a good network, especially for lesbians. In 2003, N.W.T. created a Human Rights Commission, which prohibits discrimination on several grounds, including sexual orientation. This was the first jurisdiction in Canada to specifically protect the transgendered.[311]

In 2000, I interviewed a lesbian who had lived in Iqaluit for five years. She could think of no episodes of homophobic violence; in fact, she could think of no openly gay men – and she knew only two closeted lesbians. Things have changed rapidly since then. In 2001, Iqaluit celebrated its first Gay Pride picnic, which has become an annual tradition. In 2003, a travelling Parliamentary committee examining same-sex marriage sparked debate on queer issues; two months later, Svend Robinson made northern headlines when he attended the Pride picnic. One organizer explained that some Inuit still feel 'unsafe' attending, and that the goal was 'to raise public awareness and take the stigma out of being lesbian or gay in Nunavut.'[312]

There still seems to be a certain degree of denial. Nunavut – along with Prince Edward Island and New Brunswick, has been criticized for not providing condoms in correctional centres. Premier Paul Ogilik reportedly said that condoms were unnecessary because there were no homosexual prisoners in Nunavut.[313]

Summary

Most of the queer-bashing incidents I analyzed in this book occurred in large urban centres, especially Toronto and Vancouver. Every city has its own approach to homophobic violence. At one end of the 'police-community' continuum, Dire Enfin la Violence (DELV) has been the most critical of the police. Despite Montreal's huge, highly visible queer community – and several murders and bashings – an underfunded anti-violence program finally disintegrated in 2003.

At the other end of the spectrum, Vancouver's queer community allowed police to control anti-violence programs, which led to strong discontent. Aaron Webster's murder in 2001 forced the community to face its indifference and create a new, community-based approach, which is still unfolding. Toronto's social service-oriented anti-violence program represents a 'mixed model.' Activists provide assistance, advocate on behalf of victims and liaise with police. The Anti-Violence Program (AVP) tries to remain at arm's length when advocating on behalf of victims, but has been criticized for taking a 'social work' approach to homophobic violence.

Medium-sized cities like Ottawa have provided leadership, defined issues, and created the country's longest-running liaison committee. But cracks have appeared recently, leading to criticisms that the community has become complacent. Calgary is an example of a police force divided: one hand offers support and assistance to the queer community, while the other wields a stick, as evidenced by the bathhouse raids of 2002. Some cities are becoming increasingly organized around violence (Victoria, Regina, London and Halifax); others are in stasis. Some cities are unable to capture the attention of the police; others cannot galvanize support at the grassroots. Smaller and northern communities face their own specific challenges, and would benefit from Rainbow BC's strategy of reaching out to isolated citizens and connecting them with support and services in larger centres.

Conclusion

Warfare and repression have rational objectives: to defeat a formally defined enemy, or to prevent a subjugated group from challenging, weakening, or overturning authority structures. The violence of rape, random beating, the harassment of threats, taunts, display of pictures and symbols, and so on, is irrational in the sense that it is not explicitly instrumental to an end. It is performed for its own sake, for sport or out of random frustration, and has as its object only the humiliation and degradation of its victims.

Iris Marion Young, *Justice and the Politics of Difference*

In May 2003, hundreds of people arrived in Montreal for a historic meeting: EGALE's Rainbow Visions Conference, probably the largest and most diverse gathering of queer activists in Canada. The array of workshops included the following:

- When Violence Happens at Home: Confronting Same-Sex Partner Abuse
- Queer Male Youth and the Sex Trade
- Aboriginal Anti-Homosexualism
- Everybody's Kinky! Leathersex, Fetishism, Kink, S/M and Healthy Sexuality
- Sex, Drugs and the Circuit
- Barebacking: Challenges to a Harm Reduction Approach to Safer Sex
- Transsexual Cross-Dressing
- The Politics of Polyamory
- You Don't Look Like a Lesbian: Femmes Speak Out
- Benefits of Meditation for Queers and Their Allies

Since beginning my research on homophobic violence in 1995, I had always contended that at some point, like-minded researchers and activists should link up. I had always been struck by the fact that victims, researchers, and activists were isolated in various pockets across Canada, unaware of one another's struggles and successes.

At Rainbow Visions, all of that changed. On the first full day of the conference, I sat on a queer-bashing panel with Ellen Faulkner, Ann Field, and Roy Gillis, whose research I have already cited in this book. In the afternoon, we squeezed into a small classroom to attend 'Hate Crimes and the LGBT Communities,' chaired by activists from Toronto and Vancouver. The crowd included a young woman from rural B.C., a man from St John's, a union member from the Public Service Alliance of Canada, and an aboriginal man from Ottawa. There were people from Edmonton, Sault St Marie, and Moncton. Some heterosexuals from Saint John also showed up; they said a friend of theirs had been killed, and they wanted to learn more about the issue.

The presenters identified new, troubling trends. Private security guards are harassing queers in malls, and incidents of family violence – involving fathers, uncles, and brothers – are also on the rise. A growing problem in the gay male community is homelessness. In 2000, a man was killed at the Salvation Army hostel on Sherbourne Street in Toronto, a city where many indigent gay men choose to live in bathhouses. This lack of secure housing makes them more vulnerable to crime and violence.[1] In 2002, a homeless gay man named Jude Simard was killed in Montreal's Viger Square. This park was the site of a turf war between a gang of skinheads and a gang of gay men, according to the victim's lover, who was also homeless and had also been attacked in the weeks leading to the killing.[2]

At the end of Rainbow Visions, there were hugs and tears and promises to write. This conference somehow felt different: a fundamental shift had occurred, and a new era of queer organizing in Canada had begun. Invigorated, I came back to Ottawa, the region where I had grown up, to finish this book. It's hard to sum up ten years of research. But here are the areas where I believe action is required immediately:

Youth Education

More than 40 per cent of the queer-bashing incidents I analysed involved teenaged assailants. Can there be any better reason to support anti-homophobia education in schools?

Prisons

Canada's prison system needs to confront several pressing issues: the education of prison guards, support for queer prisoners, and innovative ways to reduce the targeting of gay, lesbian, bisexual, transgendered, effeminate, less assertive, and/or physically smaller inmates.

Law Reform

The provisions for enhanced sentencing have provoked widespread condemnation – as well as boasts that the government is getting tough on hate crime. Yet there is still little empirical evidence that the approach has worked. The hate propaganda law is important, but police cannot use it to catch assailants. A separate statute for hate-motivated assault and murder would give law enforcement officials more tools to work with. It would also make it easier for researchers to track hate crimes nationally. A universal hate-crime definition would finally make the statistics between various departments more comparable and comprehensible, and would encourage some agencies to take hate crime more seriously. It will take a strong coalition of police and minority groups to compel the federal government to dust off the Hate Crimes Statistics Act.

Gun Control

The two killers profiled in this book who generated the most carnage – John Rivest (four victims) and Marcello Palma (three victims) – both had a history of mental health problems and were under psychiatric care. So why were both of them allowed to stockpile weapons?

Parole

This book provides several examples of men who bashed and killed while on parole. Parole officers need to be trained to recognize criminals who prey on queer victims – and queers have a right to be warned when these predators are released back into their communities.

Homicide

Canadians attended several vigils for Matthew Shephard, the young American gay man who was murdered so brutally in 1998. So why has there been so little outpouring of anger for the hundred-plus homicide victims I have listed in these pages? At least Shephard's killers are locked away for life. What about Garth Hill in Victoria – strangled with a belt for an agonizing four minutes? Why did no one protest that his killing was not considered a hate crime? Where was the anger when his killers were allowed to apply for parole a few years later?

The Department of Justice needs to carefully examine homicide cases involving homosexual panic and homosexual advance. Qualitative research is needed to understand how homophobia seeps into the investigation, the prosecution, and the defence of these crimes. Obviously, it is impossible to do away with self-defence and provocation in Canadian law, but prosecutors need to be re-educated – in the same way that they were taught to treat rape cases differently in the 1980s.

It would also help to learn from other countries. The New South Wales Attorney General recommends a way out of the conundrum: changes to the provocation defence that would 'preclude non-violent homosexual advances from forming the basis of the provocation defence.' This report went even further, suggesting that trials which feature violence – and the victim's 'unusual sexuality' – be tried by jury.[3] According to de Pasquale, 'jurors would be directed to reach their decision without reference to any personal sympathy or animosity towards the victim or the accused, and would also be prohibited from casting judgment on the morality of the victim's behaviour.'[4]

International Issues

Policymakers should take their cue from Cowl and review programs in other countries that get to the roots of hate-motivated violence and that have as their goal 'the reduction of discriminatory attitudes' and the fostering of 'a general climate of mutal understanding and appreciation of diversity.' Some programs aim to reduce 'youth disenfranchisement' – for example, Germany's Federal Youth Plan, which targeted at-risk youth with work experience projects, sports and cultural activities, and events that enhance 'the understanding of citizenship and pluralistic democracy.' Australia and various European countries have embraced a multiagency, cooperative approach that involves partnerships between various levels of government, non-governmental organizations, community groups, and the private sector – a move that shifts responsibility for these activities to the local and regional levels.[5]

More and more queer refugees arrive in Canada every year. Queers across Canada have the opportunity to expand their horizons and open their hearts to these refugees by following Vancouver's lead and setting up 'Rainbow Refugee Committees' to help queer refugees heal and adapt.

Legal Remedies

Canadian queer-bashing victims and the loved ones of murder victims have every right to demand justice as a part of their healing process. Here are some of their options:

- Punitive damages: Victims can demand punitive damages from queer-bashers who were convicted but served no time.
- Private prosecutions: If solid evidence exists, private prosecution is an option against offenders who were not investigated or prosecuted.
- Dangerous offenders: Prosecutors can request that offenders who have consistently targeted queers be labelled dangerous offenders and taken off the streets.
- Goods and services: Cases of queer-bashing inside commercial premises can be pursued under the Competition Act.
- Litigation: When offenders are sued, all victims benefit. If the process were coordinated by an anti-violence organization, offenders could actually contribute financially to the solution: educational and research programs.
- Class actions: Victims' and queer rights organizations can also sue police agencies and prosecutors that refuse to gather and present evidence on hate motivation. This evidence is the only way judges can make use of the enhanced sentencing provisions.
- Charter challenges: Police and prosecutors who gather evidence on hate motivation targeting other minorities – but not queers – may be violating the Charter of Rights and Freedoms.

Policing Concerns

This book includes examples of handsome undercover officers who dress in tight jeans, entrap gay men, and then arrest them for committing 'indecent acts.' Lesbians have been harassed when gathering in private spaces. In chapter 6, I showed how Daniel Webb – an Anglican priest who sued the police for entrapment – not only lost his case but was ordered to pay legal costs. Although smaller groups have been supportive, larger and more powerful national groups like EGALE – groups that have the ability to raise funds and demand law reform – should be playing a much bigger role on this front. EGALE has made occasional statements condemning police practices and violence, but it devotes most of its time and effort to less controversial legal issues.

Police officers – and officials in prisons and lock-ups – who queer-bash can and should be prosecuted under the torture statute. If child molesters can be prosecuted for sexual abuse that occurred forty years ago, then why can't the Montreal police, caught on camera beating up queers in 1990, be brought to justice? Their actions were outrageous – an affront to all Canadians. It has been reported – but cannot be verified – that as many as twelve gay men who were bashed by Montreal police later received out-of-court settlements. This raises the chilling question: How many more cases are out there?

This book offers examples of RCMP officers who targeted gays and lesbians and botched their investigations. The Mounties' system for keeping hate crimes records is rudimentary compared to the ones used by other urban forces; moreover, they have resisted the broader definition of hate crime used by other urban forces. The RCMP has no mechanism for communicating with the queer community. A national gay and lesbian organization like EGALE should initiate a dialogue with the RCMP and demand that it take queer-bashing more seriously.

During such a meeting, real cases could be discussed – like the one that occurred in Moncton in 2001. Two gay men were holding hands at a bus stop when a straight couple began screaming obscenities at them. One of the gay men, who was epileptic, was knocked to the ground; the victim had two fits and was rushed to the hospital for stitches. The RCMP concluded that the men were not gay-bashed, and the Crown dropped the charges.[6]

The current sentencing enhancement guidelines simply will not work if law enforcement agencies do not gather evidence of hate motivation. Without that evidence, the Crown and judges are powerless to recommend stronger deterrents.

- The OPP has a hate crimes unit but has no idea how many hate crimes occur in Ontario in a given year. It claims to be unaware of any queer-bashing cases whatsoever.[7] In a letter from the OPP's Hate Crimes Unit, an officer told me: 'I am unable to provide you with statistics within the OPP regarding hate crimes as the organization does not collect these.'[8] Where is the outrage from Ontario's huge, tax-paying queer community?

- The QPP and the police forces in Montreal, Quebec City, and Gatineau have produced no statistics on homophobic violence.
- The police in Edmonton and Hamilton gather hate crime statistics, but these say nothing about how many queer victims were targeted.

In many Canadian cities, when you ask the police whether they 'keep track' of queer-bashings, they say, 'Yes, on a case-by-case basis.' But when you probe further, asking for the exact number that have occurred in the past one, five, or ten years, they tell you 'zero' – or that they don't know. Moreover, police across Canada generally refuse to classify the killings of queer people as hate crimes. If you call hate crime units across the Canada and ask them how many hate crime statistics involve homicides in the queer community, the response is usually 'zero.' Why does the queer community accept this?

Striking the Right Balance

Across Canada, relations between queers and the police range from excellent to non-existent. Activists can bring about change by integrating the best elements the following communities have to offer:

- Vancouver: excellent communication between law enforcement agencies.
- Toronto: superior crime analysis and the good reputation of an organization for providing consistent and concrete support to victims in pain.
- Montreal: a critical approach toward the social roots of homophobic violence.
- Ottawa: the ability to change the way the queer community is policed.

The degree to which each community engages with the police can be located on a continuum. At one end, Montreal activists took a root causes approach to violence. When they disagreed with police actions – such as ones involving brutality, washroom arrests, or negligence – they weren't afraid to send out press releases. However, perhaps as a result of this confrontational approach, programs were underfunded and eventually perished. A Toronto-style 'social work' approach might have made the group more solvent and provided more services to victims.

At the other end of the continuum is Vancouver, where the community let the police take the lead for years. Now a more community-based approach is beginning to take root. In Ottawa, police and activists receive top marks for working together. The police set up a hate crimes unit and hired an openly gay man to work with many minority groups. Community members who disagree with the Ottawa police have a very active liaison committee to take their concerns to. Recent soul searching will make the committee even stronger.

For better or worse, Toronto's Anti-Violence Program (AVP) offers the most practical model for addressing queer-bashing in Canadian cities. Like many front-line agencies, this one is short of staff and overworked, but keeps the focus on victims. It is very accessible: since 1990, AVP has been located in the centre of the gay village, where many bashings occur. The AVP phone line provides an alternative to 911. When victims disagree with the police, AVP provides support. When friction arises between the community and the police, AVP takes a leadership role.

One criticism of AVP is that it does not focus on the increasing problem of homicide. When you look at its statistics, you find that it has several categories for crime – assault, sexual assault, and so on – but none for homicide. And yet there have been at least thirty-six queer-related homicides in Toronto since 1990. So why did AVP organize a memorial for a gay man killed in Wyoming – but not for a gay man, loved by his community, whose burnt corpse was found in a Scarborough dumpster? We need more rituals when these killings occur, so that we never get inured to the violence. In 2004, I asked the AVP coordinator why his program did not get involved in issues relating to murders in Toronto. He replied that the killing of psychiatrist Henry Durost in 2004, for example, 'was not a hate crime because robbery was a motive.' When I asked about the killing of transsexual prostitute Cassandra Do, he said: 'The killer hasn't been found. So we don't know if it was hate-motivated or not.'[9]

In Ottawa, police are quick to discuss the brutal 1989 killing of Alain Brousseau in the media and during public discussions. But at least eight other queer-related homicides have occurred in the National Capital Region since then. Brousseau's killing is a 'safe' and more clear-cut homicide, one that involves an 'innocent' (read 'straight') victim. Yet Ottawa's community stood by silently in 2003 after a drug addict killed William Goodwin, a respected civil servant, who was vilified in the local press. In contrast, Montreal activists have taken more risks, publicizing murders that were not quite so clear-cut. Montrealers learned the hard way that *all* homicides involving queer victims undermine the community. The homophobia implicit in many of these horrible killings eventually seeps into the courtrooms, media coverage, and popular discourse.

Calgary is providing a pragmatic model for medium-sized cities that do not have the resources to develop a dedicated hate crime unit. A single police officer trained in hate crime investigation, with links to the queer community, can make a huge difference – as long as the officer's expertise is recognized and acknowledged at all levels in the police department. After the bathhouse raids of 2002, this officer's role was criticized as ineffective. The Calgary police need to demonstrate that their vision of 'community policing' reflects a hands-on, proactive strategy, and not just window dressing.

One hopeful sign is the hiring of an openly gay instructor at the Ontario Police College. All police recruits are required to take his diversity course during their three-month program. One exercise exposes recruits to same-sex domestic violence. In another exercise, recruits are presented with two scenarios: in one, officers encounter a heterosexual couple having sex in a car; in the other, a gay couple is having sex. Afterwards, the recruits 'discuss the differences in their reactions to each couple.' The college is also producing anti-homophobia videos to educate police on how to be sensitive toward their colleagues.[10]

Towards the Future

I began writing about this topic in 1992. I now realize that the problem is not going away. I'll never forget the first victim services worker I interviewed in Vancouver, a woman who had seen her fair share of queer-bashing cases. She told me: 'This is a legal system, not a justice system. If you're looking for validation and justice, you won't get it. You have to go to the community to heal.'[11]

But you don't have to be on the front lines to make a difference. Canadians could develop and contribute to an organization that would:

- serve as a clearinghouse for data from across the country,
- lobby for legislative changes,
- develop educational programs for schools, community groups, and criminal justice personnel,
- encourage social service agencies to meet the needs of victims,
- support victims pursuing various legal remedies,
- alert the media to community concerns,
- monitor international issues, and educate Canadians about how they can assist, and
- become a 'centre of excellence' in the research of homophobic violence.

A group like this could also link – both electronically and physically – like-minded professionals and other interested citizens across the country. A national conference on the topic would be an excellent start.

In my conversations and correspondence with hundreds of concerned individuals over the past several years, I have noticed two things: they are sickened by this violence, and they are at a loss. I am convinced that with the right political will, Canada could be the next world leader in this area.

The expectation is already there. On New Year's Day in 1996, two gay tourists from New York, staying at the Royal York in Toronto, were confronted by fifteen thugs a few metres from the hotel entrance. They were assaulted and had to spend the night in hospital. The director of New York City's Anti-Violence Project was shocked to hear about the incident. He told *Xtra*: 'I mean, if we can't go to Canada and feel safe, where can we go?'[12]

Where, indeed?

Notes

Introduction

1 Douglas Victor Janoff 'Darkness at the Edge of Town,' *Vancouver Sun*, 12 Sept. 1992, D4.
2 Reed Hortie (1993). 'Summertime's Ugly Emotion of Hate Smothers Young Men's Fancy for Love,' *Vancouver Sun*. 24 April 1993, 24, A2.
3 See Uyen Vu, 'Montreal Hate-Crime Conundrum,' *Montreal Gazette*, 22 Aug. 1998, B1.
4 Janoff, 'Darkness at the Edge of Town.'
5 Ellen Faulkner, 'Empowering Victim Advocates: Organizing against Anti-Gay/Lesbian Violence in Canada,' *Critical Criminology* 10 (2001): 124.
6 Michael Olivero and Rodrigo Murataya, 'Homophobia and University Law Enforcement Students.' *Journal of Criminal Justice Education* 12, 2 (2001): 271–81. But see Robin Burke. *A Matter of Justice* (New York: Routledge, 1996).
7 See John Winterdyk and Douglas King, eds., *Diversity and Justice in Canada* (Toronto: Canadian Scholars Press, 1999).
8 See Douglas Victor Janoff, 'Life under Siege: Mexico's Gays Face Discrimination, Extortion and Murder.' *Xtra West*, 19 Oct. 1995, 15.
9 See Douglas Victor Janoff, 'Amsterdam 1998: Queer Global Activism for the New Millennium,' a report prepared for EGALE (1998), available at www.egale.ca/politics/politics/amsterdam.htm. See also Amnesty International USA, *Crimes of Hate, Conspiracy of Silence: Torture and Ill-Treatment Based on Sexual Identity* (New York: Amnesty International USA, 2001). There is also a proliferation of international victimization studies emerging. See, for example, Eva Tiby, 'Victimization and Fear among Lesbians and Gay Men in Stockholm,' *International Review of Victimology* 8, 2 (2001): 217–43.

10 See www.bgogemini.org and www.lambdaistanbul.org.

11 See Canadian Press, '"Lesbian" Assignment Protested by Student,' *Vancouver Sun*, 26 May 1995, B5, and Canadian Press, 'Victoria,' *Calgary Herald*. 7 Oct. 1995, A8.

12 Faulkner, 'Empowering Victim Advocates,' 124.

13 Joan Scott, 'Experience,' in Judith Butler and Joan Scott, eds., *Feminists Theorize the Political* (New York: Routledge, 1992), 25–6.

14 Gary Kinsman, *The Regulation of Desire: Homo and Hetero Sexualities*, 2nd ed. (Montreal: Black Rose, 1996).

15 Frank Mort, 'Essentialism Revisited? Identity Politics and Late Twentieth-Century Discourses of Homosexuality,' in Jeffrey Weeks, ed., *The Lesser Evil and the Greater Good: The Theory and Politics of Social Diversity* (London: Rivers Oram, 1994), 203.

16 Bruce MacDougall, *Queer Judgments: Homosexuality, Expression, and the Courts in Canada* (Toronto: University of Toronto Press, 2000), 13.

17 See Michel Foucault, *The History of Sexuality*, Volume 1, *An Introduction* (New York: Vintage, 1978).

18 Author's interview with a Canadian academic who researches homophobic violence, 6 May 1999.

19 Peter O'Neill, 'Gay-Bashing Often Gays Fighting Own, Reform MP Claims.' *Vancouver Sun*. 18 March 1995, A12.

20 Author's interviews with two Halifax gay men at community meeting in Halifax, 25 Oct. 2000.

21 Melissa Barlow, 'The Media, the Police and the Multicultural Community: Observations on a City in Crisis.' *Journal of Crime and Justice* 17, 2 (1994): 133–65.

22 Cynthia Petersen, 'A Queer Response to Bashing: Legislating against Hate,' *Queen's Law Journal* 16 (1991): 237–60.

23 Katy Méthot and Alexandra Théberge, 'Recherche sur les habitudes et mode de vie des lesbiennes,' report prepared by *Gazelle* magazine and Dire Enfin la Violence (1996), 51.

24 See, for example, Elizabeth Bartle, 'Lesbians and Hate Crimes.' *Journal of Poverty* 4, 4 (2000): 23–43.

25 Linda Bernhard, 'Physical and Sexual Violence Experienced by Lesbian and Heterosexual Women.' *Violence against Women* 6, 1 (2000): 68–79.

26 Jane Ussher and Julie Mooney-Somers, 'Negotiating Desire and Sexual Subjectivity: Narratives of Young Lesbian Avengers,' *Sexualities* 3, 2 (2000): 183–200.

27 A. Ault (1997). 'When It Happens to Men, It's "Hate" and "a Crime": Hate Crimes Policies in the Contexts of Gay Politics, Movement Organizations, and Feminist Concerns,' *Journal of Poverty* 1, 1 (1997): 49–63.

28 But see Frank King and Daryl Slade. 'Parents Cry as Woman Charged in Death,' *Calgary Herald*, 24 July 1999, B1.

1: Methodology and the Media: Reading between the Lines

1 Bonnie Belec, 'His Own Worst Enemy.' *The Telegram*, 8 Feb. 1999, 1. St John's, NF.
2 Becki Ross, *The House That Jill Built: A Lesbian Nation in Formation* (Toronto: University of Toronto Press, 1995), 18.
3 F.A. McHenry, 'A Note on Homosexuality, Crime and the Newspapers.' *Journal of Criminal Psychopathology* 2 (1941): 533.
4 Ibid., 541.
5 Albert Reiss, 'The Social Integration of Queers and Peers,' *Social Problems* 9, 2 (1961): 118–19.
6 Ted Palys, 'Research Decisions: Qualitative and Quantitative Persepctives' unpublished manuscript (1995), 176–7.
7 Laud Humphreys, *Tearoom Trade* (Chicago: Aldine, 1970), 41.
8 Ibid., 105.
9 See Gary Smith, Susan Kippax, and Murray Chapple. 'Secrecy, Disclosure and Closet Dynamics,' *Journal of Homosexuality* 35, 1 (1998): 53–73.
10 Raymond Berger, 'Passing and Social Support among Gay Men,' *Journal of Homosexuality* 23, 3 (1992): 94.
11 Julian Roberts, *Disproportionate Harm: Hate Crime in Canada* (Working document, Department of Justice Canada, 1995), x.
12 Author's interview with Julian Roberts, 11 May 1999.
13 Edward Sagarin and Donal MacNamara, 'The Homosexual as Crime Victim,' *International Journal of Criminology and Penology* 3, 1 (1975): 14.
14 Interview with the author, 21 May 1999.
15 Interview with the author, 23 June 1999.
16 Joseph Harry, 'A Probability Sample of Gay Males,' *Journal of Homosexuality* 19, 1 (1990): 90.
17 Elizabeth Stanko and Paul Curry, 'Homophobic Violence and the Self "At Risk."' *Social and Legal Studies* 6, 4 (1997): 517.
18 John L. Martin and Laura Dean. 'Developing a Community Sample for an Epidemiological Study of AIDS,' in Claire Renzetti and Raymond Lee, eds., *Researching Sensitive Topics* (Newbury Park, CA: Sage, 1993), 85.
19 Gregory Herek and Kevin Berrill, 'Documenting the Victimization of Lesbians and Gay Men: Methodological Issues,' in Gregory Herek and Kevin Berrill, *Hate Crimes: Confronting Violence against Lesbians and Gay Men.* (Newbury Park, CA: Sage, 1992), 274.
20 John Greyson. 'Security Blankets: Sex, Video and the Police,' in Martha

Gever, Pratibha Parmar, and John Greyson, *Queer Looks: Perspectives on Lesbian and Gay Film and Video* (Toronto: Between the Lines, 1993), 384.

21 Jacquelyn Nelson and George Kiefl, *Survey of Hate-Motivated Activity* (technical report prepared for the Department of Justice, Ottawa, 1995).

22 Conal Mullen, 'Police Issue Warrant in Miles Slaying.' *Edmonton Journal*, 18 November 1998, B1.

23 Letter from Edmonton homicide investigator to the author, 9 June 1999.

24 Telephone interview with the author, 4 May 1999.

25 Chad Skelton and Yvonne Zacharias 'Police on Park Murder: It's a Hate Crime,' *Vancouver Sun*, 19 Nov. 2001, A1, A2.

26 Michael Kealy, 'Taken before Their Time.' *Xtra!* 6 June 1996, 19.

27 Canadian Press 'Serial Killer Discounted in Prostitute Murders,' *Vancouver Sun*, 24 May 1996, A7.

28 Henry Hess, 'Suspect Made Advances, Hairdresser Says,' *Globe and Mail.* 4 June 1996, A3.

29 Philip Mascoll, 'Accused Man Admits He Killed Prostitutes, Court Told,' *Toronto Star*, 29 April 1999, B1.

30 Christie Blatchford, 'Witnesses Demonstrate Capacity for Self-Delusion.' *National Post*, 19 Aug. 1999, A6.

31 Sam Pazzano, 'Triple Killings "Psychotic Episode."' *Toronto Sun*, 13 Nov. 1999, 4.

32 *R. v. Palma*, [2001] O.J. No. 3283.

33 See Kevin Griffin, '50-Year-Old Swimmer Breaks World Record at Gay Games,' *Vancouver Sun*, 8 Aug. 1990, B1, B4; 'Rescued from Basher,' *Xtra!* 28 Sept. 1990, 5; Equality for Gays and Lesbians Everywhere, 'EGALE Submissions to the Senate Committee on Legal and Constitutional Affairs: re: Bill C-41 – Hate Crimes' (1995); House of Commons Standing Committee on Justice and Legal Affairs respecting Bill C-41, an Act to Amend the Criminal Code (sentencing) and other Acts in consequence thereof (1994) 1 December 1969: 6; 'History: Violence against the Gay/Lesbian/Transgendered Community,' report prepared by the Community Relations Coordinator, Hamilton-Wentworth Regional Police, 28 May 1999.

34 See Canadian Press, 'Husband Jailed in "Blowout."' *Calgary Herald*, 27 March 1993, A2; and 'EGALE Submissions to the Senate Committee.'

35 See 'DeCarlo Arrest'. *Xtra!* 10 Oct. 1996, 16; and John Kennedy, 'College St Murders,' *Xtra!* 15 Feb. 1996, 17.

36 Gretchen Drummie, 'Gay Hooker Gets Life for Sex Slaying,' *Toronto Sun*, 24 Feb. 1996, 24.

37 Karen Hiebert-Pauls, 'Ex-Winnipeger Hacked to Death,' *Winnipeg Sun*, 22 Sept. 1993, 22.

38 Sam Pazzano 'Gay Was Bound, Stabbed: Crown,' *Toronto Sun*, 21 Feb. 1996, 19.
39 Albert Noel, 'Brutal Slaying of Yukon Man Shocks Family, Colleagues,' *Montreal Gazette*, 2 Feb. 1990, A3.
40 Albert Reiss, 'The Social Integration of Queers and Peers.' *Social Problems.* 9, 2 (1961): 105.
41 Ibid., 107.
42 Edward Sagarin and Donal MacNamara, 'The Homosexual as Crime Victim,' *International Journal of Criminology and Penology* 3, 1 (1975): 16.
43 Joseph Harry, 'Derivative Deviance: The Cases of Extortion, Fag-Bashing and Shakedown of Gay Men,' *Criminology* 19, 4 (1982): 552.
44 Brian Miller and Laud Humphreys, 'Lifestyles and Violence: Homosexual Victims of Assault and Murder,' *Qualitative Sociology* 3, 3 (1980): 171.
45 Frank van Gemert, 'Chicken Kills Hawk,' *Journal of Homosexuality* 26, 4 (1994): 149–74.
46 Dire Enfin la Violence, 'Bilan.' 31 May 1997, 18.
47 Ford C. Hickson, et al. 'Gay Men as Victims of Non-Consensual Sex,' *Archives of Sexual Behavior* 23 (June 1994): 287.
48 Interview with the author, 27 April 1999.
49 519 Church Street Community Centre, Toronto, 'Assaulted or Robbed by Someone You Picked Up?' (poster). See John Sinopoli, 'Hoodlums Target Homos,' *Xtra!* 7 March 2002, 15.
50 Douglas Victor Janoff 'Gay-Bashing in Vancouver: A Case Study,' unpublished manuscript, 1996, 10.
51 'West End Man Found Slain in Apartment,' *Vancouver Sun*, 23 Dec. 1995, B9.
52 But see Donald G. Casswell, *Lesbians, Gay Men and Canadian Law* (Toronto: Emond Montgomery, 1996); Stephen Samis, 'An Injury to One Is an Injury to All' (MA thesis, Simon Fraser University, 1995); Ellen Faulkner, 'A Case Study of the Institutional Response to Anti-Gay/Lesbian Violence in Toronto' (PhD dissertation, Ontario Institute for Studies in Education, University of Toronto, 1999); Ellen Faulkner, 'Empowering Victim Advocates: Organizing against Anti-Gay/Lesbian Violence in Canada,' *Critical Criminology* 10 (2001): 123–35; Brure MacDougall *Queer Judgments: Homosexuality, Expression and the Courts in Canada* (Toronto: University of Toronto Press, 2000); Henry Chuang and Donald Addington, 'Homosexual Panic: A Review of Its Concept,' *Canadian Journal of Psychiatry* 33 (Oct. 1988): 613–17; Cynthia Petersen, 'A Queer Response to Bashing: Legislating against Hate,' *Queen's Law Journal* 16 (1991): 237–60; Derek Janhevich, 'The Criminalization of Hate: A Social Constructionist Analysis' (MA thesis, University of Ottawa, 1997); Gary Kinsman, 'Gays and

Lesbians: Pushing the Boundaries,' in *Canadian Society: Meeting the Challenges of the Twenty-First Century*, 2nd ed. (Toronto: Oxford University Press, 2001); Gary Kinsman, *The Regulation of Desire: Homo and Hetero Sexualities*, 2nd ed. (Montreal: Black Rose, 1996).

53 See *R. v. Stewart* (1995), 41 CR (4th) 102 (BCCA).

54 *R. v. Butler* (1995), 104 C.C.C. (3d) 198 (BCCA), leave to appeal to SCC refused 23 May 1996 at 211–12.

55 Letter from deputy chief to author, 17 May 1999.

56 HALO, Minutes from the meetings of the Social Service Committee of the Homophile Association of London, Ontario, from 1989 to 1998, forwarded by the former committee chair. See also 'Councillor Asks Police to Investigate Death Threat' *Toronto Star*, 22 Jan. 1993, A6; Karen Patrick, 'Verbal Basher Charged,' *Capital Xtra!* 15 Dec. 1995, 17; letter from victim to author, 3 May 1999; Mark Kershaw, 'A Year of Victories,' *Xtra West*, 7 Jan. 1999, 17; Ken Popert, 'Imperfect Stranger,' *Xtra!* 26 Jan. 1990, 7; and Rob Thomas, 'Charges Laid over Gayline Death Threat,' *Capital Xtra!* 6 May 2004, 7.

57 See R. Mikel, 'Stopping the Bashers.' *Xtra!* 26 Oct. 1990, 5; 'Bashers Jailed' *Xtra!* 21 Aug. 1992, 10; David Walberg, 'A Day in Court,' *Xtra!* 21 June 1992, 21; and Frank Prendergast, 'Basher at the Door,' *Xtra!* 22 Oct. 1998, 11.

58 See 'Man Assaulted at Knife Point' *Xtra!* 23 Nov. 1990, 17; Ian Taylor, 'Bashings Reveal a Pattern,' *Xtra!* 15 May 1992, 17; Neal Hall, 'Gay Men Warned of Suspected Killer,' *Vancouver Sun*, 2 June 1995, B1; John Kennedy, 'Crime in the Ghetto,' *Xtra!* 18 Jan. 1996, 12; '... And around Canada' *Xtra!* 2 July 1998, 20; 'A Study of Discrimination Based on Sexual Orientation' a collaborative effort by Alberta Human Rights Commission, Gay and Lesbian Awareness Society of Edmonton, Calgary Lesbian and Gay Political Action Guild, and Gay Lines of Calgary, 7 Dec. 1992; 'Wellesley Attack' *Xtra!* 1 April 2004, 21.

59 Erich Goode and Richard Troiden, 'Correlates and Accompaniments of Promiscuous Sex among Male Homosexuals,' *Psychiatry: Journal for the Study of Interpersonal Processes* 43, 1 (1980): 51–9.

60 See 'Man Sexually Assaulted in Van,' *Montreal Gazette*, 17 July 1994, A3; 'Attempted Murder,' *Xtra!* 11 Nov. 1994, 20.

61 Letter from a St John's activist to author, 23 Aug. 1999.

62 Lana Stermac, Peter Sheridan, and Alison Davidson, 'Sexual Assault of Adult Males,' *Journal of Interpersonal Violence* 11, 1 (1996): 55.

63 Ibid., 59.

64 Ibid., 58–9.

65 Margaret Munro, 'Gay Men Who Suffer Sexual Abuse More Likely to Get AIDS, Study Finds,' *Vancouver Sun*, 6 July (1996), A6. See S.A. Strathdee, R.S. Hogg, S.L. Martindale, P.G.A. Cornelisse, K. Craib, A. Schilder, J.S.G. Montaner, M.V. O'Shaughnessy, and M.T. Schecter, 'Sexual Abuse as an Independent Predictor of Sexual Risk-Taking among Young HIV-Negative Gay Men,' presented at the Vancouver International AIDS Conference, 1996.

66 Jay Paul et al. 'Understanding Childhood Sexual Abuse as a Predictor of Sexual Risk-Taking among Men Who Have Sex with Men: The Urban Men's Health Study,' *Child Abuse and Neglect* 25, 4 (2001): 557–84.

67 Cited in Stephen Parker, 'Healing Abuse in Gay Men: The Group Component,' in Mic Hunter, *The Sexually Abused Male*, Volume 2 (New York: Lexington, 1990), 179.

68 Ford C. Hickson et al. 'Gay Men as Victims of Non-Consensual Sex,' *Archives of Sexual Behavior* 23 (June 1994): 293.

69 Mitchel Rafael, 'I'll Supply the Lube,' *Fab*, 29 Aug. 2002, 4.

70 See Richard Sparks, *Television and the Drama of Crime: Moral Tales and the Place of Crime in Public Life* (Buckingham, UK: Open University Press, 1992); Eric Smith 'Fiends and High-Risk Groups: Misrepresenting and Signifying a Disease,' in Chris McCormick, ed., *Constructing Danger: The Mis/representation of Crime in the News* (Halifax: Fernwood, 1995).

71 Canadian Press, 'Tavern Must Pay Man for Injuries in Bar Brawl,' *Hamilton Spectator*, 13 Jan. 1997, A10.

72 *Murphy v. Little Memphis Cabaret Inc.* (1996), 20 OTC 313 (Ont. Gen. Div.); [1998] O.J. No. 4752 DRS 99–06766 Docket No. C26301 (Ont. CA).

73 Moira Welsh and Dale Brazao, 'Life and Death on Our Mean Streets,' *Toronto Star*, 5 Nov. 1994, A2.

74 Rob Lamberti, 'Cops Plead for Help in Hooker Slayings,' *Toronto Sun*, 17 Nov. 1997, 4.

75 Bill Dunphy, 'Bus Driver's Mysterious Death at Odds with His Life,' *Hamilton Spectator*, 5 Nov. 1997, and 'Murdered Bus Driver Was Looking for Sex,' *Hamilton Spectator*, 8 Nov. 1997.

76 Christine Cox, 'Life Term for Murder of Bus Driver,' *Hamilton Spectator*, 19 Nov. 1998, A3.

77 Author's interview with the community relations coordinator, Hamilton-Wentworth Regional Police, 17 May 1999.

78 Phillip Quisenberry 'Television News Coverage and Its Effects on the Recording of Hate Crime' (PhD dissertation, University of Kentucky, 2001).

79 James Jacobs and Kimberly Potter, *Hate Crimes: Criminal Law and Identity Politics* (New York: Oxford University Press, 1998), 53.

80 Janis Judson and Donna Bertazzoni, *Law, Media and Culture: The Landscape of Hate* (New York: Peter Lang, 2002), 84–6.

81 But see 'Show Strikes Home for Local Gay Men,' *Hamilton Spectator*, 25 Jan. 1997; Dan Nolan, 'Gay-Bashing Awareness Campaign Marks New Era for Police,' *Hamilton Spectator*, 27 Feb. 1998; Warren Gerard, 'Is Gay Bashing Out of Control?' *Toronto Star*, 29 June 1991, D1; Ingrid Peritz, 'Crimes of Ignorance, Crimes of Hate,' *Ottawa Citizen*, 20 Dec. 1992, A4; André Picard, 'Hate Slaying of Gay Man Stuns Montreal,' *Globe and Mail*, 4 Dec. 1992, A1, A2; 'Gaybashing' *Capital Xtra!* 25 March 1994, 9; Canadian Press, 'Ex-Skinhead Says He's Sorry,' Canadian Press Newswire, 23 July 1994; Delon Shurtz, 'Federal Bill Does Little to Ease Gays' Fears Bashing, Discrimination Will Still Exist on Street,' *Lethbridge Herald*, 11 May 1996; Salim Jiwa, 'Cops Seek Help in Beating by Skinheads,' *Vancouver Province*, 12 Nov. 1997, A3 and Tom Yeung, 'Skinheads Bash Gays,' *Xtra West*, 27 Nov. 1997, 9.

82 André Picard, 'Hate Slaying of Gay Man Stuns Montreal.' *Globe and Mail*, 4 Dec. 1992, A1, A2.

83 Michelle Lalonde, 'Skinhead Leader Jailed for Slaying.' *Montreal Gazette*, 20 May 1993, A3.

84 Stephanie Nolen, 'Gaybashers Killed Man in Park: Activists.' *Montreal Gazette*, 4 Dec. 1992, A1.

85 André Picard, 'Handling Murder with Kid Gloves,' *Globe and Mail*, 13 April 1993, A5.

86 Catherine Buckie, 'Youth Gets 3 Years' Detention for His Role in Jogger's Death,' *Montreal Gazette*, 7 May 1993, A4.

87 Janis Judson and Donna Bertazzoni, *Law, Media and Culture: The Landscape of Hate* (New York: Peter Lang, 2002), 88.

88 James O'Connor, '"Gay-Bashing" Didn't Prompt Murder: Police,' *Winnipeg Sun*, 12 June 1990.

89 David Kuxhaus, 'Murder Probe Lost in Tunnel Vision,' *Winnipeg Free Press*, 3 Sept. 1997, A3.

90 James O'Connor, 'Riverside Killing Ground,' *Winnipeg Sun.* 2 July 1991, 3.

91 Donna Carreiro, 'Public Killing Baffles Cops,' *Winnipeg Sun.* 14 July 1991, 5.

92 Canadian Press, 'Neo-Nazis Went after Gay Men, Crown Says.' *Globe and Mail*, 13 Aug. 1997, A7.

93 James O'Connor, 'Weather Chills Gay-Bashers,' *Winnipeg Sun*, 14 Oct. 1991, 5.

94 David Kuxhaus, 'Murder Probe Lost in Tunnel Vision,' *Winnipeg Free Press*, 3 Sept. 1997, A3.

95 Canadian Press, 'Neo-Nazis Went after Gay Men, Crown Says,' *Globe and Mail*, 13 Aug. 1997, A7.

96 Kuxhaus, 'Murder Probe Lost in Tunnel Vision.'

97 Judson Bertazzoni, *Law, Media and Culture*, 95.

98 Greg Middleton, 'Gay-Bashing "Psycho" on the Loose,' *Vancouver Province*, 2 June 1995, A5.

99 Stuart Hunter, 'Community Sounds Alarm,' *Vancouver Province*, 2 June 1995, A5.

100 Sherryl Yeager, 'Wreck Beach Visitor Tips Police about Murder Suspect,' *Vancouver Sun*, 5 June 1995, B2.

101 Clare Ogilvie, '"Predatory" Killing of Gay Man Nets Life,' *Vancouver Province*, 18 April 1996, A42.

102 Judson and Bertazzoni, *Law, Media and Culture*, 89.

103 'Foul Play Suspected,' *Vancouver Sun*, 6 April 1994, B2; Neal Hall and Lindsay Kines, 'From DOA to DNA: Getting Away with Murder,' *Vancouver Sun*, 16 Sept. 1995, A4.

104 Author's interview with local community member, 21 Sept. 1999.

105 Canadian Press, 'Man Gets 5 Years for Stabbing,' *Halifax Daily News*. 14 Apr. 1995, 11.

106 'Man Gets Jail Term for Stabbing Senior,' *Ottawa Citizen*, 13 April 1995, B3.

107 Author's interview with local community member, 21 Sept. 1999.

108 See Kathryn Campbell, 'From Deviant to Chic: The Representation of Lesbians in Canadian Media,' MA thesis, Carleton University, 1996).

109 6 May 1987, cited in Simon Watney, *Policing Desire: Pornography, AIDS, and the Media*, 2nd ed. (Minneapolis: University of Minnesota Press, 1989), 174.

110 30 August 1983, cited in Simon, *Policing Desire*, 82.

111 Karen Hiebert-Pauls, 'Dad Backs Accused Boy,' *Winnipeg Sun*, 25 Sept. 1993.

112 For example, see Sheri Zernetsch, 'Gay Families in the Media in the Age of HIV and AIDS' (MA thesis, Concordia University, 1998).

113 Matthew Mcallister, 'Medicalization in the News Media: A Comparison of AIDS Coverage in Three Newspapers,' (PhD dissertation, University of Illinois at Urbana–Champaign, 1990).

114 Peter Beharrell, 'News Variations,' in Glasgow Media Group, *The Circuit of Mass Communication: Media strategies, Representation and Audience Reception in the AIDS Crisis* (London: Sage, 1998), 54.

115 Kevin Williams, and David Miller, 'Producing AIDS News,' in *Circuit of Mass Communication*, 156.

116 Canadian Press, 'Man Jailed for Lover's Murder,' *Calgary Herald*, 5 June 1993, A7; Michael Carmichael, 'Killer Asks for Forgiveness,' *Sudbury Star*, 13 March 1998.

117 Bruce MacDougall, *Queer Judgments: Homosexuality, Expression, and the Courts in Canada* (Toronto: University of Toronto Press, 2000), 164.

118 Kevin Williams and David Miller, 'Producing AIDS News,' in *Circuit of Mass Communication*, 156–7.

119 Letter from Halifax activist to author, 25 May 1999.

120 Kathleen McLean, 'Whitewashing a Fag Basher,' *The Gazette* (Feb): 3.

121 Canadian Press, 'Crown Appeals Manslaughter Sentence,' Canadian Press Newswire, 7 June 1994.

122 McLean, 'Whitewashing a Fag Basher.'

123 Williams Miller, 'Producing AIDS News,' 158–9.

124 Dawna Dingwall, 'Lesbian Lover Attacked,' *Winnipeg Sun*, 20 Feb. 1993, 5.

125 MacDougall, *Queer Judgments*, 176–7, summarizing the words of Judge Devine in *R. v. Longpre*, [1993] MJ No. 309 (QL) (Man. Prov. Ct).

126 Dingwall, 'Lesbian Lover Attacked.'

127 David Miller and Kevin Williams, 'Sourcing AIDS News.' In *Circuit of Mass Communication*, 133–4.

128 'Not So Gay Murder' *Xtra!* 26 April 1991, 15.

129 Ibid.

130 Albert Noel, 'Killer "Not a Violent Person, Psychiatrist Told Police." *Montreal Gazette*, 18 April 1991, A1, A6.

131 James Mennie and Mike King, 'Killer Carried "Hit List" of 18,' *Montreal Gazette*, 15 April 1991, A1, A5.

132 Noel, 'Killer "Not a Violent Person."'

133 See Elizabeth Aird, 'Transsexuals' Search for Compassion Often Leads to the Streets,' *Vancouver Sun*, 16 Sept. 1995; Stephen Hume, 'Chantal's Murder a Light on the Dual Personalities of Our City,' *Vancouver Sun*, 22 Sept. 1995, A19; Doug Saunders, 'Life Harsh for Teens in Drag,' *Globe and Mail*, 24 May 1996, A1, A5; André Picard, 'Hate Slaying of Gay Man Stuns Montreal,' *Globe and Mail*, 4 Dec. 1992, A1, A2; and André Picard, 'Montreal Gays Fear Serial Killer,' *Globe and Mail*, 12 Feb. 1993, A1.

134 Joe Gataveckes, 'Victim Last Seen at Downtown Bar,' *Toronto Star*, 17 April 1995, A9, and 'Metro Police Seek Killer in Man's Beating Death,' *Toronto Star*, 31 July 1995, A14.

2: Theories of Homophobia: Why Do They Want to Hurt Us?

1 Kim Westad, 'Pair Strangled Man, Left Lover,' *Victoria Times Colonist*, 14 Jan. 1995.

2 Kim Westad, 'Two Jailed 10 Years for Killing,' *Victoria Times Colonist*, 21 Jan. 1995.

3 Westad, 'Pair Strangled Man, Left Lover.'
4 Westad, 'Two Jailed 10 Years for Killing.'
5 Bill Cleverley, 'Charges Expected against Two Men in Saanich Murder,' *Victoria Times Colonist*, 8 Feb. 1994, A2.
6 Michel Foucault, *The History of Sexuality*, Volume 1, *An introduction* (New York: Vintage Books, 1978), 140.
7 Ibid., 191.
8 Ibid., 105.
9 Ibid., 43.
10 Ibid., 44.
11 Hubert L. Dreyfus and Paul Rabinow, *Michel Foucault: Beyond Structuralism and Hermeneutics* (Chicago: University of Chicago Press, 1982), 173.
12 Barry Adam, *The Rise of a Gay and Lesbian Movement*, rev. ed. (New York: Twayne, 1995), 16, 19.
13 Ibid., 28.
14 Ibid., 56.
15 Ibid., 105.
16 Ibid., 56.
17 Ibid., 57–8.
18 Geoffrey Giles, '"The Most Unkindest Cut of All": Castration, Homosexuality and Nazi Justice,' *Journal of Contemporary History* 27, 1 (1992): 42–6.
19 Ibid., 57.
20 Elise Chenier, 'Stranger in Our Midst: Male Sexual 'Deviance' in Postwar Ontario' (PhD dissertation, Queen's University, 2001).
21 Gary Kinsman, *The Regulation of Desire: Homo and Hetero Sexualities*, 2nd ed. (Montreal: Black Rose, 1996), 150.
22 Ibid., 39–40.
23 Ibid., 170.
24 Ibid., 166–67.
25 Ibid., 190–1.
26 Ibid., 177–81.
27 Gary Kinsman, 'Constructing Gay Men and Lesbians as National Security Risks, 1950–70,' in Gary Kinsman, Dieter K. Buse, and Mercedes Steedman, eds. *Whose National Security? Canadian State Surveillance and the Creation of Enemies* (Toronto: Between the Lines, 2000), 143.
28 See Gary Kinsman and Patrizia Gentile *In the Interests of the State: The Anti-Gay, Anti-Lesbian National Security Campaign in Canada. A Preliminary Research Report* (Sudbury: Laurentian University 1998); Jim Bronskill,

'Study Will Urge Ottawa to Apologize to "Purged" Gays,' *Vancouver Sun*, 9 March 1998, A4; Kinsman and Gentile's forthcoming book, *The Canadian War on Homsexuals: National Security as Sexual Regulation.*

29 Elisa Kukla, '"Dirty" Lesbians,' *Xtra!* 15 Sept. 2000, 15.

30 Michael Riordon, 'Shock Tactics,' *Fab* (Winter 1997): 29, 76.

31 Alec Russell 'South African Doctors Say Sorry Over Biko' *Vancouver Sun*, 19 June 1997, A12.

32 Kinsman, *The Regulation of Desire*, 338.

33 Robert Meier, 'Perspectives on the Concept of Social Control,' *Annual Review of Sociology* 8 (1982): 47.

34 Howard Becker, *Outsiders: Studies in the Sociology of Deviance*, rev. ed. (New York: Free Press, 1966), 7.

35 Edwin Schur, *Labelling Deviant Behavior* (New York: Harper and Row, 1971), 8.

36 Edwin Schur. *Crimes without Victims: Deviant Behavior and Public Policy. Abortion, Homosexuality, Drug Addiction* (Englewood Cliffs, NJ: Prentice-Hall, 1965), 110–11.

37 Mary McIntosh, 'The Homosexual Role,' in Peter Nardi and Beth Schneider, eds., *Social Perspectives in Lesbian and Gay Studies: A Reader* (Santa Barbara, CA: Routledge, 1997), 68–76.

38 See Ronald Bayer, *Homosexuality and American Psychiatry: The Politics of Diagnosis* (New York: Basic Books, 1981).

39 Jeffrey Weeks, 'The Meaning of Diversity,' in Nardi and Schneider, eds., *Social Perspectives in Lesbian and Gay Studies*, 313.

40 Jeffrey Weeks, *Sexuality and Its Discontents: Meanings, Myths and Modern Sexualities* (London: Routledge, 1985), 195.

41 See David Rayside, *On the Fringe: Gays and Lesbians in Politics* (Ithaca, NY: Cornell University Press, 1998); and Timothy Lucas, 'Sexual Orientation and the Law: An Examination of the Discourse on Two Federal Acts in Canada' (MA thesis, University of Manitoba, 1999).

42 See Douglas Victor Janoff, 'Amsterdam 1998: Queer Global Activism for the New Millenium' report prepared for EGALE, 1998, available at www.egale.ca/politics/politics/amsterdam.htm.

43 For an fascinating account of the events leading up to the launching of the lawsuit, see Janine Fuller and Stuart Blackley, *Restricted Entry: Censorship on Trial*, 2nd ed. (Vancouver: Press Gang, 1996).

44 Colin Sumner, 'Foucault, Gender and the Censure of Deviance,' in Loraine Gelsthorpe and Allison Morris, eds. *Feminist Perspectives in Criminology* (Milton Keynes, UK Open University Press, 1990), 35.

45 James W. Messerschmidt, Masculinities and Crime (Lanham, MD: Rowman and Littlefield, 1993), 15.

46 Ibid., 58.

47 Brian Pronger, 'Gay Jocks: A Phenomenology of Gay Men in Athletics,' in Michael A. Messner and Donald F. Sabo, eds., Sport, Men and the Gender Order: Critical Feminist Perspectives (Champaign, IL: Human Kinetics Books, 1990), 149.

48 Pat Griffin, 'Homophobia in Sport: Addressing the Needs of Lesbian and Gay High School Athletes,' in Gerald Unks, ed., The Gay Teen: Educational Practice and Theory for Lesbian, Gay and Bisexual Adolescents (New York: Routledge, 1995), 57–60.

49 Ronald Morrow, 'Helping Teachers Provide a Safe, Inclusive Climate for Physical Education' (EdD dissertation, University of North Carolina at Greensboro, 2000).

50 Eric Messier, 'Aggressions Homophobes,' RG (Dec. 1996): 16.

51 Uyen Vu, 'Montreal Hate-Crime Conundrum,' Montreal Gazette, 22 Aug. 1998, B1.

52 Kevin Griffin, 'Witness Program, Self-Defence Course New Weapons in War on Gay-Bashing,' Vancouver Sun, 30 Aug. 1991.

53 Cindy Filipenko, 'Vancouver Bashing' Xtra, 22 July 1994, 20.

54 Eve Kosofsky Sedgwick, Epistemology of the Closet (Berkeley: University of California Press, 1990), 3.

55 Judith Butler, 'Imitation and Gender Subordination,' in H. Aberlove, M. Barale, and D. Halperin, eds., The Lesbian and Gay Studies Reader (New York: Routledge, 1993), 314.

56 Ibid., 310.

57 Simon Watney, Policing Desire: Pornography, AIDS, and the Media, 2nd ed. (Minneapolis: University of Minnesota Press, 1989), xi.

58 Ibid., 50.

59 Joshua Gamson, 'Must Identity Movements Self-Destruct? A Queer Dilemma,' in Nardi and Schneider, eds. Social Perspectives in Lesbian and Gay Studies, 589.

60 Ibid., 593.

61 Ibid., 598.

62 For a full discussion of her case and its broader implications, see Margaret Denike and Sal Renshaw, 'Transgender and Women's Substantive Equality,' discussion paper for the National Association of Women and the Law, 22–3, Feb. 2003.

63 See Wendy McLellan, 'Sex Change Does Not Limit Person's Rights, Court

Finds,' *National Post*, 9 June 2000, A4; Tom Yeung, 'Rape Centre Hearing,' *Xtra!* 11 Jan. 2001, 20; 'Rape Relief Appeals,' *Vancouver Province*, 25 June 2002, A4; and Scott Simpson, 'Transsexual Wins Rights Ruling over Rejection as Rape Counsellor,' *Vancouver Sun*, 19 January 2002, B1.

64 Camille Bains, 'Former Man Says She Felt Female Oppression as a Child,' *Vancouver Sun*, 21 February 2001, B6.

65 Holly Devor, *FTM: Female-to-Male Transsexuals in Society* (Bloomington: Indiana University Press, 1997).

66 Bernice Hausman, 'Recent Transgender Theory,' *Feminist Studies* 27, 2 (2001): 465–7.

67 Frank Mort, 'Essentialism Revisited? Identity Politics and Late Twentieth-Century Discourses of Homosexuality,' 'in Jeffrey Weeks, ed., *The Lesser Evil and the Greater Good: The Theory and Politics of Social Diversity*, (London: Rivers Oram Press, 1994), 212.

68 See Janoff, 'Amsterdam 1998.'

69 David McKirnan, 'Bisexually Active Men: Social Characteristics and Sexual Behavior,' *Journal of Sex Research* 32, 1 (1995): 65–76.

70 Constantinos Phellas, 'Sexual and Ethnic Identities of Anglo-Cypriot Men Resident in London Who Have Sex with Men' (PhD dissertation, University of Essex, 1999).

71 Manuel Fernandez, 'An Ethnography of the Macho/Loca Relationship' (PhD dissertation, University of Southern California, 1999).

72 Bert Archer, *The End of Gay* (Toronto: Doubleday Canada, 1999), 15.

73 Ibid., 24.

74 Ibid., 22.

75 Ibid., 54.

76 Ibid., 102–3.

77 Ibid., 219–20.

78 Ibid., 281–3.

79 Donald P. Green, Jack Glaser, and Andrew Rich, 'From Lynching to Gay Bashing: The Elusive Connection between Economic Conditions and Hate Crime,' *Journal of Personality and Social Psychology* 75, 1 (1998): 82–92.

80 Keith Wilson and Jennifer Huff, 'Scaling Satan,' *Journal of Psychology* 135, 3 (2001): 292–300.

81 Gregory Herek, 'The Social Context of Hate Crimes: Notes on Cultural Heterosexism,' in Gregory Herek and Kevin Berrill, eds., *Hate Crimes: Confronting Violence against Lesbians and Gay Men* (Newbury Park, CA Sage, 1992), 96.

82 Cited in Herek 'The Social Context of Hate Crimes,' 96–97.

83 George Weinberg, *Society and the Healthy Homosexual* (New York: St Martin's Press, 1972), 4–5.

84 Ibid., 8–18.

85 Ibid., 19.

86 Joseph Rupp, 'Sudden Death in the Gay World,' *Medicine, Science and Law* 10 (1970): 189.

87 Ibid., 189–91.

88 Cited in Jack Nichols, *The Gay Agenda: Talking Back to the Fundamentalists* (Amherst, NY: Prometheus Books, 1996), 57.

89 *Denver Post*, 3 September 1992, B5, cited in Carole Jenny, and Thomas A. Roesler, 'Are Children at Risk for Sexual Abuse by Homosexuals?' *Pediatrics* 94, 1 (1994): 41.

90 Jenny and Roesler, 'Are Children at Risk,' 44.

91 Simon Watney, *Policing Desire: Pornography, AIDS, and the Media*, 2nd ed. (Minneapolis: University of Minnesota Press, 1989), 47.

92 Ibid., 49–50.

93 Ibid., 39.

94 Cited in D.J. West, *Homosexuality Re-examined* (Minneapolis: University of Minnesota Press, 1977), 201.

95 Jaime Smith 'Psychopathology, Homosexuality, and Homophobia,' *Journal of Homosexuality* 15, 1/2 (1988): 61. See also D.M. Szymanski and Y.B. Chung 'The Lesbian Internalized Homophobia Scale: A Rational/Theoretical Approach,' *Journal of Homosexuality* 41, 2 (2001): 37–52.

96 Iris Marion Young, *Justice and the Politics of Difference* (Princeton, NJ: Princeton University Press), 147.

97 Alan Klein, 'Little Big Man: Hustling, Gender Narcissism, and Bodybuilding Subculture,' in Messner and Sabo, eds. *Sport, Men and the Gender Order*, 130–1.

98 Ibid., 137–8.

99 Doug Arey, 'Gay Males and Sexual Child Abuse,' in Lisa Aronson Fontes, ed., *Sexual Abuse in Nine North American Cultures: Treatment and Prevention* (Thousand Oaks, CA: Sage, 1995), 210–11.

100 Ibid., 228–30.

101 Howard J. Ehrlich, 'The Ecology of Anti-Gay Violence,' in Gregory Herek and Kevin Berrill, eds., *Hate Crimes: Confronting Violence against Lesbians and Gay Men* (Newbury Park, CA: Sage, 1992), 109.

102 Canadian Press, '30 Months Jail in Gay-Bashing,' *Toronto Sun*, 16 July 1995, 28.

103 Gary Oakes, 'Man Jailed Year for Unprovoked Attack in Parkette,' *Toronto Star*, 15 Nov. 1995, A33.

104 Alan Bustak, 'Double Lives,' *Montreal Gazette*, 5 June 1994, A1.

105 Irwin Block, 'Reverend Asked for Kinky Sex, Accused Says,' *Montreal Gazette*, 20 May 1994, A3.

106 Bustak, 'Double Lives.'

107 Ibid.

108 Block, 'Reverend Asked for Kinky Sex.'

109 Irwin Block and Mike King, 'Minister Murdered,' *Montreal Gazette*, 2 June 1994, A1.

110 Richard Burnett, 'Interview with a Murderer,' *Xtra!* 23 April 1998, 19.

111 Lisa Fitterman, 'Priest's Killer Get Life in Prison – Again,' *Montreal Gazette*, 22 Feb. 1997, A3.

112 Patrick Hopkins, 'Gender Treachery: Homophobia, Masculinity and Threatened Identities,' in Larry May and Robert Strikwerda, eds., *Rethinking Masculinity: Philosophical Explorations in Light of Feminism* (Lanham, MD: Littlefield Adams Quality Paperbacks, 1992), 131–2.

113 Ibid., 142

114 Ibid., 132–5.

115 See Lloyd Thorn and Bob Peacock, 'Enjoyed Harassing Gays until He Discovered He Was One,' *Vanouver Province.* 21 Nov. 2001, A15.

116 Hopkins, 'Gender Treachery,' 135–7.

117 Henry E. Adams, Lester Wright, Jr., and Bethany Lohr, 'Is Homophobia Associated with Homosexual Arousal?' *Journal of Abnormal Psychology* 105, 3 (1996): 441–4.

118 David Weigle, 'Affective Valence and Arousal as Motivational Indicators of Homophobia' (PhD dissertation, Texas A&M University, 2001).

119 Author's interview with Jamie-Lee Hamilton, 11 May 1999.

120 Neal Hall, 'Murder Case Had a Twist Reminiscent of Crying Game,' *Vancouver Sun*, 9 Dec. 1994, B4.

121 David Thompson, 'I Had Gay Sex with Laci's Hubby,' *The Globe.* 17 June 2003, 4, 7.

122 Hopkins, 'Gender Treachery,' 135–7.

123 'Incident at Lemon Creek,' Transcript from CBC Radio program *Ideas*, prepared by Sean Hennessey, produced by Max Allen and broadcast on 3 May 1993.

124 Sandra Hartline, 'Man Sentenced to Two Years for Assault on Homosexual,' *Vancouver Sun*, 10 Aug. 1991.

125 'Incident at Lemon Creek.'

126 Hartline, 'Man Sentenced.'

127 Hopkins, 'Gender Treachery,' 138–9

128 Cited in Rayside, *On the Fringe*, 114.

129 Canadian Press, 'Reformer Cleared over Remarks on Gays,' *Vancouver Sun*, 16 January 1997, A9.
130 Tu Thanh Ha, 'Reform to Debate Spreading Its Wings.' *Globe and Mail.* 21 February 1994, cited in Rayside, 114.
131 'Edmonton Imports the Fag Project,' *Western Report*, 29 Jan. 1996, 20.
132 *House of Commons Standing Committee on Justice and Legal Affairs respecting Bill C-41, an Act to Amend the Criminal Code (sentencing) and other Acts in consequence thereof*, transcript of hate crime discussion, 1 Dec. 1994, 69, 16.
133 Ibid., 21.
134 Ibid., 18.
135 Ibid., 19.
136 Ibid., 26.
137 Hopkins, 'Gender Treachery,' 141.
138 Ibid., 145
139 Mike Lew, *Victims No Longer* (New York: Harper and Row, 1988), 54.
140 Stephen Tomsen and Allen George, 'The Criminal Justice Response to Gay Killings: Research Findings,' *Current Issues in Criminal Justice* 9, 1 (1997): 66–8.
141 Jack Katz, *Seductions of Crime* (New York: Basic Books, 1988), 18–19.
142 *April One*, directed by Murray Battle, April One Productions, 1993.
143 Canadian Press, '"Dead Inside,"' *Ottawa Citizen*, 19 Nov. 1993, B6.
144 Canadian Press, 'N.S. Man Gets Life for Hammer Death,' *Halifax Daily News*, 20 Nov. 1993.
145 David Rodenhiser, 'Inmate Accused in Slaying of "Suspected Homosexual,"' *Halifax Daily News*, 9 Sept. 1995, 3.
146 Susanne Hiller, 'Man Who Killed His Molester Sentenced to Four-Year Term,' *Daily News*, 16 March 1996, 6.
147 Interview with Bill by author, March 2000.
148 Interview with Pete by author, 4 August 1999.
149 Bob Massecar, 'Murder Suspect Jailed on Other Charges,' *London Free Press*, 23 Aug. 1993.
150 'Man Guilty of Manslaughter,' *London Free Press*, 26 Nov. 1993.
151 Letter, 31 Aug. 1999.
152 Ann Ciasullo, 'Making Her (In) Visible: Cultural Representations of Lesbianism and the Lesbian Body in the 1990s,' *Feminist Studies* 27, 3 (2001): 577–608.
153 Gail Mason, 'Not Our Kind of Hate Crime,' *Law and Critique* 12, 3 (2001): 261–2.
154 See Liz Hardwick, 'Queer Women Take Action,' *Angles* (May 1996), 1;

Sarah Galashan, 'Four Charged in Attack outside Lesbian Nightclub,' *Vancouver Sun*, 31 July 2001, B3; Tom Yeung, 'No Shrinking Violet,' *Xtra West*, 17 April 1997, 15; Ottawa Police Service Liaison Committee, *Heard for the First Time* (June 2002) published by the Ottawa Police Service; 'A Study of Discrimination Based on Sexual Orientation,' collaborative effort by Alberta Human Rights Commission, Gay and Lesbian Awareness Society of Edmonton, Calgary Lesbian and Gay Political Action Guild, and Gay Lines of Calgary. 7 Dec. 2002.

155 *History: Violence against the Gay/Lesbian/Transgendered Community.* (Report prepared by the Community Relations Coordinator, Hamilton-Wentworth Regional Police, 28 May 1999).

156 See 'Bash Back,' *Xtra!* 7 April 1991, 7; and *History: Violence.*

157 Gail Mason, 'Not Our Kind of Hate Crime,' *Law and Critique* 12, 3 (2001): 269.

158 'Man Who Raped, Beat Prostitute Gets 4 Years,' *Toronto Star*, 8 July 1994, A26; Kalyani Vitalla, 'Man Gets Four Years for Rape, Beating,' *Globe and Mail*, 8 July 1994, A6.

159 Mason, 'Not Our Kind of Hate Crime,' 262.

160 Ibid., 273–4.

161 Joey Thompson, 'Getting Away with Murder,' *Vancouver Province*, 3 Dec. 1995, A16.

162 Larry Still, 'Ruling That Man Not Responsible in Wife's Shooting Death Stands,' *Vancouver Sun*, 7 Feb. 1995, C14.

163 Thompson, 'Getting Away with Murder.'

164 Still 'Ruling That Man Not Responsible.'

165 Thompson, 'Getting Away with Murder.'

166 'Boy Charged with Assault' *Xtra West*, 10 Dec. 1998, 7.

167 D.J. West, *Homosexuality Re-examined* (Minneapolis: University of Minnesota Press, 1977), 204.

168 Karen Franklin, 'Hate Crime or Right of Passage? Assailant Motivations in Anti-Gay Violence' (PhD dissertation, California School of Professional Psychology at Alameda, 1997).

169 Joseph Harry, 'Conceptualizing Anti-Gay Violence,' in Gregory Herek and Kevin Berrill, eds., *Hate Crimes: Confronting Violence against Lesbians and Gay Men* (Newbury Park, CA: Sage, 1992), 115.

170 Paul Van de Ven, 'Talking with Juvenile Offenders about Gay Males and Lesbians: Implications for Combating Homophobia,' *Adolescence* 30, 117 (1995): 29–31.

171 Ibid., 38–9.

172 HALO, Minutes from the meetings of the Social Service Committee of the

Homophile Association of London, Ontario, from 1989 to 1998, forwarded by the former committee chair.

173 See *History: Violence*. See also 'Rescued from Basher,' *Xtra!* 28 Sept. 1990, 5; Rory MacDonald. 'Gay Basher Sentenced,' *Capital Xtra*. 14 April 2000, 13.

174 Bruce MacDougall, *Queer Judgments: Homosexuality, Expression, and the Courts in Canada* (Toronto: University of Toronto Press, 2000) 175; Lara Bradley, 'Educate the Enemy,' *Xtra!* 17 Dec. 1998, 11. See also Gigi Suhanic, 'Couple Ambushed Near Hospital,' *Xtra!* 27 Aug. 1998, 14.

175 Bruce DeMara, 'Don't Be Afraid, Gay-Bashing Victims Say,' *Toronto Star*, 23 Oct. 1994, A15.

176 Stephen Samis, 'An Injury to One Is an Injury to All' (MA thesis, Simon Fraser University, 1995).

177 See 'Man Pleads Guilty to Assault in Gay Bar' *Ottawa Citizen*, 7 Aug. 1999, C4; Canadian Press, 'Attack on Gay Man Nets Jail,' Canadian Press Newswire, 12 Feb 1994.

178 See Marc Morrison, 'Cracked Ribs and a Swollen Eye,' *Xtra!* 11 April 1996, 13.

179 Neil Herland, 'Wilde Attack,' *Capital Xtra!* 19 May (1995), 13.

180 'Ex-Newscaster Found Dead: Boy, 15, Held,' *Montreal Gazette*, 27 Jan. 1996, A3.

181 Letter from coordinator of Dire Enfin la Violence, 14 July 1999.

182 Interview with QPP officer by author, 12 May 1999.

183 Robyn Swanson, 'Youth Paid by Masochist to Inflict Pain Sent to Jail,' *Vancouver Sun*, 1 April 1999, B7.

184 Tomsen and George, 'The Criminal Justice Response,' 56–70.

185 'Witnesses Needed,' *Xtra!* 19 Nov. 1998, 27.

186 'Teenager Guilty in Killing of "faggot,"' *Xtra!* 25 Oct. 1991, 17.

187 Peter Small, 'Youth Gets Maximum Sentence for Murder,' *Toronto Star*, 25 January 1994, A14; and *R. v. K. (M.)*, [1993] OJ No. 1400 DRS 93-10480, Action no. Y920298E (Ont. Prov. Ct.)

188 *R. v. H. (A.)* (1992), 10 O.R. (3d) 683 (Ont. Prov. Ct. Gen. Div.); Gail Swainson, 'Autopsy Confirms Manager Stabbed.' *Toronto Star*, 10 May 1994, A7.

189 Mark Totten, *Guys, Gangs and Girlfriend Abuse* (Peterborough, ON: Broadview Press, 2000), 51–2.

190 Ibid., 54.

191 Ibid., 56.

192 Ibid., 81.

193 Ibid., 122.

194 Ibid., 124–5.

195 Watney, *Policing Desire*, 126.
196 Totten, *Guys, Gangs*, 128–9.
197 Ibid., 100–3.
198 *R. v. Stewart* (1995), 41 CR (4th) 102 (BCCA).

3: The Horror of Homophobic Violence

 1 Letter to author from Miriam, 11 Aug. 1999.
 2 Kim Westad, 'Stabbing Suspect Let Out on Bail,' *Victoria Times Colonist*, 11 May 1995.
 3 Geoffery Castle, 'Rejected Dancer Jailed for Stabbing,' *Victoria Times Colonist*, 14 Dec. 1995, C14.
 4 Letter from Miriam, 11 Aug. 1999.
 5 See Clare Ogilvie, 'Gay-Bashers Jailed,' *Vancouver Province*, 25 Aug. 1995, A14; Tom Yeung, 'Bashing Victim Grateful for Friends,' *Xtra West*, 10 Dec. 1998, 7.
 6 Lana Stermac and Peter Sheridan, 'Anti-Gay/Lesbian Violence: Treatment Issues,' *Canadian Journal of Human Sexuality* 2, 1 (1993): 33–38.
 7 Cited in ibid., 36.
 8 *House of Commons Standing Committee on Justice and Legal Affairs respecting Bill C-41, an Act to Amend the Criminal Code (sentencing) and other Acts in consequence thereof*, transcript of hate crime discussion. 1 Dec. 1994, 69, 12–13.
 9 Allan Peterkin and Cathy Risdon, *Caring for Lesbian and Gay People* (Toronto: University of Toronto Press, 2003), 166–7.
10 Stermac and Sheridan, 'Anti-Gay/Lesbian Violence,' 37.
11 Charles Mandel, 'Harrison's Art Explores Fears behind Gay-Bashing,' *Globe and Mail*, 3 Feb. 1996, C14.
12 Stermac and Sheridan, 'Anti-Gay/Lesbian Violence,' 37.
13 Gregory Herek, Roy Gillis, Jeanine Cogan, and Eric Glunt, 'Hate Crime Victimization among Lesbian, Gay and Bisexual Adults,' *Journal of Interpersonal Violence*, 12, 2 (1997): 209–10.
14 Julian Roberts, 'Disproportionate Harm: Hate Crime in Canada' (working document, Department of Justice Canada, 1995), 32.
15 Roger Spencer, 'Fighting for Our Lives,' *Xtra!* 15 June 1990, 5; Canadian Press, 'Attack on Gay Man Nets Jail,' *Canadian Press Newswire*, 12 Feb. 1994.
16 Lauren Michaels, 'Basher Alert,' *Xtra!* 24 July 1992, 9; Lila Sarick, 'Gay-Bashing Incidents on Rise in Toronto,' *Globe and Mail*, 15 Oct. 1998, A12; David Kuxhaus, 'Murder Probe Lost in Tunnel Vision,' *Winnipeg Free Press*, 3 Sept. 1997, A3.

17 Patrick Kaniuga, 'Gunning for Gays?' *Winnipeg Sun*, 25 July 1994.
18 'Slasher on St Joseph' *Xtra!* 14 Oct., 26; Carle Bernier-Genest, 'A Montréal, un mois de mai entaché de violence,' *RG* (July 1998): 21.
19 Michael Kealy, 'Slashing,' *Xtra!* 20 June 1996, 49.
20 *History: Violence against the Gay/Lesbian/Transgendered Community* (Report prepared by the Community Relations Coordinator, Hamilton-Wentworth Regional Police, 28 May 1999).
21 Tom Yeung, 'Gay Bash Line a Qualified Success,' *Xtra West* 24 July 1997, 15.
22 Sarick, 'Gay-Bashing Incidents.' 'Jogger Stabbed' *Globe and Mail*, 22 April 1991, A8; Glen MacKenzie, 'Gay-Bashing Cited as Man Stabbed in Alley,' *Winnipeg Free Press*, 18 March 1996, A2; Paul Wiecek, 'Invitation Nearly Fatal,' *Winnipeg Free Press*, 6 Feb. 1994.
23 Peter Hum, 'Man Pleads Guilty to Beating Pair with Skateboard,' *Ottawa Citizen*, 21 Jan. 1999, B6.
24 'More on Gaybashing' *Xtra!* 13 Aug. 1998.
25 Gareth Kirkby, 'Starter Gun, Pepper Spray Used,' *Xtra West*, 10 Dec. 1998, 7; 'Vancouver Reels from Two Gay Bashings,' *Xtra!* 25 July 2002, 15.
26 '3 Hurt in Bar Shooting' *Montreal Gazette*, 4 April 2001, A4; 'Suspect Arrested in Strip-Bar Shooting,' *Montreal Gazette*, 6 April 2001, A7.
27 Author's interview with Vancouver victim, 3 May 1999.
28 John Lowman and Laura Fraser, *Violence against Persons Who Prostitute: The Experience in British Columbia* (1995), 157.
29 'Two Arrested, Two Sought in Pipe Beating,' *Vancouver Province*, 28 Oct. 1999, A34.
30 'Cawthra Gun Scare' *Xtra!* 8 July 1994.
31 Author's interview with Saskatoon Police officer, 12 Aug. 1999.
32 Douglas Victor Janoff, 'Darkness at the Edge of Town,' *Vancouver Sun*, 12 Sept. 1992, D4.
33 Interview with the former coordinator of the Toronto Hate Crimes Unit, 4 May 1999.
34 Douglas Wax and Victor Haddox, 'Enuresis, Fire Setting and Animal Cruelty in Male Adolescent Delinquents: A Triad Predictive of Violent Behavior,' *Journal of Psychiatry and the Law* 2, 1 (1974): 45–71.
35 R. Langevin, 'Childhood and Family Background of Killers Seen for Psychiatric Assessment: A Controlled Study,' *Bulletin of the American Academy of Psychiatry and the Law* 11, 4 (1983): 331–42.
36 Iris Marion Young, *Justice and the Politics of Difference* (Princeton, NJ: Princeton University Press, 1990), 143–6.
37 Julia Kristeva, *Powers of Horror: An Essay on Abjection* (New York: Columbia University Press, 1982) 4.

38 Young, *Justice and the Politics of Difference*, 143.
39 Wade C. Myers et al. 'Psychopathology, Biopsychosocial Factors, Crime Characteristics, and Classification of 25 Homicidal Youths.' *Journal of the American Academy of Child and Adolescent Psychiatry* 34, 11 (1995): 1483–9.
40 Victoria Swigert et al. 'Sexual Homicide,' *Archives of Sexual Behavior* 5, 5 (1976): 391–401.
41 Frank W. Kiel, 'The Psychiatric Character of the Assailant as Determined by Autopsy Observations of the Victim,' *Journal of Forensic Sciences* 10, 3 (1965): 263–71.
42 Martha Jane Reineke, *Sacrificed Lives: Kristeva on Women and Violence* (Bloomington: Indiana University Press, 1997), 2–3.
43 Michael Bell and Raul Vila, 'Homicide in Homosexual Victims: A Study of 67 cases from the Broward County, Florida, Medical Examiner's Office,' *American Journal of Forensic Medicine and Pathology* 17, 1 (1996): 65–6.
44 Ibid., 66–7.
45 Ibid., 69.
46 'Homicide' *Xtra!* 17 July (1997), 20.
47 Jack Katz, *Seductions of Crime* (New York: Basic Books, 1988), 38.
48 Karen Patrick, 'Gay Man Murdered in Chelsea Home,' *Capital Xtra!* 13 Dec. 1996, 9.
49 Kenny Yum and Caroline Mallan, 'Burned Body Baffles Police,' *Toronto Star*, 21 Dec. 1996, A20.
50 Ibid.
51 Author's interview with the former coordinator, 26 May 1999.
52 'Encounters Were Taped' *Vancouver Sun*, 20 May 1994.
53 Author's interview with close gay male friend of the victim, 27 March 1999.
54 'Tattooed Suspect Charged,' *Vancouver Province*, 23 March 1994.
55 Bill Richardson, *Scorned and Beloved: Dead of Winter Meetings with Canadian Eccentrics* (Toronto: Knopf Canada, 1997), 322.
56 Letter from close gay male friend of the murder victim, 17 August 1999.
57 Gina Harris, 'Victims of Bashings Encourage Speaking,' *Capital Xtra*, 12 Dec. 1997, 15.
58 See Cynthia Klaasen, 'Probing the Anonymous Voices of Hatred.' *View*, 16–22, Jan. 1997, 8; Naomi Lakritz, 'Some Never Learn,' *Winnipeg Sun*, 5 April 1994, 5; 'A Study of Discrimination Based on Sexual Orientation,' Collaborative effort by Alberta Human Rights Commission, Gay and Lesbian Awareness Society of Edmonton, Calgary Lesbian and Gay Political Action Guild, and Gay Lines of Calgary, 7 Dec. 1992, 'Gay-Bashing Bid Leads to Charges Against 5,' *Vancouver Province*, 23 June 1998, A10;

'Gay-Bashing Bid Leads to Charges Against 5' *Vancouver Province*, 23 June 1998, A10; 'Carlton Assault' *Xtra!* 13 Feb. 1994, 19.

59 Allan Bennett-Brown, 'Bashing Gives Victim Faith in Neighbours,' *Georgia Straight*, 29 July–5 Aug. 1999, 7.

60 See Daryl Slade, 'Woman Jailed in Robbery,' *Calgary Herald*, 6 Nov. 1997, B4.

61 *R. v. Chaisson* (1995), 102 C.C.C. (3d) 564 (NBCA), appeal allowed (1995), 99 C.C.C. (3d) 289 (SCC), cited in Bruce MacDougall, *Queer Judgments: Homosexuality, Expression and the Courts in Canada* (Toronto: University of Toronto Press, 2000), 185.

62 Interview with Saskatoon activist, 13 July, 1999.

63 See Val Skinner, 'Cop Talk,' *Xtra!* 8 July 1994, 9; Susan Hargreaves, 'Be Alert,' *Xtra!* 9 May 1996, 8; 'Vancouver Reels from Two Gay Bashings,' *Xtra!* 25 July 2002, 15.

64 Andy Riga, 'Stating the Obvious,' *Montreal Gazette*, 13 Feb. 1996, A3.

65 'Gay Men Attacked by Youths,' *Globe and Mail*, 2 Nov. 1991, A8.

66 'Halloween Homophobia' *Xtra!* 22 Nov. 1991, 1.

67 See 'Gunman Befriended, Assaulted Man,' *Montreal Gazette*, 27 May 1994, A3.

68 Author's interview with coordinator, Dire Enfin la Violence (DELV), 29 Nov. 2000.

69 See Roberta Munroe, 'Bashing "Grossly Appalling,"' *Xtra!* 27 July 1990, 5; Cathy Lord, 'Harassing Men Brings Penalty for Assault,' *Edmonton Journal*, 4 May 1995, B3; Karen Hill, 'Bashing Arrest,' *Xtra!* 2 Jan. 1997, 13.

70 See André Picard, 'Montreal Gays Fear Serial Killer,' *Globe and Mail*, 12 Feb. 1993, A1; letter from DELV, 11 May 1999.

71 Pamela Fayerman, 'Killer of Male Lover Sentenced to 4 Years,' *Vancouver Sun*, 17 Feb. 1994, B5.

72 See Andy Ivens, 'Five Young Men Go on Trial in Beating of Island Teen,' *Vancouver Province*, 20 Jan. 1998, A14; Kim Westad, 'Constible Tells Court of Vicious Beating,' *Victoria Times Colonist*, 25 June 1997, A4; and Tracy Holmes, 'Attack on Gay Couple,' *Surrey/North Delta Leader*, 8 Nov. 1998, A13.

73 Ken Popert, 'Bashing Spree,' *Xtra!* 12 July: (1991), 1.

74 'Death Threats Target Gay Pride Service,' *Toronto Star*, 28 June 1994, A5.

75 HALO, Minutes from the meetings of the Social Service Committee of the Homophile Association of London, Ontario, from 1989 to 1998, forwarded by the former committee chair.

76 See Ritchie Doucet, 'Community Questions,' *Xtra!* 17 April: 7; Eric Messier, 'Aggressions Homophobes,' *RG* (Dec. 1996), 16; Carle Bernier-Genest, 'A

Montréal, un mois de mai entaché de violence,' *RG* (July 1998), 21; 'Richards Street Bashing,' *Xtra West*, 16 May 1996, 9; Kaj Hasselriis, 'Cops Botch Gay Murder Case,' *Xtra West*. 7 Sept. 1997, 7; Jack Keating, 'Two Men Injured as Gay-Bashing on Rise,' *Vancouver Province*, 26 March 1998, A34; Tom Yeung, '911 Screws Up Again,' *Xtra West*, 2 Nov., 7.

77 See 'Witnesses Sought,' *Xtra!* 26 Oct. 1990, 5; 'Witnesses,' *Xtra!* 28 May 1993, 17; Max MacDonald, *Xtra!* 25 June 1993, 9; Bernier-Genest, 'A Montréal,' 21; 'A Community in Fear: Gays in Montreal Live with Violence,' *Maclean's*, 29 Nov. 1993, 12–13; Kim Guttormson and Glen MacKenzie, 'Slashed, Stabbed for His Jacket,' *Winnipeg Free Press*, 3 Oct. 1994; Gina Harris, 'Victims of Bashings Encourage Speaking,' *Capital Xtra*, 12 Dec. 1997, 15.

78 See 'Beating Victim Met Attacker at Gay Bar,' *Montreal Gazette*, 17 Feb. 1997, A3; Krishna Rau, 'Youth Worker "Nearly Killed,"' *Xtra!* 7 May 1998, 21.

79 Alexandra Paul, 'Beaten, Left for Dead,' *Winnipeg Free Press*, 22 Oct. 1995, p. A4.

80 Richard Tewksbury, 'Adventures in the Erotic Oasis: Sex and Danger in Men's Same-Sex, Public, Sexual Encounters,' *Journal of Men's Studies* 4, 1 (1995): 9–24.

81 See Ariel Goodman, *Sexual Addiction: An Integrated Approach* (Madison, CT: International Universities Press, 1998).

82 Doug Arey, 'Gay Males and Sexual Child Abuse,' in Lisa Aronson Fontes, ed., *Sexual Abuse in Nine North American Cultures: Treatment and Prevention* (Thousand Oaks, CA: Sage 1995), 223.

83 Ibid., 232.

84 Robert Matas, 'Park Murder Won't Stop Encounters by Gay Man,' *Globe and Mail*, 20 Nov. 2001, A3.

85 There is graphic footage of these two corpses in *Climate for Murder*, documentary film on Montreal murders produced by Arnie Gelbart and directed by Albert Nerenberg, 1994.

86 Chris Morris, 'Gay Bashers Who Beat My Brother Should Get AIDS Test,' *Montreal Gazette*, 20 April 1993, B1.

87 Interview with gay male activist in Saskatoon, 7 May 1999.

88 See Jonathan Kingstone, '"Brutal Flurry of Blows."' *Toronto Sun*, 27 May 1999, 53; Vern Smith, 'Arrest in Dowling Murder,' *Xtra!* 17 June 1999, 33; 'Tidbits,' *Xtra!* 20 April 2000, 25; 'Richard Kall,' *Xtra!* 1 June 2000, 18; 'Tidbits,' *Xtra!* 24 Aug. 2000, 18.

89 Letter from Dire Enfin la Violence, 11 May 1999.

90 Joseph Couture, 'Murdered by the 11:30 News.' *Xtra!* 25 Dec. 2003, 7.

91 Author's interview with a police officer from the Quebec City police service, 9 June 1999.

92 Louise Larouche, 'Un Préposé aux personnes agées,' *Journal de Québec,* 10 Feb. 1990, 4.

93 Isabelle Jinchereau, 'Ghislain Girard formellement accusé de meurtres avec préméditation,' *Le Soleil,* 8 Feb. 1990.

94 Interview with a police officer from the Quebec City police service, 9 June 1999.

95 Isabelle Jinchereau, 'Rien à voir avec les moeurs des victimes,' *Le Soleil,* 7 Feb. 1990, A2.

96 Conversation, Quebec City Police Service, 16 Nov. 2000.

97 See 'Circus Arrest,' *Xtra!* 27 February 1997, 'Murder at the Web' *Xtra!* 24 Feb. 2000; 'Tidbits,' *Xtra!* 20 April 2000, 25; 'Violence in the 'Hood,' *Xtra!* 9 March 2000, 16; 'Local Shrine,' *Xtra!* 23 March 2000, 22; 'Tidbits,' *Xtra!* 24 Aug. 2000, 18.

98 Linda Singer, *Erotic Welfare: Sexual Theory and Politics in the Age of Epidemic* (New York: Routledge, 1993), 40.

99 Ibid., 47.

100 Neil Herland, 'Personal Views,' *Capital Xtra!* 18 Oct. 1996, 9.

101 Gary Dimmock, 'Gunshot Victim Met Suspect Through Ad.,' *Ottawa Citizen,* 14 Aug. 1999, C1.

102 Rob Lamberti, 'Gay-Sex Line May Be Tied to Killing,' *Toronto Sun,* 14 Sept. 1995, 20.

103 Rob Lamberti, 'Drifter May Hold Clue,' *Toronto Sun,* 26 Sept. 1995, 20.

104 Thomas Claridge, 'Man Gets 12 Years for Slaying Businessman,' *Globe and Mail,* 7 Oct. 1992, A14.

105 *R. v. Cooney* (1995), 98 C.C.C (3d) 196 at 198 (Ont. CA).

106 Claridge, 'Man Gets 12 Years.'

107 Robert MacLeod, 'Accused Used Dead Man's Bank Card,' *Globe and Mail,* 17 July 1992, A11.

108 Robert MacLeod, 'Friend Killed Man, Accused Testifies,' *Globe and Mail,* 16 July 1992, A15.

109 MacLeod, 'Accused Used Dead Man's Bank Card.'

110 *R. v. Cooney,* 199.

111 Claridge, 'Man Gets 12 Years.'

112 *R. v. Cooney,* 202.

113 Ibid., 207.

114 But see Anthony D'Augelli and Arnold Grossman, 'Disclosure of Sexual

Orientation, Victimization and Mental Health among Lesbian, Gay and Bisexual Older Adults,' *Journal of Interpersonal Violence* 16, 10 (2001): 1008–27.

115 Anthony D'Augelli, 'Developmental Implications of Victimization of Lesbian, Gay and Bisexual Youths,' In Gregory Herek, ed., *Stigma and Sexual Orientation: Understanding Prejudice against Lesbians, Gay Men and Bisexuals* (Thousand Oaks, CA: Sage, 1998), 188.

116 See Canadian Press, 'B.C. Ferries Will Babysit Rowdy Teens,' *Vancouver Sun*, 19 July 1999, B8; Caroline Alphonso, 'Some Question Need for BC Teachers' New Resource Book on Homosexuality,' *Globe and Mail*, 27 Sept. 2000; 'Schools Address Homophobia,' *Perceptions*, 23 Oct. 1996, 13; Maureen Murray, 'Gay Youth Hotline Swamped with Calls,' *Toronto Star*, 25 Oct. 1994, B1; Lesbian Gay Bi Youth Line, 'Service Information,' Aug. 1999; Debbie Lee, *Safe City Project: Beyond Hatred* (report on London queer youth prepared for HALO, July 2000), 60–2; James Moran, 'By Invitation Only, Please,' *Capital Xtra!* 16 April 1999, 18.

117 Lee, *Safe City Project*, 17–18.

118 Ibid., 40.

119 Ibid., 43.

120 Ibid., 44.

121 Ibid., 45.

122 Ibid., 46.

123 Anthony D'Augelli, 'Incidence and Mental Health Impact of Sexual Orientation Victimization of Lesbian, Gay and Bisexual Youths in High School,' *School Psychology Quarterly* 17, 2 (2002): 148–67.

124 Lee, *Safe City Project*, 44.

125 Author's interview with Winnipeg hate crimes officer, 23 June 1999.

126 Author's interview with Edmonton activist, 21 May 1999.

127 See Caroline Alphonso, 'Bullied Student Wants School Board to Pay,' *Globe and Mail*, 12 Sept. 2000, A1, 2; Jonathon Gatehouse, '18-year Accused of "Taxing" Pointed Gun at Teens, Trial Told,' *Montreal Gazette*, 2 Dec. 1997, A5; interview with London activist, 10 Dec. 2002; and Ottawa Police Service Liaison Committee (2002). *Heard for the First Time*. June.

128 See 'Challenging Homophobia and Heterosexism: A Resource Guide for Educators,' brochure produced by the Elementary Teachers' Federation of Ontario.

129 Zoe Bake-Paterson, 'No Longer a Child, Not Yet an Adult.' *Xtra!* 27 May 2004, 11.

130 Alanna Mitchell, 'Welcome to Canada's Gay High School.' *Xtra!* 29 May 2004, F6.

131 Gerald Mallon, 'Sticks and Stones Can Break Your Bones: Verbal Harassment and Physical Violence in the Lives of Gay and Lesbian Youths in Child Welfare Settings.' *Journal of Gay and Lesbian Social Services* 13, 1/2 (2001): 63–81.

132 Carol-Anne O'Brien, 'The Social Organization of the Treatment of Lesbian, Gay and Bisexual Youth in Group Homes and Youth Shelters.' *Canadian Review of Social Policy* 34 (1994): 46–7.

133 Ibid., 51.

134 Gary Comstock, *Violence against Lesbians and Gay Men* (New York: Columbia University Press, 1991), 167.

135 Cited in ibid., 55.

136 David F. Duncan, 'Prevalence of Sexual Assault Victimization among Heterosexual and Gay/Lesbian University Students,' *Psychological Reports* 66 (Fall) 1990: 65–6.

137 Ken Dowler, 'Intolerance, Ignorance and Insensitivity: An Examination of Anti-Gay Attitudes and Behaviours within a University Population' (MA thesis, University of Windsor, 1998). See also Heather Ross, 'Bashers Find Homos "Gross,"' *Xtra!* 31 Dec. 1998, 12.

138 See Arif Noorani, 'More Campus Violence,' *Xtra!* 6 Dec. 1991, 9; 'Homophobia at College,' *Perceptions*, 18 March 1995, 13; Ottawa Police Service Liaison Committee. *Heard for the First Time.* June.

139 Jennifer Prittie, 'Victim a Talented Artist and Teacher.' *National Post*, 20 Jan. 2001, A2.

140 Michael Friscolanti, 'Who Killed the Prof?' *National Post*, 20 Aug. 2001, A13.

141 Karyn Sandlos, 'Remembering David Buller,' *Xtra!* 18 March 2004, 14.

142 Paul Gallant, 'Arrest in Durost Murder.' *Xtra!* 22 Jan. 2004, 8.

143 Mike King, 'Police Dodge Shot, Arrest 2 Men after Transsexual Severely Beaten,' *Montreal Gazette*, 5 Jan. 1990, A3.

144 Colin Leslie, 'Not "Normal,"' *Xtra!* 23 May 1996, 18.

145 'History: Violence against the Gay/Lesbian/Transgendered Community' (Report prepared by the Community Relations Coordinator, Hamilton-Wentworth Regional Police, 28 May 1999).

146 See Ottawa Police Service Liaison Committee, *Heard for the First Time.*

147 'Assault Arrests' *Xtra!* 10 July 2003, 21.

148 See Robert Sarti, 'Street Transsexuals Facing Greater Risks.' *Vancouver Sun*, 27 Dec. 1993, B4; Mike Bell, 'A Change of Orientation,' *Vancouver Echo*, 31 Jan. 1996, 3; Katherine Johnson and Stephanie Castle, *Prisoner of Gender* (Vancouver: Perceptions Press, 1997).

149 Interview, 11 May 1999.

150 Greg Middleton, 'Transsexual Murder Victim Is City's 2nd in Past Six Months,' *Vancouver Province*, 13 March 1994, A21.

151 J. Wallace, 'Body Cops at the Border,' *Xtra!* 21 Aug. 2003, 9.

152 Jennifer O'Connor, 'Stating the Obvious,' *Xtra!* 27 May 2004, 15.

153 Linda Singer, *Erotic Welfare: Sexual Theory and Politics in the Age of Epidemic* (New York: Routledge, 1993), 39.

154 Melissa Farley, et al. 'Prostitution in Five Countries: Violence and Post-Traumatic Stress Disorder,' *Feminism and Psychology* 8, 4 (1998): 405–26.

155 Author's interview with client support worker at Kindred House, Edmonton, 18 May 2003.

156 Thomas Calhoun and Greg Weaver, 'Male Prostitution,' in Dennis Peck and Normal Dolch, eds., *Extraordinary Behavior: A Case Study Approach to Understanding Social Problems* (Westport, CT: Praeger, 2001), 212–26.

157 Thomas Calhoun, 'Male Street Hustling,' *Sociological Spectrum* 12, 1 (1992): 35–52.

158 Donald Allen, 'Young Male Prostitutes: A Psychosocial Study.' *Archives of Sexual Behavior* 9, 5 (1980): 399–426.

159 See Edward Morse, 'Sexual Behavior Patterns of Customers of Male Street Prostitutes,' *Archives of Sexual Behavior* 21, 4 (1992): 347–57.

160 Jacqueline Boles, 'Sexual Identity and HIV: The Male Prostitute,' *Journal of Sex Research* 31, 1 (1994): 39.

161 Ibid., 42–3.

162 Dan Allman, *M Is for Mutual, A Is for Acts: Male Sex Work and AIDS in Canada* (Ottawa: Health Canada, 1999), 12.

163 John Lowman, 'Street Prostitution,' in V.F. Sacco, ed., *Deviance: Conformity and Control in Canada*, 2nd ed. (Scarborough: Prentice-Hall, 1992), 56. See also Ottawa Police Service Liaison Committee *Heard for the First Time*.

164 Interview, 11 May 1999.

165 Allman, *M Is for Mutual*, 21.

166 Letter to the editor, *Ottawa Citizen*, 10 Jan. 1994, A6.

167 Gail Swainson, 'Autopsy Confirms Manager Stabbed,' *Toronto Star.* 10 May 1994, A7; James Dubro, 'Police Follow Leads in Wilson Killing,' *Xtra!* 8 July 1994, 14.

168 John Schmied, '"Hustler" Charged in Gay Slaying.' *Toronto Sun*, 19 May 1995, 7; Gretchen Drummie, 'Accused of Murder, Gay Lover Found Unfit,' *Toronto Sun*, 10 Sept. 1997, 28.

169 'Man, 22, Charged with Murder in Fatal Stabbing of Local Actor,' *Montreal Gazette*, 22 Feb. 1995, A3.

170 'Quebec Killing Renews Call for Gay Rights,' *Globe and Mail*, 1 March, A4.

171 'Accused Pleads Guilty to Murder of Actor' *Montreal Gazette*, 21 Dec. 1995, A3.

172 'Quebec Killing Renews Call,' A4.

173 Canadian Union of Public Employees 'CUPE National President Supports Bill C-250 to Orohibit Hate Propaganda Based on Sexual Orientation,' 5 May 2003.

174 Jeremy Hainsworth, 'Trans Prostitute Killed,' *Xtra West*, 12 June 2003.

175 'Vigil for Murdered Woman,' *Xtra*, 4 Sept. 2003, 17.

176 Hubert Martinez, 'Transvestite Prostitution,' *International Criminal Police Review* 430 (May 1991): 5–12.

177 Ian Robertson and Moira MacDonald, 'Transvestites Lure Dominating Men,' *Toronto Sun*, 25 May 1996, 4.

178 See 'Good Memory Pays Off,' *Toronto Star*, 12 March 1993, A28; Sam Pazzano, '16 Years for Doped-up Sex Attacker,' *Toronto Sun*, 28 March 1998, 22; 'Assault Suspect on New Charge,' *Toronto Sun*, 15 July 1998, 24.

179 Doug Saunders, 'Life Harsh for Teens in Drag,' *Globe and Mail*, 24 May 1996, A1, A5.

180 Robert Sarti, 'Street Transsexuals Facing Greater Risks,' *Vancouver Sun*, 27 Dec. 1993, B4.

181 Author's interview with Jamie-Lee Hamilton, 11 May 1999.

182 Bruce DeMara and Wendy Darroch, 'Guard Gets Life Term for Killing Prostitute,' *Toronto Star*, 20 April 1994, A8.

183 Paul Chapman, 'Appeal for Help in Murder Probe,' *Vancouver Province*, 10 Sept. 1995, A19.

184 Elizabeth Aird, 'Transsexuals' Search for Compassion Often Leads to the Streets,' *Vancouver Sun*, 16 Sept. 1995.

185 Interview with Jamie-Lee Hamilton, 11 May 1999.

186 Kevin Berrill, 'Anti-Gay Violence and Victimization in the United States: An Overview,' In Herek and Berrill, *Hate Crimes*, 35.

187 But see Krishna Rau, 'Crime and Punishment,' *Xtra*, 10 Dec. 1998, 7.

188 Helen Plischke, 'Easy to Be Hard,' *Edmonton Journal*, 23 April 1995, B1.

189 Bruce MacDougall, *Queer Judgments: Homosexuality, Expression, and the Courts in Canada* (Toronto: University of Toronto Press, 2000), 138.

190 Conversation, 30 May 1999.

191 Michael Harris, *Con Game: The Truth about Canada's Prisons* (Toronto: McClelland & Stewart, 2002), 195.

192 Cited in Daniel Lockwood, 'Issues in Prison Sexual Violence,' in Michael Braswell, Reid Montgomery, and Lucien Lombardo, eds., *Prison Violence in America*, 2nd ed. (Cincinnati: Anderson Publishing, 1994), 101.

193 Helen Eigenberg, 'Homosexuality in Male Prisons: Demonstrating the

Need for a Social Constructionist Approach,' *Criminal Justice Review* 17, 2 (1992); 219–34.

194 Kevin Marron, *The Slammer: The Crisis in Canada's Prison System* (Toronto: Doubleday Canada, 1996), 47.

195 Helen Eigenberg, 'Rape in Male Prisons: Examining the Relationship between Correctional Officers' Attitudes toward Male Rape and Their Willingness to Respond to Acts of Rape,' in Braswell, Montgomery, and Lombardo, *Prison Violence in America* 146–7.

196 Frank Prendergast, 'Rape in Jails not Common.' *Xtra!* 6 May 1999, 18.

197 Eigenberg, 'Rape in Male Prisons,' Braswell, Montgomery, and Lombardo, *Prison Violence*, 159.

198 Ibid., 152.

199 Ibid., 159. See also Helen Eigenberg, 'Correctional Officers' Definitions of Rape in Male Prisons,' *Journal of Criminal Justice* 28, 5 (2000): 435–49.

200 Lockwood, 'Issues in Prison Sexual Violence,' In Braswell, 98.

201 Marron, *The Slammer*, 48.

202 Canadian Press, 'Time to Reflect,' *Canadian Press Newswire*, 18 Dec. 1994.

203 Ralf Jurgens, *HIV/AIDS in Prisons: Final Report* (Montreal: Canadian HIV/AIDS Legal Network and Canadian AIDS Society, 1996).

204 E-mail from CSC Legal Services, 25 Aug. 2003.

205 Krishna Rau, 'Breaking Out,' *This Magazine* (March/April 1998): 15–17.

206 David Robinson and Luisa Mirabelli, *Research Brief: Summary of Findings of the 1995 CSC National Inmate Survey* (City: Research Division, Correctional Service of Canada, March 1996), 1.

207 Ibid., 6.

208 Ibid., 16.

209 Rau, 'Crime and Punishment.'

210 Diana Fishbein, 'Sexual Preference, Crime and Punishment,' *Women and Criminal Justice* 11, 2 (2000): 67–84.

211 Quoted in Ruthann Robson, 'Convictions: Theorizing Lesbians and Criminal Justice,' in Didi Herman and Carl Stychin, eds., *Legal Inversions: Lesbians, Gay Men and the Law* (Philadelphia: Temple University Press, 1995), 185. For more on queer executions, see Michael Shortnacy, 'Guilty and Gay, a Recipe for Execution in American Courtrooms: Sexual Orientation as a Tool for Prosecutorial Misconduct in Death Penalty Cases,' *American University Law Review* 51, 2 (2001): 309–65.

212 Kathryn Ann Farr, 'Defeminizing and Dehumanizing Female Murderers: Depictions of Lesbians on Death Row,' *Women and Criminal Justice* 11, 1 (2000): 49–66.

213 'Ottawa Bars "Lesbian Love Shack" after Widow Protests,' *Vancouver Province*, 16 May 2000, A13.
214 Chris Lambie, 'Women's Jail Warden Replaced,' *Halifax Daily News*, 12 Feb. 1997, 4.
215 Dean Beeby, 'Report Cites Lesbian Relationships in Prison Trashing,' Canadian Press Newswire. 24 June 1997.
216 Mike King, 'Prison Guard Wins $143,000 in Sexual Harassment Case,' *National Post*, 13 July 1998, A3.
217 Amanda Jelowicki, 'Jail Guard's Transsexualism Raises Questions.' *Montreal Gazette*, 29 May 1999, A5; George Kalogerakis, 'Jailing Transsexual a Gender-Bender,' *Montreal Gazette*, 3 Aug. 1999, A1.
218 Marron, *The Slammer*, 69.
219 Conversation, 30 May 1999.
220 Interview, 30 April 1999.
221 Katherine Johnson and Stephanie Castle *Prisoner of Gender* (Vancouver: Perceptions Press, 1997), 46–7.
222 Ibid., 61.
223 Ibid., 66.
224 Ibid., 63–5.
225 Marina Jiminez, 'More Prisoners Claim Human Right to Sex Change,' *National Post*, 22 Nov. 1999, A1.
226 Ibid., A1.
227 Valerie Lawton, 'Transsexual Inmate Files Complaint,' *Toronto Star*, 16 Aug. 1999.
228 Dene Moore, 'Transfer to Female Prison Draws Cheers, Concerns for Transsexual.' *Montreal Gazette*, 22 Nov. 1999, A8.
229 'Sex Changes in Prison' *Xtra!* 13 Feb. 2003, 11.
230 Interview, 7 July 1999.
231 Brian Nolan, Statement submitted to the Royal Newfoundland Constabulary Public Complaints Commission, 19 July 1993.
232 Interview, 7 July 1999.
233 Nolan, statement.
234 *R. v. Devereaux* (1996), 112 CCC (3d) 243 (Nfld. CA), at 245.
235 See www3.sympatico.ca/arbutus/LEGIT.htm, Billie Jo Newman. 'Embracing Newcomers.' *Xtra!* 27 June 2002, 12.
236 Kathleen Lahey, *Are We Persons Yet? Law and Sexuality in Canada* (Toronto: University of Toronto Press, 1999), 139.
237 See Amnesty International United Kingdom, *Breaking the Silence: Human Rights Violations Based on Sexual Orientation* (London: Amnesty International, 1997); Amnesty International USA, *Crimes of Hate, Conspiracy of*

Silence: Torture and Ill-Treatment Based on Sexual Identity (New York: Amnesty International USA, 2001).

238 See www.ilga.org and www.iglhrc.org.

239 Maureen Giuliani, 'Lesbians' Experience of Human Rights Violations: A Global Perspective' (MA thesis, University of Toronto, 1997).

240 See www.ai-lgbt.org; Jeremy Parkes, 'Unsexy Human Rights,' *Xtra!* 27 June 2002, 14.

241 André-Constantin Passiour, 'Les Appuis s'organisent à Montréal,' *Fugues* (Jan. 2002): 40. See also Dan Gardner 'Gay (Pride) and Prejudice,' *Ottawa Citizen*, 23 Nov. 2003, C3, C4.

242 Jennifer O'Connor, 'Pick Up Your PEN.' *Xtra!* 19 Feb. 2004.

243 Douglas Victor Janoff, 'Amsterdam 1998: Queer Global Activism for the New Millennium,' report prepared for EGALE, 1998; available at www.egale.ca/politics/politics/amsterdam.htm.

244 Marina Jiminez, 'Gay Refugee Claimants Seeking Haven in Canada,' *Globe and Mail*. 24 April 2004, A7.

245 See Janoff, 'Amsterdam 1998.'

246 Nicole LaViolette, 'The Immutable Refugees: Sexual Orientation in *Canada (A.G.) v. Ward*,' *University of Toronto Faculty Law Review* 55, 1 (1997): 15.

247 *(A.G.) v. Ward*, [1993] 2 S.C.R. 689, reversing [1990] 2 F.C. 667, affirming (1988), 9 Imm. L.R. (2d) 48.

248 LaViolette, 'The Immutable Refugees,' 15, 3.

249 Interview with Rob Hughes of Smith and Hughes, Vancouver, 3 May 1999.

250 Interview with Nicole Laviolette, 6 July 1999.

251 Jenni Millbank, 'Imagining Otherness: Refugee Claims on the Basis of Sexuality in Canada and Australia,' *Melbourne University Law Review* 26 1 (2002): 148–9.

252 Ibid., 150–1.

253 Ibid., 155.

254 Ibid., 159–62.

255 Ibid., 163–6.

256 Joel Dupuis, 'Believe the Hype,' *Capital Xtra*, 17 Jan. 2003, 10.

257 Millbank, 'Imagining Otherness,' 171–4.

258 'Refugee Status Denied to Straight-Appearing Gay,' *Qink Magazine*, 26 Aug. 1999, 6.

259 Marina Jiminez, 'Refugee Board Says He's Safe in Mexico.' *Globe and Mail*, 4 May 2004, A1.

260 Paul Gallant, 'Allowed Back.' *Xtra!* 30 Nov. 2000.

261 'River Jordan' *Xtra!* 21 Feb. 2002, 15; Marina Jiminez 'Gay Jordanian Now "Gloriously Free in Canada."' *Globe and Mail*, 20 May 2004, A3.

262 'Transsexual Refugee' *Xtra West*, 7 Sept. 1995.

263 Lahey, *Are We Persons Yet?* 140–1.

264 Tom Godfrey, 'He/She Booted Back to Mexico,' *Toronto Sun*, 1 Sept. 1998, 5.

265 Tom Godfrey, 'Gang-Raped Lesbian Gets Refugee Status,' *Toronto Sun*, 26 Aug. 1999, 30.

266 Irene Darra, 'Chased by Police,' *Xtra*, 20 April 2000, 14.

267 'Crime non résolu' *Fugues* (Jan. 2002): 38.

268 Interview, 11 May 1999.

269 Interview with co-founder, 18 May 2003. For more information, see www.qrd.org/qrd/www/world/immigration/legit.html

4: Law, Homophobia, and Violence: Legislating against Hate

1 Kevin Griffin, 'Publicize Gay-Bashing, Activist Tells Police,' *Vancouver Sun*, 14 May 1994, A7.

2 Kevin Griffin, 'Gays Fight Back after Attack in Coffee Bar,' *Vancouver Sun*, 11 May 1994, A2.

3 Douglas Victor Janoff, 'Gay-bashing in Vancouver: A Case Study,' (unpublished paper, 1995), 6.

4 Griffin, 'Gays Fight Back.'

5 Elizabeth Aird, 'Queer Patrol Doesn't Have Limp Wrist, Only Needed Muscle,' *Vancouver Sun*, 11 June 1994, A3.

6 Doug Barr, 'Hate Season Kickoff,' *Angles* (May1994): 1.

7 Janoff, 'Gay-bashing in Vancouver,' 7–8.

8 Ibid., 6.

9 Ibid., 10–11.

10 Ibid., 8–9.

11 Raj Takhar, 'Attack on Gays Draws Sentence,' *West End Times*, 10 May 1996, 7.

12 Raj Takhar, 'Basher Pleads Guilty,' *Angles* (May 1996): 1.

13 Bruce Ryder, 'Straight Talk: Male Heterosexual Privilege,' *Queen's Law Journal* 16 (1991): 294–5.

14 Ruthann Robson, 'Convictions: Theorizing Lesbians and Criminal Justice,' Didi Herman and Carl Stychin, eds., *Legal Inversions: Lesbians, Gay Men and the Law* (Philadelphia: Temple University Press, 1995), 191.

15 Carl Stychin, *Law's Desire* (New York: Routledge, 1995), 148.

16 *R. v. Brown*, [1993] 2 All ER 75 (HL), cited in ibid., 129.

17 Ibid., 137.

18 Ibid., 102–3.

19 Larry Backer, 'Constructing a "Homosexual" for Constitutional Theory: Sodomy Narrative, Jurisprudence and Antipathy in the U.S. and Britain,' *Tulane Law Review* 71 (Dec. 1996): 563–4.
20 Associated Press, 'Gay Sex Ban Struck Down by US Supreme Court,' *Globe and Mail* website. 26 June 2003. www.globeandmail.ca/servlet/story/RTGAM.20030626.wgsex0626/BNStory.html.
21 *Bowers v. Hardwick*, 478 U.S. 186 (1986).
22 Backer, 'Constructing a "Homosexual,"' 592.
23 Gary Kinsman, 'History,' *Capital Xtra*. 17 July 2003, 13.
24 Brenda Cossman, 'Sex Law.' *Capital Xtra*, 19 June 2003, 15.
25 James Mennie, 'Montreal Judge Rules Swingers Clubs Legal, but Not Orgies,' *Ottawa Citizen*, 6 July 2003, G5.
26 Canadian Press, 'Judge Lets Potential Jurors Be Queried on Gay Bias,' Canadian Press Newswire, 11 Oct. 1996.
27 Peter Aronson, David E. Rovella, and Bob Van Voris, 'Jurors: A Biased, Independent Lot.' *National Law Journal*, 2 Nov. 1998, A1.
28 Drury Sherrod and Peter Nardi, 'Homophobia in the Courtroom: An Assessment of Biases Against Gay Men and Lesbians in a Multiethnic Sample of Potential Jurors,' In Gregory Herek, ed., *Stigma and Sexual Orientation: Understanding Prejudice against Lesbians, Gay Men and Bisexuals* (Thousand Oaks, CA: Sage 1998), 24–5.
29 Mike Blanchfield, 'Murder Denials Just "tall tales,"' *Ottawa Citizen*, 9 Dec. 1994, B7.
30 Mike Blanchfield, 'Jury Surprises Court with Acquittal in Steamer Trunk Killing,' *Ottawa Citizen*, 17 Dec. 1994, A1.
31 Mike Blanchfield, 'Crown Claims "Sex" Angle in Steamer Trunk Killing,' *Ottawa Citizen*, 14 Dec. 1994, D11.
32 Mike Blanchfield, 'Murder Denials,' B7.
33 *R. v. Gendreau* (1980), 33 Man. R. (2d) 245 (CA), cited in Donald Casswell, *Lesbians, Gay Men and Canadian Law* (Toronto: Emond Montgomery, 1996), 616.
34 See *R. v. Wilson* (1990), 59 CCC (3d) 432 (BCCA), cited in ibid., 609.
35 Bruce MacDougall, *Queer Judgments: Homosexuality, Expression, and the Courts in Canada*, (Toronto: University of Toronto Press, 2000), 259–60.
36 *R. v. Jolicoeur* (1997), unreported, BC Prov. Ct., 7 Feb., cited in Garth Barriere, 'Asking for Trouble?' *Xtra West*, 18 Sept. 1997, 17.
37 *R. v. M. (D.J.)*, [1990] OJ No. 514 (QL) (Prov. Ct.–Youth Off. Ct.); appeal dismissed, 61 CCC (3d) 129 (OCA), cited in MacDougall, *Queer Judgments*, 173.
38 Colin Leslie, 'Life Cut Short?' *Xtra!* 17 April 1992, 11.

39 Interview with local activist, 13 July 1999.

40 MacDougall, *Queer Judgments*, 175; and Lara Bradley, 'Educate the Enemy.' *Xtra!* 17 Dec. 1998, 11.

41 Interview, 26 May 1999.

42 Canadian Press, 'Gay-Basher in Court,' *Vancouver Province*, 15 Dec. 1999, A30.

43 Colin Leslie, 'Tenant Accused in Second Bashing,' *Xtra*. 3 April 1992, 1; Colin Leslie, 'Accused Basher Banned,' *Xtra*, 17 April 1992, 11.

44 Wendy Darroch, 'Pair Who Beat Man Ordered to Write Essays on Gays,' *Toronto Star*, 31 July 1996, A18; Alisa Craig, 'A Bashing or a Simple Assault?' *Xtra!* 23 May 1996, 18.

45 Kevin Rollason, 'High Court Reduces Gay-Bash Sentence,' *Winnipeg Free Press*, 14 June 1994.

46 *R. v. Gallant* (1994), 95 Man. R. (2d) 296 (CA); MacDougall, *Queer Judgments*, 174.

47 Letter, 13 April 1999.

48 Interview with VPD officer, 13 May 1999.

49 Gareth Kirkby, 'Police, Crown Give Run-Around,' *Xtra West*. 12 Nov 1998, 10.

50 Interview with VPD officer, 13 May 1999.

51 Bruce DeMara, 'Don't Be Afraid, Gay-Bashing Victims Say,' *Toronto Star*, 23 Oct. 1994, A15.

52 Gretchen Drummie, 'Man Acquitted in Gay Bashing,' *Toronto Sun*, 28 Oct. 1995, 28.

53 Glenn Sumi, 'Playing with the Truth. *Xtra!* 18 Aug. 1995, 32.

54 'History: Violence against the Gay/Lesbian/Transgendered Community' report prepared by the Community Relations Coordinator, Hamilton-Wentworth Regional Police, 28 May 1999.

55 Julia Garro, 'Armed and Dangerous,' *Xtra*, 22 Jan. 2004, 13.

56 *R. v. McDonald*, [1995] OJ No. 2137 (QL) (Ont. Prov. Ct. Gen. Div.); Sam Pazzano, 'Robber Who Preyed on Gay Men Jailed,' *Toronto Sun*, 10 Jan. 1995, 22.

57 Larry Still, 'Burnaby Woman Given Unusual Accessory Conviction,' *Vancouver Sun*, 31 May 1991, A1.

58 Sean Upton, 'Reaction of Dead Man's Lover "Odd," Court Told.' *Ottawa Citizen*. 26 March 1994, C5

59 Mike Blanchfield, 'Ottawa Man Convicted in Beating of Gay Man,' *Ottawa Citizen*, 31 March 1994, B7.

60 *R. v. Carolan* (1995), 163 AR 238 (Alta. Prov Ct.) 239, at para. 8; interview with Crown attorney's office, Calgary, 29 June 1999.

61 *R. v. Carolan.*

62 Interview, 1 July 1999.

63 Tony Lofaro, 'Gatineau Death Suspect Nabbed by Ottawa RCMP,' *Ottawa Citizen*, 21 Oct. 1994, B8.

64 Mike Shahin, 'Escaper Gets Life in Prison for Murder of Montreal Man,' *Ottawa Citizen*, 18 Jan. 1995, B2.

65 Tony Lofaro, 'Gatineau Death Suspect Nabbed by Ottawa RCMP,' *Ottawa Citizen*, 21 Oct. 1994, B8.

66 Shahin, 'Escaper Gets Life.'

67 Lofaro, 'Gatineau Death Suspect Nabbed.'

68 Shahin, 'Escaper Gets Life.'

69 Eleanor Brown, 'Suspects Arrested.' *Xtra!* 20 Aug. 1993, 12; Cynthia Amsden, 'Portrait of a Killer,' *Ottawa Citizen*, 26 April 1995, B3.

70 Paul Moloney, 'Gay Community Cautious after Two Men Beaten to Death.' *Toronto Star*, 4 Aug. 1993, A6.

71 Cal Millar, 'Police Delve into Mystery Behind 3 Stabbing Deaths,' *Toronto Star*, 7 Aug. 1993, A10.

72 Amsden, 'Portrait of a Killer.'

73 Moloney, 'Gay Community Cautious.'

74 'Warrants Issued.' *Globe and Mail*, 4 Aug. 1993, A10.

75 Millar, 'Police Delve.'

76 Mike Blanchfield, 'Outcasts Formed Deadly Brotherhood of Doomed,' *Ottawa Citizen*, 21 June 1994, A1.

77 Amsden, 'Portrait of a Killer.'

78 Bruce Ward, 'Man, Charged in Second Death, Accused in Friend's Slaying Insists: "I'm Not Gay."' *Ottawa Citizen*, 7 Aug. 1993, C1.

79 Blanchfield, 'Outcasts Formed Deadly Brotherhood.'

80 Amsden, 'Portrait of a Killer.'

81 Graeme Hamilton, 'The Torments That Sear the Soul of Michael McGray,' *National Post*, 24 March 2000, A3.

82 Erin Anderssen, 'I Got Very Good at It, Killer Says.' *Globe and Mail*, 24 March 2000, A1, A8.

83 Rory MacDonald, '"Gay Men Easy Targets for Murder," Says Killer,' *Capital Xtra*, 14 April 2000, 13.

84 Paul Cherry, 'I'm Guilty of Gay Killings: McGray.' *Montreal Gazette*, 26 April 2000, A1, A2.

85 Valerie Jenness, 'Managing Differences and Making Legislation: Social Movements, and the Racialization, Sexualization, and Gendering of Federal Hate Crime Law in the US,' *Social Problems* 46, 4 (1999): 549.

86 Gail Mason, 'Not Our Kind of Hate Crime,' *Law and Critique* 12, 3 (2001): 255–60.

87 Annjanette Rosga, 'Deadly Words: State Power and the Entanglement of Speech and Violence in Hate Crime,' *Law and Critique* 12, 3 (2001): 239–40.

88 James Jacobs and Kimberly Potter, *Hate Crimes: Criminal Law and Identity Politics* (New York: Oxford University Press, 1998), 45–6.

89 See Jack Levin and Jack McDevitt, *Hate Crimes: The Rising Tide of Bigotry and Bloodshed* (New York: Plenum Press, 1993).

90 Jacobs and Potter, *Hate Crimes*, 53.

91 Jenness, 'Managing Differences,' 559–61.

92 Ibid., 553.

93 Ibid., 557–9.

94 Valerie Jenness, 'The Hate Crime Canon and Beyond: A Critical Assessment,' *Law and Critique* 12, 3 (2001): 283–5.

95 See also Valerie Jenness and Ryken Grattet, 'The Criminalization of Hate: A Comparison of Structural and Polity Influences in the Passage of "Bias-Crime" Legislation in the United States,' *Sociological Perspectives* 39, 1 (1996): 129–54.

96 Jenness, 'The Hate Crime Canon,' 286–7.

97 Valerie Jenness and Ryken Grattet (2001). *Making Hate a Crime: From Social Movement to Law Enforcement* (New York: Sage, 2001), 1–3.

98 Ibid., 6–7.

99 Ibid., 103–6.

100 Jenness, 'The Hate Crime Canon,' 293–4.

101 Jenness and Grattet, *Making Hate a Crime*, 112.

102 Ibid., 117.

103 Ibid., 147–51.

104 Julian Roberts, 'Legislative Responses to Hate-Motivated Crime' (draft report for the Domain Seminar on Social Justice, Department of Canadian Heritage, 14–15 May 1999), 4.

105 'Kill Fags' *Xtra!* 9 June 1995, 18.

106 Doug Nairne, 'Hate Mail Case Thrown Out,' *Winnipeg Free Press*, 29 May 1997, A1.

107 Svend Robinson, 'Svend Robinson,' *Globe and Mail*, 27 May 2003. Downloaded from www.globeandmail.ca.

108 Egale Canada 'Email Update,' 11 May 2004.

109 Roberts, 'Legislative Responses,' 31.

110 Ibid., 18.

111 Ibid., 12–13.

112 Ibid., 19.

113 Ibid., 6–7.

114 Ibid., 24.

115 Ibid., 23.

116 See T. Maroney, 'The Struggle against Hate Crime: Movement at a Crossroads,' *New York University Law Review* 73 (1993): 564–620.

117 Rachel Giese, 'Hating the Hate-Crime Bill,' *This Magazine* (November, 1995): 7–9.

118 Bill Jeffery, *Standing Up to Hate: Legal Remedies Available to Victims of Hate-Motivated Activity*, Ottawa, Department of Canadian Heritage (1998), 21.

119 Martha Shaffer, 'Criminal Responses to Hate-Motivated Violence,' *McGill Law Journal* 41 (1995): 210.

120 Ibid., 213–14.

121 Ibid., 245–6.

122 Ibid., 203.

123 Ibid., 245–6.

124 Roberts, 'Legislative Responses,' 19.

125 Ibid., 32.

126 Interview, 28 Nov. 2002.

127 Eleanor Brown, 'Victim Takes on Police,' *Xtra*, 18 Feb. 1994, 15.

128 Gretchen Drummie, 'Suspect in Gay Attack Denies Kicks,' *Toronto Sun*, 11 Mar. 1995, 28.

129 Brown, 'Victim Takes on Police.'

130 Gretchen Drummie, '"Booze, Machismo, Hate": Prosecutor Explains Gay-Bashing,' *Toronto Sun*, 16 March 1995, 43.

131 Alisa Craig, 'Gaybashing Case Goes to Court,' *Xtra!* 17 March 1995, 13.

132 Gretchen Drummie, 'Attackers Get Jail,' *Toronto Sun*, 13 May 1995, 17.

133 *R. v. Cvetan*, [1999] O.J. No. 250.

134 Eleanor Brown, 'Death Won't Affect Trial,' *Xtra*, 14 Jan. 1999, 13.

135 Interview with former coordinator, 26 May 1999.

136 Jeffery, *Standing Up to Hate*, 23.

137 Ibid., 25.

138 Ibid., 15.

139 Ibid., 25.

140 Ibid., 17–19.

141 Ibid., 28.

142 Interview, 7 July 1999.

143 Jeffery, *Standing Up to Hate*, 33.

144 Interview with CHRC official, 13 August 2003.

145 Interview, 7 July 1999.

146 Jeffery, *Standing Up to Hate*, 38–40.

147 Ibid., 13–16.
148 Cited in Ibid., 43.
149 Ibid., 43–4.
150 Ibid., 43–7.

5: Homo-cide: Getting Away with It?

 1 See Vito Russo, *The Celluloid Closet,* rev. ed. (New York: Harper & Row, 1987).
 2 Stephen Tomsen and Allen George, 'The Criminal Justice Response to Gay Killings: Research Findings,' *Current Issues in Criminal Justice* 9, 1 (1997): 59–61.
 3 Ibid., 63.
 4 Donna-Marie Sonnichsen, 'Bloody Trail Traced Man's Route, Court Told.' *Halifax Mail-Star,* 14 May 1991, B1.
 5 Donna-Marie Sonnichsen, 'Accused Insane during Stabbing, Say Psychiatrists,' *Halifax Mail-Star,* 17 May 1991, B1.
 6 Donna-Marie Sonnichsen, 'Accused Murderer Insane or Provoked into Stabbing – Lawyer,' *Halifax Mail-Star,* 16 May 1991, C1.
 7 Sonnichsen, 'Accused Insane during Stabbing.'
 8 Donna-Marie Sonnichsen, 'Bloody Trail Traced Man's Route, Court Told,' *Halifax Mail-Star,* 14 May 1991, B1.
 9 Sonnichsen 'Accused Murderer Insane.'
10 Sonnichsen, 'Accused Insane during Stabbing.'
11 Sonnichsen, 'Accused Murderer Insane.'
12 Sonnichsen, 'Accused Insane during Stabbing.'
13 Donna-Marie Sonnichsen, 'Accused Ruled Insane, Found Not Guilty,' *Halifax Chronicle Herald,* 20 May 1991, D7.
14 Letter, 6 May 1999.
15 Canadian Press, 'Munroe Verdict,' Canadian Press Newswire, 18 May 1991.
16 D.J. West, *Homosexuality Re-examined* (Minneapolis: University of Minnesota Press, 1977), 203.
17 Edward Kempf, *Psychopathology* (St Louis, MO: CV Mosby, 1920), 477–8.
18 Ibid., 514.
19 Ibid., 479.
20 Ibid., 486.
21 Ibid., 491–3.
22 Ibid., 496–8.

23 Ibid., 502.
24 Ibid., 510–11.
25 Ibid., 515.
26 J.H. Cassity, 'Personality Study of 200 Murderers,' *Journal of Criminal Pathology* 2 (1941): 296–304.
27 A.M. Duval and J.L. Hoffman, 'Dementia Praecox in Military Life as Compared with Dementia Praecox in Civil Life,' *War Medicine* 1 (1941): 854–62.
28 Benjamin Karpman, 'Mediate Psychotherapy and the Acute Homosexual Panic (Kempf's Disease),' *Journal of Nervous and Mental Disease* 98 (1943): 493.
29 Burton Glick, 'Homosexual Panic: Clinical and Theoretical Considerations,' *Journal of Nervous and Mental Disease* 20 (1959): 27.
30 Ibid., 20–3.
31 Ibid., 25–7.
32 Marion Shapiro, 'Male Homosexuality and Violence,' *Quarterly* 32, 4 (1975): 35–41.
33 Hilde Marberg, 'Fragmentary Psychoanalytic Treatment of Acute Homosexual Panic.' *Psychoanalytic Review* 59, 2 (1972): 295–304.
34 Sherwyn Woods, 'Violence: Psychotherapy of Pseudohomosexual Panic.' *Archives Of General Psychiatry* 27 (1972): 255–6.
35 Lionel Ovesey and Sherwyn Woods, 'Pseudohomosexuality and Homosexuality in Men: Psychodynamics as a Guide to Treatment,' in *Homosexual Behavior: A Modern Reappraisal* (New York: Basic Books, 1980), 329.
36 Ibid., 334–5.
37 Frank W. Kiel, 'The Psychiatric Character of the Assailant as Determined by Autopsy Observations of the Victim,' *Journal of Forensic Sciences* 10, 3 (1965): 269.
38 Henry Chuang and Donald Addington, 'Homosexual Panic: A Review of Its Concept,' *Canadian Journal of Psychiatry* 33 (October 1988): 613–14.
39 Ibid., 613.
40 Alfred Freedman, Harold Kaplan, and Benjamin Sadock, eds. *Comprehensive Textbook of Psychiatry-II* (Baltimore: Williams & Wilkins, 1975), 1518.
41 Ibid., 1788.
42 Gary Comstock, 'Dismantling the Homosexual Panic Defence,' *Law and Sexuality* 2 (1992): 87.
43 Richard Walter, 'Homosexual Panic and Murder,' *American Journal of Forensic Medicine and Pathology*, 6, 1 (1985): 49–51.
44 John Gonsiorek, 'The Use of Diagnostic Concepts in Working with Gay and Lesbian Populations,' *Journal of Homosexuality* 7, 2/3 (1982): 9–11.

45 Comstock, 'Dismantling the Homosexual Panic Defence,' 89.
46 *People v. Rodriguez* 256 Cal. App. 2d 663, 64 Cal. Rptr 253 (1967), cited in Robert G. Bagnall et al. 'Burdens on Gay Litigants and Bias in the Court System,' *Harvard Civil Rights–Civil Liberties Law Review* 19 (1984): 502.
47 Bagnall, 'Burdens on Gay Litigants,' 501.
48 Ibid., 502.
49 Ibid., 507–8.
50 Ibid., 510.
51 Ibid., 512.
52 Comstock, 'Dismantling the Homosexual Panic Defence,' 80–8.
53 'Sexual Orientation and the Law' *Harvard Law Review* (1989): 36.
54 James Polchin, 'Why Do They Strike Us?' *CLAGS News* (Winter 2001): 11.
55 F.A. McHenry, 'A Note on Homosexuality, Crime and the Newspapers,' *Journal of Criminal Psychopathology* 2 (1941): 541–2.
56 Robert Mison, 'Homophobia in Manslaughter: The Homosexual Advance as Insufficient Provocation,' *California Law Review* 80, 1 (1992): 134.
57 Ibid., 133.
58 Ibid., 161.
59 Ibid., 135–6.
60 Ibid., 167.
61 *Commonwealth v. Doucette*, 462 NE 2d 1084 (Mass. 1984), cited in Mison, 'Homophobia in Manslaughter,' 168.
62 Mison, 'Homophobia in Manslaughter,' 168–9.
63 'Sexual Orientation and the Law,' 36–8.
64 See Adrian Howe, 'More Folk Provoke Their Own Demise: Homophobic Violence and Sexed Excuses – Rejoining the Provocation Law Debate, Courtesy of the Homosexual Advance Defence,' *Sydney Law Review* 19, 3 (1997): 335–65; Scott McCoy, 'The Homosexual Advance Defense and Hate Crimes Stat-utes: Their Interaction and Conflict, *Cardozo Law Review*, 22, 2 (2001): 629–63; Dirk Meure, 'Homo Panic in the High Court: The High Court in *Green v. R*,' *Griffith Law Review* 10, 20 (2001): 240–55; Bronwyn Statham, 'The Homosexual Advance Defence: "yeah, I Killed Him, but He Did Worse to Me." *Green v. R*.,' *University of Queensland Law Journal* 20, 2 (1999): 301–11; Joseph Carmel Chetcuti, 'The Dismembered Body Case: Gay Panic Defence in a Civil Law Legal System,' *Australasian Gay and Lesbian Law Journal* 6, (1997): 68–83; Kara Suffredini, 'Pride and Prejudice: The Homosexual Panic Defense,' *Boston College Third World Law Journal* 21, 2 (2001): 279–314.
65 *Green v. the Queen* (1998), 72 ALJR 19.

66 Rebecca Bradfield, 'Criminal Cases in the High Court of Australia,' *Criminal Law Journal* 22, 5 (1998): 296–303.

67 Santo de Pasquale, 'Provocation and the Homosexual Advance Defence: The Deployment of Culture as a Defence Strategy,' *Melbourne University Law Review*, 26, 1 (2002): 120.

68 Ibid., 133–4.

69 Ibid., 135–7.

70 Ibid., 140–142.

71 Christina Pei-Lin Chen, 'Provocation's Privileged Desire,' *Cornell Journal of Law and Public Policy* 10, 1 (2000): 196–7.

72 Ibid., 199–203.

73 Ibid., 216.

74 Ibid., 224–5.

75 Bruce MacDougall, *Queer Judgments: Homosexuality, Expression, and the Courts in Canada* (Toronto: University of Toronto Press, 2000), 154.

76 See Allyson Lunny, 'Provocation and "Homosexual" Advance: Masculinized Subjects as Threat, Masculinized Subjects under Threat,' *Social and Legal Studies* 12, 3 (2003): 311–33.

77 Donald G. Casswell, *Lesbians, Gay Men and Canadian Law* (Toronto: Emond Montgomery, 1996), 631–2.

78 'Youths Found Drug Dealer Dead at Home, Trial Hears,' *Ottawa Citizen*, 13, June B3.

79 Larry Still, 'Homophobe Who Killed Gay Handed Five-Year Sentence,' *Vancouver Sun*, 29 June 1995, A3.

80 Kerry Gold, '"Panic" Defence Nets 5 Years.' *Vancouver Courier*, 30 July 1995.

81 Greg McIntyre, '"Sorry" Killer Asks No Forgiveness,' *Vancouver Province*, 25 June 1995, A21.

82 Tom Yeung, 'Is a Pass Provocation for Murder?' *Xtra!* 11 Jan. 2001, 20.

83 Still, 'Homophobe Who Killed Gay.'

84 Cindy Filipenko, 'Not Guilty by Homosexual Association,' *This Magazine* (Nov. 1995): 5.

85 Yeung, 'Is a Pass Provocation?'

86 See John Kennedy, 'Victim Seeks Sense in Bashing,' *Xtra!* 8 Dec. 1995, 16.

87 Gary Oakes, 'Doctor's Killer Jailed 5 Years,' *Toronto Star*, 3 Sept. 1994, A4.

88 Peter Small and Gail Swainson, 'Man Dies after Beating at Cafe,' *Toronto Star*, 27 Feb. 1994, A7.

89 Oakes, 'Doctor's Killer Jailed 5 Years.'

90 Small and Swainson 'Man Dies after Beating at Cafe.'

91 'Man Charged with Murder after Beating Victim Dies' *Toronto Star*, 6 March 1994, A12.

92 Oakes, 'Doctor's Killer Jailed 5 Years.'

93 Alan Cairns, 'Feds Finally Reveal AWOL Killers' Names,' *Toronto Sun*, 12 Jan. 1999, 7.

94 Peter Hum and Dave Rogers, 'Gilling Convicted in Killing.' *Ottawa Citizen*, 14 May 1998, D3.

95 Brenda Branswell and Bob Harvey, 'Man, 27, Guilty of Murder,' *Ottawa Citizen*, 25 March 1996, D1.

96 Francine Dubé, 'Father Says Son Fought Off Rapist,' *Ottawa Citizen*, 30 April 1998, B8.

97 Hum and Rogers, 'Gilling Convicted.'

98 *R. v. Gilling* (1997), 34 O.R. (3d) 392 (Ont. CA), at 395.

99 Branswell and Harvey 'Man, 27, Guilty.'

100 *R. v. Gilling*, 400.

101 Dave Rogers, 'Man Sentenced to Life in Prison for Knife Attack,' *Ottawa Citizen*, 30 April 1996, C2.

102 *R. v. Gilling*, 394.

103 Branswell and Harvey, 'Man, 27, Guilty.'

104 Rogers, 'Man Sentenced to Life.'

105 Hum and Rogers, 'Gilling convicted.'

106 Peter Hum, 'Man Who Slit Friend's Throat Sentenced to 6 1/2 Years.' *Ottawa Citizen*, 2 Sept. 1998, B3.

107 'Hitchhiker Stands Trial for Strangling Alberta Man,' Canadian Press article posted at Globaltv.com Regina, 14 Nov. 2000.

108 'Witness Says Hitchhiker Murderer Looked Like Devil,' article posted at Globaltv.com Regina, 15 Nov. 2000. http://regina.globaltv.com/sk/news/stories/news-20001115-091056.html.

109 See 'Man Gets 13 Years in Death of Designer,' *Globe and Mail*, 30 Sept. 1994, A5; Eleanor Brown, 'Suspects Arrested.' *Xtra!* 20 Aug. 1993, 12; 'Jailed Five Years for Strangling' *Globe and Mail*, 9 May 1991, A14.

110 Diana Coulter, 'Man "Exploded" in Rage, Killed Homosexual Admirer with Axe,' *Edmonton Journal*, 26 Jan. 1991.

111 Mathew Ingram, '"Totally Berserk,"' *British Columbia Report*, 18 Feb. 1991, 43–4.

112 Dave Rider, 'Slain Man Met Accused in Jail,' *Toronto Sun*, 2 June 1997, 16.

113 Gretchen Drummie, 'Gay Pass Sparked Slaying, Trial Told,' *Toronto Sun*, 23 Oct. 1998, 39.

114 Thomas Claridge, 'Toronto Man to Serve 10 Years for Manslaughter of Transsexual.' *Globe and Mail*, 23 Dec. 1998, A3.

115 Drummie, 'Gay Pass Sparked Slaying.'
116 Claridge, 'Toronto Man to Serve 10 Years.'
117 Daryl Slade, 'Accused Admits to Being Angry,' *Calgary Herald*, 26 April 1995, B3.
118 Daryl Slade, 'Accused Killer Claims Self-Defence,' *Calgary Herald*, 25 April 1995, B3.
119 Daryl Slade, 'New Trial Results in Guilty Plea,' *Calgary Herald*, 2 April 1997, B2.
120 Bob Beaty, 'Crown Seeks 10 to 12 Year Sentence in Fatal Beating,' *Calgary Herald*, 14 May 1997, B4.
121 Bob Beaty, 'Seven-Year Term for Manslaughter,' *Calgary Herald*, 15 May 1997, B6.
122 Neal Hall, 'Crown Spurns Memory-Loss Defence,' *Vancouver Sun*, 14 March 1995, B5.
123 *R. v. Moore* (1996), 81 BCAC 153 (BCCA).
124 Hall, 'Crown Spurns Memory-Loss Defence.'
125 Neal Hall, 'Body Sexually Mutilated, Trial Told,' *Vancouver Sun*, 9 March 1995, A3.
126 *R. v. Moore.*
127 Hall, 'Body Sexually Mutilated.'
128 *R. v. Moore.*
129 Joey Thompson, 'Getting Away with Murder,' *Vancouver Province*, 3 Dec. 1995, A16.
130 See *R. v. Tomlinson*, [1998] S.J. No. 848; 'Panic Defence Fails' *Perceptions*, 27 Jan. 1999, 12.

6: Homophobia, Violence, and Policing in Canada

1 Gary Comstock, *Violence against Lesbians and Gay Men* (New York: Columbia University Press, 1991), 58.
2 Cited in Kevin Berrill and Gregory Herek, 'Primary and Secondary Victimization in Anti-Gay Crimes: Official Response and Public Policy,' in *Hate Crimes: Confronting Violence against Lesbians and Gay Men* (Newbury Park, CA: Sage, 1992), 294.
3 Ellen Faulkner, *Anti-Gay/Lesbian Violence in Toronto: The Impact on Individuals and Communities*, Ottawa: Research and Statistics Division, Policy Sector, Department of Justice Canada, 1997), 202.
4 Gary Kinsman, *The Regulation of Desire: Homo and Hetero Sexualities*, 2nd ed. (Montreal: Black Rose, 1996), 359–60.
5 Heather Ross, 'Mounties Track HIV Status,' *Capital Xtra!* 11 Dec. 1998, 21.

6 Gary Kinsman, 'Responsibility as a Strategy of Governance: Regulating People Living with AIDS and Lesbians and Gay Men in Ontario,' *Economy and Society* 25, 3 (1996): 394–5.

7 Kinsman, 'Responsibility as a Strategy,' 401–4.

8 Tom Warner, *Never Going Back: A History of Queer Activism in Canada* (Toronto: University of Toronto Press, 2002), 304.

9 Allyson Lunny, 'Responsibilizing a 'Community under Attack': Hate Crime and Its Constitution for Queer Communities in Canada, 1985–2003' (PhD dissertation, University of Toronto, in progress).

10 Warner, *Never Going Back*, 290.

11 Ibid., 294–5.

12 Ibid., 302.

13 Marc Burke, *Coming Out of the Blue* (London: Cassell, 1993), 41.

14 Ibid., 45–6.

15 Ibid., 50.

16 Ibid., 47.

17 Ibid., 51.

18 Ibid., 59–60.

19 Ibid., 55.

20 Robin Perelle, 'Murder Stings Vancouver,' *Xtra!* 29 Nov. 2001, 11.

21 Lance McFall, 'Forceful Denial,' *Angles* (January 1997): 2.

22 Interview with VPD officer, 30 April 1999.

23 Mia Stainsby, 'Cautiously Coming Out,' *Vancouver Sun*, 4 Nov. 1995, F11, F12.

24 For example, see 'RCMP Suit,' *Xtra!* 26 Nov. 1993, 12.

25 Stainsby, 'Cautiously Coming Out.'

26 'Deviant Cops.' *Xtra!* 29 Oct. 1993, 18.

27 Stainsby, 'Cautiously Coming Out.'

28 Ingrid Peritz, 'Coming Out of the Blue,' *Globe and Mail*, 28 July, 1999, D3.

29 Interview, 19 April 2000.

30 Warner, *Never Going Back*, 302.

31 John Sinopoli, 'Bye, Bye Judy,' *Xtra!* 16 May 2002, 16.

32 Emily Sharpe, 'Friendly Face of Policing.' *Xtra!* 29 May 2003, 15.

33 Interview, 11 May 1999.

34 Angelique Praat and Keith Tuffin, 'Police Discourses of Homosexual Men in New Zealand,' *Journal of Homosexuality* 31, 4 (1996): 57–73.

35 Diane Richardson and Hazel May, 'Deserving Victims? Sexual Status and the Social Construcion of Violence.' *Sociological Review* 47, 2 (1999): 310–13.

36 Song Cho, 'Gaybashing 101,' *Capital Xtra*, 25 Feb. 1994, 9.

37 David Roberts, 'Violence Prompts Response from Gays,' *Globe and Mail*, 29 Aug. 1991, A4. See also Margaret Philip, 'Report Documents Gay-Bashing,' *Globe and Mail*, 25 June 1997, A8; 'Alley Assault' *Xtra!* 13 Oct. 1995, 16.

38 Leslie Moran, 'Affairs of the Heart: Hate Crime and the Politics of Crime Control,' *Law and Critique* 12, 3 (2001): 336–8.

39 Miro Cernetig, 'Gay Bashing in Vancouver Routine,' *Globe and Mail*, 12 Dec. 1996.

40 Lori Culbert, 'Police Seek Witness to Attack on Park Board Chair,' *Vancouver Sun*, 12 Dec. 1996, B2.

41 Faulkner, *Anti-Gay/Lesbian Violence*, 202.

42 'Windsor beating,' *Xtra!* 10 Dec. 1993, 17.

43 'Bar Owner Quilty of Assault,' *Xtra!* 3 March 1995, 1.

44 Letter from London queer activist, 6 May 1999.

45 'Schisler in Court' *Xtra!* 5 Oct. 2000, 15.

46 Lisa Lisle, 'Victim's Pal Charged in Failed Assault' *Ottawa Sun*, 5 Dec. 2002, 5.

47 George W. Smith, 'Policing the Gay Community: An Inquiry into Textually-Mediated Social Relations,' *International Journal of the Sociology of Law* 16 (1988): 166–7.

48 See Steven Maynard, 'Through a Hole in the Lavatory Wall: Homosexual Subcultures, Police Surveillance, and the Dialectics of Discovery,' *Journal of the History of Sexuality*, 5, 2 (1994): 207–42; Steven Maynard, *Toronto the Gay* (Chicago: University of Chicago Press, forthcoming); Elisa Kukla, 'Police Obsessions,' *Xtra!* 30 Nov. 2000, 16.

49 Cited in John Greyson, 'Security Blankets: Sex, Video and the Police,' in Martha Gever, Pratibha Parmar, and John Greyson, *Queer Looks: Perspectives on Lesbian and Gay Film and Video* (Toronto: Between the Lines, 1993), 388.

50 Thomas Fleming, 'Criminalizing a Marginal Community: The Bawdy-House Raids,' in Thomas Fleming and L.A. Visano, eds., *Deviant Designations: Crime, Law and Deviance in Canada* (Toronto: Butterworths, 1983), 37.

51 Ibid., 38–41.

52 Ibid., 51.

53 Ibid., 42.

54 Ibid., 47–8.

55 Smith, 'Policing the Gay Community,' 165–6.

56 Greyson, 'Security Blankets,' 385.

57 Frederick Desroches, 'Tearoom Trade: A Law Enforcement Problem,' *Canadian Journal of Criminology* 33, 1 (1991): 1–21.

58 But see Tom Zillich, 'Bashing Season,' *The Westender*, 19 June 1997, 4; Ottawa Police Service Liaison Committee, *Heard for the First Time*. June 2002.

59 Ingrid Peritz, 'Crimes of Ignorance, Crimes of Hate,' *Ottawa Citizen*, 20 Dec. 1992, A4.

60 'Teen Pleads Guilty in Death of Teacher,' *Montreal Gazette*, 23 March 1994, A6.

61 See 'Climate for Murder,' Documentary film on Montreal murders produced by Arnie Gelbart and directed by Albert Nerenberg, 1994.

62 'Teen Pleads Guilty.'

63 André Picard, 'Gays Target of Police, Activist Alleges,' *Globe and Mail*, 13 May 1993, A2.

64 There have also been reports from Victoria Park. See 'Sex Alerts,' *Xtra!* 9 April 1998, 20.

65 Adrian Humphries, 'Gay Former Pastor Sues Police Force for Outing Him,' *National Post*, 8 Dec. 1999, A3.

66 Adrian Humphries, 'Forced Outing Made Life "Hell" for Minister,' *National Post*, 19 Feb. 2000, A10.

67 Humphries, 'Gay Former Pastor Sues Police.'

68 'Police indecency' *National Post*, 18 Feb. 2000, A19.

69 Mark Cosgrove, 'Anglican Minister Takes Cops to Court,' *Xtra!* 9 March 2000, 14.

70 'Ontario: Ex-Priest Loses Gay Sting Suit,' *National Post*, 1 July 2000, A4.

71 Kinsman, *The Regulation of Desire*, 344.

72 Jane Mulkewich, 'The Hamilton Wentworth Regional Police Gay/Lesbian/Bisexual/Transgendered Task Force: A Public Relations Success Story' report prepared by the Community Relations Coordinator, Hamilton-Wentworth Regional Police. 31 March 1998, 3.

73 Steven Maynard, 'Park Cruisers Feel Slap of Sex Sting,' *Xtra!* 16 May 2002, 4.

74 Paul Gallant, 'Is Belleville Ontario's Sodom?' *Xtra!* 20 Feb. 2003, 11.

75 Maynard, 'Park Cruisers.'

76 Steven Maynard, 'The Belleville Un-Intelligencer,' *Xtra!* 16 May 2002, 14.

77 Steven Maynard, 'Charge Dropped, Reputation Ruined,' *Xtra!* 27 June 2002, 25.

78 Gallant, 'Is Belleville Ontario's Sodom?'

79 Emily Sharpe, 'Naming Names.' *Xtra!* 30 May 2002, 16.

80 Faulkner, *Anti-Gay/Lesbian Violence*, 202.

81 Farrell Crook, 'Two Off-Duty Peel Police Officers Fined for Beatings Outside Bar,' *Toronto Star*, 28 Nov. 1992, A22.

82 Matthew Hays, 'The Cop Factor,' *This Magazine* (February 1995): 29.

83 Commission des droits de la personne et des droits de la jeunesse, *De l'illégalité à l'égalité* (Montreal: CDPDJ, 1994), 59.

84 Tara Patel, 'Marchers Protest Police Violence,' *Montreal Gazette*, 30 July 1990, A3.

85 Linda Dawn Hammond, 'Homophobic Attack on My Exhibit!' article posted at www.iprimus.ca/~dawnone/sexreply.html. 8 August 2000.

86 Commission des droits de la personne et des droits de la jeunesse, *De l'illégalité*, 59.

87 'We're Here, We're Queer,' documentary film on Montreal police brutality, Produced by Maureen Bradley and Danielle Comeau, Video Out Productions, Vancouver 1990.

88 Hays, 'The Cop Factor.'

89 Letter, 18 Oct. 2000.

90 Stephen Tomsen and Allen George, 'The Criminal Justice Response to Gay Killings: Research Findings,' *Current Issues in Criminal Justice* 9, 1 (1997): 66.

91 Canadian Press, 'Weapon Quarantine "Discrimination,"' *Calgary Herald*, 7 May 1991, A10.

92 Canadian Press, 'Halifax Man Charged in 1992 Sydney Stabbing,' *Halifax Daily News*, 31 May 1995, 4.

93 Interview, 23 Sept. 2000.

94 Canadian Press, 'Halifax Man Charged in 1992 Sydney Stabbing.' *Halifax Daily News*, 31 May 1995, 4.

95 Canadian Press, 'Prosecution Search Down to Short List,' *Halifax Daily News*, 1 June 1995, 8.

96 Canadian Press, 'Killer Asks Forgiveness,' *Halifax Daily News*, 2 May 1996, 8.

97 Beverly Ware, 'Accused Killer Goes Free,' *Halifax Herald*, 22 April 1999, A1.

98 Interview, 26 Oct. 2000.

99 Bob Beaty, 'Jury Hears Sexual Advance Incited Attack,' *Calgary Herald*, 17 May 1994, B1.

100 Bob Beaty, 'Alcohol Fuelled Anger, Trial Told,' *Calgary Herald*, 25 May 1994, B1.

101 Bob Beaty, 'Man Tells of Deadly Air Gun Attack,' *Calgary Herald*, 19 May 1994, B1.

102 Bob Beaty, 'Man Guilty of Killing Friend,' *Calgary Herald*, 26 May 1994, B1.

103 Beaty, 'Man Tells of Deadly Air Gun Attack.'

104 Beaty, 'Man Guilty of Killing Friend.'

105 Interview, 17 May 1999.
106 Ron Ryder, 'Drugs Lured Gormley to McIver's Home,' *Charlottetown Guardian*, 7 May 1996, A2.
107 Ron Ryder, 'Gormley Murderer Clarke Accused Says His Life in Danger for Telling the Truth,' *Charlottetown Guardian*, 4 May 1996, A2.
108 Canadian Press, 'Killer Gets 12 Years,' *Vancouver Sun*, 3 Aug. 1996.
109 Ibid.
110 Nigel Armstrong, 'Videotape Led to Unfair Confession, Court Hears,' *Charlottetown Guardian*, 12 May 1996, A2.
111 Ryder, 'Drugs Lured Gormley.'
112 See Bruce Owen, 'Police Decoys Bring Down Criminals,' *Winnipeg Free Press*, 10 Nov. 1995, A4.
113 Thomas Claridge, '18 Year-Old Wait for Parole Urged,' *Globe and Mail*, 16 May 1991, A12.
114 Thomas Claridge, 'Man Sentenced to Life in Murder of Homosexual,' *Globe and Mail*, 18 May 1991, A8.
115 Jennifer Balboni and Jack McDevitt, 'Hate Crime Reporting: Understanding Police Officer Perceptions, Departmental Protocol and the Role of the Victim,' *Justice Research and Policy* 3, 1 (2001): 1–28.
116 Markel Haider, 'Implementing Controversial Policy: Results from a National Survey of Law Enforcement Department Activity on Hate Crime,' *Justice Research and Policy* 3, 1 (2001): 29–61.
117 Cited in Valerie Jenness and Ryken Grattet, *Making Hate a Crime: From Social Movement to Law Enforcement* (New York: Sage, 2001), 128.
118 Jeanine Bell, 'Policing Hatred: Police Officers, Bias Crime and the Politics of Civl Rights Law Enforcement' (PhD dissertation, University of Michigan, 2000).
119 Elizabeth Stanko, 'Re-Conceptualising the Policing of Hatred: Confessions and Worrying Dilemmas of a Consultant,' *Law and Critique* 12, 3 (2001): 309–10.
120 Ibid., 311–13.
121 Ibid., 318–21.
122 Ibid., 321–3.
123 Ibid., 327–8.
124 Ellen Faulkner, 'Empowering Victim Advocates: Organizing against Anti-Gay/Lesbian Violence in Canada,' *Critical Criminology* 10 (2001): 24.
125 Bill Jeffery, *Standing Up to Hate: Legal Remedies Available to Victims of Hate-Motivated Activity*, report prepared for the Department of Canadian Heritage, 6.
126 Ibid., 11.

127 Julian Roberts, *Disproportionate Harm: Hate Crime in Canada*, working document, Department of Justice Canada, ix.

128 Susan Martin, 'Police and the Production of Hate Crimes: Continuity and Change in One Jurisdiction,' *Police Quarterly* 2, 4 (1999): 417–37.

129 Roberts, *Disproportionate Harm*, 12.

130 Julian Roberts, 'Legislative Responses to Hate-Motivated Crime,' draft Report for the Domain Seminar on Social Justice, Department of Canadian Heritage. 14–15 May 1999, 8.

131 Roberts, 'Legislative Responses,' 10.

132 Ibid., 6.

133 Jenness and Grattet, *Making Hate a Crime*, 141.

134 Lacey Sloan, Linda King, and Sandra Sheppard, 'Hate Crimes Motivated by Sexual Orientation: Police Reporting and Training.' *Journal of Gay and Lesbian Social Services* 8, 3 (1998): 25–39.

135 Roberts, 'Legislative Responses,' 30–1.

136 Secretary of State for Multiculturalism and the Status of Women 'Report: Hate and Bias Activity Roundtable,' Ottawa, 10–11 Feb. 2000, 2–5.

137 Ibid., 8–10.

138 Ibid., 11–13.

139 Ibid., 13–15.

140 Secretary of State for Multiculturalism and the Status of Women, 'A Call for Action: Hate and Bias Activity Roundtable,' draft, 27 July 2000, 12–13.

141 Secretary of State for Multiculturalism and the Status of Women 'Report: Hate and Bias Activity Roundtable,' 14–16.

142 Ibid., 22–3.

143 Ibid., 18–19.

144 Ibid., 26–8.

145 Derek Janhevich, *Hate Crime in Canada: An Overview of Issues and Data Sources*, produced by the Canadian Centre for Justice Statistics, Statistics Canada, Catalogue no. 85-551-XIE, 2001. Available at www.statcan.ca.

146 See Sandra Besserer and Catherine Trainor, 'Criminal Victimization in Canada, 1999,' *Juristat*, 1999. http://www.communityaccounts.ca/ CommunityAccounts/OnlineData/relatedsites/victimization.pdf

147 Derek Janhevich, *Hate Crime Study: Summary Results of Consultations*, produced by the Canadian Centre for Justice Statistics, Statistics Canada, Catalogue no. 85-557-XIE, 2002. http://collection.nlc-bnc.ca/100/200/301/ statcan/hate_crime_study-e/85-557-XIE02001.pdf

148 Faulkner, 'Empowering Victim Advocates,' 10.

149 Interviews, 5 and 21 May 1999.

150 Canadian Association of Chiefs of Police, Minutes from the 26–7 April 1998 meeting of the POLIS committee.

151 Interview with QPP spokesman, 26 Nov. 2002.

152 Interview, 12 May 1999.

153 Interview with inspector in charge of QPP's anti-terrorism unit, 21 June 2004.

154 Interview, 17 May 1999.

155 Interview, 17 Dec. 2000.

156 Interview, 28 Nov. 2002.

157 Interview with head of OPP Hate Crime Unit, 21 June 2004.

158 Tom Yeung, 'Victoria Forms "Hate Crime Unit,"' *Xtra West*, 6 Feb. 1997, 7.

159 Interview with BC Hate Crimes Unit Coordinator, 30 April 1999.

160 Ministry of Attorney General, *End Hate Crime: Hate/Bias Crime Police Training Notes* (Vancouver, 1998), 13–15.

161 Interview with B.C. Hate Crimes Unit Coordinator, 30 April 1999.

162 Tom Yeung, 'Hate Crimes Unit Gets Kudos,' *Xtra West*, 22 Jan. 1998, 14.

163 Tom Yeung, 'Gay Men Targetted,' *Xtra West*, 29 Oct. 1998, 7.

164 Interview, 16 June 2004.

165 Ruth Garcia, 'An Analysis of the Discrepancies in Hate Crime Reporting,' (MSc thesis, California State University, Fresno, 2001).

166 Ian MacAulay, statement to the Osoyoos RCMP, 7 Oct. 1995.

167 *R. v. Svedruzic, Hung Quoc Truong and Huan Quoc Truong* (1996), Penticton Registry (BCSC), 21 June 1996, at para. 4.

168 Randall Lampreau, statement to Osoyoos RCMP, 7 Oct. 1995.

169 Interview with the victims, 7 June 1999.

170 Brian Coutts, statement to Osoyoos RCMP, 7 Oct. 1995.

171 Interview with the victims, 7 June 1999.

172 Royal Canadian Mounted Police, Letter, including police report, to Randall Lampreau, 21 Nov. 1995.

173 Interview with the victims, 7 June 1999.

174 *R. v. Svedruzic*, at para. 7.

175 Interview with the victims, 7 June 1999.

176 *R. v. Svedruzic*, paras 47–8 and cross-examination of B. Coutts by Mr Patterson, lines 45–8.

177 Interview with the victims, 7 June 1999.

178 'Osoyoos Justice' *Xtra West*, 16 Nov. 2000, 15.

7: Urban Cowboys and Rural Rednecks: Community Resistance to Homophobic Violence

1 Duncan Hood, 'Vicious Burlington Bashing,' *Xtra!* 30 July 1998.

2 Amy Klein, 'Gun Group for Gays Targets Bashing,' *Montreal Gazette*, 9 Nov. 2003, A19.

3 Ellen Faulkner, 'Empowering Victim Advocates: Organizing against Anti-Gay/Lesbian Violence in Canada,' *Critical Criminology* 10 (2001): 123.

4 Ibid., 124.

5 Ellen Faulkner, 'A Case Study of the Institutional Response to Anti-Gay/Lesbian Violence in Toronto' (PhD dissertation, Ontario Institute for Studies in Education, University of Toronto, 1999), 88.

6 Ibid., 97–8.

7 Ibid., 51–2. See also National Coalition of Anti-Violence Programs, *Anti-Lesbian, Gay, Bisexual and Transgender Violence in 1998: A Report of the National Coalition of Anti-Violence Programs* (New York, 1999).

8 Elizabeth Stanko and Paul Curry, 'Homophobic Violence and the Self "At Risk,"' *Social and Legal Studies* 6, 4 (1997): 519–20.

9 Interview, 26 May 1999.

10 Warren Gerard, 'Is Gay Bashing Out of Control?' *Toronto Star*, 29 June 1991, D1.

11 Julian Roberts, *Disproportionate Harm: Hate Crime in Canada*, working document, Department of Justice Canada, 1995, 32.

12 Faulkner, 'A Case Study,' 184.

13 See Rachel Giese, 'Hating the Hate-Crime Bill,' *This Magazine* (November 1995): 7–9; Carol-Anne O'Brien, 'The Social Organization of the Treatment of Lesbian, Gay and Bisexual Youth in Group Homes and Youth Shelters,' *Canadian Review of Social Policy* 34 (1994): 38–9; 'Are You a Happy Homosexual?' *Toronto Life* (November 1996): 85–91; Cassandra Fernandes and Donna Costanzo, *Hate: Communities Can Respond* (Toronto: Access and Equity Centre, 1996); Rachel Giese, 'Violence Is Banal and Brutal.' *Xtra!* 10 Oct. 1996, 28.

14 'Gay Bashing,' transcript of report on CTV National News, broadcast on 2 June 1996.

15 Sharon Lem, 'Project Aids Gay-Bash Victims,' *Toronto Sun*, 22 May 1996, 25.

16 Janice Turner, 'Beyond the Bruises,' *Toronto Star*, 8 Aug. 1996, C5.

17 Faulkner, 'A Case Study,' 54.

18 Ibid., 58.

19 Faulkner, 'Empowering Victim Advocates,' 129.

20 Faulkner, 'A Case Study,' 87–8.

21 Ibid., 102.

22 Ibid., 209.

23 Interview, 26 May 1999.

24 Faulkner, 'Empowering Victim Advocates,' 126.

25 Ibid., 131–2.

26 Faulkner, 'A Case Study,' 192–3.

27 Faulkner, 'Empowering Victim Advocates,' 132.

28 Interview with former coordinator, 26 May 1999.

29 Interview, 27 April, 1999.

30 Interview, 26 May, 1999.

31 Ibid.

32 Interview with Toronto hate crimes officer, 4 May 1999.

33 Metropolitan Toronto Police Service, 'Annual Hate-Motivated Crimes: 1996,' statistical report, Hate Crime Unit – Intelligence Services, 1996, 14.

34 Toronto Police Service, *Intelligence Services Hate Crime Report,* report dated 26 Feb. 1998, downloaded from www.mtps.on.ca/int.haterpt.htm.

35 Interview, 28 Nov. 2002.

36 Faulkner, 'Empowering Victim Advocates,' 130.

37 George W. Smith, 'Policing the Gay Community: An Inquiry into Textually Mediated Social Relations,' *International Journal of the Sociology of Law* 16 (1988): 179–80.

38 LGBT Police Liaison, 'Progress Report on a Gay, Lesbian, Bisexual and Transsexual/Transgendered Community Initiative for a Toronto Police Liaison Plan,' 17 Sept. 2000.

39 Eleanor Brown, 'Acrimony at Police Meeting.' *Xtra!* 21 Sept. 2000, 11.

40 Eleanor Brown, 'Beyond Sexual Issues,' *Xtra!* 5 Oct. 2000, 15.

41 John Sinopoli, 'Police Group Polishes Image.' *Xtra!* 29 Nov. 2001, 15.

42 Presentation, Rainbow Visions Conference, Montreal, 17 May 2003.

43 Rob Granatstein, 'Gays No Fans of Fantino,' *Toronto Sun,* 8 Nov. 1999, 4.

44 Elisa Kukla, 'It's a Miracle,' *Xtra!* 23 March 2000.

45 Eleanor Brown, 'Male Cops at the Pussy Palace,' *Xtra!* 21 Sept. 2000, 11.

46 Ibid.

47 Paul Gallant, 'Pussy Palace Triumph,' *Xtra!* 7 Feb. 2002, 11.

48 'The Names,' *Xtra!* 5 Oct. 2000, 14.

49 Eleanor Brown, 'A Bureaucratic Halt at Police Board,' *Xtra!* 5 Oct. 2000, 14.

50 Shannon Kari, 'Police Told Lesbian Party Was to Be a "Sex-o-rama,"' *Ottawa Citizen,* 7 June 2002, A8.

51 Eleanor Brown, 'The New Spin,' *Xtra!* 19 Oct. 2000, 15.

52 'Tipped Off? *Xtra!* 2 Nov. 2000, 15.

53 'March on HQ,' *Xtra!* 5 Oct. 2000, 14.

54 'Charges Laid,' *Xtra!* 19 Oct. 2000, 15.

55 Eleanor Brown, 'Under the Rug,' *Xtra!* 2 Nov. 2000, 15.

56 Mariana Valverde, 'A Pussy-Positive Judgment,' *Xtra!* 7 Feb. 2002, 18.

57 Brown, 'Male Cops at the Pussy Palace.'

58 Brown, 'A Bureaucratic Halt.'
59 'Xtra Named.' *Xtra!* 30 Nov. 2000, 16.
60 Eleanor Brown, 'Cops Sue Kyle Rae,' *Xtra!* 16 Nov. 2000, 16.
61 Shannon Kari, 'Bathhouse Furore Left Toronto Police Steaming,' *Ottawa Citizen*, 6 June 2000, A9.
62 Emily Sharpe, 'Don't Cross the Cops.' *Xtra!* 27 June 2002, 13.
63 Rachel Giese, 'Pussy Pals.' *Xtra!* 30 Nov. 2000, 25.
64 Interview with Montreal police communications spokesman, 5 Dec. 2000.
65 See Claudine Metcalfe, 'Attention C'est Chaud!' *Fugues* (June 1999): 38.
66 Commission des droits de la personne et des droits de la jeunesse, *De l'illegalité à l'égalité* (Montreal: Commission des droits de la personne et des droits de la jeunesse, 1994), 66.
67 Ingrid Peritz, 'Crimes of Ignorance, Crimes of Hate,' *Ottawa Citizen*, 20 Dec. 1992, A4.
68 Alexander Norris, 'Hear Us Out or We'll Name Biased Cops, Gays Warn Police Chief,' *Montreal Gazette*, 27 Feb. 1993, A3.
69 André Picard, 'Montreal Gays Fear Serial Killer,' *Globe and Mail*, 12 Feb. 1993, A1.
70 'Montreal Gays Vow to Take Up Arms,' *Montreal Gazette*, 15 Feb. 1993, A4.
71 '*Climate for Murder*,' documentary film on Montreal murders produced by Arnie Gelbart and directed by Albert Nerenberg, 1994.
72 Michelle Lalonde and Philip Authier, 'Gays Fault Media, Police Handling of Latest Killings,' *Montreal Gazette*, 13 Feb. 1913, A3; 'Reward Increased in Gay Killings' *Montreal Gazette*, 17 Feb. 1993, A3.
73 See '*Climate for Murder*.'
74 Canadian Press, 'Gays, Police Meet in Wake of Murders,' *Globe and Mail*, 3 Dec. 1993, A5.
75 Dire Enfin la Violence, 'Bilan,' 31 May 1997, 12.
76 Ibid.
77 Dire Enfin la Violence, 'Rapport des Activités, mars à octobre' (1998), 3–4.
78 Ibid., 6–7.
79 Ibid., 10–12.
80 Pierre Tremblay, Eric Boucher, and Marc Ouimet, 'Rhetoric of Victimization: A Case Study of the Gay Village,' *Canadian Journal of Criminology*, 40, 1 (1998): 14.
81 Ibid., 4.
82 Ibid., 10.
83 Ibid., 14–15.
84 Douglas Buckley-Couvrette et al. 'Réponse au Professeur Pierre Tremblay et al.,' *Canadian Journal of Criminology* 40, (1998): 21–5.

85 Chris Taylor, 'Gay-on-Gay Violence Shocking,' *Montreal Gazette*, 24 May 1997, A3.

86 Dire Enfin la Violence, 'Rapport des activités, mai à octobre,' (1999), 21.

87 Dire Enfin la Violence, 'Rapport des Activités, mars à octobre' (1998), 5.

88 Dire Enfin la Violence, 'Rapport des activités, novembre 1999 à mai 2000' (2000), 5.

89 Uyen Vu, 'Montreal Hate-Crime Conundrum,' *Montreal Gazette*, 22 Aug. 1998, B1.

90 Interview with coordinator, Dire Enfin la Violence, 19 April 2000.

91 Yves Lafontaine, 'Un photographe de *Fugues* attaqué sauvagement,' *Fugues* (Oct. 2001): 68.

92 André-Constantin Passiour, 'Deux touristes américains attaqués,' *Fugues* (Oct. 2001): 70.

93 André-Constantin Passiour, 'L'Enfer d'un couple gai de banlieu,' *Fugues* (Feb. 2001): 36.

94 Matthew Hays, 'Canadian Beauty,'*Xtra!* 30 May 2002, 22.

95 'Montreal Murder' *Xtra!* 16 May 2002, 16.

96 Interview, 29 Nov. 2000.

97 E-mail interview with former coordinator, 1 Dec. 2002.

98 André-Constantin Passiour, 'Une Fermeture définitive,' *Fugues* (April 2003), 30.

99 Brian Morton, 'Sensitivity Training Applauded,' *Vancouver Sun*, 17 Sept. 1992, B4.

100 Jeff Lee, 'Police Get Orders on Gay-Bashing,' *Vancouver Sun*, 16 Sept. 1992, A1.

101 Kevin Griffin, 'Witness Program, Self-Defence Course New Weapons in War on Gay-Bashing,' *Vancouver Sun*, 30 Aug. 1991.

102 Elizabeth Aird, 'Queer Patrol Doesn't Have Limp Wrist, Only Needed Muscle,' *Vancouver Sun*, 11 June 1994, A3.

103 Tom Yeung, 'Catch the Re-Runs of Davie's Angels,' *Xtra West*, 19 Feb. 1998, 11.

104 Tom Yeung, 'Fighting Back,' *Xtra West*, 29 May 1997, 9.

105 Ibid.

106 Hoddy Allan, 'A Matter of Response,' *Xtra West*, 29 May 1997, 10.

107 Tom Yeung, 'Inspecting the Top Brass,' *Xtra West*, 13 Nov. 1997, 19.

108 Letter from B.C. Hate Crimes Unit Coordinator, 23 Nov. 1999.

109 Tom Zillich, 'Bashing Season,' *Westender*, 19 June 1997, 4.

110 Vancouver Police Department, 'Bashline Volunteer Orientation Manual,' volunteer application package, 1997.

111 Douglas Victor Janoff, Copy of letter to Vancouver Police Department, 30 Sept 1997.

112 Douglas Victor Janoff, notes taken after discussion with a gay-bashing victim who called the Vancouver Police Department's Bashline, 13 Oct. 1997.

113 Tom Yeung, 'What Caused Allan's Injuries?' *Xtra West*, 4 March 1999, 7.

114 Gareth Kirkby, 'Police Actions Questioned,' *Xtra West*, 26 June 1997, 7.

115 Tom Yeung, 'Oh, What a Letdown,' *Xtra West*, 13 May 1999, 7.

116 Letter, 13 April 1999.

117 Rob McMahon, 'Time for Action on Bashings,' *Xtra West*, 25 Nov. 1999, 4–5.

118 Interview, 20 May 1999.

119 Tom Yeung, 'Community Abandons Bashline,' *Xtra West*, 28 Oct. 1999, 7, and 10.

120 Yeung, 'Oh, What a Letdown.'

121 Interview, 20 May 1999.

122 Letter from Bashline official, 18 Oct. 2000.

123 Kim Bolan, 'Killers "Likely Serial Gay Bashers,"' *Vancouver Sun*, 21 Nov. 2001, B1, B6.

124 Mark Hume, 'Arrest Made in "Gay Bashing" BC murder,' *National Post*, 13 Feb. 2003, A13.

125 Ian Bailey, '1,500 Mourn Man Killed in Gay-Bashing,' *National Post*, 19 Nov. 2001, A8.

126 Dene Moore, 'Witnesses Step Forward in Beating Death of Gay Man,' *Edmonton Journal*, 20 Nov. 2001, A13.

127 Hume, 'Arrest Made in "Gay Bashing."'

128 Gareth Kirkby, 'First Arrest in Webster Killing,' *Capital Xtra*, 13 March 2003, 7.

129 'Police Offering $10,000,' *Vancouver Province*, 20 Dec. 2001, A4.

130 Kirkby, 'First Arrest.'

131 Rod Mickleburgh, 'Teen Gets 3 Years for Hate-Crime Killing,' *Globe and Mail*, 19 Dec. 2003, A1.

132 Gareth Kirkby, 'Why Not Murder?' *Xtra*, 16 Oct. 2003, 20; Rod Mickleburgh, 'Court Erupts After Man Freed in Bashing Death,' *Globe and Mail*, 11 December 2004.

133 See also Chad Skelton and Yvonne Zacharias, 'Police on Park Murder: It's a Hate Crime.' *Vancouver Sun*, 19 Nov. 2001, A1, A2; Jack Keating, 'Vancouver Killing Sparks Anger in Gay Community,' *Montreal Gazette*, 20 Nov. 2001, A10; Yvonne Zaccharias, 'Mourners Grieve for Victim of Stanley Park Beating,' *Vancouver Sun*, 26 Nov. 2001, B3; Patricia Bailey, 'Police Investigate Second Park Beating,' *Vancouver Sun*, 12 Dec. 2001,

A1; Robert Matas, 'Vancouver Gays Outraged by Killing,' *Globe and Mail,* 19 Nov. 2001, A11; Peter McKnight, 'Hate Laws Can Be Used Against You,' *Vancouver Province,* 3 Dec. 2001, A12; Peter O'Neil, 'Jaffer Blasts Senator for Remarks on Gays.' *Vancouver Sun,* 23 Nov. 2001, A14; Mark Wilson, 'Crime Trend Down Despite Gay Slaying,' *Vancouver Province,* 21 Nov. 2001, A6; Yvonne Zaccharias, 'Inside Stanley Park's Gay Sex Scene,' *Vancouver Sun,* 20 Nov. 2001, A1.

134 Kim Bolan, 'Killers "Likely Serial Gay Bashers,"' *Vancouver Sun,* 21 Nov. 2001, B1, B6.

135 Bailey, '1,500 Mourn.'

136 'More Than 100 Meet to Battle Homophobia,' *Vancouver Province,* 29 Nov. 2001, A3.

137 Presentation by a staff member from The Centre at the EGALE Rainbow Visions conference in Montreal, 17 May 2003.

138 Interview, 9 Dec. 2002.

139 Presentation by a staff member from the Centre at the EGALE Rainbow Visions conference.

140 Interview with Ottawa hate crime officer, 15 June 2004.

141 David Pepper, 'A Criminal Negligence: Making Police Respond to Gay Bashing.' *Outcome* (1993): 34–5.

142 David Pepper and Carroll Holland, *Moving toward a Distant Horizon,* 3rd ed. of public summary of the final report of the Action Plan Project funded by the Ottawa Police Services Board (Ottawa, 1999), 52.

143 Ibid., 40.

144 Mike Blanchfield, 'Judge Wipes Out Officer's Conviction,' *Ottawa Citizen,* 8 March 1993, B2.

145 'Charges against Ottawa Officer Withdrawn,' *Ottawa Citizen,* 9 Nov. 1994, B8.

146 Philip Hannan, 'Mental Bruises of Bashings,' *Capital Xtra!* 26 Aug. 1994, 1.

147 Philip Hannan, 'Man Charged with Careless Driving,' *Capital Xtra!* 28 Oct. 1994, 13.

148 Peter Nogalo, 'Unexpected Encounters,' *Capital Xtra!* 27 June 1997, 11.

149 Bonnie Van Toen, 'RCMP Busy Policing Poodles at Remic,' *Capital Xtra,* 23 June 2000, 17.

150 Rory MacDonald, 'Assault Complaints Point to the Same Suspect,' *Capital Xtra,* 27 Sept. 2002, 7.

151 Rory MacDonald, 'Assaults Could Go Back Several Years,' *Capital Xtra,* 25 Oct. 2002, 8.

152 Lee Greenberg, Elaine O'Connor, and Fiona Isaacson, 'Police Warned Gays about Dating Services,' *Ottawa Citizen,* 6 Dec. 2002, F1.

153 Rory MacDonald, 'Communication Breakdown,' *Capital Xtra*, 6 Dec. 2002, 9.

154 Rory MacDonald, 'New Developments in Murder and Assault Cases,' *Capital Xtra*, 22 May 2003, 11.

155 Letter from OPS Liaison Committee coordinator to the committee, 23 Dec. 2002.

156 Andrew Seymour, 'Cops Hunt for Predator After Gay Men Attacked,' *Ottawa Sun*, 5 Dec. 2002, 5.

157 Rory MacDonald, 'Assault on Leather Men,' *Capital Xtra*, 19 June 2003, 11.

158 John Steinbachs, 'Relatives Suffer Agonizing Wait,' *Ottawa Sun*, 5 Dec. 2002, 3.

159 Laura Czekaj, 'Sadness Tinged by Fear,' *Ottawa Sun*, 7 Dec. 2002, 3.

160 John Steinbachs and Andrew Seymour, 'Hate Unit Eyes Murder,' *Ottawa Sun*, 5 Dec. 2002, 3.

161 John Steinbachs, Andrew Seymour, and Lisa Lisle, 'Cops See Eerie Similarities,' *Ottawa Sun*, 6 Dec. 2002, 3.

162 Jake Rupert, 'Suspect Charged in Raynsford Beating Death,' *Ottawa Citizen*, 17 Jan. 2002, B1.

163 Rory MacDonald, 'What Makes a Hate Crime,' *Capital Xtra*, 22 May 2003, 31.

164 Andrew Seymour, 'Grim Find in Condo,' *Ottawa Sun*, 8 July 2003, 3.

165 Laura Czekaj and Lisa Lisle, 'Man Faces Murder Charge,' *Ottawa Sun*, 12 July 2003, 7.

166 Sean McKibbon, 'Killed in Drunken Binge,' *Ottawa Sun*, 20 Jan. 2004, 4.

167 Interview, 21 Aug. 2003.

168 Ottawa Police Service Liaison Committee, *Heard for the First Time* (June 2002). Available at www.ottawapolice.ca.

169 Carla Wilson, 'Beacon Hill Volunteer Group Trying to Halt Attacks on Night Park,' *Victoria Times Colonist*, 6 Dec. 1994.

170 Ian Dutton, 'Hate in Action.' *Victoria Times-Colonist*, 30 July A1.

171 See 'Gay Basher Sought,' *Vancouver Province*, 1 July 2001, A4.

172 Interview, 2 Dec. 2002.

173 Interview with a Victoria police officer, 15 June 2004.

174 'A Study of Discrimination Based on Sexual Orientation' A collaborative effort by the Alberta Human Rights Commission, the Gay and Lesbian Awareness Society of Edmonton, the Calgary Lesbian and Gay Political Action Guild, and Gay Lines of Calgary, 7 Dec. 1992.

175 Letter, 16 June 1999.

176 Charles Mandel, 'Turning Hate into Art,' *Edmonton Journal*, 5 Dec. 1995, B6.

177 *Vriend v. Alberta*, [1994] 6 WWR 414 , per Russel J, rev'd , 132 DLR 595, per McClung, O'Leary, JJ, Hunt J dissenting, reinstated (1998), 156 DLR 385 (SCC), per Cory and Iacobucci JJ.

178 'Dealing with the Sickos,' *Xtra!* 23 April 1998, 17.

179 Interview, 21 May 1999.

180 Tom Warner, *Never Going Back: A History of Queer Activism in Canada* (Toronto: University of Toronto Press, 2002), 291.

181 'Edmonton Imports the Fag Project,' *Western Report* 11, (1996): 20.

182 Interview, 21 May 1999.

183 Letter from the coordinator of the Edmonton Gay and Lesbian Community Centre. 3 Jan. 2001.

184 Interview with EPS officer, 10 Dec. 2002.

185 Letter, 14 May 1999.

186 Letter from Calgary activist, 14 May 1999.

187 Ibid.

188 Letter from Hate Crime Coordinator, Calgary Police Service, 23 Oct. 2000.

189 '... and around Canada,' *Xtra!* 2 July 1998, 20.

190 'Cruising Alerts,' *Xtra!* 27 Aug. 1998, 19.

191 EGALE, Press release on Calgary bathhouse raid. 18 Dec. 2002.

192 Robin Perelle, 'Bathhouse on Trial,' *Capital Xtra*, 13 March 2003, 10.

193 Amy Steele, 'Fishing in a Bathhouse,' *Xtra!* 15 April 2004, 15.

194 EGALE, Press release on Calgary bathhouse raid.

195 Perelle, 'Bathhouse on Trial.'

196 CJSW FM press release, 17 June 2003.

197 Interview, 12 Aug. 1999.

198 Letter from Saskatoon Gay and Lesbian Health Services, 27 Nov. 2002.

199 Interview, 13 July 1999.

200 Interview, 7 May 1999.

201 'Fearing for His Safety' *Perceptions*, 10 Sept. 1997, 10.

202 Letter from Regina victim, 5 Oct. 2000.

203 Interview with the Community Relations Coordinator, 22 April 1999.

204 Interview with the Cultural Relations Unit spokesman, 9 Dec. 2002.

205 Ibid.

206 'Police Get Tip on "Gay-Bashing,"' *Winnipeg Sun*, 12 June 1992.

207 Canadian Press, 'Gays Band Together against Bashers,' *Winnipeg Free Press*, 14 Sept. 1991, L11.

208 Allison Bray, 'Thugs on Bikes Chase, Choke Victim,' *Winnipeg Free Press*, 17 Aug. 1991, 1, 4.

209 Donna Carreiro, 'Gay-Bashing "Epidemic" Frustrates City Police,' *Winnipeg Sun*, 13 Jan. 1992.

210 James O'Connor, 'Riverside Killing Ground,' *Winnipeg Sun*, 2 July 1991, 3.

211 Canadian Press, 'Gays Band Together against Bashers.'

212 'Squad to Probe Attacks on Gays,' *Winnipeg Free Press*, 8 Sept. 1993.

213 Gay-Bashing Tactic,' *Winnipeg Sun*, 18 July 1993.

214 Melanie Verhaeghe, 'Basher Suspect Caught,' *Winnipeg Sun*, 28 July 1993.

215 Naomi Lakritz, 'Some Never Learn,' *Winnipeg Sun*, 5 April 1994, 5.

216 David Kuxhaus, 'Try Them as Adults, Gay-Bash Victim Says,' *Winnipeg Free Press*, 20 July 1995, B1.

217 Interview, 23 June 1999.

218 Ibid.

219 Interview, 14 May 1999.

220 Michael Cook, 'Gaybashing in Winnipeg? You Bet!' *Swerve* (May 2000): 9.

221 Rainbow Resource Centre 'Community Safety Project,' 2000.

222 Interview with an activist, Rainbow Resource Centre, 25 Nov. 2002.

223 Interview with the Diversity Coordinator, Winnipeg Police Service, 25 Nov. 2002.

224 Interview with an activist, Rainbow Resource Centre.

225 Katie Chalmers and David Schmeichel 'Vigil Will Honour Murdered Gay,' *Winnipeg Sun.* Jan. 21.

226 'Uncertainty over Murder' *Swerve* (Feb. 2002).

227 'Vigil Achieves Peaceful Closure' *Swerve* (Feb. 2002).

228 Interview with an activist, Rainbow Resource Centre.

229 'Uncertainty over murder.'

230 Eleanor Brown, 'Sarnia Man Nurtures Hate,' *Xtra!* 22 July 1994, 1.

231 Interview with Gary Kinsman, 27 April 1999.

232 See Michael Carmichael, 'Judge Fines and Lectures Gay Basher,' *Sudbury Star*, 19 Nov. 1998.

233 'Sudbury Conviction' *Xtra!* 6 March 2003, 15.

234 'Family Asks Homos to Avoid Funeral' *Xtra!* 13 Jan. 2000, 18.

235 Julian Roberts, *Disproportionate Harm: Hate Crime in Canada*, working document, Department of Justice Canada, 8.

236 Canadian Press, 'Bar "Doesn't Want Gays."' *Halifax Daily News*, 5 May 1996, 14.

237 Letter from HALO activist, 6 May 1999.

238 Interview, 10 May 1999.

239 Gerald Hannon, 'The Kiddie-Porn Ring That Wasn't,' *Globe and Mail*, 11 March 1995, D1, D5.

240 Ibid.

241 Shannon Bell and Joseph Couture, 'Justice and Law: Passion, Power, Prejudice and So-Called Pedophilia,' in Dorothy Chunn and Dany Lacombe, eds., *Law as a Gendering Practice* (Toronto: Oxford University Press, 2000), 41–3.

242 Ibid., 44.

243 Ibid., 47–8.

244 Letter from HALO activist, 6 May 1999.

245 Julian Fantino, Letter signed 9 Dec. 1996.

246 Julian Fantino, Letter signed 5 Feb. 1997.

247 'London Alert' *Xtra!* 11 Jan. 2001, 20.

248 Interview with community activist, 10 Dec. 2002.

249 Letter from a London Police Service officer, 31 Aug. 1999.

250 Interview with hate crimes officer, 9 Dec. 2002.

251 Ali Grant, *Geographies of Oppression and Resistance: Contesting the Reproduction of the Heterosexual Regime'* (PhD dissertation, McMaster University, 1997).

252 Interview, 17 May 1999.

253 Ibid.

254 Mulkewich, 'The Hamilton Wentworth Regional Police Gay/Lesbian/ Bisexual/Transgendered Task Force,' 6–7.

255 Interview, 27 April 1999.

256 Tanya Gulliver, 'Hamilton Reels from Bashing,' *Xtra!* 4 March 2004, 7.

257 Tanya Gulliver, 'Hamilton Rallies around Victim.' *Xtra!* 18 March 2004, 27.

258 Interview, 20 May 1999.

259 Serge Gauthier, 'Un autre tabassage homophobe,' *RG* (Jan. 2000): 8.

260 Roberts, *Disproportionate Harm*, 27.

261 Interview, 22 April 1999.

262 Interview with Halifax police spokesman, 9 Dec. 2002.

263 See 'Man Shot in Leg, Arm' *Halifax Daily News*, 7 July 1999, 8.

264 David Rodenhiser, '"Sadistic" Attack Brings Two-Year Jail Sentence,' *Halifax Daily News*, 10 Feb. 1993.

265 Letter from Halifax activist, 25 May 1999.

266 Ibid.

267 Sean Martin, 'Streetwise Advice,' *Wayves* 1, 7 (1995).

268 Interview with a Halifax gay man, 26 Oct. 2000.

269 NSRAP, Minutes of meeting with police representatives. Sept. 2000.

270 'Gay Bashing,' ATV, 6 p.m. Maritime newscast, broadcast 25 Oct. 2000.

271 Interviews with two Halifax gay men at NRG bar in Halifax, 25 Oct. 2000.

272 Interview with activist, NSRAP, 26 Nov. 2002.
273 Brenda Kossowan, 'Gay Discrimination Doesn't Exist: Politician,' *Red Deer Advocate*, 11 May 1996.
274 Brenda Kossowan, 'Gay Bashing Is Still a Reality in the Heartland,' *Red Deer Advocate*, 11 May 1996.
275 Andrea Maynard, 'Homosexuals Find Refuge at City Tavern,' *Red Deer Advocate*, 16 Nov. 1996.
276 Ian Mackenzie, 'Fort McMurray Manslaughter,' *Xtra!* 26 June 2003, 4.
277 'Prairie Attack,' *Xtra*, 22 Dec. 1995, 16.
278 'Windsor Murder,' *Xtra!* 21 July 1995, 18.
279 'Bar Bashing,' *Xtra!* 26 March 1998, 21.
280 Eleanor Brown, 'Sarnia Man Nurtures Hate,' *Xtra!* 22 July 1994, 1.
281 Eleanor Brown, 'A Small Town's Indifference,' *Xtra!* 9 July 1993, 11.
282 Charles Mandel, 'Harrison's Art Explores Fears Behind Gay-Bashing,' *Globe and Mail*, 3 Feb. 1996, C14.
283 'Peterborough Pride,' *Xtra!* 18 Sept. 2003, 21.
284 Interview, 28 April 1999.
285 'Kingston Bashings,' *Capital Xtra!* 23 June 2000, 14.
286 Rory MacDonald, 'Arrests in Kingston Murder,' *Capital Xtra*, 22 May 2003, 15.
287 Interviews with police spokesman, 21 May 1999 and 26 Nov. 2002.
288 Interview, 17 May 1999.
289 Letter from coordinator, 23 Nov. 2000. See also Tom Killorn, 'PEI Task Force Establishing to Combat Anti-Gay Crimes,' *Charlottetown Guardian*, 1 Feb. 2001, A5.
290 'Safe Spaces Moncton,' Posted at safespaces.org/safespaces/moncton.html. 15 Nov. 2000.
291 Interview with Safe Spaces Moncton coordinator, 14 Nov. 2000.
292 Kelly Toughill, 'N.B. gays Cheer Victory in Hard-Fought Rights Battle,' *Toronto Star*, 21 Oct. 1998, A2.
293 Letter from member of Rainbow Alliance, a Saint John queer organization, 15 Nov. 2000.
294 See Canadian Press, 'Unusual Plea Adds AIDS to Problem of Gay-Bashing,' *Winnipeg Free Press*, 20 April 1993; Toughill, 'N.B. Gays Cheer'; Canadian Press, 'Hundreds Rally for Beaten Man,' *Guardian.* 15 Nov. 1999, A1.
295 'Gay-Bashing Brings Charges,' *National Post*, 27 Nov. 1999, A4.
296 'Gay Bashings in Fredericton,' *Capital Xtra!* 10 Dec. 1999, 14.
297 Interview, 9 Dec. 2002.
298 'MP Attacker Sentenced.' *Xtra!* 18 March 2004, 27.
299 Letter from a St John's activist, 23 Aug. 1999.

300 Interview with a St John's gay man, 22 June 1999.
301 Letter, 19 May 1999.
302 Interview with a St John's gay man, 22 June 1999.
303 Michael Riordon, *Out Our Way: Gay and Lesbian Life in the Country* (Toronto: Between the Lines, 1996).
304 Joseph Harry, 'Conceptualizing Anti-Gay Violence,' in Gregory Herek and Kevin Berrill, eds., *Hate Crimes: Confronting Violence against Lesbians and Gay Men* (Newbury Park, CA: Sage, 1992), 118–19.
305 Sherri Aikenhead, 'Someone to Talk To,' *Halifax Daily News*, 1 April 1996, 17.
306 Kathleen McLean, 'Queens' Land It Ain't,' *The Gaezette*, July 1994.
307 Debbi Christinck, 'Accused Asked if Victim Was Gay: Witness,' *Ottawa Citizen*, 18 Jan. 2003, D3.
308 Letter from victim, 6 Oct. 2000. See also Laverne Monette and Darcy Albert, *Voices of Two-Spirited Men: A Survey of Aboriginal Two-Spirited Men across Canada* (Toronto: Ryerson University Centre for Quality Service Research, 2001).
309 But see John Bermingham, 'Gay Campers Forced to Flee,' *Vancouver Province*, 14 July 1994, A5; 'Cruising Alerts' *Xtra!* 27 Aug. 1998, 19.
310 Letter, 13 Aug. 1999.
311 'Up North' *Capital Xtra.* 6 Dec. 2003, 11.
312 Denise Rideout, 'North of 60,' *Capital Xtra*, 19 June 2003, 13.
313 'Up North.'

Conclusion

1 Presentation, Rainbow Visions Conference, Montreal, 17 May 2003; 'Tidbits' *Xtra!* 20 April 2000, 25.
2 Yves Lafontaine, 'Le sans-abri tué dans le Square Viger était gai,' *Fugues.* (Nov. 2002): 26.
3 New South Wales Attorney-General's Department Working Party on the Review of the Homosexual Advance Defence, *Homosexual Advance Defence: Final Report of the Working Party*, Sept. 1998 www.agd.nsw.gov.au/clrd1.nsf.
4 Santo de Pasquale, 'Provocation and the Homosexual Advance Defence: The Deployment of Culture as a Defence Strategy,' *Melbourne University Law Review.* 26, 1 (2002): 119–20.
5 Terrence Cowl, *Responding to Hate: An International Comparative Review of Program and Policy Responses to Hate Group Activities*, Department of Canadian Heritage (Ottawa, 1995), 7–11.

6 'Aggression à Moncton' *RG* (March 2002), 22.

7 Interviews; 17 May 1999 and 19 Dec. 2000.

8 Letter from a detective of the OPP's Hate Crimes Unit, 4 Dec. 2000.

9 Interview with AVP Coordinator, 21 June 2004.

10 John Sinopoli, 'Is Police Sensitivity an Oxymoron?' *Xtra!* 27 June 27 2002, 22.

11 Victor Janoff, 'Gay-Bashing in Vancouver: A Case Study,' unpublished paper, 1995 (see 255n1).

12 Colin Leslie, 'Goons Bash Tourists on New Year's,' *Xtra!* 18 Jan. 1996, 1.

Selected Bibliography

Books and Dissertations

Adam, Barry. *The Rise of a Gay and Lesbian Movement.* Rev. ed. New York: Twayne, 1995.

Amnesty International United Kingdom. *Breaking the Silence: Human Rights Violations Based on Sexual Orientation.* London. Amnesty International UK, 1997.

Amnesty International USA. *Crimes of Hate, Conspiracy of Silence: Torture and Ill-Treatment Based on Sexual Identity.* New York: Amnesty International USA, 2001.

Burke, Marc. *Coming Out of the Blue.* London: Cassell, 1993.

Butler, Judith. *Gender Trouble: Feminism and the Subversion of Identity.* New York: Routledge, 1990.

Crichlow, Wesley. *Buller Men and Batty Bwoys: Hidden Men in Toronto and Halifax Gay Communities.* Toronto: University of Toronto Press, 2003.

Devor, Holly. *FTM: Female-to-Male Transsexuals in Society.* Bloomington: Indiana University Press, 1997.

Foucault, Michel. *The History of Sexuality.* Vol. 1. *An Introduction.* New York: Vintage, 1978.

Fuller, Janine, and Stuart Blackley. *Restricted Entry: Censorship on Trial,* 2nd ed. Vancouver: Press Gang, 1996.

Herek, Gregory, ed. *Stigma and Sexual Orientation: Understanding Prejudice against Lesbians, Gay Men and Bisexuals.* Thousand Oaks, CA: Sage, 1998.

Herek, Gregory, and Kevin Berrill, eds. *Hate Crimes: Confronting Violence against Lesbians and Gay Men.* Newbury Park, CA: Sage, 1992.

Jenness, Valerie, and Ryken Grattet. *Making Hate a Crime: From Social Movement to Law Enforcement.* New York: Sage, 2001.

Johnson, Katherine, and Stephanie Castle. *Prisoner of Gender.* Vancouver: Perceptions Press, 1997.

Kinsman, Gary. *The Regulation of Desire: Homo and Hetero Sexualities*, 2nd ed. Montreal: Black Rose, 1996.

Kinsman, Gary, and Patrizia Gentile. *The Canadian War on 'Queers': National Security as Sexual Regulation* (forthcoming).

Lahey, Kathleen. *Are We 'Persons' Yet? Law and Sexuality in Canada.* Toronto: University of Toronto Press, 1989.

Lunny, Allyson. 'Responsibilizing a "Community under Attack": Hate Crime and Its Constitution for Queer Communities in Canada, 1985–2003.' PhD dissertation, Centre of Criminology, University of Toronto, in progress.

MacDougall, Bruce. *Queer Judgments: Homosexuality, Expression and the Courts in Canada.* Toronto: University of Toronto Press, 2000.

Maynard, Steven. *Toronto the Gay.* Chicago: University of Chicago Press, forthcoming.

Peterkin, Allan, and Cathy Risdon. *Caring for Lesbian and Gay People.* Toronto: University of Toronto Press, 2003.

Rayside, David. *On the Fringe: Gays and Lesbians in Politics.* Ithaca, NY: Cornell University Press, 1998.

Ross, Becki. *The House that Jill Built: A Lesbian Nation in Formation.* Toronto: University of Toronto Press, 1995.

Schur, Edwin. *Crimes without Victims: Deviant Behavior and Public Policy; Abortion, Homosexuality, Drug Addiction.* Englewood Cliffs, NJ: Prentice-Hall, 1965.

Totten, Mark. *Guys, Gangs and Girlfriend Abuse.* Peterborough, ON: Broadview Press, 2000.

Warner, Tom. *Never Going Back: A History of Queer Activism in Canada.* Toronto: University of Toronto Press, 2002.

Weeks, Jeffrey. *Sexuality and Its Discontents: Meanings, Myths and Modern Sexualities.* London: Routledge, 1985.

Young, Iris Marion. *Justice and the Politics of Difference.* Princeton, NJ: Princeton University Press, 1990.

Scholarly Articles

Arey, Doug. 'Gay Males and Sexual Child Abuse.' Pp. 200–35 in Lisa Aronson Fontes, ed., *Sexual Abuse in Nine North American Cultures: Treatment and Prevention.* Thousand Oaks: Sage, 1995.

Bell, Shannon and Joseph Couture 'Justice and Law: Passion, Power, Prejudice and So-Called Pedophilia.' Pp. 40–59 in Dorothy Chunn and Dany Lacombe, eds., *Law as a Gendering Practice*. Toronto: Oxford University Press, 2000.

Boles, Jacqueline. 'Sexual Identity and HIV: The Male Prostitute.' *Journal of Sex Research* 31, 1 (1994): 39–46.

Butler, Judith. 'Imitation and Gender Subordination.' Pp. 307–20 in H. Aberlove, M. Barale, and D. Halperin, eds., *The Lesbian and Gay Studies Reader*. New York: Routledge, 1993.

De Pasquale, Santo. 'Provocation and the Homosexual Advance Defence: The Deployment of Culture as a Defence Strategy.' *Melbourne University Law Review* 26, 1 (2002): 110–34.

Faulkner, Ellen. 'Empowering Victim Advocates: Organizing Against Anti-Gay/Lesbian Violence in Canada.' *Critical Criminology* 10 (2001): 123–35.

Fleming, Thomas. 'Criminalizing a Marginal Community: The Bawdy-House Raids.' Pp. 37–60 in Thomas Fleming and L.A. Visano, eds., *Deviant Designations: Crime, Law and Deviance in Canada*. Toronto: Butterworths, 1983.

Giles, Geoffrey. '"The Most Unkindest Cut of All": Castration, Homosexuality and Nazi Justice.' *Journal of Contemporary History* 27, 1 (1992): 41–51.

Hopkins, Patrick. 'Gender Treachery: Homophobia, Masculinity and Threatened Identities,' Pp. 129–51 in Larry May and Robert Strikwerda, eds., *Rethinking Masculinity: Philosophical Explorations in Light of Feminism*. Lanham, MD: Littlefield Adams, 1992.

Kinsman, Gary. 'Responsibility as a Strategy of Governance: Regulating People Living with AIDS and Lesbians and Gay Men in Ontario.' *Economy and Society* 25, 3 (1996): 393–409.

– 'Constructing Gay Men and Lesbians as National Security Risks, 1950–70.' Pp. 143–53 in Gary Kinsman, Dieter K. Buse, and Mercedes Steedman, eds., *Whose National Security? Canadian State Surveillance and the Creation of Enemies*. Toronto: Between the Lines, 2000.

Klein, Alan. 'Little Big Man: Hustling, Gender Narcissism, and Bodybuilding Subculture.' Pp. 127–39 in Michael A. Messner and Donald F. Sabo, eds., *Sport, Men and the Gender Order: Critical Feminist Perspectives*. Champaign, IL: Human Kinetics, 1990.

Lunny, Allyson. 'Provocation and "Homosexual" Advance: Masculinized Subjects as Threat, Masculinized Subjects under Threat.' *Social and Legal Studies* 12, 3 (2003): 311–33.

Martin, John L., and Laura Dean. 'Developing a Community Sample for an Epidemiological Study of AIDS.' Pp. 82–99 in Claire Renzetti and Raymond Lee, eds., *Researching Sensitive Topics*. Newbury Park, CA: Sage, 1993.

Mason, Gail. 'Not Our Kind of Hate Crime.' *Law and Critique* 12, 3 (2001): 253–78.

McHenry, F.A. 'A Note on Homosexuality, Crime and the Newspapers.' *Journal of Criminal Psychopathology* 2 (1941): 531–48.

McIntosh, Mary. 'The Homosexual Role.' Pp. 68–76 in Peter Nardi and Beth Schneider, eds., *Social Perspectives in Lesbian and Gay Studies: A Reader*. Santa Barbara, CA: Routledge, 1997.

Miller, Brian and Laud Humphreys.'Lifestyles and Violence: Homosexual Victims of Assault and Murder.' *Qualitative Sociology* 3, 3 (1980): 169–85.

O'Brien, Carol-Anne. 'The Social Organization of the Treatment of Lesbian, Gay and Bisexual Youth in Group Homes and Youth Shelters.' *Canadian Review of Social Policy* 34 (1994): 37–57.

Pei-Lin Chen, Christina. 'Provocation's Privileged Desire.' *Cornell Journal of Law and Public Policy* 10, 1 (2000): 195–235.

Reiss, Albert. 'The Social Integration of Queers and Peers.' *Social Problems* 9, 2 (1961): 102–20.

Rubin, Gayle. 'Thinking Sex.' Pp. 3–64 in Linda S. Kauffman, ed., *American Feminist Thought at Century's End: A Reader*. Cambridge, MA: Blackwell, 1993.

Rupp, Joseph. 'Sudden Death in the Gay World.' *Medicine, Science and Law* 10 (1970): 189–91.

Sagarin, Edward, and Donal MacNamara. 'The Homosexual as Crime Victim.' *International Journal of Criminology and Penology* 3, 1 (1975): 13–25.

Scott, Joan. 'Experience.' Pp. 22–40 in Judith Butler and Joan Scott, eds., *Feminists Theorize the Political*. New York: Routledge, 1992.

Shaffer, Martha. 'Criminal Responses to Hate-Motivated Violence.' *McGill Law Journal* 41 (1995): 199–250.

Smith, George W. 'Policing the Gay Community: An Inquiry into Textually-Mediated Social Relations.' *International Journal of the Sociology of Law* 16 (1988): 163–183.

Stanko, Elizabeth. 'Re-Conceptualising the Policing of Hatred: Confessions and Worrying Dilemmas of a Consultant.' *Law and Critique* 12, 3 (2001): 309–29.

Stanko, Elizabeth, and Paul Curry. 'Homophobic Violence and the Self "at Risk."' *Social and Legal Studies* 6, 4 (1997): 513–32.

Tomsen, Stephen, and Allen George. 'The Criminal Justice Response to Gay Killings: Research Findings.' *Current Issues in Criminal Justice* 9, 1 (1997): 56–70.

Tremblay, Pierre, Eric Boucher, and Marc Ouimet. 'Rhetoric of Victimization: A Case Study of the Gay Village' *Canadian Journal of Criminology* 40, 1 (1998): 1–20.

Newspaper, Newsletter, and Magazine Articles

Aird, Elizabeth. 'Transsexuals' Search for Compassion Often Leads to the Streets.' *Vancouver Sun*, 16 Sept. 1995.

Amsden, Cynthia. 'Portrait of a Killer.' *Ottawa Citizen*, 26 April 1995, B3.

Armstrong, Nigel. 'Videotape Led to Unfair Confession, Court Hears.' *The Charlottetown Guardian*, 12 May 1999, A2.

Blatchford, Christie. 'Witnesses Demonstrate Capacity for Self-Delusion.' *National Post*. 19 Aug. 1999, A6.

Burnett, Richard. 'Interview with a Murderer.' *Xtra!* 23 April 1998, 19.

Bustak, Alan. 'Double Lives.' *Montreal Gazette*, 5 June 1994, A1.

Cherry, Paul. 'I'm Guilty of Gay Killings: McGray.' *Montreal Gazette*, 26 April 2000, A1, A2.

Crook, Farrell. 'Two Off-Duty Peel Police Officers Fined for Beatings Outside Bar.' *Toronto Star*, 28 Nov. 1992, A22.

Gold, Kerry. '"Panic" Defence Nets 5 Years.' *Vancouver Courier*, 30 July 1995.

Hays, Matthew. 'The Cop Factor.' This Magazine (February 1995): 29.

Hannon, Gerald. 'The Kiddie-Porn Ring That Wasn't.' *Globe and Mail*, 11 March 1995, D1, D5.

Hume, Stephen. 'Chantal's Murder a Light on the Dual Personalities of Our City.' *Vancouver Sun*, 22 Sept. 1995, A19.

Janoff, Victor. 'Darkness at the Edge of Town.' *The Vancouver Sun*, 12 Sept. 1992, D4.

– 'Life under Siege: Mexico's Gays Face Discrimination, Extortion and Murder.' *xtra West* 19 Oct. 1995, 15.

McLean, Kathleen. 'Whitewashing a Fag Basher.' *Gaezette*. Feb. 1994, 3.

Rau, Krishna. 'Breaking Out.' *This Magazine* (March/April 1998): 15–17.

– 'Crime and Punishment.' *xtra*. 10 Dec. 1998, 7.

Riordon, Michael. 'Shock Tactics.' *Fab* (Winter 1997): 29, 76.

Saunders, Doug. 'Life Harsh for Teens in Drag.' *Globe and Mail*, 24 May 1996, A1, A5.

Film and Radio Documentaries

Incident at Lemon Creek. Transcript from CBC Radio program *Ideas*, prepared by Sean Hennessey, produced by Max Allen and broadcast on 3 May 1993.

Climate for Murder Documentary film on Montreal murders, produced by Arnie Gelbart and directed by Albert Nerenberg, 1994.

We're Here, We're Queer. Documentary film on Montreal police brutality, produced by Maureen Bradley and Danielle Comeau. Video Out Productions, Vancouver, 1990.

Reports

Allman, Dan. *M Is for Mutual, A Is for Acts: Male Sex Work and AIDS in Canada*. Ottawa: Health Canada, 1999.

Commission des droits de la personne du Quebec. *Rapport du Comité Interne de la Commission sur la Violence et la Discrimination à l'égard des Lesbiennes et des Gais*. Montreal: Commission des droits de la personne du Québec. 29 June 1993.

Commission des droits de la personne et des droits de la jeunesse. *De l'illegalité à l'égalité*. Montreal: Commission des droits de la personne et des droits de la jeunesse. May 1994.

Faulkner, Ellen. *Anti-Gay/Lesbian Violence in Toronto: The Impact on Individuals and Communities*. Research and Statistics Division, Policy Sector, Ottawa, Department of Justice Canada, 1997.

Janoff, Victor. 'Amsterdam 1998: Queer Global Activism for the New Millennium.' Report prepared for EGALE, 1998. www.egale.ca/politics/politics/ amsterdam.htm.

Jeffery, Bill. *Standing Up to Hate: Legal Remedies Available to Victims of Hate-Motivated Activity*. Ottawa: Department of Canadian Heritage, 1998.

Lee, Debbie. *Safe City Project: Beyond Hatred*. Report on London queer youth, prepared for HALO. London, ON: HALO Support Services, July 2000.

Mulkewich, Jane. 'The Hamilton Wentworth Regional Police Gay/Lesbian/ Bisexual/Transgendered Task Force: A Public Relations Success Story.' Hamilton: Hamilton Wentworth Regional Police Service. 31 March 1998.

Ottawa Police Service Liaison Committee. *Heard for the First Time*. Ottawa: Ottawa Police Service. June, 2002.

Pepper, David, and Carroll Holland. *Moving toward a Distant Horizon*. 3rd ed. Ottawa: Ottawa Police Service, 1999.

Roberts, Julian. 'Legislative Responses to Hate-Motivated Crime.' Draft report for the Domain Seminar on Social Justice (14–15 May, 1999). Gatineau: Department of Canadian Heritage, 1999.

Index

Manitoba: community approaches in
Winnipeg, 229–30; homicide, 27–
8, 230; homophobic violence, 30,
32–3, 229; policing issues, refusal
to acknowledge hate crimes, 27,
164, 229–30; other issues, 177,
181, 193

manslaughter. *See* homicide
Mason, Gail, 56–7
media issues, 25–33, 36, 105, 221–3
medical issues, 67
methodological issues, 15–17, 20–2
Mison, Robert, 141–2
murder. *See* homicide

Nazis and Neo-Nazis. *See* hate
groups
New Brunswick: homicide, 60–1, 77;
homophobic violence, 74–5, 239–
40, 249; policing issues, 240, 249
Newfoundland: community approaches, 240; homophobic
violence, 13, 24, 97–8, 240;
policing issues, 97–8, 170, 240
Northwest Territories, 242
Nova Scotia. Halifax: community
approaches, 235–7; homicides, 55,
132–3; homophobic violence, 235–
7; policing issues, 235–7; other
parts of Nova Scotia: homicides,
32, 179; homophobic violence, 32,
241; policing issues, 179, 241
Nunavut, 242–3

Ontario
drug/alcohol issues, 114–15;
perpetrator: prostitute, 89; —,
teenager, 60–1; robberies, 18,
181–2; sexual advance allega-

tion, 151; victims —, female, 26;
—, homeless, 245; —, transgendered, 17–18, 90–1, 151;
violence: extreme, 72–3, 84–5,
60–1; —, in urban settings, 148–
9; —, in victim's home 78, 80–
81, 85
homophobic violence: in urban
settings, 76, 111; in victim's
home, 110–11; multiple perpetrators, 75, 112–13, 125, 253;
robbery, 113; transgendered
victim, 85
non-urban parts of Ontario: drug/
alcohol issues, 241; extreme
violence, 54–5, 179; in victim's
home, 238; sexual advance allegation, 29; homophobic violence:
—, in prisons, 91–2; —, in urban
settings, 239; —, in victim's
home, 80, 238; —, multiple perpetrators, 26, 238–9; policing
issues, 165, 167–70, 173–4,
179, 188–9
policing issues: bathhouse raids,
166–7, 207–8; hate crime investigations, 16, 124, 181, 205–6;
other types of targeting, 171–3,
177; refusal to acknowledge hate
crimes, 16, 81, 114–5, 148;
violence against queers, 165–6,
175
Ontario, cities
Hamilton: community approaches,
26, 234; homicide, 26; homophobic violence, 85, 234; policing issues, 169, 173, 194–5, 234
London: community approaches,
231–4; homicide, 55–6; homophobic violence, 58, 82–3,